BASIC AND CLINICAL SCIENCE COURSE

Clinical Optics

Section 3

2007–2008

(Last major revision 2005–2006)

**AMERICAN ACADEMY
OF OPHTHALMOLOGY**

The Eye M.D. Association

LEO

LIFELONG

EDUCATION FOR THE

OPHTHALMOLOGIST®

The Basic and Clinical Science Course is one component of the Lifelong Education for the Ophthalmologist (LEO) framework, which assists members in planning their continuing medical education. LEO includes an array of clinical education products that members may select to form individualized, self-directed learning plans for updating their clinical knowledge. Active members or fellows who use LEO components may accumulate sufficient CME credits to earn the LEO Award. Contact the Academy's Clinical Education Division for further information on LEO.

The American Academy of Ophthalmology is accredited by the Accreditation Council for Continuing Medical Education to provide continuing medical education for physicians.

The American Academy of Ophthalmology designates this educational activity for a maximum of 40 *AMA PRA Category 1 Credits*™. Physicians should only claim credit commensurate with the extent of their participation in the activity.

The Academy provides this material for educational purposes only. It is not intended to represent the only or best method or procedure in every case, nor to replace a physician's own judgment or give specific advice for case management. Including all indications, contraindications, side effects, and alternative agents for each drug or treatment is beyond the scope of this material. All information and recommendations should be verified, prior to use, with current information included in the manufacturers' package inserts or other independent sources, and considered in light of the patient's condition and history. Reference to certain drugs, instruments, and other products in this publication is made for illustrative purposes only and is not intended to constitute an endorsement of such. Some material may include information on applications that are not considered community standard, that reflect indications not included in approved FDA labeling, or that are approved for use only in restricted research settings. The FDA has stated that it is the responsibility of the physician to determine the FDA status of each drug or device he or she wishes to use, and to use them with appropriate patient consent in compliance with applicable law. The Academy specifically disclaims any and all liability for injury or other damages of any kind, from negligence or otherwise, for any and all claims that may arise from the use of, any recommendations or other information contained herein.

Basic and Clinical Science Course

Section 3

Faculty Responsible for This Edition

Kevin M. Miller, MD, *Chair,* Los Angeles, California

Darren L. Albert, MD, Montreal, Quebec

Penny A. Asbell, MD, New York, New York

Neal H. Atebara, MD, Honolulu, Hawaii

Robert J. Schechter, MD, Los Angeles, California

Ming X. Wang, MD, PhD, Nashville, Tennessee

Christie Morse, MD, Concord, New Hampshire
   Practicing Ophthalmologists Advisory Committee for Education

Dr. Miller states that he has an affiliation with Alcon Laboratories and Hoya Holdings and that he receives financial compensation from STAAR Surgical.

The other authors state that they have no significant financial interest or other relationship with the manufacturer of any commercial product discussed in the chapters that they contributed to this publication or with the manufacturer of any competing commercial product.

Recent Past Faculty

Aazy A. Aaby, MD

Mathias Fellenz, MD, FRCS(C)

Perry Rosenthal, MD

Constance E. West, MD

In addition, the Academy gratefully acknowledges the contributions of numerous past faculty and advisory committee members who have played an important role in the development of previous editions of the Basic and Clinical Science Course.

American Academy of Ophthalmology Staff

Richard A. Zorab, *Vice President, Ophthalmic Knowledge*
Hal Straus, *Director, Publications Department*
Carol L. Dondrea, *Publications Manager*
Christine Arturo, *Acquisitions Manager*
Nicole DuCharme, *Production Manager*
Stephanie Tanaka, *Medical Editor*
Steven Huebner, *Administrative Coordinator*

AMERICAN ACADEMY
OF OPHTHALMOLOGY
The Eye M.D. Association

655 Beach Street
Box 7424
San Francisco, CA 94120-7424

Contents

General Introduction

The Basic and Clinical Science Course (BCSC) is designed to meet the needs of residents and practitioners for a comprehensive yet concise curriculum of the field of ophthalmology. The BCSC has developed from its original brief outline format, which relied heavily on outside readings, to a more convenient and educationally useful self-contained text. The Academy updates and revises the course annually, with the goals of integrating the basic science and clinical practice of ophthalmology and of keeping ophthalmologists current with new developments in the various subspecialties.

The BCSC incorporates the effort and expertise of more than 80 ophthalmologists, organized into 13 section faculties, working with Academy editorial staff. In addition, the course continues to benefit from many lasting contributions made by the faculties of previous editions. Members of the Academy's Practicing Ophthalmologists Advisory Committee for Education serve on each faculty and, as a group, review every volume before and after major revisions.

Organization of the Course

The Basic and Clinical Science Course comprises 13 volumes, incorporating fundamental ophthalmic knowledge, subspecialty areas, and special topics:

1. Update on General Medicine
2. Fundamentals and Principles of Ophthalmology
3. Clinical Optics
4. Ophthalmic Pathology and Intraocular Tumors
5. Neuro-Ophthalmology
6. Pediatric Ophthalmology and Strabismus
7. Orbit, Eyelids, and Lacrimal System
8. External Disease and Cornea
9. Intraocular Inflammation and Uveitis
10. Glaucoma
11. Lens and Cataract
12. Retina and Vitreous
13. Refractive Surgery

In addition, a comprehensive Master Index allows the reader to easily locate subjects throughout the entire series.

References

Readers who wish to explore specific topics in greater detail may consult the journal references cited within each chapter and the Basic Texts listed at the back of the book.

These references are intended to be selective rather than exhaustive, chosen by the BCSC faculty as being important, current, and readily available to residents and practitioners.

Related Academy educational materials are also listed in the appropriate sections. They include books, audiovisual materials, self-assessment programs, clinical modules, and interactive programs.

Study Questions and CME Credit

Each volume of the BCSC is designed as an independent study activity for ophthalmology residents and practitioners. The learning objectives for this volume are given on page 1. The text, illustrations, and references provide the information necessary to achieve the objectives; the study questions allow readers to test their understanding of the material and their mastery of the objectives. Physicians who wish to claim CME credit for this educational activity may do so by mail, by fax, or online. The necessary forms and instructions are given at the end of the book.

Conclusion

The Basic and Clinical Science Course has expanded greatly over the years, with the addition of much new text and numerous illustrations. Recent editions have sought to place a greater emphasis on clinical applicability, while maintaining a solid foundation in basic science. As with any educational program, it reflects the experience of its authors. As its faculties change and as medicine progresses, new viewpoints are always emerging on controversial subjects and techniques. Not all alternate approaches can be included in this series; as with any educational endeavor, the learner should seek additional sources, including such carefully balanced opinions as the Academy's Preferred Practice Patterns.

The BCSC faculty and staff are continuously striving to improve the educational usefulness of the course; you, the reader, can contribute to this ongoing process. If you have any suggestions or questions about the series, please do not hesitate to contact the faculty or the editors.

The authors, editors, and reviewers hope that your study of the BCSC will be of lasting value and that each section will serve as a practical resource for quality patient care.

Objectives

Upon completion of BCSC Section 3, *Clinical Optics*, the reader should be able to:

- Compare and contrast physical and geometrical optics

- Discuss the clinical and technical relevance of such optical phenomena as interference, coherence, polarization, diffraction, and scattering

- Review the basic properties of laser light and how they affect laser–tissue interaction

- Outline the principles of light propagation and image formation and work through some of the fundamental equations that describe or measure such properties as refraction, reflection, magnification, and vergence

- Explain how these principles can be applied diagnostically and therapeutically

- Describe the clinical application of Snell's law and the lens maker's equation

- Identify optical models of the human eye and describe how to apply them

- Define the various types of visual perception and function, including visual acuity, brightness sensitivity, color perception, and contrast sensitivity

- Summarize the steps for performing streak retinoscopy

- Summarize the steps for performing a manifest refraction using a phoropter or trial lenses

- Describe the use of the Jackson cross cylinder

- Describe the indications for prescribing bifocals and common difficulties encountered in their use

- Review the materials and fitting parameters of both soft and rigid contact lenses

- Explain the optical principles underlying various modalities of refractive correction: spectacles, contact lenses, intraocular lenses, and refractive surgery

- Discern the differences among these types of refractive correction and describe how to apply them most appropriately to the individual patient

- Discuss the basic methods of calculating intraocular lens powers and the advantages and disadvantages of the different methods

- Describe the conceptual basis of multifocal IOLs and how the correction of presbyopia differs between these IOLs and spectacles

- Recognize the visual needs of low vision patients and how to address these needs through optical and nonoptical devices and/or appropriate referral

- Describe the operating principles of various optical instruments in order to use them more effectively

CHAPTER 1

Physical Optics

What is light? This question has been the subject of vigorous debate for centuries. One school of thought supported the wave theory, originally stated by Christian Huygens and amplified by Young and Maxwell. Opposed to this school were those who championed the corpuscular theory, originated by Newton and supported by Planck. Ultimately, however, both theories are necessary to account for all the phenomena associated with light. The science of quantum mechanics, which evolved from Planck's quantum theory, successfully addresses the dual nature of light by comprehending both the particle and the wave aspects of light.

The description of optical phenomena is currently divided into the areas of physical optics, geometrical optics, and quantum optics. *Physical optics* describes those phenomena that are most readily understood in terms of light's wave properties. *Geometrical optics* conceives of light as rays and deals with the imaging properties of lenses and mirrors. *Quantum optics* is concerned with the interaction of light and matter and considers light as having both wave and particle (photon) characteristics.

In brief, light behaves like a *wave* as it passes through air, a vacuum, or transparent materials. Light exhibits some characteristics of *particles* (photons) when it is being generated or absorbed. The *ray model* is a simplified method for describing the propagation of light. Although it ignores the effects of diffraction and other physical optics phenomena, it provides a powerful method for calculations involving lenses and images.

Because our primary interest is in propagation of light through media, including transparent ocular tissues, we concentrate on the wave and ray descriptions of light, with only occasional references to its photon characteristics.

Wave Theory

Water waves provide a good analogy for understanding light waves. When a wave travels along the water's surface, particles at the surface move up and down as the wave passes but they do not move along with the wave. In the case of light, no material substance moves as the light wave propagates. Rather, at each point the electric field increases, decreases, and reverses direction as the wave passes (Fig 1-1). The electric field is always perpendicular to the direction of propagation.

Two principal characteristics of a wave, as illustrated in Figure 1-1, are its wavelength (λ) and amplitude *(A)*. *Wavelength* is determined by the distance between crests of the wave. *Amplitude* is the maximum value attained by the electric field as the wave propagates. It determines the intensity of the wave. The third characteristic of a wave, not

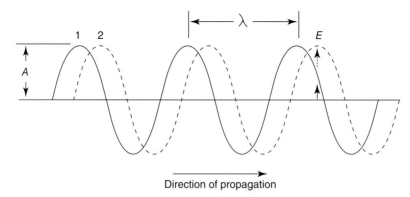

Direction of propagation

Figure 1-1 Instantaneous "snapshot" of a light wave. *1* represents the light at a particular instant; *2* represents the wave a short time later, after it has moved a fraction of 1 wavelength to the right. The wavelength, *λ*, is the distance between crests of the wave. The electric field, *E*, at a particular point, is represented by the *solid line* for wave 1 and by the *dashed line* for wave 2. The amplitude of the wave, *A*, is the maximum value of the electric field. The frequency is the number of wave crests that pass a fixed point per second and is dependent on the speed of the wave. *(Redrawn by C. H. Wooley.)*

shown in Figure 1-1, is the *frequency,* which is the number of wave crests that pass a fixed point per second. Finally, multiple waves may be described as "in phase," which doubles the intensity; "out of phase," where they cancel each other; or at some level in between, resulting in an intermediate level of intensity (Fig 1-2).

In addition to an electric field, a light wave has a magnetic field that increases and decreases with the electric field. As indicated in Figure 1-3, the magnetic field *(H)* is perpendicular both to the direction of propagation of the light and to the electric field. The magnetic field is less important than the electric field and is often omitted in descriptions of a light wave.

Figure 1-4 illustrates the electromagnetic wave spectrum, including the very small portion occupied by visible light. In common usage, the term *light* refers to the visible portion of the electromagnetic wave spectrum, but it can be applied to radiation in the infrared and near-ultraviolet portions of the spectrum as well. Although the visible light region is normally defined as 400–700 nanometers (nm), the boundaries are not precise, and under certain conditions the eye's sensitivity extends well into the infrared and ultraviolet regions. For example, in aphakia, without the UV absorption of the natural lens, the retina is able to detect wavelengths well below 400 nm. X-rays also produce a response in the retina, but these waves are not focused by the optical components of the eye.

The speed of light in a vacuum *(c)* is one of the fundamental constants of nature, almost exactly 3×10^8 m/sec. The wavelength of a light wave is related to its frequency *(v)* by the equation

$$\lambda v = c$$

When light travels through any transparent medium *(m)* other than a vacuum, its velocity *(v)* is reduced. The index of refraction *(n)* of the medium is defined as the ratio

A

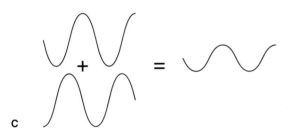

B

Figure 1-2 When light waves are fully "in phase" with one another, their superposition results in a doubling of the light intensity **(A)**. When they are fully "out of phase," they cancel each other out, and the resulting light intensity is zero **(B)**. When they are in between these 2 extremes, the resulting light intensity is at an intermediate level **(C)**. *(Illustrator C. H. Wooley.)*

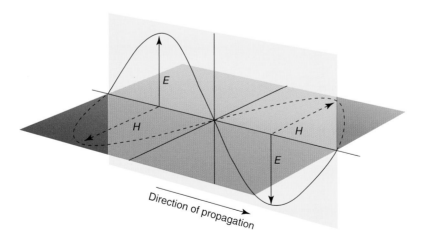

C

Figure 1-3 A magnetic field always accompanies the electric field in any electromagnetic wave. The magnetic field, represented by *H,* is always perpendicular to the electric field. *(Redrawn by Jonathan Clark.)*

Figure 1-4 The electromagnetic spectrum. *(Reproduced with permission from Steinert RF, Puliafito CA. The Nd:YAG Laser in Ophthalmology: Principles and Clinical Applications of Photodisruption. Philadelphia: Saunders; 1985. Redrawn by C. H. Wooley.)*

of the speed of light in a vacuum to the speed of light in the given material and is written as

$$n_m = c/v$$

Lens materials have unique indices of refraction. The index of refraction of typical CR-39 plastic lenses is 1.50, whereas the "high-index lenses" have an index of refraction of 1.66. The higher the index of refraction, the thinner, and, therefore, more attractive, the lens. This is important for patients with higher refractive errors who prefer "thin lenses."

The frequency of a wave does not change on traveling through a transparent medium, but the wavelength (λ_m) becomes shorter, as governed by the relationship

$$\lambda/\lambda_m = n_m$$

Photon (Particle) Aspects of Light

When light interacts with matter, individual quanta of energy (photons) are emitted or absorbed. The amount of energy *(E)* per photon is equal to Planck's constant multiplied by the frequency and is written as

$$E = h\nu$$

where ν is the frequency of the light wave and h is *Planck's constant:* 6.626×10^{-34} J/sec. Because the frequency of blue light is greater than that of red light (see Fig 1-4), a photon of blue light has greater energy than a photon of red light.

The diagnostic use of fluorescein demonstrates a practical application of this principle. For example, a photon of blue light is absorbed by an individual fluorescein molecule. When the molecule reemits light (fluoresces), the emitted photon has a lower energy, lying in the yellow-green portion of the spectrum. The remaining energy is converted into heat or chemical energy. As a general rule, light emitted through fluorescence has a longer wavelength than the excitation light.

The particle–wave duality extends to other fundamental concepts as well. The electron, for example, behaves like a wave with a wavelength much shorter than that of light. Because diffraction effects are much reduced at shorter wavelengths (see Diffraction, later), extremely high resolution can be obtained with the electron microscope.

Interference and Coherence

Interference occurs when 2 light waves originating from the same source are brought together. Interference occurs most readily when the light is monochromatic; that is, it lies within a narrow band of wavelengths. But interference can also be obtained with white light under optimum conditions.

In Figure 1-5, the curved lines represent the crests of the waves at a particular instant. Where the crests coincide (for example, at *A*), a maximum of intensity is produced because the energy of the electromagnetic fields is added together *(constructive interference)*. Where the crest of 1 wave coincides with the trough of the other wave *(B)*, the 2 electromagnetic fields cancel each other, and intensity is minimized *(destructive interference)*. If the 2 waves are exactly equal in amplitude, the destructive interference will be complete, and the light intensity will be zero. Thus, in Figure 1-5, the screen displays a series of light and dark bands corresponding to areas of constructive and destructive interference.

The term *coherence* describes the ability of 2 light beams, or different parts of the same beam, to produce interference. *Spatial,* or lateral, coherence defines the ability of 2 separated portions of the same wave (*P* and *Q* in Fig 1-5) to produce interference.

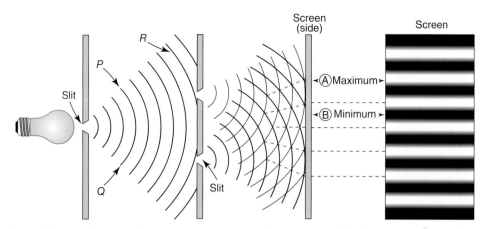

Figure 1-5 Interference. *A* represents constructive interference; *B* indicates destructive interference. *(Redrawn by Jonathan Clark.)*

Temporal, or longitudinal, coherence is the ability of 1 wave of a beam to interfere with a different wave within the same beam (*P* and *R*). A large, white light source has a coherence close to zero. However, if the light is passed through a narrow slit, as in Figure 1-5, the spatial coherence between *P* and *Q* improves, approaching unity as the slit approaches zero width. Temporal coherence is improved by using a filter to select a narrow band of wavelengths, thereby making it highly monochromatic. Laser light is highly coherent. Most gas lasers approach perfect temporal coherence, meaning that a portion of the beam can be made to interfere with a much later portion of the beam.

Applications of Interference and Coherence

Interference resulting from the high degree of coherence in laser light can lead to serious problems in some laser applications. However, interference effects can also be put to practical use, as in *laser interferometry,* a technique for evaluating retinal function in the presence of a cataractous lens. A laser beam is split into 2 beams, which then pass through different parts of the pupil. Where the beams again overlap on the retina, interference fringes are formed, even if the beams have been diffused by the cataract.

One of the most important applications of interference is in *antireflection films* (Fig 1-6) and interference filters (Fig 1-7). If the 2 reflected beams in Figure 1-6 are equal in amplitude but exactly half a wavelength out of phase, the resulting destructive interference will cause the beams to cancel each other and thereby prevent reflection for a given wavelength. Modern low-reflection coatings consist of several thin layers of transparent materials designed to give a reflection of only a few tenths of a percent over the visible spectrum. Films are typically prepared by evaporation of the material in a vacuum chamber and deposition on the glass surface.

The *interference filter* (see Fig 1-7) is designed so that successive rays transmitted through the filter are exactly in phase and therefore interfere constructively. This condition applies exactly for only 1 wavelength, and therefore the filter transmits only that wavelength and a narrow band of wavelengths on either side. Other wavelengths are

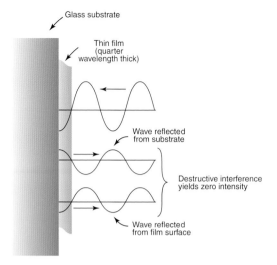

Figure 1-6 Destructive interference by an antireflection film. *(Redrawn by C. H. Wooley.)*

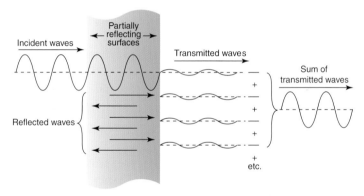

Figure 1-7 The interference filter transmits only that wavelength for which the internally reflected waves are in phase with one another. *(Redrawn by C. H. Wooley.)*

reflected by the interference filter. The reflecting layers can be thin films of metal such as silver or aluminum. More frequently they consist of multiple thin layers of transparent materials, with the thickness of each layer chosen to give the desired reflectance.

Thin layers can also be designed so that the transmission (or reflection) has the characteristic properties of a sharp cutoff filter. For example, a so-called *cold mirror* has a multilayer coating designed to reflect the visible (cold) light and transmit the infrared wavelengths. The excitation filter used in fluorescein angiography transmits short wavelengths, below about 500 nm, that cause fluorescein to fluoresce. The barrier filter used in the fundus camera transmits only the long wavelengths, above about 500 nm. Therefore, the fluorescent emission is received by the film, but all excitation light is excluded.

Polarization

In general, the human eye is not sensitive to polarization of light. Nevertheless, polarization has a number of applications in visual science and ophthalmology, as we shall see.

A good analogy for polarization is light waves moving through a picket fence. The fence lets only waves of a certain direction through, blocking the rest of the waves. *Plane-polarized*, or *linearly polarized*, light consists of waves that all have their electric fields in the same plane.

In a different analogy, we could turn one end of a rope in a circular motion. The wave would then travel along the rope as a circular oscillation. Similarly, in *circularly polarized light*, the electric field at any point rotates rapidly. In *elliptically polarized light*, the electric field both rotates and changes amplitude rapidly as the wave passes.

Unpolarized light consists of a random mixture of various plane-polarized beams. *Partial polarization*, as the name implies, produces a mixture of unpolarized light and polarized light (plane, circular, or elliptical).

One way to produce plane-polarized light is to pass a beam of unpolarized light through a polarizing filter (eg, sheet plastic). This is analogous to passing a vibrating rope through a picket fence so that only the vertical vibration is transmitted. Certain crystals, particularly calcite, can be used to polarize light. As will be seen later, reflection can also cause complete or partial polarization. Even the sky acts as a partial polarizer by means of the scattering properties of air molecules.

Applications of Polarization

One exception to the eye's lack of sensitivity to polarization is the Haidinger brush phenomenon. This can be demonstrated clinically by rotating a polarizer continuously in front of a uniform blue field. A normal subject will see a rotating structure that looks like a double-ended brush or a propeller. This phenomenon is useful in localizing the fovea during sensory testing and in evaluating the status of the nerve fiber layer of Henle at the macula.

Polarizing sunglasses are sometimes useful in reducing the glare from reflected sunlight. In boating, for example, sunlight reflected from the water surface is partially polarized. Because the predominant polarization is horizontal (see Fig 1-9 later in the chapter), the sunglasses are constructed to pass only the vertical polarization. Similarly, in driving, the light reflected from the road surface and from the painted or glass surfaces of other automobiles is also partially polarized, usually horizontally.

Certain materials such as glass or plastic, when stressed, will change the state of polarized light. A heat-treated ophthalmic lens, for example, will exhibit a distinctive pattern when placed between crossed polarizing sheets. People who wear polarizing sunglasses may be especially aware of stress patterns in glass doors and auto rear windows.

Polarized light is used in some ophthalmic instruments to eliminate the strong reflex from the cornea. The viewer looks through a polarizer that is placed 90° to the polarization of the light incident on the examined eye. The polarizer eliminates the light that is specularly reflected from the cornea, while partially transmitting the light diffusely reflected from the retina.

Polarizing projection charts are especially useful because they can be made to test 1 eye at a time while the patient is viewing binocularly through a pair of special polarizing glasses. For example, alternate letters on a Snellen chart can be polarized at 90° to each other and therefore are seen by each eye separately. Other charts provide sensitive tests for binocular functions or abnormalities such as stereopsis, fixation disparity, and aniseikonia.

Diffraction

Diffraction is the ability of light to bend around edges. All waves are subject to diffraction when they encounter an obstruction, an aperture, or another irregularity in the medium. Diffraction changes the direction of the wave; in the case of light, this corresponds to a bending of the light ray. The shorter the wavelength, the less the change of direction.

Diffraction is seldom seen alone; rather, it is usually combined with other effects, such as interference or refraction. One example in which diffraction dominates is in the light streaks seen through windshields that have been repeatedly rubbed by windshield wipers. Each fine scratch diffracts the light into directions perpendicular to the scratch— that is, into a plane of rays normal to the diffracting groove. Another example is the pattern seen when viewing a distant light through fine-woven curtain material. Again, the diffraction is in a direction perpendicular to the diffracting material—in this case, the threads. With cross-woven material, a 2-dimensional array of bright spots is seen. Here, diffraction is mixed with interference, producing discrete spots of light rather than continuous streaks.

Diffraction sets a limit on visual acuity when the pupil size is less than about 2.5 mm (for the person with emmetropia). The image formed on the retina from a distant small source takes the form of concentric light and dark rings surrounding a bright central disk, the *Airy disk* (Fig 1-8). The diameter, *d*, of the central disk increases as the pupil size decreases according to the equation

$$d = 2.44 f\lambda / a$$

where: λ = wavelength
a = diameter of the aperture (pupil)
f = focal length of the optical system (the eye)

This equation illustrates another property of diffraction: that longer wavelengths (red) diffract more than shorter wavelengths (blue) and therefore form a larger-diameter Airy disk. The best resolution obtainable from an optical instrument is limited by diffraction. The minimum resolvable distance is approximately equal to the radius of the Airy disk. Because of this, telescopes generally increase in resolution as the aperture of the objective lens is increased. However, ground-based astronomical telescopes larger than 10 inches in diameter are limited in resolution by atmospheric turbulence, the same phenomenon that gives rise to the familiar twinkling of stars. A space telescope operating in the relative vacuum high above the earth's atmosphere is unaffected by atmospheric conditions.

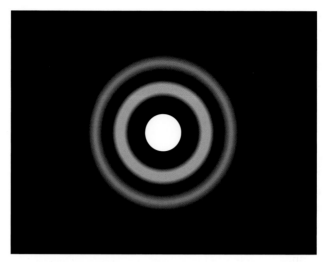

Figure 1-8 Diffraction pattern produced by a small circular aperture. The central bright spot is called an *Airy disk*. *(From Campbell CJ.* Physiological Optics. *Hagerstown, MD: Harper & Row; 1974:20.)*

An Airy disk is seldom seen directly, even when the viewer looks at a small source through a small pupil, usually because of aspherical irregularities in the cornea and the crystalline lens. In this way, diffraction combines with other aberrations to increase the blur circle size on the retina. (Blur circles are discussed in Chapter 2, under Image Quality.)

Because diffraction sets a limit on an optical system's resolution, there is a degree of precision in the fabrication of optical components beyond which any improvement in the image is negligible. This limit is given by the *Rayleigh criterion:* If the wavefront produced by the optical system is within one-quarter wavelength of being perfect, further improvement will not result in significantly better resolution. This tolerance has a practical application in setting standards for the fabrication of optical components.

Scattering

Scattering of light occurs at irregularities in the light path, such as particles or inclusions in an otherwise homogeneous medium. Scattering caused by very small particles, such as the molecules in the atmosphere, is called *Rayleigh scattering.* Although Rayleigh scattering is generally very weak, it varies according to wavelength, with greater scattering at shorter wavelengths. The sky appears blue because blue light from the sun is scattered more than sunlight of longer wavelengths. Larger particles, such as dust in the air, scatter light more intensely and with less dependence on wavelength.

Scattering of light in ocular tissues can result from various pathological conditions. Corneal haze is caused by excess water in the stroma, which disrupts the very regular, close-packed collagen structure of the stroma. In an early cataract, large molecules in the lens structure cause scattering. Anterior chamber flare is caused by protein in the aqueous humor.

Such scattering material interferes with vision in 2 ways. The primary effect is that of glare, starbursts, and halos. For example, when light from a source such as the sun or an oncoming headlight reaches the eye, a fraction of the light scattered within the ocular media falls on the retina. That which falls in the foveal area reduces the contrast and tends to obscure detail in the image of interest. The second effect, particularly important when the scattering is intense, is a reduction in the light available to form the image on the retina.

Reflection

The laws of reflection as they affect light rays and the formation of images are discussed in Chapter 2, Geometrical Optics).

The magnitude of the reflection at an interface between 2 media depends primarily on the difference in index of refraction between the first and second media. An air–glass interface reflects approximately 4% (at normal incidence). The air–cornea interface reflects about 2%, whereas the cornea–aqueous interface reflects only about 0.02%.

Reflection from an interface also depends strongly on the angle of incidence. As illustrated in Figure 1-9, polarization becomes important for oblique incidence. At 1 particular angle (known as the *Brewster angle*) for every interface, only 1 polarization is reflected. The fact that 1 polarization is reflected more strongly than the other enables polarizing sunglasses to block reflected light, as explained in the earlier discussion of polarization and in the following paragraph.

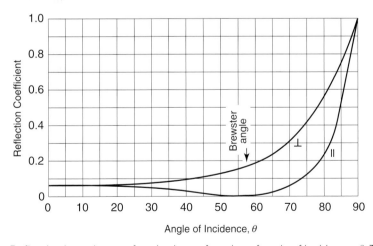

Figure 1-9 Reflection by a glass surface in air as a function of angle of incidence, θ. The symbol $\perp$ indicates the polarization perpendicular to the plane of incidence; $\parallel$ denotes the polarization parallel to the plane of incidence. At grazing incidence, 90°, the reflection coefficient approaches 100%. In this example, the glass has an index of refraction of 1.51; the Brewster angle for this index is 56.5°. At the Brewster angle, θ_B, the reflection of the parallel component is essentially zero. *(From Ditchburn RW. Light. 2nd ed. London: Blackie and Son; 1952: Fig 14.3. Redrawn by C. H. Wooley.)*

Total reflection occurs when light from a medium with a high index of refraction encounters a medium with a lower index at oblique incidence (see Total Internal Reflection in Chapter 2). The basis for transmission of light in fiberoptics is total reflection at the internal surface of the fiber. The fiber usually consists of a high-index core glass surrounded by a lower-index cladding glass. Total reflection occurs at the interface between the 2 glasses. This interface must remain free of dirt, contamination, and contact with any other material that might degrade the total reflection.

Reflection from metals such as silver or aluminum can be as high as 85% to 95%. As with other materials, the reflectivity increases with the angle of incidence. Mirrors used in ophthalmic instruments usually consist of an aluminum layer that has been vacuum-evaporated on a glass substrate and then overcoated with a protective thin film of transparent material such as silicon monoxide to prevent oxidation and scratching of the aluminum surface.

Semitransparent mirrors, sometimes used as 1-way mirrors, often consist of a metallic layer thin enough to transmit a fraction of the incident light. They are not 100% efficient in that a substantial fraction of the light is also absorbed. In critical applications, partially reflecting mirrors can be made of other materials so that only a negligible fraction is lost to absorption.

Metallic reflection *partially* polarizes the reflected light. As with other materials, the perpendicular component is more strongly reflected than the parallel component. However, with metals there is no angle at which only 1 polarization is reflected; therefore, the polarization of the reflected light is never complete.

Transmission and Absorption

Transmission is the passing of radiant energy through a medium or space. It is measured in terms of transmittance, the percentage of energy that can pass through a particular medium. For absorbing materials, the transmittance is often a function of wavelength.

Absorption is usually expressed as an *optical density* (OD). An optical density of 1 means a transmittance of 10%. Other values are 2 (0.01) = 1%; and 3 (0.001) = 0.1%.

In general, the expression for optical density is OD = log $1/T$, where T is the transmittance. See also Chapter 4, Clinical Refraction, for a discussion of absorptive lenses.

Duke-Elder S, Abrams D, eds. *System of Ophthalmology.* Vol V, *Ophthalmic Optics and Refraction.* St Louis: Mosby; 1970:30–36.

Illumination

The quantitative measurement of light is carried out in 2 different ways. *Radiometry* measures light in terms of power, the basic unit being the *watt*. For example, the *irradiance* on a surface is the number of watts per square meter incident on that surface.

Photometry measures light in units based on the response of the eye. The basic unit is the *candela,* a more precisely defined replacement for the old unit, the candle. A point source with output of 1 candela emits a total of 4π (ie, $\approx$12.6) *lumens.* The *illuminance* on a surface is the number of lumens per square meter incident on that surface. The *luminance* of a surface is the amount of light reflected or emitted by the surface.

If a source has a known output in watts, can we determine its output in lumens? Yes, provided we know the spectral properties of the lamp—that is, power at each wavelength. The output at each wavelength is multiplied by the sensitivity of the eye to that wavelength, and the results are summed to obtain the total response of the eye to light from that source. For example, if the source is monochromatic, with a wavelength at the peak of the eye's photopic sensitivity (555 nm), the conversion factor is 685 lumens per watt. At other wavelengths the factor is less, falling to approximately zero at 400 and 700 nm (Figs 1-10 and 1-11).

The *apostilb* is defined as the luminance of a perfectly diffusing surface that is emitting or reflecting 1 lumen per square meter. It is encountered in perimetry, where the luminance of the background and of the targets is often specified in apostilbs.

Brightness is a subjective term referring to the sensation produced by a given illuminance on the retina. The commonly used radiometric and photometric terms are summarized in Table 1-1.

The clinician should be familiar with levels of illumination frequently recommended by illumination engineers (Table 1-2). It should be noted that the recommended foot-

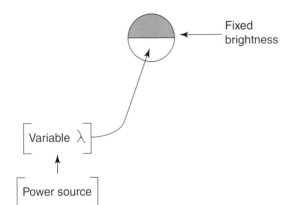

Figure 1-10 Schematic arrangement for measuring the spectral sensitivity of the eye. The subject is light-adapted. For λ_x, a certain amount of power (W_x) will be needed to match the standard brightness. A curve can then be constructed of W_x versus λ_x (see Fig 1-11). *(Redrawn by C. H. Wooley.)*

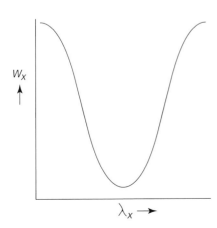

Figure 1-11 The amount of power (W_x) at each wavelength (λ_x) needed to match a standard brightness in the arrangement of Figure 1-10. This curve is inverted with respect to the familiar photopic luminosity curve. The greatest energy efficiency is roughly in the middle of the visible spectrum, at a wavelength of 555 nm. *(Redrawn by C. H. Wooley.)*

Table 1-1 Principal Types of Light Measurement

Description	Radiometric Measure		Photometric Measure	
	Type	Units	Type	Units
Quantity of light leaving a source or passing through a region of space	Radiant flux	Watts = joules/second	Luminous flux	Lumens (1 candle emits 4π lm)
Light emitted per unit solid angle	Radiant intensity	Watts/steradian (1 sr = 1 unit of solid angle)	Luminous intensity (candle power)	1 candela* = 1 lm/sr
Quantity of light per unit area incident on a surface or at an image	Irradiance	Watts/square meter	Illuminance	1 lux = 1 lumen/square meter; 1 footcandle = 1 lumen/square ft
Light reflected or emitted by a surface, per unit area and per unit solid angle	Radiance	Watts/steradian/square meter	Luminance	1 apostilb = $(1/\pi)$ lumen/square meter/sr; 1 footlambert = $(1/\pi)$ lumen/square ft/sr
Illuminance at the retina, adjusted for pupil size			Retinal illuminance	Trolands (luminance of 1 candle/square meter viewed through 1-square-mm pupil)

* A standard (new) candle is called a candela.

(Modified from Armington JC. *The Electroretinogram*. New York: Academic Press; 1974:75.)

Table 1-2 Recommended Illumination Levels

Office, kitchen	150 footcandles
Reading	70 footcandles
Refracting lane:	
Wall chart	25–50 footcandles
Projector	10 footcandles
Operating table	2500 footcandles

candles are a measure of the luminous power impinging on a surface, not that which is reflected into the eye. An ideal 100-watt lamp bulb provides about 600 footcandles of illumination 3 feet away and 150 footcandles 6 feet away.

Michaels DD. *Visual Optics and Refraction: A Clinical Approach.* St Louis: Mosby; 1985: 14–16.

Laser Fundamentals

Laser is an acronym for *light amplification by stimulated emission of radiation*—a phrase that highlights the key events in producing laser light. In the most simplified sequence, an energy source excites the atoms in the *active medium* (a gas, solid, or liquid) to emit a particular wavelength of light. The light thus produced is amplified by an optical feed-back system that reflects the beam back and forth through the active medium to increase its coherence, until the light is emitted as a laser beam. This process is described in greater detail in the following sections.

Properties of Laser Light

Lasers are only one of many sources of light energy. The unique properties of laser light, however, make it particularly suitable for many medical applications. These properties are *monochromaticity, directionality, coherence, polarization,* and *intensity.*

Monochromaticity

Lasers emit light at only 1 wavelength or sometimes at a combination of several wavelengths that can be separated easily. Thus a "pure," or monochromatic, beam is obtained. Although the wavelength spread is not infinitesimally small, a gas laser emission line can be as narrow as 0.01 nm, compared with the 300-nm span of wavelengths found in white light. At best, a filter might reduce the transmission of white light to a color range (band width) of 5 nm at the expense of most of the white light's energy. For medical purposes, the color of light can be used to enhance absorption or transmission by a target tissue with a certain absorption spectrum. The wavelength specificity of a laser greatly exceeds the absorption specificity of pigments in tissues. In addition, monochromatic light is not affected by chromatic aberration in lens systems. Thus, monochromatic light can be focused to a smaller spot than can white light.

Directionality

The second property of laser-emitted light is *directionality*. Lasers emit a narrow beam that spreads very slowly. As explained later in this chapter, lasers amplify only those photons that travel along a very narrow path between 2 mirrors. This process serves as a very efficient mechanism for collimating light. In a typical laser, the beam increases by about 1 mm in diameter for every meter traveled. Directionality makes it easy to collect all of the light energy in a simple lens system and focus this light to a small spot.

Coherence

Coherence, meaning that all the propagated energy from the source is in phase, is the term most often associated with lasers (see Fig 1-5 and the earlier discussion, Interference and Coherence). Laser light projected onto a rough surface produces a characteristic sparkling quality known as *laser speckle.* This phenomenon occurs because the irregular reflection of highly coherent light creates irregular interference patterns, or speckle. Coherence of laser light is utilized to create the interference fringes of the laser interferometer. In therapeutic ophthalmic lasers, coherence, like directionality, is important because it improves focusing characteristics.

Polarization

Many lasers emit linearly polarized light. *Polarization* is incorporated in the laser system to allow maximum transmission through the laser medium without loss caused by reflection. The specific polarization of the light beam is not currently used in medical applications.

Intensity

In most medical applications, the most important property of lasers is *intensity.* Intensity is the power in a beam of a given angular size, and the physical correlate of the perception of "brightness" is the intensity per unit area. In medical laser applications, the 4 important radiometric terms are *energy* (J), *power* (W), radiant energy density (J/cm^2), and *irradiance* (W/cm^2) (Table 1-3). The laser output is quantitated in either joules or watts.

Table 1-3 Radiometric Terminology for Medical Lasers

Term	Unit
Radiant energy	joule*
Radiant power	watt
Radiant energy density	joules/cm^2
Irradiance	watts/cm^2
Radiant intensity	watts/sr†
Radiance (brightness)	watts/sr cm^2

* 1 joule = 1 watt × 1 sec.
† Steradian is the unit of solid angle. There are 4π steradians in a sphere.

(From Steinert RF, Puliafito CA. *The Nd:YAG Laser in Ophthalmology: Principles and Clinical Applications of Photodisruption.* Philadelphia: Saunders; 1985.)

Recall that energy is work, and power is the rate at which work is done. One joule = 1 watt × 1 second, or 1 W = 1 J/sec. The tissue effect is then determined by the focal point spot size, which determines energy density and irradiance (or, less properly stated, "power density"). In ophthalmic lasers, spot size is conventionally given as the diameter. Thus, a 50-μm spot size has an area of π $(25 \times 10^{-4})^2$ cm², or about 2×10^{-5} cm².

In an ophthalmic laser with a continuous beam of light, such as argon and krypton, the control panel meter gives the power in watts; in a pulsed laser, such as the Nd:YAG, the meter reading gives the energy per pulse in joules. This specification is convenient because the continuous laser beam has a constant power, but the energy varies according to the shutter setting (for example, 100 mW for 0.2 second delivers 20 mJ). In the case of pulsed lasers, the beam is intermittent, varying in strength over the course of the pulse, and thus has both average and peak power. A single discrete pulse, however, carries a determinate amount of energy that can be readily measured. Knowledge of any two of the variables of energy, power, and time allows ready calculation of the third variable.

In sum, directionality, coherence, polarization, and, to some degree, monochromaticity enhance the most important characteristic of lasers, which is light intensity. The sun has a power of 10^{26} watts but emits energy in all directions at a great distance from the earth. Thus, a simple 1-mW helium neon laser has 100 times the radiance of the sun. Their intense radiance, combined with monochromaticity that can target selected tissues and avoid others on the basis of spectral absorption, makes lasers a unique tool in medicine. This is particularly true in ophthalmology, as the eye is designed to allow light transmission to most of its structures. Figure 1-12 summarizes the major properties of laser light in comparison with a conventional light source.

Elements of a Laser

All ophthalmic lasers currently in use require 3 basic elements: (1) an *active medium* to emit coherent radiation; (2) energy input, known as *pumping;* and (3) *optical feedback,* to reflect and amplify the appropriate wavelengths.

In 1917, Albert Einstein explained the mathematical relationships of 3 atomic transition processes: *absorption, spontaneous emission,* and *stimulated emission.* According to the fundamental principles of quantum physics, certain atomic energy transitions are highly probable, or "allowed." Light energy can readily induce such an allowed transition, causing the energy of the atom to move from its ground state (E_0) to an excited state (E_1). The atom absorbs a quantum of energy at a predictable frequency appropriate to cause the specific transition. If the source of illumination is white light, a discrete frequency (line spectrum) will be subtracted from the illuminating beam. Each atomic element has a characteristic line spectrum. This process is known as *absorption* (Fig 1-13A).

Because the lowest energy state is the most stable, the excited atom soon emits a quantum of energy at the same frequency in order to return to the ground state. This process can occur without external stimulation (*spontaneous emission;* Fig 1-13B) or as a result of stimulation by a photon of light at the same frequency (*stimulated emission;* Fig 1-13C). Spontaneous emission occurs randomly in time, whereas stimulated emission

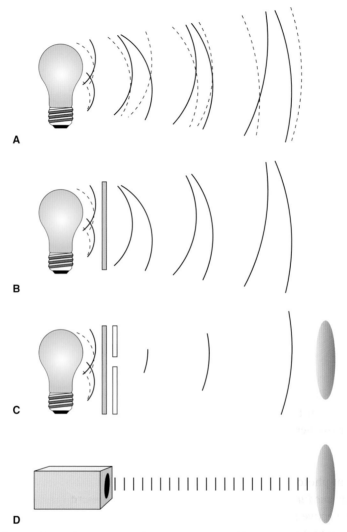

Figure 1-12 Comparison of properties of incandescent and laser light sources. **A,** The incandescent bulb emits incoherent, rapidly divergent light with a broad mixture of wavelengths *(solid and broken waves)*. **B,** A narrow-band pass filter absorbs all but a narrow portion of the spectrum *(solid waves)* but, in doing so, absorbs much of the light energy. **C,** Directionality and coherence are improved by the addition of a pinhole aperture, but still more energy is lost; a lens system collects some of the light and brings it to a focus. **D,** A laser emits monochromatic, directional, coherent light that is readily collected by a lens system and brought to a much smaller focal area. Compared with the incandescent source, the power and irradiance of the laser system are many orders of magnitude greater. *(Reproduced with permission from Steinert RF, Puliafito CA. The Nd:YAG Laser in Ophthalmology: Principles and Clinical Applications of Photodisruption. Philadelphia: Saunders; 1985. Redrawn by Jonathan Clark.)*

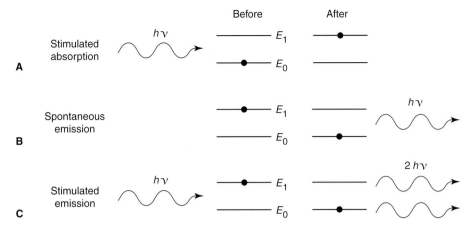

Figure 1-13 Schematic representation of an electron moving between the lowest energy (ground) state (E_0) and an allowed excited state (E_1) in conjunction with absorption of a quantum of light energy ($\Delta E = E_1 - E_0 = h\nu$). **A,** Stimulated absorption. **B,** Spontaneous emission. **C,** Stimulated emission. *(Reproduced with permission from Steinert RF, Puliafito CA. The Nd:YAG Laser in Ophthalmology: Principles and Clinical Applications of Photodisruption. Philadelphia: Saunders; 1985. Redrawn by C. H. Wooley.)*

is in phase with the stimulating wave. Therefore, stimulated emission is coherent. After absorption, the majority of energy release is through spontaneous emission occurring incoherently in all directions, and only a small fraction of the energy is normally released as coherent stimulated emission. The laser environment, however, amplifies only the stimulated emission.

As indicated in Figure 1-13C, stimulated emission occurs when an incident photon of the proper frequency interacts with an atom in the upper energy state. The result is the emission of a photon of the same wavelength and the return of the atom to its lower energy state. The emitted photon also has the same phase and direction of propagation as the incident photon.

The *active medium* is an atomic or molecular environment that supports stimulated emission. The active medium allows a large number of atoms to be energized above the ground state so that stimulated emission can occur. The particular atomic energy transition determines the wavelength of the emission ($E = h\nu = hc/\lambda$). Lasers are usually named for the active medium. The medium can be a gas (argon, krypton, carbon dioxide, argon-fluoride excimer, or helium with neon), a liquid (dye), a solid (an active element supported by a crystal, such as neodymium supported by yttrium-aluminum-garnet [Nd:YAG] and erbium supported by yttrium-lanthanum-fluoride [Er:YLF]), or a semiconductor (diode).

The second requirement for a laser is a means for imparting energy to the active medium so that a majority of the atoms are in an energy state higher than the ground state. This condition is known as a *population inversion* because it is the inverse of the usual condition in which the majority of atoms are in the ground energy state. The energy input that makes possible population inversion is known as *pumping*. Gas lasers are usually pumped by electrical discharge between electrodes in the gas. Dye lasers are often pumped by other lasers. Solid crystals are usually pumped by incoherent light such as the xenon arc flash lamp.

Once population inversion in an active medium has been achieved, *optical feedback* is required to promote stimulated emission and suppress spontaneous emission. The laser cavity acts as an optical resonator. Mirrors are placed at each end of a beam path to reflect light back and forth through the active medium, in which pumping maintains a population inversion (Fig 1-14). Each time the light wave resonates through the active medium, the total coherent light energy is increased through stimulated emission. Spontaneous emission, which occurs randomly in all directions, rarely strikes a mirror and therefore is not amplified.

The last element in this schematic laser design is a mechanism for releasing some of the oscillating laser light from the cavity. This is achieved by making one of the mirrors fully reflective and the other mirror only partially reflective. A portion of the light waves striking the second mirror is emitted from the cavity as the laser beam. The reflectivity of the mirror is selected to satisfy the requirements for efficient amplification in a particular system. For example, if a laser has a 98% reflective mirror, the light waves are coherently amplified by stimulated emission during an average of 50 round-trips through the active medium before they are emitted as the laser beam.

Laser Sources

Solid-state laser sources commonly used in medical applications are ruby and Nd:YAG. Refractive surgery uses excimer lasers (ablative procedures) and, less commonly, infrared holmium-YLF (IntraLase) and holmium:YAG lasers (laser thermal keratoplasty [LTK]). Argon, krypton, carbon dioxide, and argon-fluoride excimer are the most important gas

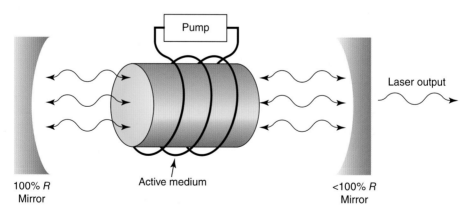

Figure 1-14 Elementary laser schematic illustrating the active medium within the optical resonance cavity formed by the mirrors and the pump, which creates a population inversion in the active medium. One mirror is fully reflective (100% *R*), whereas the other is partially transparent (<100% *R*). As drawn, the mirror is 66% reflective, and the average light wave makes 3 round-trips through the active medium before being emitted. *(Reproduced with permission from Steinert RF, Puliafito CA. The Nd:YAG Laser in Ophthalmology: Principles and Clinical Applications of Photodisruption. Philadelphia: Saunders; 1985. Redrawn by Jonathan Clark.)*

laser sources used in medicine. The dye laser is the only liquid laser used in ophthalmology.

In 1975, it was shown that rare gas atoms in metastable excited states could react with halogens to form diatomic rare gas halides in a bound excited dimer *(excimer)* state. Decay of these excimer molecules to a weakly bound or unbound ground state is accompanied by emission of a photon with ultraviolet frequency. Excimer lasers efficiently produce high-power ultraviolet irradiation. A number of different excimer molecules can be created, and each is associated with a specific transition and emission wavelength: argon fluoride, or ArF (193 nm); krypton fluoride, or KrF (249 nm); and xenon fluoride, or XeF (351 nm).

Semiconductor diode lasers are solid-state lasers that are extremely compact and highly efficient. These laser sources are commonly used in communications applications and in digital information and audio systems. Increased power output of semiconductor diode lasers now makes them feasible for retinal photocoagulation and for some glaucoma applications.

Laser–Tissue Interaction

Although Einstein had developed the basic theory of laser emission more than 40 years earlier, it was not until 1960 that Theodore Maiman built the first successful laser with a ruby crystal medium.

Even before the invention of lasers, light energy had been employed therapeutically to heat and permanently alter target tissue. This early phototherapy had its origins in observations of solar retinitis and was used in the treatment of numerous retinal disorders and glaucoma. A laser could now achieve similar effects in a more controlled manner. The term *photocoagulation* refers to the selective absorption of light energy and conversion of that energy to heat, with a subsequent thermally induced structural change in the target. These processes and their therapeutic results depend on laser wavelength and laser pulse duration. A variety of photocoagulating lasers are currently in clinical use: argon, krypton, dye, holmium, and the solid-state gallium arsenide lasers.

A second category of laser–tissue interaction uses high-peak-power pulsed lasers to ionize the target and rupture the surrounding tissue. In clinical practice, this process (known as *photodisruption*) uses laser light as a pair of virtual microsurgical scissors, reaching through the ocular media to open tissues such as lens capsule, iris, inflammatory membranes, and vitreous strands without damaging surrounding ocular structures. Currently, the Nd:YAG and Er:YAG lasers are the principal photodisruptive lasers used in clinical ophthalmology.

A third category of laser–tissue interaction, called *photoablation,* arose from the insight that high-powered ultraviolet laser pulses can precisely etch the cornea in the same manner that they etch synthetic polymers. The high energy of a single photon of 193-nm ultraviolet light exceeds the covalent bond strength of corneal protein. The high absorption of these laser pulses precisely removes a submicron layer of cornea without opacifying adjacent tissue, owing to the relative absence of thermal injury. A decade of laboratory and clinical investigation has brought excimer laser photoablation to clinical use in refractive surgery and corneal therapeutics. (See also BCSC Section 13, *Refractive Surgery.*)

Figure 1-15 shows some typical laser wavelengths.

Campbell CJ. *Physiological Optics.* Hagerstown, MD: Harper & Row; 1974.

Rubin ML, Walls GL. *Fundamentals of Visual Science.* Springfield, IL: Charles C Thomas; 1969.

Figure 1-15 Typical laser wavelengths. *(Adapted from Steinert RF, Puliafito CA. The Nd:YAG Laser in Ophthalmology: Principles and Clinical Applications of Photodisruption. Philadelphia: Saunders; 1985. Redrawn by Jonathan Clark.)*

CHAPTER **2**

Geometrical Optics

Geometrical optics deals primarily with imaging: how to produce images using light and how to manipulate image features such as size, brightness, and location. As its name implies, geometrical optics can be understood largely in terms of geometrical principles. In contrast, physical optics emphasizes the wave nature of light, and quantum optics (not covered in this text) emphasizes the particle nature of light and the interaction of light and matter. Geometrical optics models light as rays, which emanate from object points and focus to image points.

Pinhole Imaging

The simplest imaging device is a pinhole aperture. Here's a simple experiment. Make a pinhole near the center of a large sheet of aluminum foil, light a candle, and extinguish all other illumination in the room. Hold a sheet of plain white or, better, waxed paper about 2 feet from the candle, and place the pinhole midway between the paper and the candle. Observe an inverted image of the candle flame on the paper (Fig 2-1).

The image is faint, but the object's features are faithfully duplicated. Moreover, the characteristics of the image are readily manipulated. For instance, moving the pinhole closer to the candle while keeping the paper stationary yields a larger image.

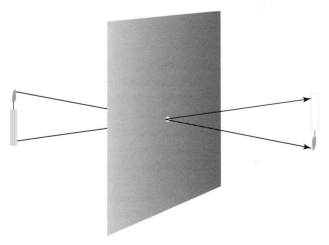

Figure 2-1 Pinhole imaging. *(Illustration developed by Edmond H. Thall, MD, and Kevin M. Miller, MD, and rendered by C. H. Wooley.)*

The object may be treated as a collection of points. Geometrical optics regards every object point as a *point source* of light. A point source (ie, a point in the mathematical sense) is infinitesimally small and radiates light equally in all directions. Although point sources do not exist, some objects may be treated as point sources for practical purposes. For example, stars other than our own sun, by virtue of their enormous distances from the earth, behave as point sources. The point source is mainly a conceptual tool: it is usually easier to understand an optical system by concentrating on the light radiating from only a few object points.

For every object point there is a unique, corresponding image point. Thus, a 1-to-1 correspondence exists between object points and image points. In optics, the term *conjugate* refers to the correspondence between object and image points. An object point and its corresponding image point constitute a pair of *conjugate points* (Clinical Example 2-1). An image point is said to be conjugate to its corresponding object point and vice versa. It is common practice to use a letter to identify a specific point in the object and the same letter with a prime to indicate the conjugate image point (eg, *A* and *A'*).

A *ray* is a geometrical construct that indicates the route (or routes) light follows as it travels from an object point to the conjugate image point. Rays represent only a path; they do not indicate the amount (ie, intensity) or wavelengths of the light traveling along the path. An arrowhead on the ray indicates the direction light travels; however, too many arrowheads can clutter illustrations. To minimize this problem, light is conventionally depicted as traveling from left to right unless indicated otherwise.

A *pencil* of light is a small bundle of rays that travel in the same direction. The smaller a pencil (the narrower the pinhole or aperture forming it), the more it behaves like a single ray of light.

Pinhole imaging has been known for millennia, but pinhole images are usually too faint to be useful. Only in rare situations is pinhole imaging practical. For instance, a solar eclipse can be safely observed by using a pinhole to image the sun on a piece of paper. Of course, one should not look through the pinhole to directly view the sun!

CLINICAL EXAMPLE 2-1

The concept of conjugate points can be illustrated by retinoscopy. When performing retinoscopy, the examiner observes the light reflex emanating from the subject's pupil. The examiner's retina is conjugate to the subject's pupil (Fig 2-2A). At the point of neutrality in the refraction, the subject's retina is conjugate with the peephole of the retinoscope (Fig 2-2B). After being adjusted for the working distance, the subject's retina is conjugate with optical infinity (Fig 2-2C). (Retinoscopy is covered in detail in Chapter 4, Clinical Refraction.)

Another example of conjugacy is demonstrated by direct ophthalmoscopy. After being compensated for the refractive errors of the eyes of the examiner and subject by dialing an appropriate working lens into the ophthalmoscope, the 2 retinas are conjugate (Fig 2-3). Because light entering the subject's eye is intense and distracting, and little light illuminates the inside of the examiner's eye, the subject cannot see the examiner's retina.

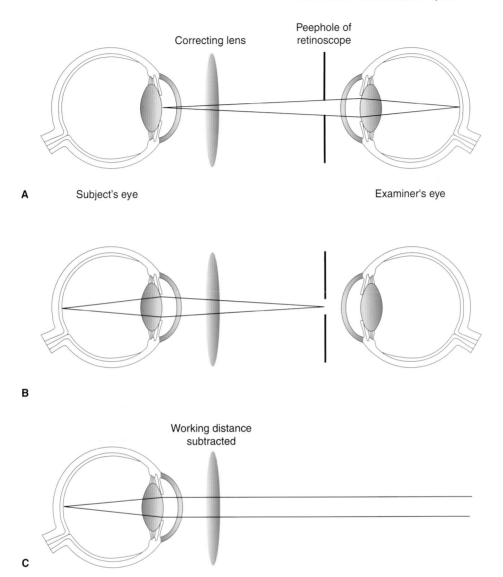

Figure 2-2 A, In retinoscopy, the examiner's eye is conjugate with the subject's pupil. **B,** At the point of neutrality, the subject's retina is conjugate with the peephole of the retinoscope. **C,** After the working distance has been subtracted, the subject's retina is conjugate with optical infinity. *(Illustration developed by Kevin M. Miller, MD, and rendered by C. H. Wooley.)*

Now what happens if we punch several pinholes in aluminum foil, separated by a few inches, and repeat the pinhole-imaging experiment? Several complete images of the flame appear simultaneously (Fig 2-4). Each object point is a point source radiating light in all directions. Some light from each object point traverses every pinhole and produces an image. Note that only a small amount of light from each object point is necessary to yield a complete image. The pinhole restricts the brightness, not the size, of the image.

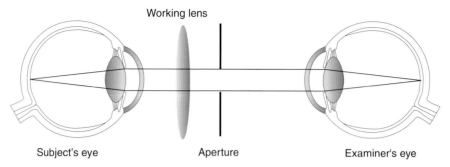

Figure 2-3 In direct ophthalmoscopy, the retina of the examiner is conjugate with the retina of the subject. *(Illustration developed by Kevin M. Miller, MD, and rendered by C. H. Wooley.)*

Figure 2-4 Multiple pinholes produce distinct, complete images. *(Illustration developed by Edmond H. Thall, MD, and Kevin M. Miller, MD, and rendered by C. H. Wooley.)*

Imaging with Lenses and Mirrors

Repeat the pinhole-imaging demonstration, but replace the pinhole with a +6 D spherical trial lens, and note the improvement in the image. Vary the distances among the candle, lens, and paper, and observe the variety of different image characteristics that can be obtained from the same lens (Fig 2-5). Different lenses provide an even broader range of images.

Compared with the pinhole, the lens allows much more light from each object point to traverse the lens and ultimately contribute to the image. Generally, lenses produce better images than pinholes. However, lenses do have some disadvantages. Place a lens at a fixed distance from the candle and note that the image appears in only 1 location. In pinhole imaging, an image appears at any location behind the aperture. Changing the distance between an object and a lens causes the distance between the image and the lens to change, but the image still forms in only 1 location.

Mirrors produce images in much the same way as lenses (Fig 2-6). The comments made in this section regarding lenses also apply to mirrors.

Most optical systems are rotationally symmetric about their long axis. This axis of symmetry is the *optical axis* (see Figs 2-5 and 2-6). Although the human eye is not truly rotationally symmetric, it is nearly symmetric, and theoretical models of the eye often

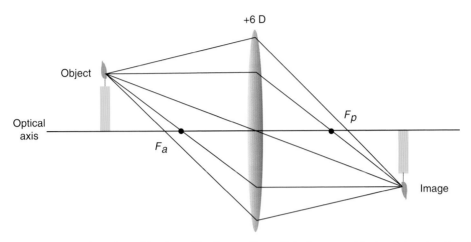

Figure 2-5 Basic imaging with a lens. The lens collects light from an object point and redirects the light to a small spot in the image. *(Illustration developed by Kevin M. Miller, MD, and rendered by C. H. Wooley.)*

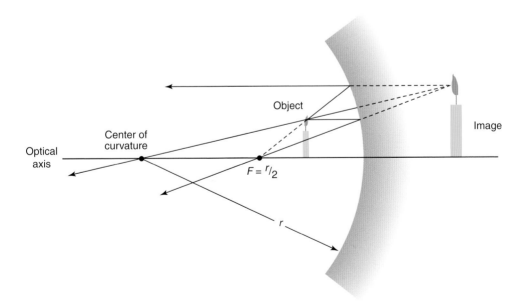

Figure 2-6 Basic imaging with a mirror. In this example, an upright, magnified, and virtual image is produced because the object is located inside the focal point, *F*. *(Illustration developed by Kevin M. Miller, MD, and rendered by C. H. Wooley.)*

approximate the eye as a rotationally symmetric system. (See the discussion of schematic eyes in Chapter 3, Optics of the Human Eye.)

Object Characteristics

Objects may be characterized by their location with respect to the imaging system and by whether they are luminous. Objects that can be felt or touched, that are located in front of an imaging system, are known as *real objects*. Objects that cannot be felt or touched, that are located behind an imaging system, are known as *virtual objects*. These concepts will be developed more fully later.

If an object point produces its own light, such as the candle flame in the previous illustrations, it is called *luminous*. If it does not produce its own light, it can only be imaged if it is reflective and illuminated.

Image Characteristics

Images can be described by characteristics such as magnification, location, depth of focus, quality, and brightness. Some of these features will be discussed briefly.

Magnification

The most important characteristic of an image is its magnification. Magnification can be classified as transverse, axial, or angular.

The ratio of image height to corresponding object height is known as *transverse magnification* (Fig 2-7):

Transverse magnification = image height/object height

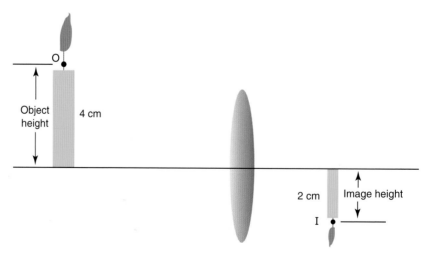

Figure 2-7 Transverse magnification is the ratio of image height to object height. Object height and image height may be measured from any pair of off-axis conjugate points. In this illustration, an object point, *O*, on the wick, and its conjugate, *I*, are used to measure object and image height. *(Illustration developed by Edmond H. Thall, MD, and Kevin M. Miller, MD, and rendered by C. H. Wooley.)*

To calculate transverse magnification, any off-axis object point and its conjugate image point may be used. Object and image heights are measured perpendicularly from the optical axis. By convention, object or image height is considered positive when the point is above the optical axis and negative when the point is below the axis.

In general usage, magnification means *enlargement;* however, in optics the term *magnification* refers to making images larger or smaller than the object. An image is a scale model of the object, and magnification is the scale factor. Inverted images are indicated by a minus sign, whereas images with the same orientation as the object (upright images) have a positive magnification. For instance, in Figure 2-7 the object height is +4 cm and the image height is −2 cm; thus, the transverse magnification is −0.5, meaning that the image is inverted and half as large as the object. A magnification of +3 means the image is upright and 3 times larger than the object.

Transverse magnification applies to linear dimensions. For example, a 4 cm × 6 cm object imaged with a magnification of 2 produces an 8 cm × 12 cm image. Both width and length double, yielding a fourfold increase in image area.

The word *power* is sometimes used synonymously with transverse magnification. This usage is unfortunate because "power" has several different meanings, and confusion often arises. Other uses of the word include refracting power, resolving power, prism power, angular magnification, and light-gathering power. Generally, the multiplication sign, ×, is used to indicate magnification. The transverse magnification of microscope objectives, for example, is sometimes expressed by this convention.

Most optical systems have a pair of *nodal points* (Fig 2-8). Occasionally, the nodal points overlap, appearing as a single point, but technically they remain a pair of overlapping nodal points. The nodal points are always on the optical axis and have an important property. From any object point, a unique ray passes through the anterior nodal point. This ray emerges from the optical system along the line connecting the posterior nodal point to the conjugate image point (Fig 2-9). These rays form 2 angles with the

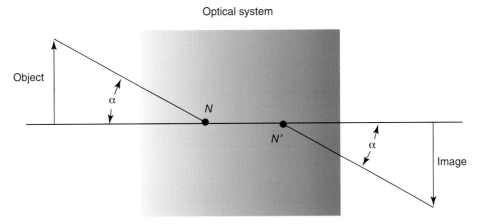

Figure 2-8 The anterior and posterior nodal points (*N* and *N'*, respectively) of an optical system. Any ray from an object point to the anterior nodal point will emerge along the line joining the posterior nodal point and the image point. The angles formed by these rays with the optical axis are identical. *(Illustration developed by Kevin M. Miller, MD, and rendered by C. H. Wooley.)*

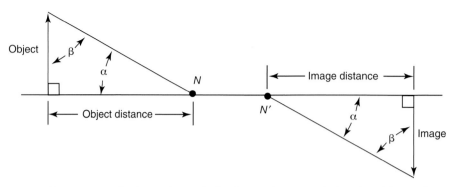

Figure 2-9 Lines perpendicular to the optical axis may be extended to the object points and image points. The triangles formed by these lines are similar. *(Illustration developed by Kevin M. Miller, MD, and rendered by C. H. Wooley.)*

optical axis. The essential property of the nodal points is that these 2 angles are equal for any choice of object point. Because of this property, the nodal points are useful for establishing a relationship among transverse magnification, object distance, and image distance. (See Quick Review of Angles, Trigonometry, and the Pythagorean Theorem.)

No matter where an object is located, both the object and the image subtend equal angles with respect to their nodal points. Therefore, the 2 triangles in Figure 2-9 are similar, and the lengths of corresponding sides of similar triangles are proportional. Thus,

$$\text{Transverse magnification} = \frac{\text{image height}}{\text{object height}} = \frac{\text{image distance}}{\text{object distance}}$$

As a practical matter, object and image distances must obey a sign convention consistent with the established convention for transverse magnification (ie, negative when the image is inverted). Object and image distances are always measured along the optical axis. For the purpose of calculating transverse magnification, object distance is measured from the anterior nodal point to the object, and image distance is measured from the posterior nodal point to the image. For a simple thin lens immersed in a uniform medium such as air, the nodal points overlap in the center of the lens. Object and image distances are negative when they point to the left and positive when they point to the right (see Fig 2-9).

Quick Review of Angles, Trigonometry, and the Pythagorean Theorem
It is useful to review a few basic principles of geometry and trigonometry. A circle can be divided angularly into 360° or 2π radians. π is approximately 3.14, so 360° corresponds approximately to 6.28 radians. It is frequently necessary to convert back and forth between degrees and radians when solving optics problems. A degree can be subdivided into 60′ (minutes); each minute can be subdivided into 60″ (seconds).

The sum of the angles in a triangle equals 180° or π radians. For any right angle triangle with sides *a, b,* and *c* (Fig 2-10) and angle θ between sides *b* and *c,* the trigonometric functions are defined as follows:

Trigonometric Function	Inverse Function
$\sin\theta = \dfrac{a}{c}$	$\theta = \arcsin\dfrac{a}{c}$
$\cos\theta = \dfrac{b}{c}$	$\theta = \arccos\dfrac{b}{c}$
$\tan\theta = \dfrac{a}{b}$	$\theta = \arctan\dfrac{a}{b}$

The Pythagorean theorem states that $c^2 = a^2 + b^2$; as a result, therefore, $c = \sqrt{a^2 + b^2}$. Triangles are said to be similar when their angles are equal. When 2 triangles have identical angles, their sides are proportional. Triangles *A* and *B* in Figure 2-11 are similar.

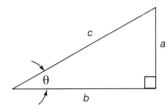

Figure 2-10 Right-angle triangle with sides *a, b,* and *c* and angle θ between sides *b* and *c.* *(Illustration developed by Kevin M. Miller, MD, and rendered by C. H. Wooley.)*

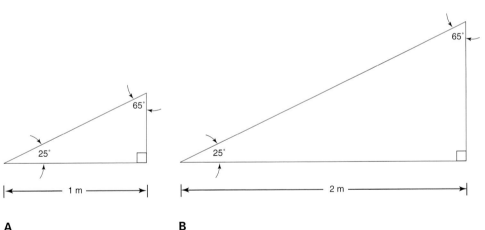

A   **B**

Figure 2-11 Triangles in **A** and **B** are similar because their angles are equal. *(Illustration developed by Kevin M. Miller, MD, and rendered by C. H. Wooley.)*

Here is a simple experiment. Use a pinhole to image the sun onto a piece of paper 50 cm behind the pinhole. What is the size of the image? Assume that the sun subtends an angle of 0.5° and that the nodal points for pinhole imaging overlap in the middle of the pinhole. The situation is illustrated in Figure 2-12.

From trigonometry:

$$\tan(0.25°) = \frac{x}{50 \text{ cm}} = \frac{x}{500 \text{ mm}}$$

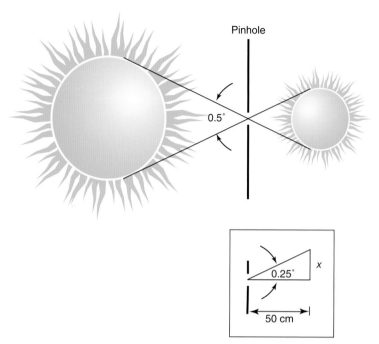

Figure 2-12 Pinhole imaging of the sun. The drawing is obviously not to scale. The inset shows the geometry of the situation; x is the radius of the image. *(Illustration developed by Kevin M. Miller, MD, and rendered by Jonathan Clark.)*

Thus,

$$x = (500 \text{ mm})\tan(0.25°) = 2.2 \text{ mm}$$

The radius of the image is 2.2 mm, which is fairly small, and the diameter or overall height of the image is 4.4 mm.

Axial magnification, also known as *longitudinal magnification*, is measured along the optical axis. For small distances around the image plane, axial magnification is the square of the transverse magnification.

Axial magnification = (transverse magnification)²

Angular magnification is the ratio of the angle subtended by an object at the eye using a lens or magnifier divided by the angle subtended by the object without the lens or magnifier. The standard viewing distance is 25 cm. More will be said about simple magnifiers later.

Image Location

Another important characteristic of an image is its location. Refractive errors result when images formed by the ocular media are located off the retina. Image location is specified as the distance (measured along the optical axis) between a reference point associated with the optical system and the image.

The reference point depends on the situation. As discussed earlier, the reference point can be the posterior nodal point. However, it is often more convenient to use the back surface of a lens as a reference point. The back lens surface is usually not at the same location as the posterior nodal point, but it is easier to locate than the nodal point.

Most often, image distance is measured from the posterior principal point to the image. The principal points (discussed later in the chapter) are, like the nodal points, another pair of useful reference points on the axis. In fact, the nodal and principal points often, but not always, overlap.

Whatever reference point is used to measure image distance, the sign convention is always the same. When the image is to the right of the reference point, image distance is positive; when the image is to the left of the reference point, the distance is negative.

Depth of Focus

In most optical systems, image location is somewhat indefinite. Perform the basic imaging demonstration with a lens as described in the earlier section Imaging with Lenses and Mirrors, and notice that the paper can be held anywhere within a range of a few millimeters and the image remains sharp (Fig 2-13). Outside of this region, the image is decidedly blurry, but within it, the image appears acceptably sharp. The size of this region represents the depth of focus, which may be small or large depending on several factors. (See Clinical Example 2-2.) In the past, depth of focus was of concern only in the management of presbyopia. However, it is an important concept in refractive surgery as well.

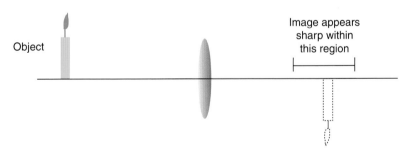

Figure 2-13 Depth of focus. The image remains equally sharp within a small region. The length of this region is the depth of focus. *(Illustration developed by Edmund H. Thall, MD, and Kevin M. Miller, MD, and rendered by C. H. Wooley.)*

CLINICAL EXAMPLE 2-2

Pinholes are often placed over the naked eye to screen for uncorrected refractive errors, and over existing glasses and contact lenses to look for residual refractive errors. What is the depth of focus of a pinhole?

Images can form at any distance behind a pinhole, unlike the corresponding situation with lenses and mirrors. Therefore, a pinhole has infinite depth of focus.

Depth of focus applies to images. *Depth of field* is the same idea applied to objects. If a camera or other optical system is focused on an object, nearby objects are also in focus (Fig 2-14). Objects within the range of depth of field will be in focus, whereas objects outside the depth of field will be out of focus.

Image Quality

Careful examination reveals that some details in an object are not reproduced in the image. Images are imperfect facsimiles, not exact scaled duplicates of the original object. Fundamentally, detail is lost because object points are imaged as diffuse spots rather than as perfect points.

Consider an object 50 cm in front of a pinhole 1 mm in diameter. Paper is placed 50 cm behind the pinhole, so the magnification is −1. A small pencil of rays from each object point traverses the aperture (Fig 2-15).

Each object point produces a 2-mm-diameter spot in the image. These spots are called *blur circles*, although this term is somewhat misleading in that off-axis object points produce elliptical spots in the image. Further, this analysis ignores diffraction effects that make the spot even larger and more irregular. In any case, if 2 object points are widely separated, their images will also be separate. However, when the object points are close (but still distinctly separate), their images overlap. Because the space between object points is not present in the image, detail has been lost.

To some extent, the loss of detail can be mitigated by using a smaller pinhole (Fig 2-16). For example, a 0.5-mm pinhole will produce 1-mm-diameter blur circles, and the object points could be closer together before their images overlapped. A smaller pinhole gives a dimmer, but more detailed, image. Nevertheless, there is always some loss of detail.

Detail is lost because the blur circle is larger than a point. A smaller blur circle preserves more detail, but the only way to avoid any loss of detail is to produce a perfect

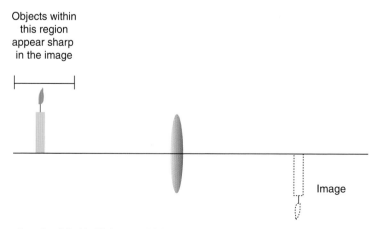

Figure 2-14 Depth of field. Objects within the depth of field are clear in the image. *(Illustration developed by Edmund H. Thall, MD, and Kevin M. Miller, MD, and rendered by C. H. Wooley.)*

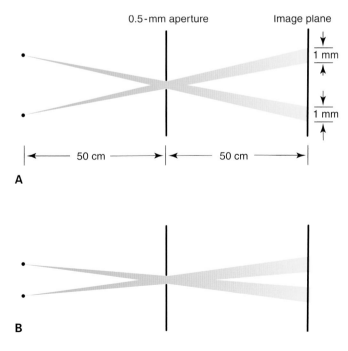

Figure 2-15 A, In pinhole imaging, a small pencil of rays from each object point traverses the aperture, producing a small spot in the image. **B,** If the object points are too close to each other, their images overlap. *(Illustration developed by Kevin M. Miller, MD, and rendered by C. H. Wooley.)*

Figure 2-16 A, A smaller pinhole restricts light from a single object point to a smaller spot in the image. **B,** Object points can be closer together before their images overlap, and thus the image contains more detail. This analysis ignores diffraction effects. *(Illustration developed by Kevin M. Miller, MD, and rendered by C. H. Wooley.)*

point image of each object point. Theoretically, if a perfect point image could be produced for every point of an object, the image would be an exact duplicate of the object. A perfect point image of an object point is called a *stigmatic image.* "Stigmatic" is derived from the Greek word *stigma,* which refers to a sharply pointed stylus.

Loss of detail occurs in lens and mirror imaging as well, because light from an object point is distributed over a region of the image rather than being confined to a perfect image point (Fig 2-17). Generally, lenses focus light from a single object point to a spot 10–100 μm across. This is better than a typical pinhole, but the shape of the spot can be very irregular. The term *blur circle* is especially misleading when applied to lenses and mirrors. A better term is *point spread function,* which describes the way light from a single object point is spread out in the image.

To summarize, a *stigmatic* image is a perfect point image of an object point. However, in most cases, images are not stigmatic. Instead, light from a single object point is distributed over a small region of the image known as a blur circle or, more generally, a point spread function. The image formed by an optical system is the spatial summation of the point spread function for every object point. The amount of detail in an image is related to the size of the blur circle or point spread function for each object point. The smaller the point spread, the better the resemblance between object and image.

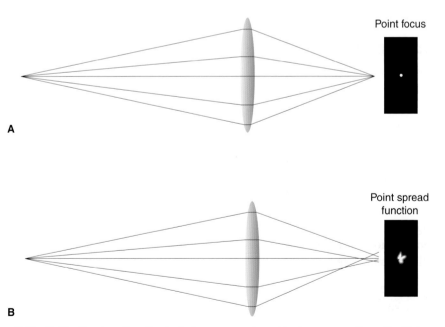

Figure 2-17 A, Textbooks often illustrate images produced by lenses as stigmatic. **B,** In most cases, however, the images are not stigmatic. The point spread function reveals how faithfully an imaging system reproduces each object point. The final image is the spatial summation of the point spread function for all object points. *(Illustration developed by Kevin M. Miller, MD, and rendered by C. H. Wooley.)*

Brightness and Irradiance

The word *brightness* is often used imprecisely. Brightness describes a visual perception: the response of the nervous system to light entering the eye. The individual's perception of brightness depends not only on the amount of light reaching the retina but also on many other factors such as the degree of dark adaptation and presence of pathology. *Irradiance* is a better term for discussing image characteristics. It is a purely physical measure of the amount of light per unit area of an image.

The relationship between irradiance and brightness is similar to the relationship between wavelength and color. If light of a given wavelength is observed by 2 people, one with normal color vision and the other with anomalous color perception, these 2 observers will "see" different colors. *Wavelength* is a physical property of the light itself, whereas *color* depends on the visual system. Likewise, *irradiance* depends only on light itself; *brightness* is a perception.

Clinically, the most important use of irradiance is in the calibration of various testing apparatuses such as perimeters. Periodic calibration is essential to the reproducibility of visual tests.

Light Propagation

An intensive investigation of light propagation was begun in the late 1500s. Numerous experiments measuring light deviation were carried out, and the data were collected and summarized as laws. These laws are summarized in the following sections.

Optical Media and Refractive Index

Light can travel through a variety of materials, such as air, glass, plastics, liquids, crystals, some biological tissues, the vacuum of space, and even some metals. A *medium* is any material that transmits light.

Light travels at different speeds in different media. Light moves fastest in a vacuum and slower through any material. The *refractive index* of an optical medium is the ratio of the speed of light in a vacuum to the speed of light in the medium and is usually denoted in mathematical equations by the lowercase letter *n*. The speed of light in a vacuum is 299,792,458 m/s. This is approximately 300,000 km/s or 186,000 miles/s. In 1983 the Système International defined a meter as the distance light travels in a vacuum during 1/299,792,458 of a second. Refractive index is always greater than or equal to 1. In computations, it is often easier to work with the refractive index of a material than directly with the speed of light.

$$n = \frac{\text{speed of light in vacuum}}{\text{speed of light in medium}}$$

Refractive index is quite sensitive to a material's chemical composition. A small amount of salt or sugar dissolved in water changes its refractive index. Because refractive index is easy to measure accurately, chemists use it to identify compounds or determine their purity. Glass manufacturers alter the refractive index of glass by adding small amounts of rare earth elements. Until recently, clinical labs screened for diabetes by measuring the refractive index of urine. Table 2-1 lists the refractive indices of various tissues and materials of clinical interest.

Refractive index varies with temperature and barometric pressure, but these changes are usually small enough to be ignored. One exception is silicone polymer. The refractive index of polymerized silicone at room temperature (20°C) differs enough from its index at eye temperature (35°C) that manufacturers of silicone intraocular lenses (IOLs) have to account for the variation.

Refractive index also varies with wavelength. As discussed in Chapter 1, Physical Optics, light can be regarded as an electromagnetic wave of various wavelengths. The visual system perceives different wavelengths of light as different colors, with long wavelengths appearing red, intermediate wavelengths appearing yellow or green, and short wavelengths appearing blue. In a vacuum, all wavelengths travel at the same speed. In any other medium, short wavelengths usually travel more slowly than long wavelengths. This phenomenon is called *dispersion.*

In the human eye, chromatic dispersion leads to *chromatic aberration.* If yellow wavelengths are focused precisely on the retina, blue light will be focused in front of the retina and red light will be focused behind the retina. (See Clinical Example 2-3.)

Some media, such as quartz, are optically inhomogeneous. That is, the speed of light through the material depends on the direction of light propagation through the material.

Table 2-1 Refractive Index (Helium D Line) for Some Materials of Clinical Interest

Material	Refractive Index
Air	1.000
Water	1.333
Cornea	1.376
Aqueous and vitreous humor	1.336
Spectacle crown glass	1.523
Polymethylmethacrylate (PMMA)	1.492

CLINICAL EXAMPLE 2-3

You may notice that red objects appear nearer than blue objects when they are displayed against a black background (Fig 2-18). This effect stands out in slide presentations that are rich in red and blue text and is known as *chromostereopsis.* It occurs because the human eye has approximately 0.5 D of chromatic aberration. Even individuals with red-green color blindness can observe the effect. To bring red print into focus, the eye must accommodate. To bring blue print into focus, the eye must relax accommodation. As a result, red print appears closer than blue print. The accommodative effort required to bring the various pieces of a chromatic image into focus impart to it a 3-dimensional quality.

Figure 2-18 Chromostereopsis is demonstrated by this illustration of red and blue print on a black background. The illustration is not very dramatic unless rendered on a computer monitor or projected onto a screen. *(Illustration developed by Kevin M. Miller, MD, and rendered by C. H. Wooley.)*

Law of Rectilinear Propagation

The law of rectilinear propagation states that light in a single medium travels along straight-line paths called *rays* (Fig 2-19). The light ray is the most fundamental construct in geometrical optics. Of particular note, rays traversing an aperture continue in straight lines in geometrical optics. A bundle of light rays traveling close to each other in the same direction is known as a *pencil* of light.

The law of rectilinear propagation is inaccurate insofar as it does not account for the effect of diffraction as light traverses an aperture (see Chapter 1, Physical Optics). The basic distinction between physical optics and geometrical optics is that the latter, being based on the law of rectilinear propagation, ignores diffraction. For clinical purposes, diffraction effects are rarely important. However, in situations where diffraction effects are significant, geometrical optics is invalid.

Optical Interfaces

The boundary separating 2 different optical media is called an *optical interface*. Typically, when light strikes an interface, some light is transmitted through the interface, some is reflected, and some is absorbed or converted to heat by the interface. The amount of light transmitted, reflected, and absorbed depends on several factors.

Rays and pencils of light undergo specular reflection and transmission at smooth optical interfaces (Fig 2-20). Pencils of light undergo diffuse reflection and transmission

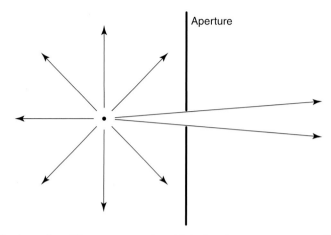

Figure 2-19 The law of rectilinear propagation. Light in a homogeneous medium propagates along straight line paths originating from a point source. A ray is a geometrical construct that represents a light path. Notice that rays traversing an aperture continue along a straight line. *(Illustration developed by Edmond H. Thall, MD, and Kevin M. Miller, MD, and rendered by C. H. Wooley.)*

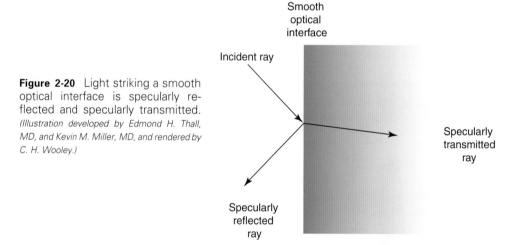

Figure 2-20 Light striking a smooth optical interface is specularly reflected and specularly transmitted. *(Illustration developed by Edmond H. Thall, MD, and Kevin M. Miller, MD, and rendered by C. H. Wooley.)*

at rough optical interfaces (Fig 2-21). If a pencil of light is stopped down to a single ray, it is reflected and transmitted specularly by a rough interface.

Specular Reflection: Law of Reflection

In specular reflection, the direction of the reflected ray bears a definite relationship to the direction of the incident ray. To express a precise relationship between incident rays and reflected rays, it is necessary to construct an imaginary line perpendicular to the optical interface at the point where the incident ray meets the interface. This imaginary line is a *surface normal* (Fig 2-22). The surface normal and the incident ray together define an imaginary plane known as the plane of incidence and reflection. The angle

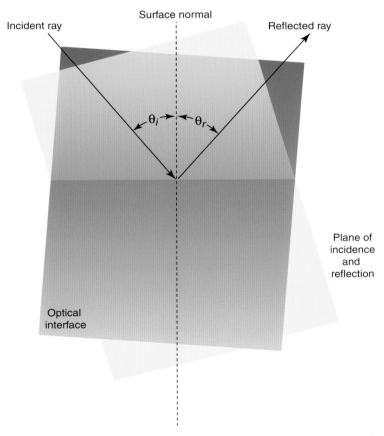

Figure 2-21 A pencil of light striking a rough optical interface is diffusely reflected and diffusely transmitted. *(Illustration developed by Kevin M. Miller, MD, and rendered by C. H. Wooley.)*

Figure 2-22 Illustration showing the definitions of angle of incidence, angle of reflection, surface normal, and the plane of incidence and reflection *(yellow). (Illustration developed by Edmond H. Thall, MD, and Kevin M. Miller, MD, and rendered by C. H. Wooley.)*

formed by the incident ray and surface normal is the *angle of incidence* θ_i. Note that this is not the angle between the incident ray and the optical interface. The reflected ray and the surface normal form the *angle of reflection* θ_r.

The *law of reflection* states that the reflected ray lies in the same plane as the incident ray and the surface normal (ie, the reflected ray lies in the plane of incidence) and that $\theta_i = \theta_r$ (Fig 2-23).

The amount of light reflected from a surface depends on θ_i and the plane of polarization of the light. The general expression for reflectivity can be derived from Fresnel's equations, which are beyond the scope of this text. The reflectivity at normal incidence is simple and depends only on the optical media bounding the interface. The *reflection coefficient* for normal incidence is given by

$$R = \left(\frac{n_2 - n_1}{n_2 + n_1} \right)^2$$

The reflection coefficient can be used to calculate the amount of light transmitted at an optical interface if absorption losses are minimal. (See Clinical Example 2-4.)

Specular Transmission: Law of Refraction

In specular transmission, the transmitted ray's direction bears a definite relation to the incident ray's direction. Again, a surface normal is constructed, and the angle of incidence and the plane of incidence and transmission are defined just as they were for reflection (Fig 2-24). The angle formed by the transmitted ray and the surface normal is the *angle of refraction*, also known as the *angle of transmission*. The angle of transmission θ_t is preferred in this text because the angle of refraction θ_r might otherwise be confused with the angle of reflection θ_r.

At the optical interface, light undergoes an abrupt change in speed that, in turn, usually produces an abrupt change in direction. The *law of refraction*, also known as

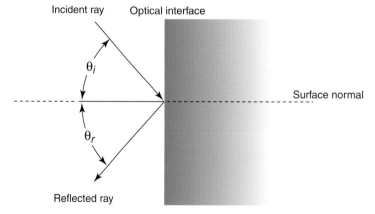

Figure 2-23 The law of reflection. Compared to the previous figure, the optical interface here is vertical instead of horizontal. The surface normal, incident ray, and reflected ray all lie in the same plane (in this case the plane of the paper). The angle of incidence equals the angle of reflection. *(Illustration developed by Edmond H. Thall, MD, and Kevin M. Miller, MD, and rendered by C. H. Wooley.)*

How much more reflective is an acrylic IOL than a silicone IOL? Assume that the index of refraction of acrylic is 1.55 and the index of refraction of silicone is 1.43.

An IOL is immersed in aqueous, which has an index of refraction of 1.33. The reflectivity coefficient of an acrylic IOL inside the eye is

$$R_{acrylic} = \left(\frac{1.55 - 1.33}{1.55 + 1.33}\right)^2 = 0.00584 = 0.584\%$$

The reflectivity coefficient of a silicone IOL inside the eye is

$$R_{silicone} = \left(\frac{1.43 - 1.33}{1.43 + 1.33}\right)^2 = 0.00131 = 0.131\%$$

Therefore, an acrylic IOL is 0.584/0.131 = 4.46 times more reflective than a silicone IOL.

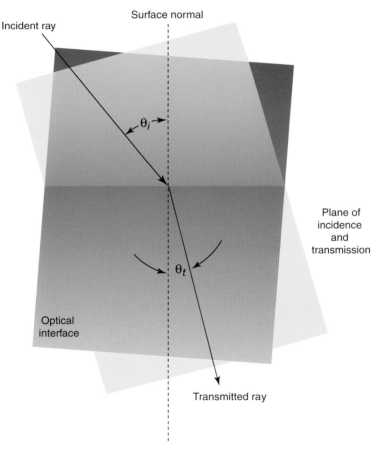

Figure 2-24 Illustration showing the definitions of angle of incidence, angle of transmission, surface normal, and the plane of incidence and transmission *(yellow)*. *(Illustration developed by Edmond H. Thall, MD, and Kevin M. Miller, MD, and rendered by C. H. Wooley.)*

Snell's law, in honor of its discoverer, states that the refracted or transmitted ray lies in the same plane as the incident ray and the surface normal and that

$$n_i \sin\theta_i = n_t \sin\theta_t$$

where

n_i = refractive index of incident medium
n_t = refractive index of transmitted medium
θ_i = angle of incidence
θ_t = angle of transmission

When light travels from a medium of lower refractive index to a medium of higher refractive index, it bends toward the surface normal. Conversely, when light travels from a higher to a lower refractive index, it bends away from the surface normal (Fig 2-25; Clinical Example 2-5).

Normal Incidence

Normal incidence occurs when a light ray is perpendicular to the optical interface. In other words, the surface normal coincides with the ray. If the interface is a refracting

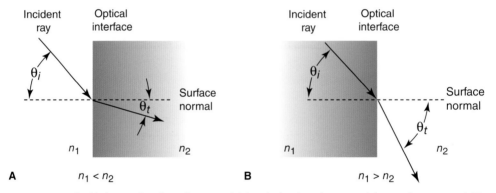

Figure 2-25 A, Light moving from lower to higher index bends toward the surface normal. **B,** Conversely, light moving from higher to lower index bends away from the surface normal. *(Illustration developed by Edmond H. Thall, MD, and Kevin M. Miller, MD, and rendered by C. H. Wooley.)*

CLINICAL EXAMPLE 2-5

Imagine you are fishing from a pier and you spot a "big one" in front of you a short distance below the surface of the water. You don't have a fishing rod, but instead you are armed with a spear (Fig 2-26). How should you throw the spear to hit the fish?

From your knowledge of Snell's law, you know that the fish is not where it appears to be. If you throw the spear at the fish, you will certainly miss it. What you have to do is throw the spear in front of the virtual fish, the one you see, to hit the real fish.

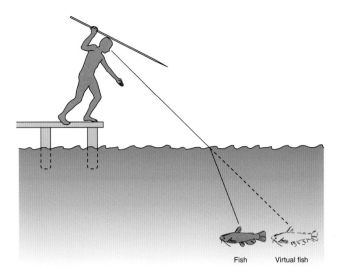

Figure 2-26 The fisherman must throw the spear in front of the virtual fish to hit the actual fish. *(Illustration developed by Kevin M. Miller, MD, and rendered by Jonathan Clark.)*

surface, the ray is undeviated. Light changes speed as it crosses the interface but does not change direction. If the surface reflects specularly, rays and pencils of light will be reflected back along a 90° angle to the surface.

Total Internal Reflection

Total internal reflection (TIR) occurs when light travels from a high-index medium to a low-index medium and the angle of incidence exceeds a certain *critical angle.* Under these circumstances, the incident ray does not pass through the interface; all its energy is reflected instead of transmitted. The law of reflection governs the direction of the reflected ray.

Figure 2-27A shows a light ray traveling from a high-index medium (spectacle crown glass) into a low-index medium (air). In this situation, the transmitted ray bends away from the surface normal, and thus the angle of transmission exceeds the angle of incidence. As the angle of incidence increases, the angle of transmission increases even more. Eventually, the angle of transmission equals 90°. At this point, the transmitted ray grazes along the optical interface (Fig 2-27B).

The critical angle is the angle of incidence that produces a transmitted ray 90° to the surface normal. The critical angle θ_c can be calculated from Snell's law:

$$n_i \sin\theta_c = n_t \sin 90°$$

The sine of 90° is 1; thus,

$$n_i \sin\theta_c = n_t$$

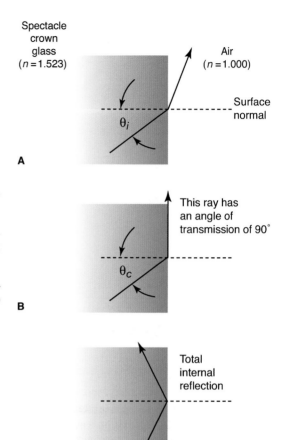

Figure 2-27 **A,** When light travels from a high-index medium to a low-index medium, it bends away from the surface normal. **B,** At the critical angle, θ_c, the refracted light travels in the optical interface. **C,** Beyond the critical angle, all light is reflected by the interface. In **A** and **B,** light is also reflected by the interface, but this is not drawn. *(Illustration developed by Kevin M. Miller, MD, and rendered by C. H. Wooley.)*

Rearranging gives

$$\sin\theta_c = \frac{n_t}{n_i}$$

So, the angle of transmission is 90° when the angle of incidence is

$$\theta_c = \arcsin\frac{n_t}{n_i}$$

In the current example, $n_i = 1.000$ and $n_t = 1.523$, so the critical angle is 41.0°.

What happens when the angle of incidence exceeds the critical angle? As Figure 2-27C shows, the angle of transmission increases as the angle of incidence increases, but the angle of transmission cannot exceed 90°. Consequently, refraction cannot occur. Indeed, Snell's law has no valid mathematical solution (in real numbers) when the critical angle is exceeded. Instead, the incident ray is 100% reflected.

TIR is a rather curious phenomenon. Consider light traveling from spectacle crown glass to air. If the angle of incidence is 10°, the light transmits easily as it crosses the interface. However, if the angle of refraction is 45°, the interface becomes an impenetrable barrier! The interface is transparent to some rays and opaque to others. Physicists have devoted a great deal of attention to this phenomenon.

TIR has great practical value. In the early 1600s, it was difficult to make a good mirror. The best surfaces could specularly reflect only about 80% of incident light, and the rest was diffusely reflected, which made these surfaces nearly useless as imaging devices. However, TIR is just that—total. When TIR occurs, 100% of the light is reflected. In the past, often the only way to make a practical mirror was to use internally reflecting prisms. Today, TIR is still used in prisms found in binoculars, slit lamps, and operating microscopes, to give just a few examples. Clinically, however, TIR can be a nuisance, such as when you are trying to examine the anterior chamber angle (Clinical Example 2-6).

Dispersion

With the exception of a vacuum, which always has a refractive index of 1.000, refractive indices are not fixed values. They vary as a function of wavelength. In general, refractive

---

CLINICAL EXAMPLE 2-6

TIR makes it impossible to view the eye's anterior chamber angle without the use of a contact lens. Light from the angle undergoes TIR at the air–cornea interface (Fig 2-28A). Light from the angle never escapes the eye. The problem is overcome by using a contact lens to eliminate the air at the surface of the cornea (Fig 2-28B). Light travels from the cornea (or coupling gel) to the higher-index contact lens. TIR never occurs when light travels from lower to higher index, so light enters the contact lens and is reflected from the mirror. TIR does not occur at the front surface of the contact lens because the angle of incidence is less than the critical angle.

Assuming the refractive index of the tear film on the front surface of the cornea is 1.333, the critical angle for the air–tear interface is

$$\theta_c = \arcsin \frac{1}{1.333} = 48.6°$$

From trigonometry, we can estimate the angle at which light rays from the trabecular meshwork strike the air–tear interface. The situation is illustrated in Figure 2-29 with average anatomic dimensions. The effect of the back surface of the cornea is ignored because it has relatively little power and this is only a rough calculation. From basic trigonometry,

$$\theta_i = \arctan \frac{5.5}{3.5} = 57.5°$$

Interestingly, this rough calculation shows that θ_c is exceeded by only a few degrees. When the cornea is ectatic (as in some cases of keratoconus), the angle of incidence is less than θ_c and the angle structures are visible without a goniolens.

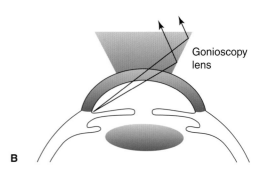

Figure 2-28 **A,** Light from the anterior chamber angle undergoes total internal reflection (TIR) at the air–tear film interface. **B,** A contact lens prevents TIR and allows visualization of the angle structures. *(Illustration developed by Kevin M. Miller, MD, and rendered by C. H. Wooley.)*

Figure 2-29 Average anatomic dimensions of the anterior segment. *(Illustration developed by Kevin M. Miller, MD, and rendered by C. H. Wooley.)*

indices are higher for short wavelengths and lower for long wavelengths. As a result, blue light travels more slowly than red light in most media, and Snell's law predicts a greater angle of refraction for blue light than for red light (Fig 2-30).

The *Abbe number,* also known as the V-number, is a measure of a material's dispersion. Named for the German physicist Ernest Abbe (1840–1905), the Abbe number *V* is defined as

$$V = \frac{n_\mathrm{D} - 1}{n_\mathrm{F} - n_\mathrm{C}}$$

where n_D, n_F, and n_C are the refractive indices of the Fraunhofer D, F, and C spectral lines (589.2 nm, 486.1 nm and 656.3 nm, respectively). Low-dispersion materials, which demonstrate low chromatic aberration, have high values of *V*. High-dispersion materials have low values of *V*. Abbe numbers for common optical media typically range from 20 to 70.

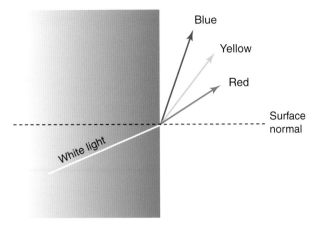

Figure 2-30 Chromatic dispersion. *(Illustration developed by Kevin M. Miller, MD, and rendered by C. H. Wooley.)*

Reflection and Refraction at Curved Surfaces

For the sake of simplicity, the laws of reflection and refraction were illustrated at flat optical interfaces. However, most optical elements have curved surfaces. To apply the law of reflection or refraction to curved surfaces, the position of the surface normal must be determined, because the angles of incidence, reflection, and refraction are defined with respect to the surface normal. Once the position of the surface normal is known, the laws of refraction and reflection define the relationship between the angle of incidence and the angles of refraction and reflection, respectively.

There is a mathematical procedure for determining the position of the surface normal in any situation, but the details of it are beyond the scope of this discussion. However, for some geometrical shapes, the position of the surface normal is easy to determine. In particular, the normal to a spherical surface always intersects the sphere's center. For example, Figure 2-31 shows a ray incident on a spherical surface. The incident ray is 2 cm above, and parallel to, the optical axis. The surface normal is found by connecting the point where the ray strikes the surface to the center of the sphere. The angle of incidence and the sine of the angle of incidence are determined by simple trigonometry.

Fermat's Principle

The mathematician Pierre de Fermat believed that natural processes occur in the most economical way. Fermat's principle, as applied to optics, implies that light travels from one point to another along the path requiring the least time. Historically, the laws of reflection and refraction were discovered by careful experimental measurements before Fermat's time. However, both the law of refraction and the law of reflection can be mathematically derived from Fermat's principle without the need for any measurements.

Suppose that the law of refraction were unknown, and consider light traveling from a point source in air, across an optical interface, to some point in glass (Fig 2-32). Unaware of Snell's law, we might consider various hypothetical paths that light might

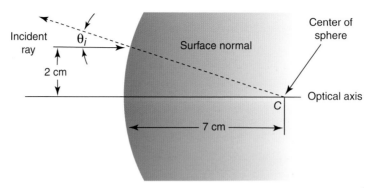

Figure 2-31 A ray 2 cm above and parallel to the optical axis is incident on a spherical surface. The surface normal is found by connecting the point where the ray strikes the surface to the center of the sphere (point *C*). The angle of incidence is found using similar triangles and trigonometry (arctan $2/7 = 16.6°$). *(Illustration developed by Edmond H. Thall, MD, and Kevin M. Miller, MD, and rendered by C. H. Wooley.)*

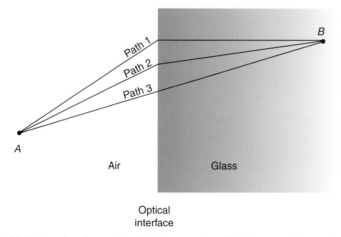

Figure 2-32 Light traveling from *A* to *B* follows only path 2 because it requires the least time. Light does not travel along either path 1 or 3. *(Illustration developed by Edmond H. Thall, MD, and Kevin M. Miller, MD, and rendered by C. H. Wooley.)*

follow as it moves from point A to point B. Path 3 is a straight line from A to B and is the shortest total distance between the points. However, a large part of path 3 is inside glass, where light travels more slowly. Path 3 is not the fastest route. Path 1 is the longest route from A to B but has the shortest distance in glass. Nevertheless, the extreme length of the overall route makes this a fairly slow path. Path 2 is the best compromise between distance in glass and total path length, and this is the path light will actually follow.

Using mathematics beyond the scope of this text, it can be shown that the optimal path is the one predicted by Snell's law. Thus, Snell's law is a consequence of Fermat's principle.

Fermat's principle is an important conceptual and practical tool. The concept of *optical path length (OPL)* enhances the practical utility of Fermat's principle. OPL is the actual distance light travels in a given medium multiplied by the medium's refractive index. For instance, if light travels 5 cm in air ($n = 1.000$) and 10 cm in glass ($n = 1.523$), the OPL is 5 cm $\times$ 1.000 + 10 cm $\times$ 1.523 = 20.2 cm. According to Fermat's principle, light follows the path of minimum OPL.

Figure 2-33 shows light from an object point traveling along 2 different paths to the image point. According to Fermat's principle, for both paths to intersect at the image point, the time required to travel from object to image point (or alternatively, the OPL) must be absolutely identical for each path. If the time required for light to travel along each path is not exactly identical, the paths will not intersect at the image point.

Light traveling path 1 from object to image point traverses a relatively thick part of the lens. Light traveling the longer path 2 goes through less glass. If the lens is properly shaped, the greater distance in air is perfectly compensated for by the shorter distance in glass. So the time required to travel from object to image—and, thus, the OPL—is identical for both paths.

Stigmatic Imaging Using a Single Refracting Surface

By the early 1600s, the telescope and microscope had been invented. Although useful, the images produced by these early devices were often not very good because their lenses did not focus stigmatically or even nearly stigmatically.

At the time, lens makers were not very particular about the shape of the surfaces that were ground on the lens. It seemed that any curved surface produced an image, so lens surfaces were carefully polished but haphazardly figured (ie, shaped). However, as ideas such as stigmatic imaging and Snell's law developed, it became clear that the shape of the lens surfaces was intimately connected to the quality of the image. As the 17th century continued, efforts began to improve image quality by carefully figuring the lens surfaces.

The question arose, What surface produces the best image? Descartes applied Fermat's principle to the simplest situation possible—a single refracting surface. Consider a single object point and a long glass rod (Fig 2-34). Descartes realized that if the end of the rod were figured in a nearly elliptical shape, a stigmatic image would form in the glass. This shape became known as a Cartesian ellipsoid, or Cartesian conoid.

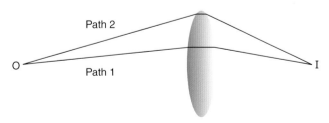

Figure 2-33 Light traveling the shorter distance from object to image point traverses a thick part of the lens. Light traveling the longer path goes through less glass. If the lens is properly shaped, the greater distance in air is perfectly compensated for by the shorter distance in glass, and the time required to travel from object to image is identical for both paths. *(Illustration developed by Edmond H. Thall, MD, and Kevin M. Miller, MD, and rendered by C. H. Wooley.)*

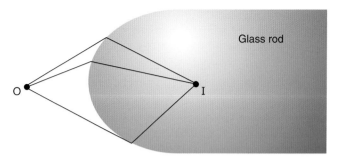

Figure 2-34 The Cartesian conoid is a single refracting surface that produces a stigmatic image for a single object point. *(Illustration developed by Edmond H. Thall, MD, and Kevin M. Miller, MD, and rendered by C. H. Wooley.)*

Some readers may be troubled by the fact that the image forms in glass instead of air, but this is not a problem. After all, in a myopic eye the image forms in the vitreous cavity, and in an emmetropic eye it forms on the retina. Once a stigmatic image is produced, the rod can be cut and a second Cartesian ellipsoid placed on the back surface (Fig 2-35). The final image is also stigmatic. The Cartesian ellipsoid produces a stigmatic image of only 1 object point. All other object points image nonstigmatically.

Until about 1960, it was impossible to manufacture a Cartesian ellipsoid. The only surfaces that could be accurately figured were spheres, cylinders, spherocylinders, and flats. Now aspheric surfaces are relatively easy to manufacture.

Descartes established that a single refracting surface could, at best, produce a stigmatic image of only 1 object point. By means of mathematics beyond the scope of this text, it can be demonstrated that an optical system can produce a stigmatic image for only as many object points as there are "degrees of freedom" in the optical system. A single lens has 3 degrees of freedom *(df)*: the front surface, the back surface, and the lens thickness. A combination of 2 lenses has 7 *df*: the 4 lens surfaces, the 2 lens thicknesses, and the distance between the lenses. Most optical systems generally have many lenses to improve image quality.

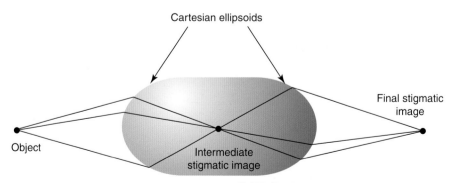

Figure 2-35 A combination of Cartesian ellipsoids also gives a stigmatic image. *(Illustration developed by Edmond H. Thall, MD, and Kevin M. Miller, MD, and rendered by C. H. Wooley.)*

First-Order Optics

For centuries, the sphere was the only useful lens surface that could be manufactured. Descartes proved that lenses with spherical surfaces do not produce stigmatic images, but common experience shows that such lenses can produce useful, if not perfect, images. Consequently, the properties of spherical refracting surfaces have been carefully studied.

Today, the accepted approach for studying the imaging properties of any lens is the method called *exact ray tracing*. In this technique, the paths of several rays, all originating from a single object point, are traced using Snell's law. A computer carries out the calculations to as high a degree of accuracy as necessary, usually between 6 and 8 significant figures.

Figure 2-36 shows an exact ray trace for a single spherical refracting surface. Because the image is not stigmatic, the rays do not converge to a single point. However, there is one location where the rays are confined to the smallest area, and this is the location of the image. The distribution of rays at the image location indicates the size of the blur circle or point spread function. From the size of the blur circle, the image quality can be determined. From the location of the image, other properties, such as magnification, can be determined. Ultimately, all image properties can be determined using an exact ray trace.

After the discovery of Snell's law, it was realized that exact ray tracing could be used to analyze optical systems. However, exact ray tracing requires extensive trigonometric calculations. Until relatively recent advances in computer technology, the computational requirements made the technique of exact ray tracing impractical. Today, such calculations are easily performed on personal computers, using software that can trace hundreds of rays in a second.

Beginning in the 1600s, methods of analyzing optical systems were developed that either greatly reduced or eliminated the need for calculation. These methods are based on approximations—that is, these methods do not give exact answers. Nevertheless, carefully chosen approximations can yield results that are very close to the exact answer while greatly simplifying the mathematics.

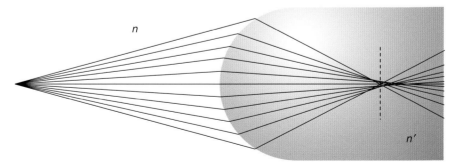

Figure 2-36 An exact ray trace for a single refracting surface. The image is not stigmatic. However, at one particular location, indicated by the *dotted line,* the rays are confined to the smallest area. This is the image location. *(Illustration developed by Edmond H. Thall, MD, and Kevin M. Miller, MD, and rendered by C. H. Wooley.)*

The trick is to choose approximations that provide as much simplification as possible while retaining as much accuracy as possible. In this regard, the mathematician Carl Gauss (1777–1855) made many contributions to the analysis of optical systems. Gauss's work, combined with that of others, developed into a system for analyzing optical systems that has become known as *first-order optics*.

Ignoring Image Quality

To determine image quality, it is necessary to know how light from a single object point is distributed in the image (ie, the point spread function). To determine the point spread function, hundreds of rays must be accurately traced. In Gauss's day, manufacturing techniques rather than optical system design limited image quality. Accordingly, there was little interest in theoretically analyzing image quality. Interest lay instead in analyzing other image features, such as magnification and location.

To determine all image characteristics except image quality requires tracing only a few rays. If image quality is ignored, analysis of optical systems is reduced from tracing hundreds of rays to tracing just 2 rays. In Gauss's time, exactly tracing even 2 rays was a daunting task, however, especially if the optical system consisted of several lenses.

Paraxial Approximation

To exactly trace a ray through a refracting surface, a coordinate system must be established. By convention, the origin of the coordinate system is located at the vertex, the point where the optical axis intersects the surface. Also by convention, the y-axis is vertical, the z-axis coincides with the optical axis, and the x-axis is perpendicular to the page (Fig 2-37). An arbitrary object point is selected, and an arbitrary ray is drawn from that object point to the refracting surface.

The first difficulty in making an exact ray trace is determining the precise coordinates (y, z) of the position where the ray strikes the refracting surface. The formula for finding

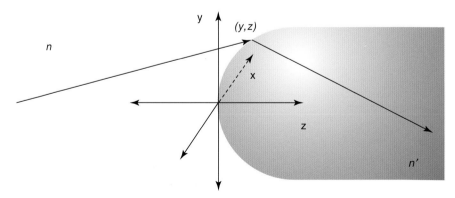

Figure 2-37 To exactly trace a ray through a refracting surface, it is necessary to establish a coordinate system (the x-, y-, and z-axes) and then find the precise coordinates (y, z) of the point where the ray intersects the surface. *(Illustration developed by Edmond H. Thall, MD, and Kevin M. Miller, MD, and rendered by C. H. Wooley.)*

the intersection of a ray with a spherical surface requires fairly complicated calculations involving square roots (and extracting square roots was no mean feat in the 1600s).

Instead of trying to trace an arbitrary ray through an optical system, it is easier to deal with rays extremely close to the optical axis, so-called *paraxial rays*. A refracting surface that is sufficiently close to the optical axis may be treated as flat. Just as the earth's surface seems flat to a human observer, a refracting surface "seems" flat to a paraxial ray (Fig 2-38).

Note that for a ray to be paraxial, it must hug the optical axis over its entire course from object to image. A ray from an object point far off axis is not paraxial even if it strikes the refracting surface near the axis (Fig 2-39).

Treating a lens as a flat plane instead of a sphere eliminates the calculation necessary to find the intersection of the ray and the surface. The intersection of the ray with the surface is specified simply as a distance from the optical axis (*h* in Figure 2-40).

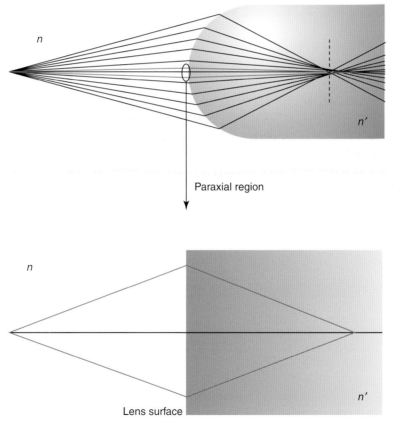

Figure 2-38 The paraxial region. The enlargement shows the paraxial region with the vertical scale greatly increased but the horizontal dimensions unchanged. Notice that in the paraxial region the lens is essentially flat. The paraxial rays are shown in *red. (Illustration developed by Edmond H. Thall, MD, and Kevin M. Miller, MD, and rendered by C. H. Wooley.)*

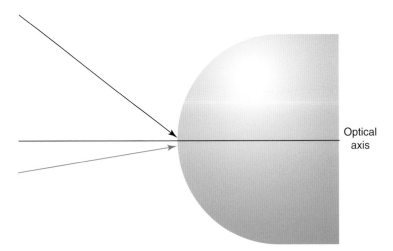

Figure 2-39 Both rays strike the refracting surface in the paraxial region. However, because it is close to the optical axis over its entire path, only the lower ray is a paraxial ray. *(Illustration developed by Edmond H. Thall, MD, and Kevin M. Miller, MD, and rendered by C. H. Wooley.)*

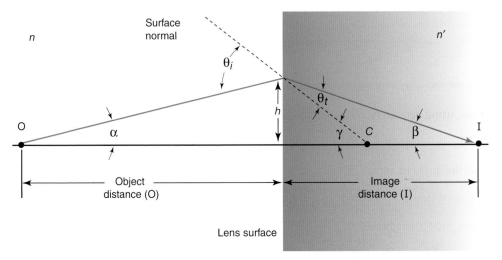

Figure 2-40 Detail of the paraxial region with the vertical scale greatly enlarged relative to the horizontal scale. The lens is spherical but appears flat in the paraxial region. The center of the lens is indicated by point C. The points O and I represent the object point and its image, respectively. θ_i and θ_t indicate the angles of incidence and transmission, respectively. *(Illustration developed by Edmond H. Thall, MD, and Kevin M. Miller, MD, and rendered by C. H. Wooley.)*

Small-Angle Approximation

To trace a paraxial ray, begin with an object point at or near the optical axis and extend a ray from the object point to the refracting surface, represented by a flat vertical plane (see Fig 2-40). The next step is to determine the direction of the ray after refraction.

To determine the direction of the refracted ray, apply Snell's law. The angle of incidence is θ_i and the angle of transmission is θ_t. Thus,

$$n \sin\theta_i = n' \sin\theta_t$$

Now the polynomial expansion for the sine function is

$$\sin\theta = \theta - \frac{\theta^3}{3!} + \frac{\theta^5}{5!} - \frac{\theta^7}{7!} \cdots$$

where the angle θ is expressed in radians. If the angle θ is small, the third-order term $\theta^3/3!$ and every term after it become insignificant, and the sine function can be approximated as

$$\sin\theta \approx \theta$$

This is the mathematical basis of the (essentially equivalent) terms *small-angle approximation, paraxial approximation*, and *first-order approximation*. Only the first-order term of the polynomial expansion needs to be used when the analysis is limited to paraxial rays, which have a small angle of entry into the optical system.

The angles appear large in the bottom part of Figure 2-38 because of the expanded vertical scale, but the upper part shows that in the paraxial region these angles are quite small.

Using the small-angle approximation, Snell's law becomes

$$n\theta_i = n'\theta_t$$

Now, using geometry and Figure 2-40, the angle of incidence θ_i is

$$\theta_i = \alpha + \gamma$$

and the angle of transmission θ_t is

$$\theta_t = \gamma - \beta$$

Thus, Snell's law becomes

$$n(\alpha + \gamma) = n'(\gamma - \beta)$$

or

$$n\alpha + n'\beta = \gamma(n' - n)$$

Now, the small-angle approximation also works for tangents:

$$\tan\alpha \approx \alpha \qquad \tan\beta \approx \beta \qquad \tan\gamma \approx \gamma$$

and

$$\tan\alpha = -\frac{h}{o}$$

The negative sign is used because the object distance (o) is considered a negative distance because it goes backward from the lens to the object point.

$$\tan\beta = -\frac{h}{i} \qquad \tan\gamma = \frac{h}{r}$$

Thus,

$$-\frac{nh}{o} + \frac{n'h}{i} = \frac{h(n'-n)}{r}$$

Canceling the common factor h gives

$$-\frac{n}{o} + \frac{n'}{i} = \frac{n'-n}{r}$$

Rearranging yields

$$\frac{n}{o} + \frac{(n'-n)}{r} = \frac{n'}{i}$$

Finally, we define the refractive power of the surface, $P = [(n'-n)/r]$. Thus,

$$\frac{n}{o} + P = \frac{n'}{i}$$

This is called the *lens maker's equation*. The ratio *n/o* is the *reduced object vergence* and the ratio *n'/i* is the *reduced image vergence*. Vergence is discussed in detail in the section Ophthalmic Lenses.

The Lens Maker's Equation

The lens maker's equation (LME) is one of the most important equations in ophthalmology. Unfortunately, it is also one of the most misused equations in all of ophthalmology.

Fundamentally, the LME says 2 things. First, the location of the image depends on the location of the object. In other words, every object is imaged in a different, unique position. Consider a specific example wherein the refractive index of a glass rod is 1.5 and the radius of curvature is 0.1 m. Suppose an object is in air with $n = 1.0$. The LME becomes

$$\frac{1}{o} + \frac{1.5-1.0}{0.1\,\text{m}} = \frac{1.5}{i}$$

or

$$\frac{1}{o} + 5\,\text{m}^{-1} = \frac{1.5}{i}$$

Note the units of reciprocal, or inverse, meters. Suppose the object is 1 m in front of the lens. Object distances are negative, so

$$\frac{1}{-1\,m} + 5\,m^{-1} = 4\,m^{-1} = \frac{1.5}{i}$$

$$i = \frac{1.5}{4\,m^{-1}} = 0.375\,m$$

Thus, the image is 37.5 cm behind the refracting surface.

If the object moves closer to the lens—say to 50 cm—similar calculations yield an image distance of 0.5 m, or 50 cm. Thus, as the object moves closer to the lens, the image moves farther away. The object and image always move in the same direction (in this case, to the right) (Fig 2-41). However, the object and image do not move by the same amount.

The LME also establishes a relationship between the shape of the refracting surface and its optical function. The radius of the spherical refracting surface affects the image characteristics. The *refractive power* (or simply *power*) of a spherical refracting surface is

$$P = \frac{(n' - n)}{r}$$

To demonstrate the significance of power, consider 2 spherical refractive surfaces, both constructed from glass rods ($n = 1.5$). Suppose that 1 refracting surface has a radius of 10 cm, as in the previous example, and the other has a radius of 20 cm. If an object is 1 m in front of each surface, where is the image? As shown in the previous example, the first surface has a power of 5.0 D and produces an image 37.5 cm behind the surface. The second surface has a power of 2.5 D and forms an image 1 m behind the refracting surface. Notice that the second surface has half the power, but the image is more than

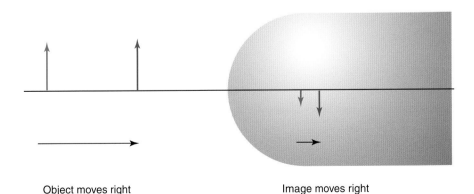

Object moves right   Image moves right

Figure 2-41 When the object moves closer to the refracting surface, the image moves farther away. Stated another way, both the object and image move in the same direction. When the object moves to the right, the image moves to the right and vice versa. *(Illustration developed by Edmond H. Thall, MD, and Kevin M. Miller, MD, and rendered by C. H. Wooley.)*

twice as far behind the refracting surface. The relationship between power and image characteristics is explored further in later discussions.

Unfortunately, in recent years the concept of refractive power has been misapplied, particularly in the field of refractive surgery. Refractive power applies only to spherical surfaces, and the cornea is not spherical. In general, every point on an aspheric surface is associated with infinitely many curvatures. There is no such thing as a single radius of curvature. The sphere is a very special case: a single radius of curvature characterizes the entire sphere. A single radius can characterize no other shape, and refractive power should not be applied to any nonspherical surface.

In addition, power is a paraxial concept; thus, it applies only to a small area near the optical axis. Power is not applicable to nonparaxial regions of the cornea. In the paraxial region, imaging is stigmatic (ie, paraxial rays focus to a common point). Even for spherical surfaces, outside the paraxial region rays do not focus to a single point (Fig 2-42). That is, outside this region, rays do not focus to the location predicted by the LME.

Ophthalmic Lenses

In this section, we build upon the basic principles of first-order optics to show how both simple lenses and complex multielement optical systems can be modeled. We also demonstrate how imaging problems are solved.

Vergence and Reduced Vergence

The LME has an interesting physical interpretation based on the idea of *vergence*. Typically, light diverges from object points and then traverses a lens, which converges the light to image points. The amount of divergence or convergence can be quantified.

First, if rays diverge from a point, the vergence is negative; if rays converge to a point, the vergence is positive. Consider a lens close to an object point (Fig 2-43A). The lens collects a large fraction of the light radiating from the object point. When the lens is

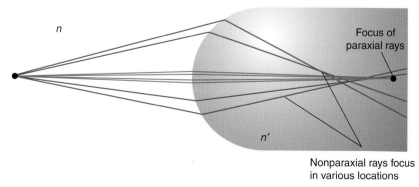

Figure 2-42 Rays in the paraxial region focus stigmatically. Rays outside the paraxial region do not focus at the image point, decreasing image quality. *(Illustration developed by Edmond H. Thall, MD, and Kevin M. Miller, MD, and rendered by C. H. Wooley.)*

Figure 2-43 A, Close to an object point light is strongly divergent, so a lens placed close to the object point collects a large fraction of the light radiated from the point. **B,** Farther from an object point light is much less divergent, so a lens collects a much smaller portion of the light radiated by the object point. *(Illustration developed by Kevin M. Miller, MD, and rendered by C. H. Wooley.)*

moved away from the object point, it collects a smaller amount of the light radiated by the object point because the light is less divergent (Fig 2-43B). Close to the lens, the light is more divergent; farther from the lens, the light is less divergent. Similarly, close to an image point, light is more convergent; farther from the image point, light is less convergent.

Vergence is therefore inversely proportional to distance from the object point or to the image point. Vergence is the reciprocal of distance. The distances used most often in ophthalmology are 4 m, 2 m, 1 m, 0.5 m, 0.33 m, 0.25 m, and 0.2 m. The reciprocals of these distances are, respectively, 0.25 m^{-1}, 0.5 m^{-1}, 1 m^{-1}, 2 m^{-1}, 3 m^{-1}, 4 m^{-1}, and 5 m^{-1}. For convenience, the reciprocal meter (m^{-1}) is given another name, the *diopter* (D).

As light travels away from an object point or toward an image point, its vergence constantly changes (Fig 2-44). To calculate the vergence of light at any point on a ray, one must know the location of the object or image point associated with the ray. Conversely, if one knows the vergence at some point along a ray, the position of the object or image point can be determined.

Reduced vergence is vergence multiplied by the refractive index of the medium. This term can be confusing because reduced vergence is numerically larger than vergence. For example, 1 m in front of an image point, light traveling in glass ($n = 1.5$) has a vergence of +1.0 D but a reduced vergence of +1.5 D. Confusing or not, however, the term *reduced vergence* is too well entrenched to be changed.

The LME can be interpreted in terms of reduced vergence. Light from an object point diverges, but the degree of divergence decreases as the light moves farther from the

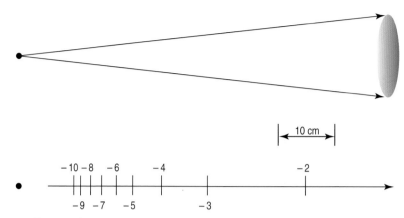

10 cm

- 10 - 8 - 6   - 4   - 2
- 9 - 7   - 5   - 3

Figure 2-44 Every point on a ray has a different vergence. The numbers indicate vergence in diopters. The linear scale is shown for comparison. *(Illustration developed by Edmond H. Thall, MD, and Kevin M. Miller, MD, and rendered by C. H. Wooley.)*

object point. Eventually, the light encounters the refracting surface, and just as it reaches the surface, it has a reduced vergence of n/o. The refracting surface suddenly changes the light's vergence by an amount equal to its power. As the light leaves the refracting surface, it has a reduced vergence of $(n/o) + P$, but because the light is converging to an image point, this must equal n'/i.

Calculations using the LME are inconvenient because they involve reciprocal distances. Vergence is a way to simplify the calculations. By means of reduced vergence, the LME

$$\frac{n}{o} + P = \frac{n'}{i}$$

can be written in a very simple form:

$$U + P = V$$

where U = reduced object vergence and V = reduced image vergence.

Consider an object in air 50 cm in front of a +5 D refracting surface with $n = 1.5$. Where is the image? Light diverging from the object has a negative vergence. When the light reaches the lens, it has a reduced vergence of −2 D. The lens adds +5 D, for a final reduced vergence at the lens of +3 D. The plus sign indicates the light converges as it leaves the lens. Dividing the reduced vergence by the index of the glass gives a vergence of +2 D, so the image is 50 cm behind the refracting surface.

The most common mistake in working with vergence calculations is ignoring the negative sign for divergent light. One way to avoid this mistake is to deal with the signs first, rather than with the numbers. For instance, in the previous problem, many people would begin by converting distance to diopters—that is, the object is 50 cm from the lens, so the vergence is +2 D. Having performed the conversion, it is easy to forget about the minus sign. It is better to deal with the sign first. In the previous problem, begin by noting that light diverges from the object so it has a negative value; then write down the sign and convert distance to vergence. Get in the habit of always writing the sign in front of the vergence, even when the sign is positive. In the preceding example, for instance, a plus sign precedes the vergences: +5 D and +3 D. If you encounter difficulties with a vergence calculation, check the signs first. The problem is most likely a dropped minus sign. (See Clinical Example 2-7.)

Transverse Magnification for a Single Spherical Refracting Surface

In the LME, object and image distances are measured from the vertex—that is, the point where the surface intersects the optical axis. To calculate transverse magnification using the equation given earlier, object and image distances should be measured from the nodal points. The nodal points overlap on a single spherical refracting surface at the center of curvature. Rays intersecting the center of curvature strike the surface at normal incidence and are undeviated (Fig 2-45).

If o and i are, respectively, the object and image distances for the LME, and r is the radius of curvature, then

$$\text{Transverse magnification} = \frac{i-r}{o-r}$$

It might appear that the denominator should be $o + r$ instead of $o - r$. However, $o - r$ is correct because the sign convention makes object distances negative. By algebraic manipulation, this can be converted to a very simple equation involving reduced vergence:

$$\text{Transverse magnification} = \frac{U}{V}$$

CLINICAL EXAMPLE 2-7

Imagine you are having a difficult time outlining the borders of a subretinal neovascular membrane on a fluorescein angiogram. You pull out a 20 D indirect ophthalmoscopy lens and use it as a simple magnifier. If you hold the lens 2.5 cm in front of the angiogram, where is the image?

Light from the angiogram enters the 20 D lens with a reduced vergence of

$$U = -\frac{1}{0.025\ \text{m}} = -40\ \text{D}$$

It exits the lens with a reduced vergence of

$$-40\ \text{D} + 20\ \text{D} = -20\ \text{D}$$

The light is divergent as it exits the lens; therefore, the virtual image you see is on the same side of the lens as the angiogram. It is located (1/20 D) = 0.05 m = 5 cm in front of the lens. Because the image is twice as far from the lens as the object, the transverse magnification is 2.

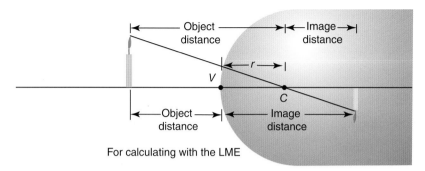

Figure 2-45 For the lens maker's equation (LME), object and image distances are measured from the vertex *(V)*. For calculating transverse magnification, object and image distances are measured from the nodal points, which are both located at the center of curvature *(C)*. The distance between the *C* and *V* is the radius of curvature, *r*. *(Illustration developed by Edmond H. Thall, MD, and Kevin M. Miller, MD, and rendered by C. H. Wooley.)*

Reduced vergence not only simplifies calculations with the LME but also simplifies calculation of magnification. Use of reduced vergence obviates the need for object or image distances, nodal points, or radius of curvature.

Thin-Lens Approximation

The LME deals with a single refracting surface, but, of course, lenses have 2 surfaces. According to the LME, when light from an object strikes the front surface of a lens, its (reduced) vergence changes by an amount equal to the power of the front surface P_f. The vergence continues to change as the light moves from the front to the back surface; this is known as the *vergence change on transfer* P_t. The back lens surface changes the vergence by an amount equal to the back-surface power P_b. Thus,

$$\frac{n}{o} + P_f + P_t + P_b = \frac{n'}{i}$$

The powers of the front and back lens surfaces are easily calculated, but the vergence change on transfer is difficult to calculate. However, because the vergence change on transfer is small in a thin lens, it can be ignored to arrive at the *thin-lens approximation*. The total lens power is the sum of the front- and back-surface powers. Thus,

$$\frac{n}{o} + P = \frac{n'}{i}$$

This is the *thin-lens equation* (TLE). The TLE and LME appear to be the same. However, there is an important difference: in the LME, *P* is the power of a single surface; in the TLE, *P* is the combined power of the front and back surfaces.

For example, if a +5 D thin lens has water (*n* = 1.33) in front and air in back and an object is 33 cm in front of the lens, where is the image? Light from the object strikes the lens with a reduced vergence of $(-1.33/0.33$ m$) = -4$ D. The lens changes the vergence by $+5$ D, so light leaves the lens with a vergence of $+1$ D, forming an image 1 m behind the lens.

The transverse magnification is the ratio of reduced object vergence to reduced image vergence. In the preceding example, the magnification is -4, indicating that the image is inverted and 4 times as large as the object.

Lens Combinations

Most optical systems consist of several lenses. For instance, consider an optical system consisting of 2 thin lenses in air. The first lens is $+5$ D, the second lens is $+8$ D, and they are separated by 45 cm. If an object is placed 1 m in front of the first lens, where is the final image and what is the transverse magnification?

In paraxial optics, the way to analyze a combination of lenses is to look at each lens individually. The TLE shows that the first lens produces an image 25 cm behind itself with a magnification of -0.25. Light converges to the image and then diverges again. The image formed by the first lens becomes the object for the second lens. The image is 20 cm in front of the second lens; thus, light strikes the second lens with a vergence of -5 D and forms an image 33 cm behind the second lens. The transverse magnification for the second lens alone is $(-5$ D$/3$ D$) = -1.66$. The total magnification is the product of the individual magnifications $-1.66 \times -0.25 = 0.42$.

Note that it is absolutely essential to calculate the position of the image formed by the first lens. Only after locating the first image is it possible to calculate the vergence of light as it reaches the second lens.

Any number of lenses can be analyzed in this way. Locate the image formed by the first lens and use it as the object for the second lens. Repeat the process for each subsequent lens. The overall transverse magnification is the product of the transverse magnifications produced by each individual lens.

Virtual Images and Objects

Many people find the subject of virtual images and virtual objects to be the most difficult aspect of geometrical optics. Virtual images and objects can be understood in terms of a few simple rules. The trick is to not "overthink" the subject.

Consider an object 10 cm in front of a $+5$ D thin lens in air (Fig 2-46A). Light strikes the lens with a vergence of -10 D and leaves with a vergence of -5 D. In this case, unlike in all the previous examples, light emerges with a negative vergence, which means that light is still diverging after crossing the lens. No real image is produced. The reader can easily verify this by repeating the basic imaging demonstration with a $+5$ D spherical convex trial lens. Note that no image appears, no matter where the paper is held.

Now, suppose a $+6$ D thin lens is placed 5 cm behind the first lens. Will an image form? If so, what are its characteristics? Light has a vergence of -5 D, but as the light crosses the 5 cm to the second lens, its vergence changes (the vergence change on transfer). As discussed, in order to determine the vergence at the second lens, it is nec-

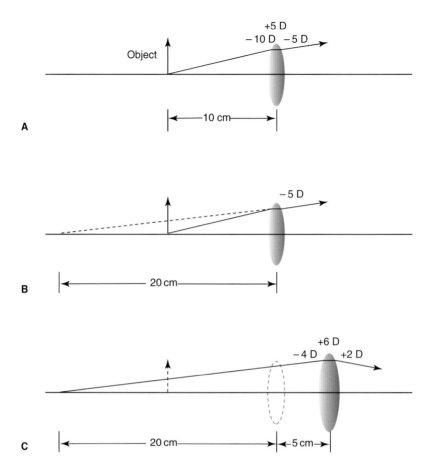

Figure 2-46 Light exits the +5 D lens with a vergence of −5 D **(A),** producing a virtual image 20 cm in front of the lens **(B).** The virtual image becomes the object for the +6 D lens, which in turn produces a real image 50 cm to the right of the lens **(C).** *(Illustration developed by Kevin M. Miller, MD, and rendered by C. H. Wooley.)*

essary to find the location of the image formed by the first lens. However, if the first lens does not form an image, how can the vergence at the second lens be calculated?

The solution is to use a mathematical trick. Light leaving the first lens has a vergence of −5 D. The same vergence would be produced by an object 20 cm away if the first lens were not present (Fig 2-46B).

So, light leaving the second lens appears to be coming from an object 20 cm away from the first lens and 25 cm away from the second lens. Using the imaginary object as a reference point, it is easy to see that the vergence at the second lens is −4 D. When light leaves the second lens, it has a vergence of +2 D, forming a real image 50 cm behind the second lens (Fig 2-46C).

In this example, an imaginary reference point was used to determine the vergence at the second lens. In geometrical optics, this reference point is commonly called the *virtual image* formed by the first lens. A virtual image is a mathematical convenience that allows all of the formulas developed so far (LME, TLE, transverse magnification) to be used even when a lens does not form a real image.

Mathematically, virtual images are used in exactly the same way as real images. In Figure 2-46, the first lens forms a virtual image 20 cm to the left. The transverse magnification for the first lens is $(-10\ \text{D}/-5\ \text{D}) = 2$. Thus, the virtual image is upright and twice as large as the original object. This virtual image now becomes the object for the second lens. The vergence at the second lens is -4 D, and after traversing the second lens, the vergence is $+2$ D. The image now formed is real and 50 cm to the right of the second lens. The transverse magnification for the second lens is -2 D. The total magnification is therefore $2 \times -2 = -4$. The final image is inverted and 4 times larger than the original. Again, this can be verified with trial lenses.

Objects may be virtual also. Consider an object 50 cm in front of a $+3$ D thin lens in air. A $+2$ D thin lens in air is placed 50 cm behind the first lens. The first lens forms a real image 1 m to the right. However, before the light can reach this image, it strikes a second lens. The image formed by the first lens is the object for the second lens, but this object is on the wrong side of the lens. Thus, it is called a *virtual object* (Fig 2-47).

Here, unlike in all the previous examples, light is convergent when it strikes the second lens (vergence $= +2$ D). The second lens increases the vergence to $+4$ D, forming a real image 25 cm behind the second lens. The transverse magnification for the first lens is -2 and for the second lens $+0.5$, for a total magnification of -1.

A common misconception is that inverted images are real and upright images are virtual. This is not the case. The correct rule is very simple: For any individual lens, the object is virtual when light striking the lens is convergent, and the object is real when light striking the lens is divergent. When light emerging from the lens is convergent, the image is real, and when light emerging from a lens is divergent, the image is virtual.

Focal Points and Planes

The $+5$ D lens in Figure 2-48A has an *anterior focal point* F_a that is $(1/5\ \text{D}) = 0.2$ m $= 20$ cm in front of the lens. By definition, light emanating from F_a exits the lens collimated and comes to a focus at plus optical infinity. The same is true of light ema-

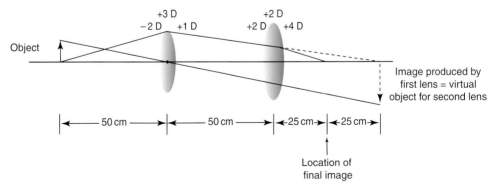

Figure 2-47 The real image formed by the $+3$ D lens is the virtual object for the $+2$ D lens. *(Illustration developed by Kevin M. Miller, MD, and rendered by C. H. Wooley.)*

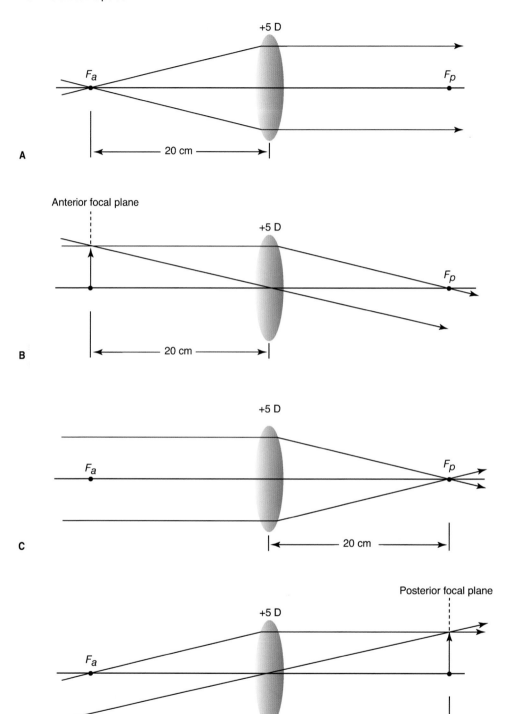

Figure 2-48 **A,** Light that emanates from the anterior focal point, F_a, leaves the lens collimated. **B,** All object points in the anterior focal plane focus to plus optical infinity. **C,** Collimated on-axis light from minus optical infinity focuses to the posterior focal point, F_p. **D,** Collimated off-axis rays focus to the posterior focal plane. *(Illustration developed by Kevin M. Miller, MD, and rendered by C. H. Wooley.)*

nating from any point in the *anterior focal plane* (Fig 2-48B). Collimated light entering a lens from minus optical infinity images to the *posterior focal point* F_p (Fig 2-48C). Collimated off-axis rays from minus infinity focus to the *posterior focal plane* (Fig 2-48D). For a thin lens immersed in a uniform optical medium such as air or water, F_a and F_p are equidistant from the lens. For a convex (plus-power) spherical lens, F_a is located anterior to the lens and F_p is located posterior to the lens. For a concave (minus-power) spherical lens, the points are reversed: F_a is posterior to the lens and F_p is anterior to the lens. To avoid confusion, some writers prefer the terms F and F' instead of F_a and F_p.

Paraxial Raytracing Through Convex Spherical Lenses

From any object point, 3 simple rays can be drawn through a thin lens to locate a corresponding point in the image. Only 2 rays are actually needed. The same rays can be used to find corresponding points if a thick lens or a multielement lens system can be modeled by first-order optical principles. The first 2 rays traverse F_a and F_p. The final ray, known as the *central ray* or *chief ray,* traverses the nodal points. For a thin lens immersed in a medium with a uniform refractive index, the nodal points overlap at the optical center of the lens. The central ray traverses the nodal point undeviated; that is, it does not change direction with respect to the optical axis as it passes through the lens.

It is customary to represent objects as arrows to show size and orientation. The tip of an arrow represents a single object point. Suppose an object is placed 20 cm in front of a +10 D lens immersed in air (Fig 2-49).

A ray can be drawn from the tip of the object through F_a. This ray emerges from the lens parallel to the optical axis and heads off to plus infinity. A second ray can be drawn that parallels the optical axis until it enters the lens. It emerges from the lens and passes through F_p on its way to plus infinity. The intersection of these 2 rays defines the corresponding image point. It can be seen that the image in this example is inverted. The location of the image can be determined by vergence calculations. The vergence of light entering the lens is $(-1/0.2 \text{ m}) = -5$ D. By the LME, the vergence of light exiting the lens is -5 D $+ 10$ D $= +5$ D. The image is located $(1/5 \text{ D}) = 0.2$ m $= 20$ cm to the right of the lens. Because the object and image are equidistant from the lens, the transverse magnification is -1. The central ray can also be drawn through the optical center of the lens to confirm the location of the image.

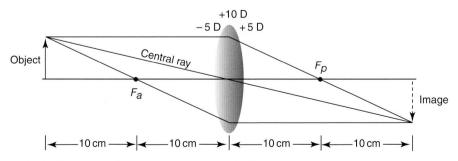

Figure 2-49 Raytracing through a convex spherical lens. *(Illustration developed by Kevin M. Miller, MD, and rendered by C. H. Wooley.)*

Now what if the object in the previous example is moved closer so that it is 5 cm in front of the lens instead of 20 cm in front (inside F_a), as shown in Figure 2-50A? The ray that leaves F_a and passes through the object point emerges from the lens parallel to the optical axis. The ray that enters the lens parallel to the optical axis exits through F_p. Finally, the central ray traverses the optical center of the lens undeviated. On the back side of the lens, these 3 rays are divergent. So where is the image? If you are an observer on the back side of the lens, you see the image point as the backward extension of all 3 rays (Fig 2-50B).

By the LME, the vergence of light exiting the lens is -10 D. The image is located $(1/-10 \text{ D}) = 10$ cm to the left of the lens. The image is upright and virtual, and by similar triangles, its transverse magnification is $+2$. This is the optical basis of a simple, handheld plus lens magnifier. An object positioned inside the focal point of a plus spherical lens will produce a magnified, upright, virtual image. Try this simple experiment with the lens you use for indirect ophthalmoscopy.

Concave Lenses

In the examples we have used thus far, the lenses have been convex, or positive. Light emerges from a convex lens more convergent or, at least, less divergent than it entered. In contrast, a concave, or negative, lens makes light more divergent.

Negative lenses are not very useful in and of themselves. A negative lens cannot produce a real image of a real object. Instead, a negative lens is usually used in combi-

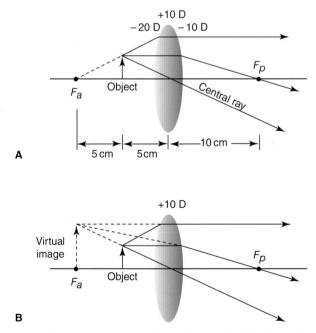

Figure 2-50 Raytracing through a convex spherical lens. **A,** This time the object is located inside the anterior focal point. **B,** The image is magnified, upright, and virtual and is located to the left of the object. *(Illustration developed by Kevin M. Miller, MD, and rendered by C. H. Wooley.)*

nation with a positive lens to alter image characteristics. For instance, suppose that an object is 1 m in front of a +6 D thin lens in air. The image is 20 cm behind the lens and the magnification is −0.2 (Fig 2-51A). Suppose it is not convenient to have the image so close to the lens and that it would be better to have the image 50 cm behind the lens.

For a +6 D lens to produce a real image 50 cm behind itself, the object must be 25 cm in front of the lens. As a practical matter, however, the position of the object usually cannot be changed. Instead, the problem can be solved by placing a negative thin lens between the +6 D lens and the object so the negative lens produces a virtual image 25 cm in front of the +6 D lens (Fig 2-51B).

As another example, a −5.55 D thin lens placed 10 cm in front of the +6 D thin lens (90 cm from the object) produces a virtual image 15 cm in front of the negative lens and 25 cm in front of the +6 D lens. The virtual image becomes a real object for the +6 D lens, which forms an image 50 cm behind itself. The overall magnification is −0.33.

Many different negative thin lenses could be used. Each different power of negative lens must be placed at a different distance from the +6 D lens. In particular, a −8.17 D lens placed 85.7 cm away from the object also produces a virtual image 25 cm in front of the +6 D lens, yielding a final real image in the desired location. Moreover, the final image has the same −0.25 magnification as the original image. So, in this case, it is

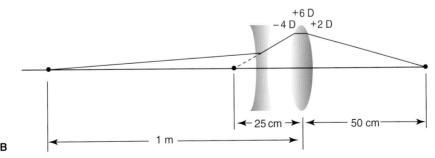

Figure 2-51 Negative lenses are used to change the characteristics of images formed by positive lenses. **A,** An object placed 1 m in front of a +6 D lens images 20 cm behind the lens. **B,** A concave (negative) spherical lens can be placed in front of the +6 D lens to move the final image location to 50 cm. *(Illustration developed by Kevin M. Miller, MD, and rendered by C. H. Wooley.)*

possible to select a negative lens that changes the final image location without changing its size.

Paraxial Raytracing Through Concave Spherical Lenses

The principles of paraxial raytracing are the same for concave spherical lenses as for convex spherical lenses. Consider a -2 D lens. Its F_a is $(1/-2$ D$) = 50$ cm behind the lens. By definition, a ray of light directed through F_a will exit the lens parallel to the optical axis (Fig 2-52A). Similarly, a virtual object in the anterior focal plane of a concave lens will image to plus infinity. A ray of light entering the lens parallel to the optical axis will pass through F_p after exiting the lens (Fig 2-52B). Similarly, a real object at minus optical infinity will produce a virtual image in the posterior focal plane of a concave lens.

Now let's consider an object placed 100 cm in front of the lens. The 3 usual rays can be drawn (Fig 2-53). A virtual image is formed 33 cm in front of the lens. By similar triangles, the transverse magnification is $+0.33$. No matter where a real object is placed in front of a minus lens, the resulting image is upright, minified, and virtual.

Objects and Images at Infinity

If an object is placed 50 cm in front of a $+2$ D thin lens in air, where is the image? Light emerges from the lens with a vergence of 0. A vergence of 0 means that light is neither convergent nor divergent, so it is collimated. In this example, light rays emerge parallel to one another, neither converging to a real image nor diverging from a virtual image. In this case, the image is said to be at *infinity*.

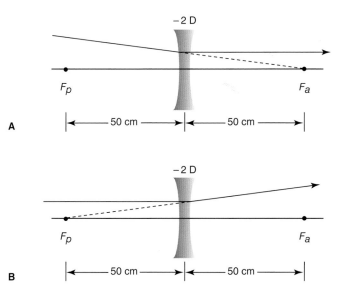

Figure 2-52 A, Incoming light directed through the anterior focal point, F_a, of a concave spherical lens exits the lens collimated. **B,** Collimated incoming light parallel to the optical axis leaves the lens as if it had come through the posterior focal point, F_p. *(Illustration developed by Kevin M. Miller, MD, and rendered by C. H. Wooley.)*

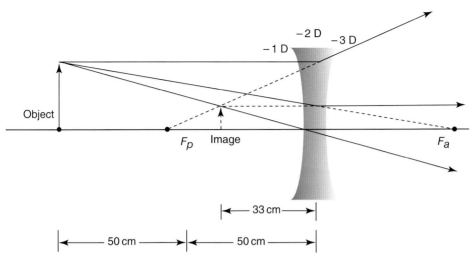

Figure 2-53 No matter where a real object is placed in front of a concave (negative) spherical lens, the image is upright, minified, and virtual. *(Illustration developed by Kevin M. Miller, MD, and rendered by C. H. Wooley.)*

Objects can be at infinity as well. If a second lens is placed anywhere behind the first one, light striking the second lens has a vergence of 0, neither convergent nor divergent. The object is at infinity. As a practical matter, a sufficiently distant object may be regarded as at infinity. Clearly, an object like the moon, which is 400 million meters away, has a vergence of essentially 0. For clinical work, objects more than 20 ft (6 m) distant may be regarded as being at optical infinity. An object 6 m away has a vergence of about −0.17 D; clinically, this is small enough to be ignored. When determining a refractive correction, few patients can notice a change of less than 0.25 D.

Some people think that objects in the anterior focal plane are imaged in the posterior focal plane. This is not true. Objects in the anterior focal plane image to plus infinity; objects at minus infinity image in the posterior focal plane.

Principal Planes and Points

If an object's position changes in front of a lens, both the location and magnification of the image change. Most optical systems have one particular object location that yields a magnification of 1. In other words, when an object is located in the correct position, the image will be upright and the same size as the object. The *principal planes* are perpendicular to the optical axis and identify the object and image locations that yield a magnification of 1. The principal planes are also called the *planes of unit magnification.*

Consider an optical system consisting of 2 thin lenses in air (Fig 2-54). The first lens is +6 D, the second lens is +15 D, and the 2 lenses are separated by 35 cm. An object located 50 cm in front of the first lens is imaged 25 cm behind the first lens with a magnification of −0.5. The real image becomes a real object for the second lens, which produces a real image 20 cm behind the second lens with a magnification of −2. The *anterior principal plane* of this system is 50 cm in front of the first lens; the *posterior*

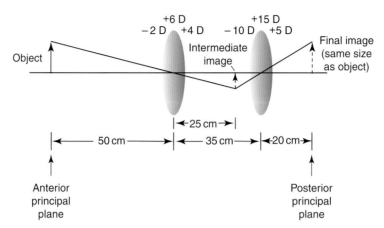

Figure 2-54 These 2 thin lenses in air produce an image that is upright, real, and the same size as the object. *(Illustration developed by Kevin M. Miller, MD, and rendered by C. H. Wooley.)*

principal plane is 20 cm behind the second lens. Often, both the anterior and posterior principal planes are virtual; in some cases, the posterior principal plane is in front of the anterior principal plane.

The intersection of the anterior and posterior principal planes with the optical axis defines, respectively, the *anterior* and *posterior principal points*. Like the nodal points, the principal points are an important pair of reference points.

Collectively, the nodal points, focal points, and principal points are called the *cardinal points*, because these 3 pairs of points completely describe the first-order properties of an optical system. Notice that 2 pairs of cardinal points are conjugate. The posterior principal point is the image of the anterior principal point, and the same relationship holds for the nodal points. However, the focal points are not conjugate. Two pairs of cardinal points are associated with planes: the focal points and the principal points. However, there is no such thing as a nodal plane associated with a nodal point.

Modeling an Unknown Optical System

In the previous examples, we showed how vergence calculations could be used to determine image location and magnification for a single lens or a combination of 2 lenses. However, most optical systems consist of many lenses. A typical 35-mm camera lens contains between 6 and 12 individual lenses. Vergence calculations become tedious for such systems; it is easier to analyze image characteristics graphically.

Thick lenses and complex optical systems can be modeled using principal planes, nodal points, and focal points if the optical surfaces are spherical and we restrict the analysis to paraxial rays. The location of each point or plane can be determined experimentally.

Consider an unknown optical system that contains any number of optical elements (Fig 2-55A). We will treat it as a "black box." A real object placed in front of the black box will image somewhere in space. If the image forms in front of the box, it is virtual. If it forms behind the box, it is real. Now consider a single ray of light that leaves a point

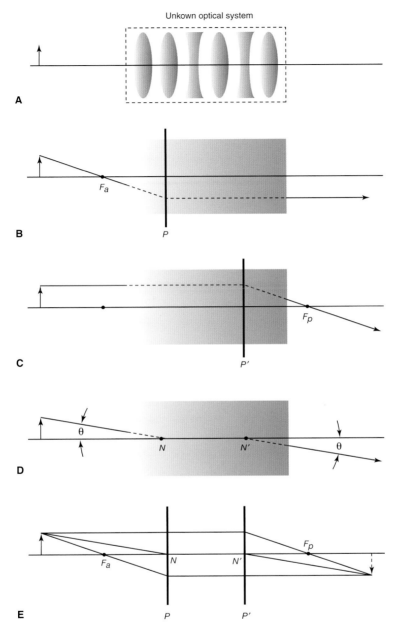

Figure 2-55 **A,** An unknown "black box" optical system may contain any number of optical elements. **B,** A ray of light from an object point is traced that leaves the system parallel to the optical axis. The intersection of this ray with the optical axis defines the anterior focal point, F_a. The intersection of rays entering and leaving the optical system defines the location of the anterior principal plane, P. **C,** Another ray of light from the same object point enters the optical system parallel to the optical axis and exits through the posterior focal point, F_p. The intersection of the 2 rays entering and leaving the system defines the posterior principal plane, P'. **D,** The nodal points are defined by entering and exiting rays that intersect the optical axis at the same angle. If the refractive indices of the media bounding the optical system are the same on both sides, the nodal points correspond to the principal points. **E,** The final model simplifies the complex unknown optical system. *(Illustration developed by Kevin M. Miller, MD, and rendered by C. H. Wooley.)*

on the object, such as the tip of the arrow in the drawing. The ray can be modeled experimentally using a laser pointer. At some angle of entry into the box with respect to the optical axis, the ray will exit the box parallel to the optical axis. The extension inside the box of the entering and exiting rays defines the location of the *anterior principal plane* P (Fig 2-55B). Similarly, a ray of light entering the black box parallel to the optical axis will exit the box at some angle to the optical axis. The intersection of these 2 rays inside the box defines the location of the *posterior principal plane P'* (Fig 2-55C). The intersection of the principal planes and the optical axis defines the principal points. If the indices of refraction of the media on either side of the black box are the same, the nodal points, N and N', correspond to the locations of the principal points (Fig 2-55D). The focal points, F_a and F_p, are determined the same way as for a thin lens. The result is an optical model that simplifies the complicated optical system (Fig 2-55E). If the media bounding the system are different (eg, the human eye has air on one side and vitreous gel on the other side), the nodal points "pull" in the direction of the medium with the higher refractive index. The anterior focal length of the system is the distance from F_a to the anterior principal point, not the distance to the first lens in the black box. The posterior focal length is the distance from F_p to the posterior principal point.

Thick Lenses

The thin-lens approximation is invalid in some clinical settings. For example, IOLs are treated as thick lenses. Consider a lens of arbitrary thickness (Fig 2-56).

The combined power of a thick lens P is not simply the sum of the individual surface powers; instead (as described under Thin-Lens Approximation), it includes the vergence change on transfer P_t:

$$P = P_f + P_b + P_t$$

where

P_f = power of the first lens surface
P_b = power of the second lens surface

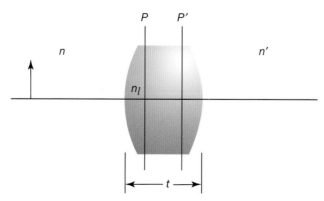

Figure 2-56 An example of a thick lens. *(Illustration developed by Kevin M. Miller, MD, and rendered by C. H. Wooley.)*

The vergence change on transfer is

$$P_t = -\frac{t}{n_l} P_f P_b$$

where

t = lens thickness
n_l = index of refraction of the lens

Thus, the power of a thick lens equals

$$P = P_f + P_b - \frac{t}{n_l} P_f P_b$$

Note that when powers P, P_f, and P_b are in diopters, t should be in meters. A lens with a front-surface power of $+5.0$ D, a back-surface power of $+10.0$ D, and a thickness of 1 cm, constructed from glass with an index of $n_l = 1.5$, has a total power of $+14.7$ D. In this case, the power of the thick lens is one third of a diopter less than it would be if it were a thin lens. The difference is attributable to the vergence change that occurs as light travels from the front surface to the back surface.

Focal Lengths

For any optical system, the distance from the anterior principal point to the anterior focal point is the *anterior focal length (AFL)*. Similarly, the *posterior focal length (PFL)* is the distance from the posterior principal point to the posterior focal point.

Following the sign convention, focal lengths are negative when the focal point is to the left of the principal point and positive when the focal point is to the right of the principal point. For instance, a $+5$ D thin lens in air has an AFL of -20 cm and a PFL of $+20$ cm.

For any optical system, focal lengths and refractive power P are related by

$$\text{AFL} = \frac{n_o}{P} \qquad \text{PFL} = \frac{n_i}{P}$$

For any optical system, the distance from the anterior principal point to the anterior nodal point is always equal to the distance from the posterior principal point to the posterior nodal point. The distance between principal point and nodal point follows the sign convention and is given by

$$\text{Distance} = \text{AFL} + \text{PFL}$$

For instance, for a $+5$ D thin lens in air, AFL + PFL = -20 cm + 20 cm = 0. Thus, the nodal points and principal points overlap. For a $+5$ D thin lens with water ($n = 1.33$) in front and air in back, the AFL = -26.6 cm and the PFL = 20 cm. Thus, the nodal points are 6.6 cm to the left of the principal points.

Gaussian Reduction

Thus far, we have discussed the properties of a single optical system. The treatment of refractive errors usually involves adding a lens to an existing optical system, the patient's eye. Gaussian reduction describes what happens when 2 optical systems (such as a corrective lens and the eye) are combined.

When 2 optical systems—each with its own cardinal points—are combined, a totally new optical system is created that can be described by a new set of cardinal points. The thick-lens equation, discussed in a previous section, can be used to reduce the 2 individual systems to a single system with its own cardinal points. In general, the combined system's cardinal points and power differ from those of either of the individual systems. Clinically, Gaussian reduction is most important in conjunction with the correction of ametropias (discussed in Chapter 4, Clinical Refraction) and in calculating IOL implant power (see Chapter 6, Intraocular Lenses).

Knapp's Law, the Badal Principle, and the Lensmeter

One problem of treating refractive errors is that the corrective lens usually changes the size of the retinal image. Many patients can tolerate a small change in image size, but problems arise if the image size disparity between the 2 eyes is too large. The brain can fuse images that are up to 8% different in size. According to Knapp's law, the size of the retinal image does not change if the posterior nodal point of the correcting lens is placed at the anterior focal point of the eye.

Consider a thin lens in air that produces an image such as that shown in Figure 2-57A. The image is located where the orange and red rays intersect. However, the image size is entirely determined by the red ray alone. The red ray emerges parallel to the axis, and the image height is the distance between the red ray and the axis, regardless of where the orange ray intersects.

For whatever reason, suppose it is desirable to change the image location. This can be accomplished by placing another lens in front of the first lens, as shown in Figures 2-57B and 2-57C. The correcting lens, also a thin lens in air, can be placed in almost any position (although the power of the correcting lens will change depending on the position). However, the only way to change the image position without also changing the image size is to locate the correcting lens so that the red ray is unchanged.

When the center of the correcting lens (to be precise, the posterior nodal point of the correcting lens) coincides with the anterior focal point of the original lens, the red ray trace does not change (Fig 2-57B). Consequently, image size does not change. Knapp's law states that retinal image size does not change when a spectacle lens is placed in the eye's anterior focal plane. The anterior focal point of the eye is about 17 mm in front of the cornea (see Chapter 3, Optics of the Human Eye). Although it is possible to wear glasses so the spectacle lens is 17 mm in front of the eye, most people prefer to wear them at a corneal vertex distance of 10 mm to 15 mm.

Figure 2-57C shows a correcting lens of different power placed without regard to Knapp's rule. In this case, both the image location and the image size change.

Manual lensmeters make use of the same principle, although for completely different reasons. When applied to lensmeters, Knapp's law is called the *Badal principle*. One type

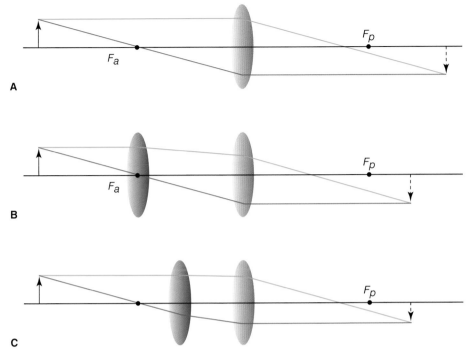

Figure 2-57 Illustration of Knapp's law. Ray trace **(A)** shows the image location and size for a single thin lens in air. A second thin lens *(green)* is used to change the image location in ray trace **(B).** According to Knapp's law, the image size does not change if the posterior nodal point of the second lens coincides with the anterior focal point of the original lens. Ray trace **(C)** shows that another correcting lens (different power) can be placed to change the image location by the same amount, but the image size also changes. *(Illustration developed by Kevin M. Miller, MD, and rendered by C. H. Wooley.)*

of optometer used for performing objective refraction is based on a variation of Knapp's law wherein the posterior focal plane of the correcting lens coincides with the anterior nodal point of the eye. The effect is the same. Retinal image size remains constant. In this application, the law is called the *optometer principle.* Optical engineers use a variation of Knapp's law called *telecentricity* to improve the performance of telescopes and microscopes. Regardless of the name, the basic principle remains the same.

Afocal Systems

Consider an optical system consisting of 2 thin lenses in air (Fig 2-58). The lens powers are $+2$ D and -5 D, respectively. Where is F_p for this system? The posterior focal point is where incoming parallel rays focus. However, as the ray trace shows, rays entering the system parallel to the optical axis emerge parallel to the axis. This system has no focal points; in other words, it is an *afocal system.*

If an object is 2 m in front of the first lens, where is the image and what is the transverse magnification? Vergence calculations show that the image is virtual, 44 cm to the left of the second lens (14 cm to the left of the first lens), and that the transverse magnification is 0.4. If an object is 4 m in front of the first lens, vergence calculations show that the image is virtual, 76 cm to the left of the second lens, and that the transverse magnification is exactly 0.4. In afocal systems, the transverse magnification is the same for every object regardless of location.

Where are the principal planes for this system? Actually, it has no principal planes. Remember, the principal planes are the unique conjugates with a transverse magnification of 1. In this system, the transverse magnification is always 0.4 and never 1. If the transverse magnification were equal to 1, it would be 1 for every pair of conjugates. Consequently, there would be no unique set of planes that could be designated principal planes. In general, afocal systems do not have cardinal points. (See Clinical Example 2-8.)

Afocal systems are used clinically as telescopes or low vision aids. The 2 basic types of refracting telescopes are the *Galilean telescope* (named for, but not invented by, Galileo) and the *Keplerian telescope* (invented by Johannes Kepler). The Galilean telescope consists of 2 lenses. The first lens, the *objective lens,* is always positive and usually has a low power, whereas the second lens, the *eyepiece,* or *ocular,* is always negative and usually has a high power. The lenses are separated by the difference in their focal lengths. The afocal system depicted in Figure 2-58 is a Galilean telescope.

The Keplerian, or astronomical, telescope also consists of 2 lenses, a low-power objective and a high-power ocular, but both are positive and separated by the sum of their

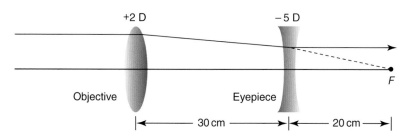

Figure 2-58 The Galilean telescope is an example of an afocal system. The lenses are separated by the difference in focal lengths. *F* is simultaneously the posterior focal point of the plus lens and the anterior focal point of the minus lens. *(Illustration developed by Kevin M. Miller, MD, and rendered by C. H. Wooley.)*

CLINICAL EXAMPLE 2-8

Using trial lenses, duplicate this optical system by holding a −5 D lens up to your eye and a +2 D lens 30 cm in front of the eye so that you are looking through both lenses at the same time. Objects appear 2.5 times larger. Why do objects appear this much larger when the transverse magnification is 0.4?

A transverse magnification of 0.4 means that the image is 2.5 times smaller than the object. However, this particular optical system forms images that are 6.25 times closer than corresponding objects. The closer proximity of the image more than compensates for the smaller size of the image. The net effect is that objects appear 0.40 × 6.25, or 2.5, times larger!

focal lengths. The image is inverted. For comparison, construct a Keplerian telescope using $+2$ D and $+5$ D trial lenses.

For each telescope:

$$\text{Transverse magnification} = \frac{P_{obj}}{P_{eye}} = \frac{f_{eye}}{f_{obj}}$$

$$\text{Axial magnification} = m^2$$

where

P_{obj} = power of the objective lens
P_{eye} = power of the eyepiece or ocular
f_{eye} = focal length of the eyepiece (negative for concave lenses)
f_{obj} = focal length of the objective lens
m = transverse magnification

Each form of telescope has advantages and disadvantages. The advantage of a Galilean telescope is that it produces an upright image and is shorter than a Keplerian telescope. These features make the Galilean telescope popular as a spectacle-mounted visual aid or in surgical loupes.

Conversely, the Keplerian telescope uses light more efficiently, making faint objects easier to see (Fig 2-59). In the Keplerian design, all the light from an object point collected by the objective lens ultimately enters the eye. In the Galilean design, some of the light

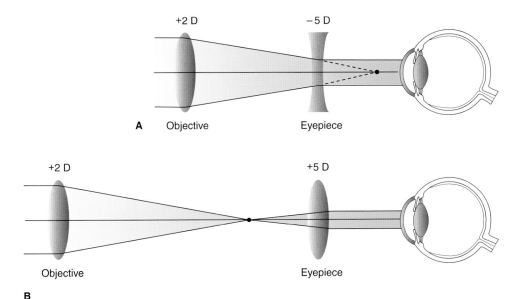

Figure 2-59 Comparison of Galilean and Keplerian telescopes. In the Galilean telescope **(A),** some of the light collected by the objective is lost. In the Keplerian telescope **(B),** all the light collected enters the eye. *(Illustration developed by Kevin M. Miller, MD, and rendered by C. H. Wooley.)*

collected by the objective is lost. Because astronomical observation is largely a matter of making faint stars visible, all astronomical telescopes are of the Keplerian design. The inverted image is not a problem for astronomers, but inverting prisms can be placed inside the telescope. Common binoculars and handheld visual aids are usually of the Keplerian design.

Ophthalmic Prisms

An ophthalmic prism is a wedge of transparent plastic or glass with a triangular cross section having an apex and a base (Fig 2-60). Low-power prisms with small apex angles may be incorporated into spectacle lenses and contact lenses. The doubling in keratometers is achieved with low-power prisms. High-power prisms with large apex angles are used to measure angles of strabismus, to produce the doubling in the measuring head of the Goldmann tonometer, and to apply laser treatment to the periphery of the fundus.

Plane Parallel Plate

The simplest prism has an apex angle of 0°; that is, the 2 faces are parallel. When a light ray traverses a plane parallel plate (such as a piece of window glass), it is refracted at both surfaces; but because the bending is equal and opposite at the 2 surfaces, no deviation results. However, lateral displacement occurs for all incident rays that are not perpendicular to the surfaces (Fig 2-61).

When the surfaces of a wedge of glass are not parallel, light rays undergo a net deviation, and an ophthalmic prism is created.

Angle of Deviation

In any prism with an apex angle greater than 0°, the total angle of deviation of light that passes through it is the sum of the deviations produced at each of the surfaces (see Fig 2-60). The 2 deviations may be in the same direction or in opposite directions, depending on the angle of incidence, but the total deviation is always in the direction of the base of the prism (Fig 2-62).

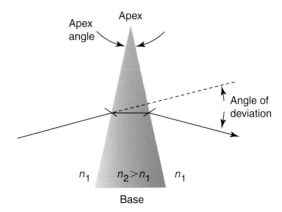

Figure 2-60 Cross section of a prism. Light rays are always bent toward the base of a prism. *(Illustration developed by Edmond H. Thall, MD, and Kevin M. Miller, MD, and rendered by C. H. Wooley.)*

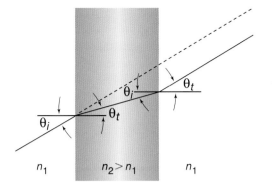

Figure 2-61 Plane parallel plate. The light ray obeys the same laws at entry and exit; the result is lateral displacement without angular deviation. *(Illustration developed by Edmond H. Thall, MD, and Kevin M. Miller, MD, and rendered by C. H. Wooley.)*

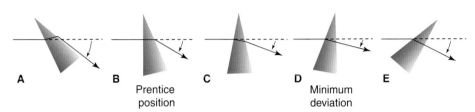

A   B   C   D   E

Prentice
position

Minimum
deviation

Figure 2-62 Variation of the angle of deviation depending on the angle of incidence. *(Illustration developed by Edmond H. Thall, MD, and Kevin M. Miller, MD, and rendered by C. H. Wooley.)*

The minimum angle of deviation produced by a prism occurs when the light ray undergoes equal bending at the 2 surfaces, as in Figure 2-62D. The angle of deviation is greater in any other situation.

Prism Diopter

Prism power is defined by the amount of deviation produced as a light ray traverses a prism. The deviation is determined by the centimeters of deflection measured 100 cm from the prism (Fig 2-63). The amount is expressed in prism diopters Δ.

The term *prism diopter* should never be shortened to "prisms" or "diopters" because the meaning becomes entirely different. For angles under 100Δ (45°), each 2Δ are approximately equal to 1°, but strictly speaking, the relationship is a trigonometric one.

From Figure 2-63, it is apparent that the relationship between θ and Δ is

$$\tan \theta = \frac{\Delta}{100 \text{ cm}}$$

Therefore,

$$\Delta = 100 \tan \theta$$
$$\theta = \arctan \frac{\Delta}{100}$$

Plastic prisms and prism bars are calibrated according to the angle of minimum deviation. They should be held with their rear surface in the frontal plane of the patient to achieve, approximately, the calibrated effect (Fig 2-64).

Prisms made of glass (not widely used) are calibrated according to the Prentice position—that is, with 1 face of the prism perpendicular to the line of sight. All of the bending occurs at the opposite face (see Fig 2-62B). The strabismus that is neutralized is greater than the minimum deviation for that prism. If the rear surface of a 40Δ glass prism is erroneously held in the frontal plane, only 32Δ of effect will be achieved. This is the manner in which prism in spectacle lenses is measured on a lensmeter, with the back surface of the spectacle lens flat against the nose cone of the lensmeter.

Displacement of Images by Prisms

If a prism is introduced into the path of light rays that are converging to form an image, all the light rays are bent toward the base of the prism, and the image is also displaced toward the base of the prism (Fig 2-65). In this case, the image is real, so real images are displaced toward the base of a prism.

Figure 2-63 Definition of prism diopter. *(Illustration developed by Edmond H. Thall, MD, and Kevin M. Miller, MD, and rendered by C. H. Wooley.)*

Figure 2-64 Correct positions for holding glass and plastic orthoptic prisms. *(Illustration developed by Edmond H. Thall, MD, and Kevin M. Miller, MD, and rendered by C. H. Wooley.)*

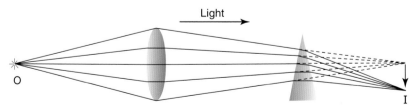

Figure 2-65 Real images displace toward the base of a prism. *(Illustration developed by Edmond H. Thall, MD, and Kevin M. Miller, MD, and rendered by C. H. Wooley.)*

What happens if instead we turn the light around, making the image the object, and then view the object through the prism? We will see that the prism forms a virtual image of the object, which is displaced toward the apex of the prism (Fig 2-66). Stated another way, if a prism is introduced before an eye that is looking at an object, the eye will have to shift toward the apex of the prism to maintain fixation. In general, virtual images are displaced toward the apex of a prism, although the light rays themselves are bent toward the base. The images we see when looking through prisms are always virtual images. This phenomenon is the source of the common teaching that a prism displaces images toward its apex.

Prismatic Effect of Lenses (Prentice's Rule)

A spherical lens behaves like a prism at every point on its surface except at its optical center. In plus lenses, the prism power bends light rays toward the optical axis. In minus lenses, the light bends away from the optical axis. Prism power increases as the distance from the optical center increases, in proportion to the dioptric power of the lens. This relationship is expressed mathematically by Prentice's rule (Fig 2-67). By similar triangles,

$$\frac{h}{100 \text{ cm}} = \frac{\Delta}{\frac{100 \text{ cm}}{D}}$$

$$\Delta = hD \text{ (Prentice's rule)}$$

where h is in centimeters.

The prismatic effect of lenses becomes important clinically in patients with anisometropia in the vertical meridian. If the distance correction is different for the 2 eyes, prismatic effects are produced in the reading position, leading to vertical misalignment of the visual axes. Prismatic effects must be anticipated in the design of bifocal lenses to minimize image displacement and jump (see Chapter 4, Clinical Refraction).

Prismatic effect can be added to an ordinary spectacle lens simply by decentering it in the frame so that the visual axis in primary position passes through an off-center portion of the lens. Whether the desired amount of prism can be added by decentration depends on the power of the lens and the size of the lens blank. For example, adding 5Δ of base-out (BO) prism to a $+1$ D spherical spectacle lens would require decentering

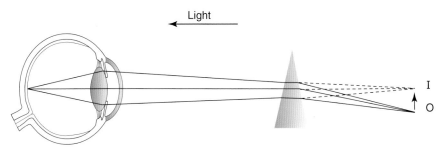

Figure 2-66 Virtual images displace toward the apex of a prism. *(Illustration developed by Edmond H. Thall, MD, and Kevin M. Miller, MD, and rendered by C. H. Wooley.)*

the lens temporally by 5 cm! In this case, decentration would not work, and prism would simply have to be ground into the lens.

How can one quickly tell with a lensmeter whether a spectacle lens has been decentered or whether prism has been ground into the lens? Simply by locating the optical center by moving the lens about until the lensmeter target is centered. If the greatest distance from the optical center to the edge of the lens is more than half the diameter of the usual lens blank (diameter = 60 mm), prism must have been ground into the lens.

Remember that prism in a spectacle lens is read at the position of the visual axis in primary position. A washable felt-tip marker is helpful in marking this position before transferring the glasses from the patient's face to the lensmeter.

Vector Addition of Prisms

Prismatic deviations in different directions are additive by straightforward vector addition. Vectors combine information about magnitude and direction. For instance, if 6Δ base up (BU) and 8Δ BO before the left eye are needed to correct a strabismic deviation, a single prism of 10Δ with base up and out in the 37° meridian accomplishes the same purpose (Fig 2-68).

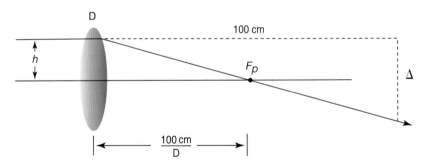

Figure 2-67 Prentice's rule. The prism power of a lens at any point on its surface, in prism diopters, Δ, is equal to the distance away from the optical center, h, in centimeters times the power of the lens in diopters. *(Illustration developed by Kevin M. Miller, MD, and rendered by C. H. Wooley.)*

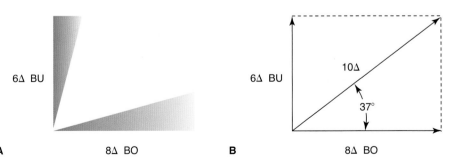

Figure 2-68 Vector addition of horizontal and vertical prisms. **A,** The magnitude of the sum vector is $\sqrt{8^2 + 6^2}$. **B,** The angle of the sum vector is arctan (6/8). BU = base up; BO = base out. *(Illustration developed by Kevin M. Miller, MD, and rendered by C. H. Wooley.)*

When prescribing an oblique prism, remember to specify the direction of the base properly. A prism before the left eye cannot simply be specified as "base in in the 37° meridian." It must be specified as either "base up and out in the 37° meridian" or "base down and in in the 37° meridian."

A rotary prism (Risley prism), mounted on the front of most phoropters, consists of 2 prisms of equal power that are counter-rotated with respect to one another to produce prism power varying from 0 (prisms neutralize each other) to the sum of the 2 powers (prisms aligned in the same direction). Intermediate values may be determined by vector addition and are marked on the dial of the prism housing. The Risley prism is particularly useful in measuring phorias (often in conjunction with the Maddox rod) and fusional vergence amplitudes.

Prism Aberrations

In addition to chromatic aberration (producing colored fringes at the edges of objects viewed through the prism), prisms have other aberrations, such as asymmetrical magnification and curvature of field. Although these aberrations are usually insignificant, they occasionally produce symptoms, even with low-power ophthalmic prisms.

Fresnel Prisms

Fresnel (pronounced *fre-nell'*) prisms, which are equivalent to side-by-side strips of long, narrow, thin prisms (Fig 2-69), are sometimes used to avoid the weight and some of the aberrations of conventional prisms.

The most popular form of Fresnel prism is a membrane molded from clear polyvinyl chloride. Known as a Press-On Prism, it is applied with water to the back surface of an ordinary spectacle lens, in the desired orientation. Visual acuity suffers somewhat from light scattering at the groove edges, but the chromatic aberration of the prisms themselves produces most of the visual decrement. The advantages of these prisms far outweigh the

Figure 2-69 Cross-sectional construction of a Fresnel prism as compared to a conventional ophthalmic prism. *(Redrawn from Duane TD, ed.* Clinical Ophthalmology. *Hagerstown, MD: Harper & Row; 1976: vol 1, chap 52, fig 52-2.)*

disadvantages, however, and they are widely used in the fields of strabismus and orthoptics. Fresnel lenses are also available with concentric groove construction to approximate spherical lenses.

Mirrors

As discussed earlier in this chapter (under Imaging with Lenses and Mirrors), many of the vergence and ray tracing concepts we developed for lenses also apply to mirrors. In the following pages, we consider some points specific to mirrors.

Reflecting Power

We can define the reflecting power of mirrors in the same way we define the refracting power of lenses: by the amount of vergence produced by the mirror.

- Convex mirrors add negative vergence (like minus lenses).
- Concave mirrors add positive vergence (like plus lenses).
- Plane mirrors add no vergence.

The focal length of a mirror in meters is equal to the reciprocal of the power of the mirror in diopters, and vice versa:

$$P_m = \frac{1}{f}$$

where

P_m = reflecting power of a mirror in diopters
f = focal length of the mirror in meters

Mirrors are often specified, however, not by focal length, but by radius of curvature. Because refractive index does not apply to reflective surfaces, the relationship between radius of curvature r and focal length is simple:

$$f = \frac{r}{2}$$

The focal length is half the radius of curvature. Therefore,

$$P_m = \frac{2}{r}$$

Reversal of Image Space

The basic vergence relationship, $U + P = V$, can be applied directly to mirrors if one remembers that the mirror reverses the image space. The incoming side of the mirror is the same as the outgoing side. If the incoming light rays are traveling from left to right, they will travel from right to left upon reflection. In this case, converging image rays (plus vergence) form a real image to the left of the mirror, and diverging image rays (minus vergence) appear to come from a virtual image to the right of the mirror.

Central Ray for Mirrors

The central ray for mirrors (Fig 2-70) is just as useful as the central ray for lenses, because if image location is determined by vergence calculation, the central ray immediately indicates the orientation and size of the image. Note that, in using the ratio of image distance to object distance to calculate the size of the image, the image and object distances can be measured either from the center of curvature of the mirror or from the surface of the mirror.

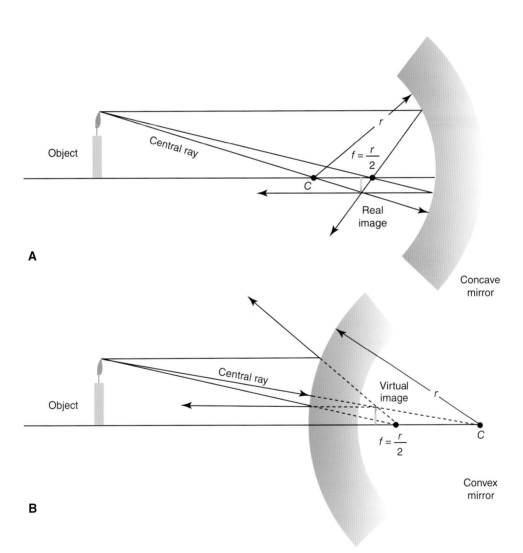

Figure 2-70 Raytracing for concave **(A)** and convex **(B)** mirrors. The central ray for mirrors is different from the central ray for lenses in that it passes through the center of curvature of the mirror, not through the center of the mirror. *(Illustration developed by Kevin M. Miller, MD, and rendered by C. H. Wooley.)*

Vergence Calculations

Because a *plane mirror* adds no vergence to light but simply reverses its direction, vergence does not change when light is reflected.

For example, light from an object 1 m to the left of a plane mirror has a vergence of -1 D at the mirror. On reflection, the vergence will still be -1 D; however, in tracing imaginary extensions of the reflected image rays to the far side of the mirror (into virtual image space), the virtual image is located 1 m to the right of the mirror.

In general, plane mirrors create upright virtual images from real objects, with the virtual image located as far behind the mirror as the real image is in front. Note that, as illustrated in Figure 2-71, only half a full-length plane mirror is needed to see one's entire body.

A *concave mirror* (eg, makeup mirror, shaving mirror, or the internal limiting membrane of the fovea) adds positive vergence to incident light. It therefore has positive, or converging, power. If parallel rays strike the mirror, they reflect and converge toward a point halfway to the center of curvature. Note that the focal point F of a concave mirror is not unique, for any central ray can serve as an optical axis. Note further that the anterior and posterior focal points of a concave mirror are in exactly the same place.

As an example, consider an object 1 m to the left of a concave mirror with a radius of curvature of 50 cm. Where is the image?

The power of the mirror is equal to $1/f$, where $f = (r/2)$.

$$f = \frac{r}{2} = \frac{0.5}{2} = 0.25\,\text{m}$$

$$P_m = \frac{1}{f} = \frac{1}{0.25\,\text{m}} = +4\,\text{D}$$

$$U + P_m = V$$

$$-1\,\text{D} + (+4\,\text{D}) = +3\,\text{D}$$

$$\text{Transverse magnification} = \frac{U}{V} = \frac{-1\,\text{D}}{3\,\text{D}} = -0.33$$

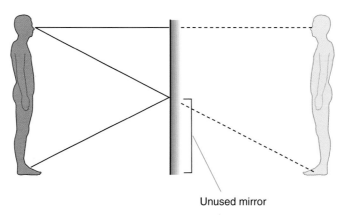

Unused mirror

Figure 2-71 Using a half-length mirror for a full-length view. *(Illustration developed by Edmond H. Thall, MD, and Kevin M. Miller, MD, and rendered by C. H. Wooley.)*

Therefore, the image is located 1/3 m (33 cm) to the left of the mirror, in real image space. It is also minified and inverted.

A *convex mirror* adds negative vergence to incident light. It therefore has negative, or diverging, power. The anterior and posterior focal points, which coincide, are virtual focal points located halfway between the surface of the mirror and the center of curvature.

If the preceding example used a convex, rather than a concave, mirror with the same radius of curvature, the power of the mirror would be −4 D.

$$U + P_m = V$$
$$-1\,D + (-4\,D) = -5\,D$$
$$\text{Transverse magnification} = \frac{U}{V} = \frac{-1\,D}{-5\,D} = +0.20$$

In this case, the image rays are diverging, and a virtual image will appear to be located 20 cm to the right of the mirror. The image is minified and erect.

Optical Aberrations

In paraxial optics, the focus is always stigmatic. As discussed earlier, paraxial rays focus to a single point. Marginal or nonparaxial rays, however, do not necessarily focus stigmatically. Deviations from stigmatic imaging are called *aberrations*. Aberrations can be divided into monochromatic and chromatic forms. The 2 most common monochromatic aberrations are defocus (myopic and hyperopic spherical errors) and regular astigmatism. The clinical application of wavefront aberrometry has made it possible to measure *higher-order aberrations,* which were previously lumped into a catchall term—*irregular astigmatism.* Examples of higher-order aberrations include coma, spherical aberration, and trefoil. Spherical aberration has become a particularly relevant higher-order aberration with the increasing application of keratorefractive surgery.

Regular Astigmatism

Unlike a spherical lens surface, which has the same curvature—and, thus, the same refracting power—in all meridians, an *astigmatic lens* surface is warped in a particular manner. The curvature of an astigmatic lens varies from a minimum value to a maximum value, with the extreme values located in meridians 90° apart. Thus, the refracting power varies from one meridian to the next, and an astigmatic surface cannot bring a pencil of light rays to a point focus. Instead, 2 focal lines are formed. The complicated geometrical envelope of a pencil of light rays refracted by a spherocylindrical lens is called the *conoid of Sturm* (Fig 2-72).

The conoid of Sturm has 2 focal lines, each parallel to one of the principal meridians of the spherocylindrical lens. All the rays in the pencil pass through each of the focal lines. The cross sections of the conoid of Sturm at various points along its length, including the portion of the conoid external to the 2 focal lines, are generally ellipses. At the dioptric mean of the 2 focal lines, there is a cross section of the conoid of Sturm that

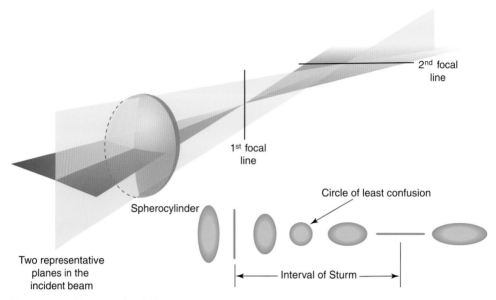

Two representative planes in the incident beam

Spherocylinder

1st focal line

2nd focal line

Circle of least confusion

Interval of Sturm

Figure 2-72 The conoid of Sturm. *(Illustration developed by Kevin M. Miller, MD, and rendered by Jonathan Clark.)*

is circular. This circular patch of light rays is called the *circle of least confusion;* it represents the best overall focus of the spherocylindrical lens. The circle of least confusion occupies the position where all the rays would be brought to focus if the lens had a spherical power equal to the average spherical power of all the meridians of the spherocylindrical lens. This average spherical power of a spherocylindrical lens is called the *spherical equivalent* of the lens. It can be calculated by the following relationship:

$$\text{Spherical equivalent (D)} = \text{sphere (D)} + \frac{\text{cylinder (D)}}{2}$$

Although the cross section of each pencil of rays forming the conoid of Sturm is relatively easy to appreciate, the images produced by spherocylindrical lenses of extended objects, which are composed of an infinite number of pencils of light, are of somewhat different configuration (Fig 2-73).

When calculating object and image relationships for spherocylindrical lenses, we must treat each principal meridian separately, applying the basic vergence relationship or graphical analysis. Once image positions are determined by these methods, we return to the 3-dimensional conoid of Sturm to understand the cross-sectional configurations of the pencils or beams of light that are intercepted by a screen (ie, by the retina of the eye) at various positions.

The simplest form of astigmatic lens is a *planocylindrical* lens, either plus or minus, as shown in Figure 2-74. The Maddox rod is an example of a high-power, clinically useful cylindrical lens (Fig 2-75).

The general form of an astigmatic surface is a *spherocylinder,* or torus, which might be likened to the surface of a curved barrel or American football (Fig 2-76). The meridians

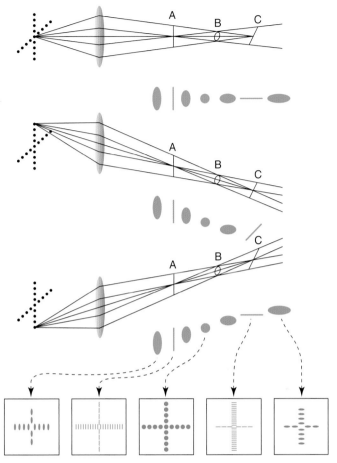

Figure 2-73 Images of an extended object (a cross) formed by a spherocylindrical lens at various distances from the lens. Note that a line of the cross will appear clear only if the image is observed in the focal plane of one of the focal lines of the conoid of Sturm and, furthermore, only if the line is parallel with that particular focal line. *(Modified from Michaels DD.* Visual Optics and Refraction. *2nd ed. St Louis: Mosby; 1980: p 60; fig 2-37.)*

of greatest and least curvature—and therefore the meridians of greatest and least power of an astigmatic lens—are known as the *principal meridians* of that surface or lens. Although a spherocylindrical lens may be thought of as the combination of 2 planocylinders, it is more convenient to think of it as the combination of a spherical lens and a cylindrical lens. The orientation of the cylindrical lens is specified by the axis position according to conventional notation (Fig 2-77). Note that the 0° meridian is the same as the 180° meridian and that the 180° notation is always used for this meridian. Note also that cylinders are symmetrical after rotating 180°, so an axis of 1° is equivalent to 181°, 2° is equivalent to 182°, and so on. The smaller of the 2 numbers is always recorded.

The powers in the principal meridians and the cylinder axis of spherocylindrical lenses may be specified in several ways. The common graphical method is called the

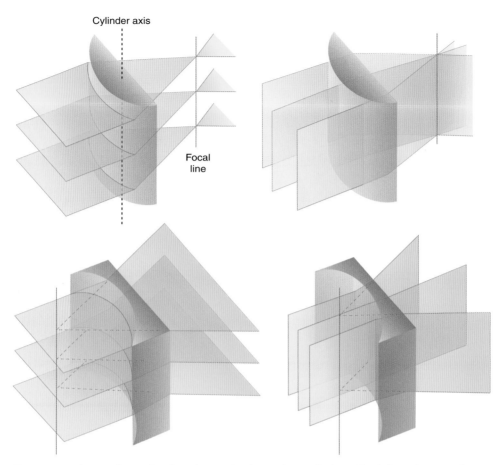

Cylinder axis

Focal
line

Figure 2-74 Image formation by plus and minus planocylinders. Each lens has maximum power in the horizontal meridian (perpendicular to the axis of the cylinder, which is in the vertical meridian) and no power in the vertical meridian. Light rays are bent only in the horizontal direction in passing through the lenses, forming vertical focal lines (a real focal line in the case of the plus cylinder and a virtual focal line in the case of the minus cylinder). Note that the focal lines formed by planocylinders are always parallel to their axes. *(Illustration developed by Kevin M. Miller, MD, and rendered by Jonathan Clark.)*

power cross. A cross is drawn oriented in the principal meridians, and each arm of the cross is labeled with the power acting in that meridian (Fig 2-78). The most common written notation specifies a sphere power, a cylinder power, and the axis of the cylinder. Note that the following examples of spherocylindrical expression are entirely equivalent. Remember that the maximum power of a cylinder is in the meridian 90° away from the axis of the cylinder. To avoid errors in transcription and lens manufacture, it is helpful to notate the axis using all 3 digits and dropping the ° notation.

Combined cylinder form: $+1.00 \times 180 + 4.00 \times 090$
Plus cylinder form: $+1.00 + 3.00 \times 090$
Minus cylinder form: $+4.00 - 3.00 \times 180$

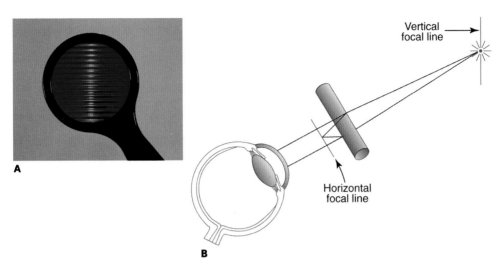

Figure 2-75 The Maddox rod. **A,** This high-powered cylindrical lens is used clinically to form a line image from a point source of light. **B,** The real focal line produced by a Maddox rod is formed so close to the rod and so close to the patient's eye that the patient cannot focus on it. However, every astigmatic lens produces 2 focal lines perpendicular to each other; in the case of the Maddox rod, the second focal line is a virtual focal line passing through the point light source. *(Photograph courtesy of Kevin M. Miller, MD. Illustration developed by Kevin M. Miller, MD, and rendered by C. H. Wooley.)*

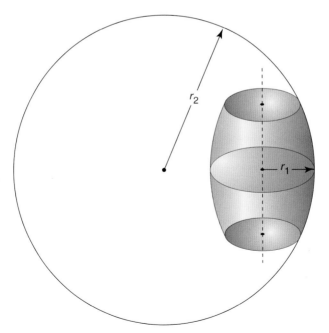

Figure 2-76 Toric surfaces having major and minor radii of curvature. *(Illustration developed by Kevin M. Miller, MD, and rendered by Jonathan Clark.)*

Figure 2-77 Meridian convention for specification of cylinder axis, the so-called *TABO* convention, named after the optical committee that adopted it in 1917. *(Photograph courtesy of Kevin M. Miller, MD.)*

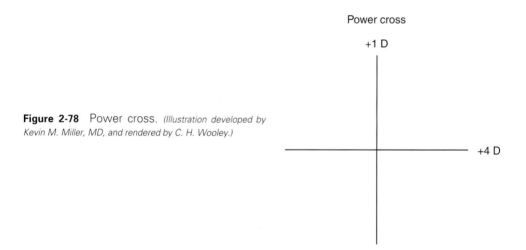

Figure 2-78 Power cross. *(Illustration developed by Kevin M. Miller, MD, and rendered by C. H. Wooley.)*

The spherical equivalent power of this lens is $(+1 D + 4 D)/2 = +250$ D. (See Clinical Example 2-9.)

Transposition

Sometimes we need to be able to transpose the notation for a spherocylindrical lens from plus cylinder form to minus cylinder form and vice versa. The 2 forms are simply different ways of specifying the same lens. One method of transposing is to convert the first cylinder form to the power cross notation and then convert the power cross notation to

Imagine you have just performed streak retinoscopy on 1 eye of a child under general anesthesia using a rack of spherical lenses. The child received cyclopentolate cycloplegia. A +5 D sphere neutralizes the retinoscopic reflex in the 85° meridian. A +3 D sphere neutralizes the reflex in the 175° meridian. Assuming a working distance of 67 cm, what is the appropriate refractive correction for this child's eye?

Subtracting the working distance equivalent of 1.5 D from each measurement, we construct a power cross (Fig 2-79). The power cross can be broken into spherical and cylindrical components, if necessary. Remember that the +2.00 D power acting in the 85° meridian has its axis in the 175° meridian. The equivalent lens in spherocylindrical notation is

$$+1.50 + 2.00 \times 175$$

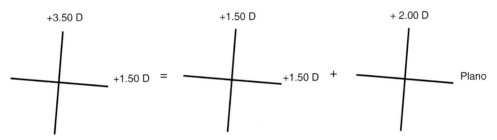

Figure 2-79 A power cross can be decomposed into spherical and cylindrical components. *(Illustration developed by Kevin M. Miller, MD, and rendered by C. H. Wooley.)*

the second cylinder form. In practice, a shorthand method is often used. To convert a prescription from 1 cylinder form to the other:

- Add the sphere and cylinder powers together to obtain the new sphere.
- Change the sign of the cylinder to obtain the new cylinder.
- Rotate the axis 90° to obtain the new axis.

Check to see that the plus and minus cylinder forms in these examples can be correctly transposed to one another.

Combining Spherocylindrical Lenses

Spherocylindrical lenses can be added to one another to produce a single equivalent spherocylindrical lens. In fact, if any number of spherocylindrical lenses are combined, the result is always an equivalent spherocylindrical lens having principal meridians 90° apart. Similarly, a single spherocylindrical lens may be resolved into any number of component spherocylindrical lenses, provided that certain trigonometric rules are followed.

It is easy to add spherocylindrical lenses together if the principal meridians are aligned with one another. In this simple scenario, the principal meridians of the resultant lens are the same as those of the components. Combining 2 spherical lenses (placed close together) yields the algebraic sum of the 2 lens powers. Combining 2 cylinders at the same axis is just as simple and yields a resultant cylinder power that is just the algebraic sum of the 2 cylinder powers; the axis remains unchanged. For cylinders separated by 90°, the situation is also straightforward. One of the cylinders can be transformed into a cylinder with opposite sign at the same axis as the other cylinder, and then the cylinders can be added algebraically as before.

Combining Cylinders at Oblique Axes

It is more difficult to add spherocylindrical lenses when the principal meridians are not aligned with one another. A simple way of doing it is to read the power of the lens combination with a lensmeter.

Because cylinders have a power and axis, it might seem that cylinders could be treated as vectors and that the procedure for combining cylinders would be the procedure for combining vectors. Unfortunately, this is not completely true. Consider that a +1.00 cylinder at axis 180 is the same as a +1.00 cylinder at axis 0. If we add the vectors that correspond to these 2 angles, we get 0, and it is clear that if we add the 2 cylinders, we get +2.00 at either axis 0 or, equivalently, axis 180. Thus, it is clear, cylinders cannot be treated as vectors for the purpose of combination.

The correct procedure is to begin by ensuring that the 2 cylinders to be combined are both positive or negative in sign. If the signs are different, transpose one into the notation of the other. Then associate each cylinder with a vector whose length is the magnitude of the cylinder and whose axis is twice the axis of the cylinder (Fig 2-80). These associated vectors are then added in the usual way. The resultant vector is transformed back to a cylinder. The final cylinder has the magnitude of the resultant vector, but the final cylinder axis is half of the resultant vector axis.

The spherical power of the resultant is equal to the sum of the spherical equivalents of the 2 spherocylinders to be combined. The spherical part of the resultant spherocylinder is determined by the following rule:

$$P_{\text{resultant sphere}} = P_{\text{first sphere}} + P_{\text{second sphere}} + \frac{P_{\text{first cylinder}} + P_{\text{second cylinder}} - P_{\text{resultant cylinder}}}{2}$$

An example will illustrate the technique. Combine

$$+1.00 - 2.00 \times 105 \qquad \text{and} \qquad -5.00 + 3.00 \times 040$$

A transformation of the first spherocylinder to positive cylinder notation gives the equivalent problem of combining:

$$-1 + 2 \times 015 \qquad \text{and} \qquad -5 + 3 \times 040$$

Figure 2-80 shows the associated vectors (with angles doubled) representing the cylinders. The resultant vector may be found by adding the horizontal and vertical components of the individual vectors:

Horizontal component = $2 \cos 30° + 3 \cos 80° = 2.25$
Vertical component = $2 \sin 30° + 3 \sin 80° = 3.95$

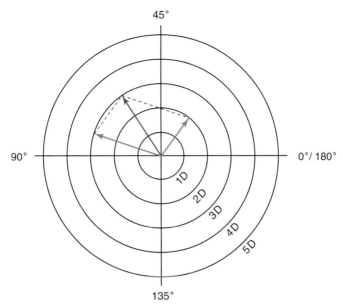

Figure 2-80 Illustration showing how cylinders can be represented by vectors on a double-angle polar coordinate grid. Cylinder power is proportional to the length of the vectors. Cylinder axis is half the angle between the vector and the horizontal axis. *(Illustration developed by Kevin M. Miller, MD, and rendered by C. H. Wooley.)*

By the Pythagorean theorem, the resultant vector has

$$\text{Magnitude} = \sqrt{2.25^2 + 3.95^2} = 4.55$$

and

$$\text{Double angle} = \arctan\left(\frac{3.95}{2.25}\right) \approx 60°$$

The resultant cylinder axis is half this amount, or approximately 30°, and the corresponding resultant cylinder is approximately +4.55 × 030.
    The resultant sphere is

$$P_{\text{resultant sphere}} = -1 - 5 + \frac{2 + 3 - 4.55}{2} = -5.78$$

The final spherocylinder result is approximately

    $-5.75 + 4.50 \times 030$

Spherical Aberration

Spherical aberration causes night myopia and some cases of fluctuating vision following keratorefractive surgery. Although a spherical surface focuses rays stigmatically in the paraxial region (according to the LME), rays outside that region do not focus to a point. For a positive spherical surface, the farther a ray is from the axis, the more anterior its focus (see Fig 2-36).

Spherical aberration has 2 effects. First, image quality (or visual acuity) decreases because the focus is not stigmatic. Second, the image location changes from the position predicted by the LME and vergence equations to the location of the best focus. Roughly speaking, the best focus is achieved where the rays are confined to the smallest area. In the human eye, spherical aberration shifts the focus anteriorly, making the patient slightly more myopic than would be expected from vergence calculations.

Spherical aberration exacerbates myopia in low light (night myopia). In brighter conditions, the pupil constricts, blocking the more peripheral rays and minimizing the effect of spherical aberration. As the pupil enlarges, more peripheral rays enter the eye and the focus shifts anteriorly, making the patient slightly more myopic in low-light conditions. Typically, the amount of myopic shift is about 0.50 D.

Spherical aberration accounts for some cases of fluctuating vision following kera-torefractive surgery. Normally, the cornea is flatter peripherally than centrally, which decreases spherical aberration. Radial keratotomy makes the cornea more spherical, increasing spherical aberration. LASIK and PRK can make the central cornea flatter than the peripheral cornea. In general, the effect of spherical aberration increases as the fourth power of the pupil diameter. Doubling pupil diameter increases spherical aberration 16 times. Thus, a small change in pupil size can cause a significant change in refraction. This possibility should be considered in patients who have fluctuating vision despite stable K readings and well-healed corneas following keratorefractive surgery. (See Clinical Example 2-10.)

Chromatic Aberration

Thus far in our analysis of aberrations we have ignored the effect of wavelength. Ophthalmic lenses and the human eye are often treated as though they focus all wavelengths identically, but this is not true. Most lenses introduce dispersion. Dispersion in the human

---

CLINICAL EXAMPLE 2-10

What causes halos to form around distant point lights at night after LASIK when a pupil dilates widely?

This problem is typically encountered when a high correction is performed and a small optical zone results. If a pupil remains small enough to allow only light that has been refracted by the treated cornea to reach the fovea, the image will be relatively stigmatic (Fig 2-81A). If, however, the pupil opens widely under scotopic conditions, light refracted by the untreated peripheral cornea will enter the eye and form a myopic defocus on the retina. This defocused light, an effect of surgically induced spherical aberration, will be perceived as a halo (Fig 2-81B).

Small pupil

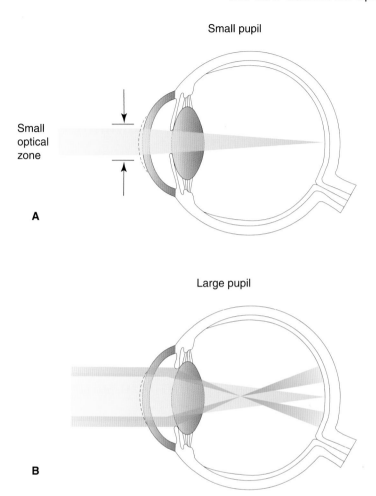

Small
optical
zone

A

Large pupil

B

Figure 2-81 A, If the treated optical zone is larger than the entrance pupil, the image focuses stigmatically. **B,** If the optical zone is smaller than the entrance pupil, light refracting through the untreated peripheral cornea will cause spherical aberration. A patient viewing a distance point light source will see halos around the light. *(Illustration developed by Kevin M. Miller, MD, and rendered by C. H. Wooley.)*

eye causes *chromatic aberration,* in which blue light focuses in front of red light (Fig 2-82). The difference between the blue and red foci is about 0.5 D in the average eye, but it can be much more. Even if all monochromatic aberrations could be compensated for or eliminated by contact lenses or refractive surgery, chromatic aberration and diffraction would still limit the optical resolving power of the eye.

Chromatic compensation is common in microscope, telescope, and camera lenses but is not yet available in spectacle, contact, or intraocular lenses. Blue-blocking, red-blocking, and other colored sunglasses improve visual acuity by decreasing chromatic aberration. They do so, however, at the cost of reducing the color content of the perceived image.

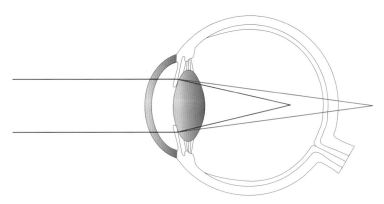

Figure 2-82 Chromatic aberration in the human eye. *(Illustration developed by Kevin M. Miller, MD, and rendered by C. H. Wooley.)*

CHAPTER 3

Optics of the Human Eye

The Human Eye as an Optical System

The eyes play such an integral role in our ability to study the world around us that it is easy to overlook the fact that they obey many of the same principles as optical instruments. When designing a complex optical system such as an operating microscope, for instance, an engineer must also take into account the optics of the human eye, which follow the same optical principles as microscopes. This chapter introduces conceptual tools ("schematic eyes") that were developed to help us understand the remarkable inner workings of the eye's optics. Also covered are the various methods used to measure the eye's ability to "see" and a review of the types of refractive errors of the human eye.

Schematic Eyes

Many attempts have been made to understand the optics of the human eye. The major challenges lie in the complexity of some of the eye's optical elements and their "imperfections" as compared to mathematical ideals. Simplifications and approximations make models easy to understand and use but also detract from their ability to explain all the complexities and subtleties of the eye. In one example, the anterior surface of the cornea is not spherical—rather, it tends to flatten toward the limbus. In another example, the center of the crystalline lens is usually decentered with respect to the cornea and the visual axis of the eye.

Many mathematical models of the eye's optical system have been developed over the years, based on careful anatomic measurements and equally careful approximations. Notable models were developed by Listing, Donders, Tscherning, and von Helmholtz. Gullstrand, a professor of ophthalmology in Sweden, developed a schematic eye model that so closely approximated the human eye that he was awarded the Nobel Prize in 1911. The dimensions of the Gullstrand schematic eye are illustrated in Figure 3-1 and listed in Table 3-1.

As useful as the Gullstrand schematic eye is in modeling the optics of the eye, it is cumbersome for certain clinical calculations and can be simplified further. Because the principal points of the cornea and lens are fairly close to each other, we can substitute for them a single intermediate point. In a similar fashion, the nodal points of the cornea and lens can be combined into a single nodal point for the eye. Thus, we can treat the eye as if it were a single refracting element, an ideal spherical surface separating 2 media

Figure 3-1 Optical constants of Gullstrand's schematic eye. **A,** Refractive indices of the media and positions of the refracting surfaces. **B,** Positions of the cardinal points, which are used for optical calculations. *(Illustration by C.H. Wooley.)*

of different refractive indices: 1.0 for air and 1.33 for the eye (Fig 3-2). This is known as the *reduced schematic eye.*

Using this concept of the reduced schematic eye, the reader should be able to calculate the retinal image size of an object in space, such as a Snellen letter. This calculation utilizes the simplified nodal point, through which light rays entering or leaving the eye pass undeviated. Retinal image size can be calculated by using the geometric principle of similar triangles if the following information is given: (1) the actual size of a Snellen letter's height on the eye chart, (2) the distance from the eye chart to the eye, and (3) the distance from the nodal point to the retina (17 mm). The formula for this calculation is as follows:

$$\frac{\text{Retinal image height}}{\text{Snellen letter height}} = \frac{\text{nodal point to retina distance}}{\text{chart to eye distance}}$$

Table 3-1 The Schematic Eye

	Accommodation Relaxed	Maximum Accommodation
Refractive index		
Cornea	1.376	1.376
Aqueous humor and vitreous body	1.336	1.336
Lens	1.386	1.386
Equivalent core lens	1.406	1.406
Position		
Anterior surface of cornea	0	0
Posterior surface of cornea	0.5	0.5
Anterior surface of lens	3.6	3.2
Anterior surface of equiv. core lens	4.146	3.8725
Posterior surface of equiv. core lens	6.565	6.5275
Posterior surface of lens	7.2	7.2
Radius of curvature		
Anterior surface of cornea	7.7	7.7
Posterior surface of cornea	6.8	6.8
Equivalent surface of cornea		
Anterior surface of lens	10.0	5.33
Anterior surface of equiv. core lens	7.911	2.655
Posterior surface of equiv. core lens	− 5.76	− 2.655
Posterior surface of lens	− 6.0	− 5.33
Refracting power		
Anterior surface of cornea	48.83	48.83
Posterior surface of cornea	− 5.88	− 5.88
Equivalent surface of cornea		
Anterior surface of lens	5.0	9.375
Core lens	5.985	14.96
Posterior surface of lens	8.33	9.375
Corneal system		
Refracting power	43.05	43.05
Position of first principal point	− 0.0496	− 0.0496
Position of second principal point	− 0.0506	− 0.0506
First focal length	− 23.227	− 23.227
Second focal length	31.031	31.031
Lens system		
Refracting power	19.11	33.06
Position of first principal point	5.678	5.145
Position of second principal point	5.808	5.255
Focal length	69.908	40.416
Complete optical system of eye		
Refracting power	58.64	70.57
Position of first principal point, H	1.348	1.772
Position of second principal point, H'	1.602	2.086
Position of first focal point, F	− 15.707	− 12.397
Position of second focal point, F'	24.387	21.016
First focal length	− 17.055	− 14.169
Second focal length	22.785	18.930
Position of first nodal point, N	7.078	
Position of second nodal point, N'	7.332	
Position of fovea centralis	24.0	24.0
Axial refraction	− 1.0	− 9.6
Position of near point		− 102.3

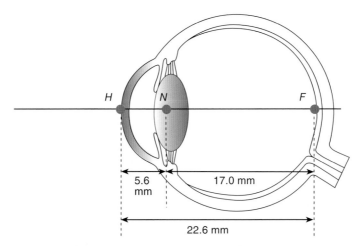

Figure 3-2 Dimensions of the reduced schematic eye, defined by the anterior corneal surface *(H)*, the simplified nodal point of the eye *(N)*, and the fovea *(F)*. The distance from the simplified nodal point to the fovea is 17 mm, and the distance from the anterior corneal surface to the nodal point is 5.6 mm. The refractive index for air is taken to be 1.0, and the simplified refractive index for the eye is 1.333. *(Illustration by C. H. Wooley.)*

Although technically, in a clinical setting, the distance from the eye chart to the nodal point should be measured, it is much easier to measure the distance to the surface of the cornea. The 5.5 mm between the corneal surface and nodal point is usually insignificant.

As an example, if the distance between the nodal point and the retina is 17 mm, the distance between the eye chart and the eye is 20 feet (6000 mm), and the height of a Snellen letter is 60 mm, the resulting image size on the retina is 0.17 mm.

> Katz M, Kruger PB. The human eye as an optical system. In: Tasman W, Jaeger EA, eds. *Duane's Clinical Ophthalmology.* Philadelphia: Lippincott Williams & Wilkins; 2003.

Important Axes of the Eye

There is occasionally confusion in the ophthalmic literature regarding the terms used to describe the axes of the eye. Following are some important definitions:

Visual axis The line connecting the fixation point and the fovea.

Pupillary axis The line passing through the midpoint of the entrance pupil that is perpendicular to the corneal surface.

Principal line of vision The line passing through the object of regard, perpendicular to the corneal surface.

Optical axis A line that best approximates the line passing through the optical centers of the cornea and lens and the fovea. Because the lens is usually decentered with respect to the cornea and the visual axis, no single line can precisely pass through each of these points. However, because the amount of decentration is small, the best approximation of this line is taken to be the optical axis.

Angle kappa (κ) The angle between the pupillary axis and the visual axis (Fig 3-3).

Angle alpha (α) The angle between the eye's optical axis and its visual axis. This angle is taken as positive when the visual axis in object space lies on the nasal side of the optical axis.

Pupil Size and Its Effect on Visual Resolution

The size of the blur circle on the retina generally increases as the size of the pupil increases. If a pinhole aperture is placed immediately in front of an eye, it acts as an artificial pupil, and the size of the blur circle is reduced correspondingly (Fig 3-4; Clinical Problems 3-1).

   The pinhole aperture is used clinically to measure *pinhole visual acuity.* If visual acuity improves when measured through a pinhole aperture, a refractive error is usually present. Thus, the pinhole can be used to screen quickly for refractive errors. The most useful pinhole diameter for general clinical purposes (refractive errors from −5 D to +5 D) is 1.2 mm. If the pinhole aperture is made smaller, the blurring effects of diffraction around the edges of the aperture overwhelm the image-sharpening effects of the small pupil. To obtain a useful pinhole vision for refractive errors greater than 5 D, it is usually

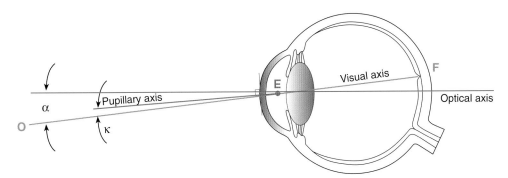

Figure 3-3 Angle kappa (κ). The pupillary axis *(red line)* is represented schematically as the line passing through the midpoint of the entrance pupil *(E)* that is perpendicular to the corneal surface. The visual axis *(green line)* is defined as the line connecting the fixation point *(O)* and the fovea *(F)*. If all the optical elements of the human were in perfect alignment, these 2 lines would overlap. In actuality, however, the fovea is normally displaced from its expected position. The angle between the pupillary axis and the visual axis is called *angle kappa* (κ). Angle kappa is considered positive when the fovea is located temporally and downward from the expected position, as is the usual case. Angle alpha (α) is the angle between the eye's optical axis and its visual axis. This angle is taken as positive when the visual axis in object space lies on the nasal side of the optical axis, as is normally the case. *(Courtesy of Neal H. Atebara, MD. Redrawn by C.H. Wooley.)*

Figure 3-4 Light rays from each point on an object *(the upright arrow)* form a blur circle on the retina of a myopic eye. The retinal image is the composite of all blur circles, the size of each being proportional to the diameter of the pupil **(A)** and the amount of defocus. If a pinhole is held in front of the eye, the blur circles decrease in size, thus sharpening the overall retinal image **(B)**. *(Courtesy of Neal H. Atebara, MD. Redrawn by C. H. Wooley.)*

CLINICAL PROBLEMS 3-1

Why do persons with uncorrected myopia squint?
To obtain a pinhole effect (or rather a stenopeic slit effect). Better visual acuity results from smaller blur circles (or even smaller blur "slits").

Does pupil size affect the measured near point of accommodation?
Yes. With smaller pupil size, the eye's depth of focus increases, and objects closer than the actual near point of the eye remain in better focus.

Why are patients less likely to need their glasses in bright light?
One reason is that the bright light causes the pupil to constrict, allowing the defocused image to be less blurred on the retina.

necessary, in addition to the pinhole, to use a lens that corrects most of the refractive error.

It can also be useful to check pinhole visual acuity after the best refractive correction has been determined. The most helpful findings are obtained with the pupil dilated. For example, if visual acuity improves when a pinhole is held over the best correction, optical irregularities such as corneal and lenticular light-scattering translucencies or irregular astigmatism are likely to be present, with the pinhole restricting light to a relatively uniform area of the eye's optics. (This technique also can be useful in identifying optical causes of monocular diplopia.) If visual acuity is worse when tested through a pinhole aperture over the best correction, macular disease must be considered. A diseased macula is often unable to adapt to the reduced amount of light entering through the pinhole, and visual acuity can decrease markedly.

It is worth mentioning that, because of the refractive effects of the cornea, the image of the pupil as viewed by the clinician is larger than the actual pupil. This larger image is called the *entrance pupil*. The entrance pupil is about 13% larger than the actual pupil and is situated about 3 mm behind the anterior surface of the cornea. This phenomenon can be readily seen during corneal transplant surgery. When the corneal button is removed, the pupil appears smaller than it did with the cornea intact.

Visual Acuity

Clinicians often think of visual acuity primarily in terms of Snellen acuity, but it is important to recognize that visual perception is a far more complex process than is implied by this simple measuring system. Indeed, there are a multitude of ways to measure visual function. Measurement of the minimum brightness of a target so that it may be distinguished from its background is called the *minimum visible threshold;* the smallest visual angle at which 2 separate objects can be discriminated is called the *minimum separable threshold;* the smallest detectable amount of misalignment of 2 line segments is called *Vernier acuity.* A patient's ability to recognize progressively smaller letters or forms is called the *minimum legible threshold,* of which Snellen acuity is the most common variant in clinical practice.

Snellen acuity is measured with test letters constructed so that the letters as a whole subtend an angle of *5 minutes of arc,* whereas each stroke of the letter subtends 1 minute of arc. Letters of different sizes are designated by the distance at which the letters subtend an angle of 5 minutes (Fig 3-5). The Snellen chart is designed to measure visual acuity in angular terms. However, the accepted convention does not specify acuity in angular measure but uses a notation in which the numerator is the *testing distance* (in feet or meters), and the denominator is the *distance at which a letter subtends the standard visual angle of 5 minutes.* Thus, on the 20/20 line (6/6 in meters), the letters subtend an angle of 5 minutes when viewed at 20 feet. On the 20/40 line (6/12 in meters), the letters

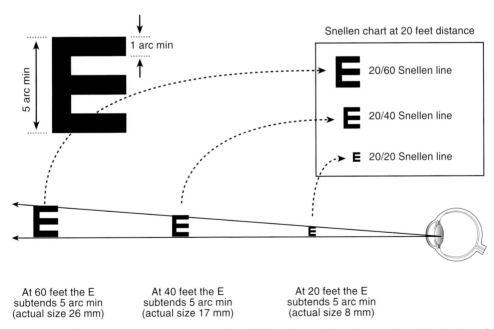

Figure 3-5 Snellen letters are constructed such that they subtend an angle of 5 minutes of arc when located at the distance specified by the denominator. For example, if a Snellen E is 26 mm in height, it subtends 5 arc minutes at 60 feet. Correspondingly, a 26-mm letter occupies the 20/60 line of the Snellen chart at the standard testing distance of 20 feet. *(Courtesy of Neal H. Atebara, MD. Redrawn by C. H. Wooley.)*

subtend an angle of 10 minutes when viewed at 20 feet or 5 minutes when viewed at 40 feet. Conversions from the Snellen fraction to the *minimum angle of resolution or recognition* (MAR) and the *base-10 logarithm of the minimum angle of resolution or recognition* (logMAR) are shown in Table 3-2.

The standard Snellen eye chart, although widely accepted, is not perfect. The letters on different Snellen lines are not related to one another by size in a geometric or logarithmic sense. For example, the increase in letter size going from the 20/20 line to the 20/25 line is different from that going from the 20/25 line to the 20/30 line. In addition, certain letters (such as C, D, O, and G) are inherently harder to recognize than others (such as A and J) because there are more letters of the alphabet with which they can be confused. For these reasons, alternative visual acuity charts have been developed (eg, ETDRS, Bailey-Lovie) and popularized in clinical trials (Fig 3-6). Acuity devices that display optotypes on video monitors have also become popular because they allow presentation of a random assortment of optotypes and eliminate problems with memorization seen in patients who visit the office frequently.

Westheimer G. Visual acuity. In: Kaufman PL, Alm A, eds. *Adler's Physiology of the Eye*. 10th ed. St. Louis: Mosby; 2003.

Contrast Sensitivity and the Contrast Sensitivity Function

An often-underappreciated variable in measuring visual function is the *contrast* of an optotype with its background. In general, the higher the contrast between an optotype (eg, Snellen letter) and its background, the easier it is to read. One reason good illumination makes it is easier to read a book is that more light creates a brighter background and therefore a higher contrast against the black letters on the page. If the brightness of an object (I_{min}) and the brightness of its background (I_{max}) are known, the degree of

Table 3-2 Visual Acuity in Different Notations

	Snellen Fraction		Minimum Angle		Decimal
Feet	Meters	4-Meter Standard	of Resolution	LogMAR	Notation
20/10	6/3	4/2	0.5	−0.3	2.0
20/15	6/4.5	4/3	0.75	−0.1	1.5
20/20	6/6	4/4	1.0	0.0	1.0
20/25	6/7.5	4/5	1.25	0.1	0.8
20/30	6/9	4/6	1.5	0.2	0.7
20/40	6/12	4/8	2.0	0.3	0.5
20/50	6/15	4/10	2.5	0.4	0.4
20/60	6/18	4/12	3.0	0.5	0.3
20/80	6/24	4/16	4.0	0.6	
20/100	6/30	4/20	5.0	0.7	0.2
20/120	6/36	4/24	6.0	0.8	
20/150	6/45	4/32	8.0	0.9	
20/200	6/60	4/40	10.0	1.0	0.1
20/400	6/120	4/80	20.0	1.3	0.05

Figure 3-6 Modified ETDRS visual acuity chart produced by the Lighthouse. The chart is intended for use at 4 m but can also be used at 2 m or 1 m with appropriate scaling. *(Photograph courtesy of Kevin M. Miller, MD.)*

contrast between the object and its background can be measured using the following formula:

$$\frac{I_{max} - I_{min}}{I_{max} + I_{min}}$$

Thus, on a page where the letters are printed with perfectly black ink (ie, totally nonreflecting) on perfectly white paper (ie, 100% reflecting), the contrast will be 100%. Snellen acuity is commonly tested with targets, either illuminated or projected charts, that *approximate* 100% contrast. When we measure Snellen visual acuity, therefore, we are measuring the smallest optotype at approximately 100% contrast that can be resolved by the visual system. In everyday life, however, 100% contrast is rarely encountered, and most visual tasks must be performed in lower-contrast conditions.

To take contrast sensitivity into account when measuring visual function, some investigators have borrowed a concept from physical optics known as the *modulation transfer function* (MTF). Consider a target in which the light intensity varies from some peak value to zero in a sinusoidal fashion. The contrast is 100%, but instead of looking like a bar graph, it looks like a bar graph with softened edges. The number of light bands per unit length or per unit angle is called the *spatial frequency.* Spatial frequency is closely related to Snellen acuity; for example, the 20/20 E is composed of bands of light and dark, where each band is 1 minute of arc. Thus, 20/20 Snellen acuity corresponds (for a 100% contrast target) roughly to 30 cycles per degree of resolution when expressed in spatial frequency notation. If we take sine wave gratings with various spatial frequencies and describe how the optical system alters the contrast of each of them, we have a set of information that constitutes the MTF.

In clinical practice, we present a patient with targets of various spatial frequencies and peak contrasts. A plot is then made of the minimum resolvable contrast target that can be seen for each spatial frequency. The minimum resolvable contrast is the *contrast threshold*. The reciprocal of the contrast threshold is defined as the *contrast sensitivity*, and the manner in which contrast sensitivity changes as a function of the spatial frequency of the targets is called the *contrast sensitivity function* (CSF) (Fig 3-7). A typical contrast sensitivity curve obtained with sinusoidal gratings is shown in Figure 3-8. As just discussed, there is a degree of correspondence between the expected Snellen acuity and the contrast sensitivity curve. Contrast sensitivity can also be tested with optotypes of variable contrast (such as Pelli-Robson or Regan charts), which may be easier for patients to use. Which of these approaches is more useful clinically remains controversial.

As with any test of visual function, it is important to perform the test with the best possible optical correction in place. In addition, luminance must be kept constant when CSF is tested, because mean luminance has an effect on the shape of the normal CSF. In

Figure 3-7 Contrast sensitivity grating. In this example, the contrast diminishes from bottom to top and the spatial frequency of the pattern increases from left to right. The pattern appears to have a hump in the middle at the frequencies for which the human eye is most sensitive to contrasts. *(Image courtesy of Brian Wandell, PhD.)*

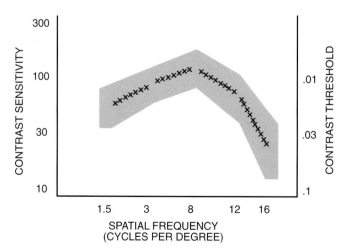

Figure 3-8 A typical contrast sensitivity curve is noted as x-x-x. The *shaded area* represents the range of normal values for 90% of the population. Expected deviations from the normal due to specific diagnoses are noted in the text discussion. *(Developed by Dr. Arthur P. Ginsburg and licensed under U.S. Patent #4,365,873 by Vistech Consultants, Inc. Courtesy of Stereo Optical Company, Inc, Chicago.)*

low luminance, the low spatial frequency falloff disappears and the peak shifts toward the lower frequencies. In brighter light, there is little change in the shape of the normal CSF through a range of luminance for the higher spatial frequencies. Generally, contrast sensitivity is measured at normal room illumination, which is about 30–70 footlamberts.

Contrast sensitivity is affected by various conditions of the eye, both physiologic and pathologic. Pupil size has an effect on contrast sensitivity, as it does on Snellen acuity. With miotic pupils, diffraction reduces contrast sensitivity; with large or dilated pupils, optical aberrations may interfere with performance. Contrast sensitivity can also be affected by any corneal pathology that causes distortion or edema. Lens changes, particularly incipient cataracts, may significantly decrease CSF, even with a normal Snellen acuity. Retinal pathology may affect contrast sensitivity more (as with retinitis pigmentosa or central serous retinopathy) or less (certain macular degenerations) than it does Snellen acuity. Glaucoma may produce a significant loss in the midrange. Retrobulbar optic neuritis may also be associated with a notch-type pattern loss. Amblyopia is associated with a generalized attenuation of the curve.

Marmor MF, Gawande A. Effect of visual blur on contrast sensitivity. Clinical implications. *Ophthalmology.* 1988;95:139–143.

Miller D. Glare and contrast sensitivity testing. In: Tasman W, Jaeger EA, eds. *Duane's Clinical Ophthalmology.* Philadelphia: Lippincott Williams & Wilkins; 1992.

Refractive States of the Eyes

The refractive state of the eye can be considered in 2 ways. First, the *focal point* concept may be employed. The location of the image formed by an object at optical infinity through a nonaccommodating eye determines its refractive state. Objects focusing anterior or posterior to the retina form a blurred image on the retina, whereas objects that focus on the retina form a sharp image. Alternatively, the *far point* concept may be used. The far point is the point in space that is conjugate to the fovea of the nonaccommodating eye; it is where the fovea images if the optics are reversed and the fovea is made the object.

Emmetropia is the refractive state in which parallel rays of light from a distant object are brought to focus on the retina in the nonaccommodating eye (Fig 3-9A). The far

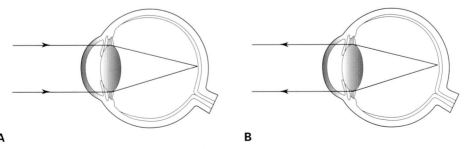

A   B

Figure 3-9 Emmetropia with accommodation relaxed. **A,** Parallel light rays from infinity focus to a point on the retina. **B,** Similarly, light rays emanating from a point on the retina focus at the far point of the eye at optical infinity. *(Illustration by C. H. Wooley.)*

point of the emmetropic eye is at infinity, and infinity is conjugate with the retina (Fig 3-9B). *Ametropia* refers to the absence of emmetropia, where the far point of the eye is not at infinity.

Ametropia can be classified by presumptive etiology as *axial* or *refractive*. In *axial ametropia*, the eyeball is either unusually long (myopia) or short (hyperopia). In *refractive ametropia*, the length of the eye is statistically normal, but the refractive power of the eye is abnormal: excessive power in myopia or too little power in hyperopia. *Aphakia* is an example of extreme refractive hyperopia unless the aphakic eye was highly myopic (>20 D) preoperatively. An ametropic eye requires either a diverging or a converging lens to image a distant object on the retina. (For the measurement and spectacle correction of refractive errors, see Chapter 4, Clinical Refraction. For contact lens correction of ametropias, see Chapter 5, Contact Lenses.)

Ametropias may also be classified by the nature of the mismatch between the optical power and length of the eye. In *myopia*, the eye possesses too much optical power for its axial length. In the myopic eye (with accommodation relaxed), light rays from an object at infinity converge too soon and thus focus in front of the retina, resulting in a *defocused image* on the retina (Fig 3-10A); likewise, the far point of the eye images in front of the eye, between the cornea and optical infinity (Fig 3-10B). In *hyperopia*, the eye does not possess enough optical power for its axial length. In the hyperopic eye (with accommodation relaxed), an object at infinity attempts to focus light behind the retina, again producing a defocused image on the retina (Fig 3-11A); the far point of the eye (actually a virtual point rather than a real point in space) is located behind the retina (Fig 3-11B).

In *astigmatism*, light rays do not focus to a single point. Whereas simple myopic and hyperopic eyes are *stigmatic* optical systems that focus light rays from infinity to a single point, variations in the curvature of the cornea or lens at different meridians prevent the light rays in an astigmatic eye from focusing to a single point. In an astigmatic eye, there is no single focal point, but rather a set of 2 *focal lines*. Each astigmatic eye can be classified by the orientations and relative positions of these focal lines. If 1 focal line lies in front of the eye and the other is on the retina, the condition is classified as *simple myopic astigmatism*. If both focal lines lie in front of the retina, the condition is classified as *compound myopic astigmatism*. If 1 focal line lies behind the retina and the other is on the retina, it is classified as *simple hyperopic astigmatism*. If both focal lines lie behind the

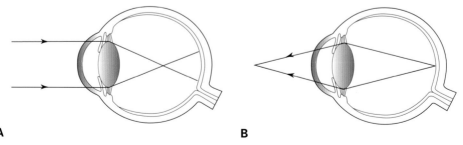

A   **B**

Figure 3-10 Myopia with accommodation relaxed. **A,** Parallel light rays from infinity focus to a point anterior to the retina, forming a blurred image on the retina. **B,** light rays emanating from a point on the retina focus to a far point in front of the eye, between optical infinity and the cornea. *(Illustration by C. H. Wooley.)*

retina, it is classified as *compound hyperopic astigmatism.* If 1 focal line lies in front and the other behind the retina, it is classified as *mixed astigmatism* (Fig 3-12).

If the principal meridians of astigmatism have constant orientation at every point across the pupil, and if the amount of astigmatism is the same at every point, the refractive condition is known as *regular astigmatism* and is correctable by cylindrical spectacle lenses. Regular astigmatism may itself be classified into *with-the-rule* and *against-the-rule*

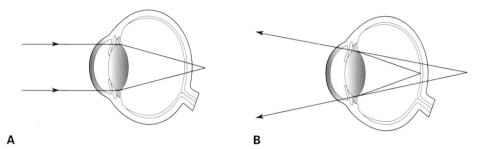

A   **B**

Figure 3-11 Hyperopia with accommodation relaxed. **A,** Parallel light rays from infinity focus to a point posterior to the retina, forming a blurred image on the retina. **B,** Light rays emanating from a point on the retina are divergent as they exit the eye, appearing to have come from a virtual far point behind the eye. *(Illustration by C. H. Wooley.)*

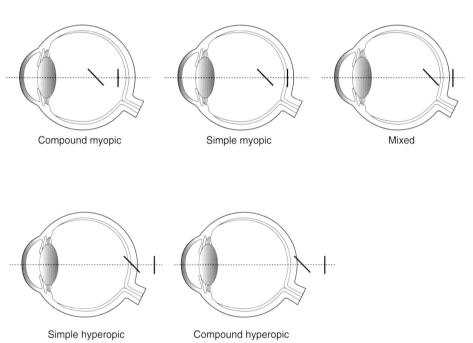

Compound myopic   Simple myopic   Mixed

Simple hyperopic   Compound hyperopic

Figure 3-12 Types of astigmatism. The locations of the focal lines with respect to the retina define the type of astigmatism. The main difference between the types of astigmatism depicted in the illustration is the spherical equivalent refractive error. All of the astigmatisms depicted are "with-the-rule" astigmatisms—that is, they are corrected with a plus cylinder whose axis is vertical. If they were "against-the-rule" astigmatisms, the positions of the vertical and horizontal focal lines would be reversed.

astigmatism. In *with-the-rule* astigmatism (the more common type in children), the vertical meridian is steepest (resembling an American football lying on its side), and a correcting plus cylinder should be used at or near axis 90°. In *against-the-rule* astigmatism (the more common type in older adults), the horizontal meridian is steepest (resembling an American football standing on its end), and a correcting plus cylinder should be used at or near axis 180°. The term *oblique astigmatism* is used to describe regular astigmatism in which the principal meridians do not lie at, or close to, 90° or 180°.

In *irregular astigmatism*, the orientation of the principal meridians or the amount of astigmatism changes from point to point across the pupil. Although the principal meridians are 90° apart at every point, it may sometimes appear by retinoscopy or keratometry that the principal meridians of the cornea, as a whole, are not perpendicular to one another. All eyes have at least a small amount of irregular astigmatism, but only recently have instruments such as corneal topographers and wavefront aberrometers been able to measure them clinically. These *higher-order* irregularities in the refractive properties of the cornea and lens have been characterized by Zernicke polynomials, mathematical shapes that approximate various types of irregular astigmatism more closely than the simple "American football" model. Zernicke polynomials include such shapes such as aspherical aberration, coma, and trefoil.

Anisometropia refers to any difference in the spherical equivalents between the 2 eyes. Uncorrected anisometropia in children may lead to amblyopia, especially if 1 eye is hyperopic. Fortunately, anisometropia in children can usually be corrected fully without symptomatic effects. Although adults may be annoyed by uncorrected anisometropia, they may be totally intolerant of initial spectacle correction. Unequal image size, or *aniseikonia*, may occur, and the prismatic effect of the glasses will vary in different directions of gaze, inducing *anisophoria*. Anisophoria is usually more bothersome than aniseikonia for patients with spectacle-corrected anisometropias.

Aniseikonia is a difference in the size or shape of the images formed in the 2 eyes. The most common cause is the differential magnification inherent in the spectacle correction of anisometropia. Even though aniseikonia is difficult to measure, anisometropic spectacle correction can be prescribed in such a manner as to reduce aniseikonia. Magnification can be reduced by making the front surface power of a lens less positive. Decreasing center thickness also decreases magnification. Decreasing vertex distance decreases both the magnifying effect of plus lenses and the minifying effect of minus lenses (these effects become increasingly noticeable as lens power increases). Contact lenses may provide a better solution than spectacles in most patients with anisometropia, particularly in children (in whom fusion may be possible). For a fuller discussion of contact lens correction of anisometropia, see Chapter 5, Contact Lenses.

Unilateral aphakia is an extreme example of hyperopic anisometropia arising from refractive ametropia. Spectacle correction produces an intolerable aniseikonia of about 25%; contact lens correction produces aniseikonia of about 7%, which is usually tolerated. Aniseikonia may be reduced still further, if necessary, by adjusting the powers of contact lenses and simultaneously worn spectacle lenses to provide the appropriate minifying or magnifying effect by the Galilean telescope principle. For further information on correcting aphakia, see Chapter 4, Clinical Refraction; Chapter 5, Contact Lenses; and Chapter 6, Intraocular Lenses.

Accommodation is the mechanism by which the eye changes refractive power by altering the shape of its crystalline lens by mechanisms described by Helmholtz. The posterior focal point is moved forward in the eye during accommodation (Fig 3-13A). Correspondingly, the far point moves closer to the eye (Fig 3-13B). *Accommodative effort* occurs when the ciliary muscle contracts in response to parasympathetic stimulation, thus allowing the zonule fibers to relax. The outward-directed tension on the lens capsule is decreased and the lens becomes more convex. The movement of the equatorial edge of the lens is thus away from the sclera during accommodation and toward the sclera again when accommodation is relaxed. *Accommodative response* results from the increase in lens convexity (primarily the front surface). It is evident that as the lens loses elasticity from the aging process, the accommodative response wanes, even though the amount of ciliary muscle contraction or accommodative effort is virtually unchanged. The accommodative response of the eye may be expressed as *amplitude of accommodation* (in diopters of change in lens power) or as *range of accommodation* (the distance between the far point of the eye and the nearest point at which the eye can maintain focus, or near point). In calculating the additional spectacle lens requirement for a patient with presbyopia, the amplitude in diopters is a more useful measurement. In appraising an individual's ability to perform a specific visual task, the range in meters or centimeters is more informative.

Glasser A, Kaufman PL. The mechanism of accommodation in primates. *Ophthalmology.* 1999;106:863–872.

Epidemiology of Refractive Errors

An interplay among corneal power, lens power, anterior chamber depth, and axial length determines an individual's refractive status. All 4 elements change continuously as the eye grows. On average, babies are born with about 3.0 D of hyperopia. In the first few months, this hyperopia may increase slightly, but it then declines to an average of about

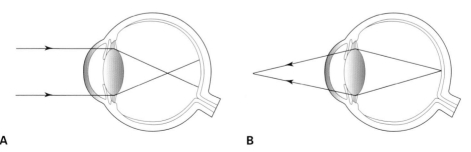

A   **B**

Figure 3-13 Emmetropia with accommodation stimulated. **A,** Parallel light rays now come to a point locus in front of the retina, forming a blurred image on the retina. **B,** Light rays emanating from a point on the retina focus to a near point in front of the eye, between optical infinity and the cornea. *(Illustration by C. H. Wooley.)*

1.0 D of hyperopia by age 1, due to marked changes in corneal and lenticular powers, as well as axial growth. By the end of the second year, the anterior segment attains adult proportions; however, the curvatures of the refracting surfaces continue to change measurably. One study found that average corneal power decreased 0.1–0.2 D, and lens power decreased about 1.8 D, between ages 3 and 14 years.

From birth to age 6 years, the axial length of the eye grows by about 5 mm, and one might expect from this a high prevalence of myopia in infants. However, most infants are actually emmetropic, with only a 2% incidence of myopia at 6 years. This phenomenon is due to a still undetermined mechanism called *emmetropization*. During the first 6 years of life, as the eye grows by 5 mm, a compensatory loss of 4 D of corneal power and 2 D of lens power keeps most eyes close to emmetropia. It appears that the immature human eye develops so as to reduce refractive errors.

Lawrence MS, Azar DT. Myopia and models and mechanisms of refractive error control. *Ophthalmol Clin North Am.* 2002;15:127–133.

Refractive Errors. Preferred Practice Pattern. San Francisco: American Academy of Ophthalmology; 2002.

Vision Problems in the U.S. Prevalence of Adult Vision Impairment and Age-Related Eye Disease in America. Schaumburg, IL: Prevent Blindness America; 2002.

Zadnik K, Mutti DO. Biology of the eye as an optical system. In: *Duane's Clinical Ophthalmology* (vol 1, ch 34). Philadelphia: Lippincott Williams & Wilkins; 2003.

Developmental Myopia

The prevalence of myopia increases steadily with increasing age. Myopia in American children has been estimated at 3% among those 5 to 7 years old, 8% among those 8 to 10 years old, 14% among those 11 to 12 years old, and 25% among those 12 to 17 years old. In particular ethnic groups, a similar trend of increasing prevalence with age has been demonstrated, although the percentages in each age group may differ. Ethnic Chinese children, for example, have much higher rates of myopia at all ages. A national study in Taiwan found the prevalence was 12% among 6-year-old children and 84% among those 16 to 18 years old. Similar rates have been found in Singapore and Japan.

Different subsets of myopia have been characterized. *Juvenile-onset myopia,* defined as myopia with an onset between 7 and 16 years of age, is due primarily to growth in axial length. Risk factors include esophoria, against-the-rule astigmatism, premature birth, family history, and intensive near work. In general, the earlier the onset of myopia, the greater the degree of progression. In the United States, the mean rate of childhood myopia progression is reported at about 0.5 D per year. In about 75% of teens, refractive errors stabilize at about age 15 or 16. In those who do not experience stabilization, progression often continues into the 20s or 30s.

Adult-onset myopia begins at about 20 years of age. Extensive near work is a risk factor for the development of myopia at this age. A study of West Point cadets found myopia requiring corrective lenses in 46% at entrance, 54% after 1 year, and 65% after 2 years. The probability of myopic progression was related to the degree of initial refractive error. It is estimated that as many as 20% to 40% of patients with low hyperopia and with emmetropia who have extensive near-work requirements become myopic before age 25, as compared to less than 10% of persons without such demands. Older Naval Academy recruits have a lower rate of myopia development than younger recruits over a 4-year curriculum (15% for 21-year-olds versus 77% for 18-year-olds). Some young adults are at risk for myopic progression even after a period of refractive stability. It has been theorized that persons who regularly perform considerable near work undergo a process similar to emmetropization; however, in such cases, the "emmetropization" is for the customary close working distance and results in a myopic shift.

The etiologic factors involving myopia are complex, with both genetic and environmental factors playing roles to varying extents in different forms of myopia. Regarding a genetic role, identical twins are more likely to have a similar degree of myopia than fraternal twins, siblings, or parent and child. Identical twins separated at birth and having different work habits do not show significant differences in refractive error. Some forms of severe myopia suggest dominant, recessive, and even sex-linked inheritance patterns. However, studies of ethnic Chinese in Taiwan show an increase in the prevalence and severity of myopia over the span of 2 generations, a finding that implies that genetics alone are not entirely responsible for myopia. As mentioned, some studies have reported that near work is associated with a higher prevalence and progression of myopia, although other studies have not, especially with respect to middle distance activities, such as those that involve video display terminals. Higher educational achievement has been strongly associated with a higher prevalence of myopia, although the cause of the association is not clear. Nutrition has been implicated in the development of some refractive errors. Studies from Africa find that children suffering malnutrition have an increased prevalence of high ametropia, astigmatism, and anisometropia.

Animal models of myopia may help our understanding of the mechanisms underlying eye growth. When monkeys, tree shrews, and birds are deprived of visual stimuli early in life, they become myopic. When chicks are given plus spectacle lenses, their eyes become more hyperopic; when they are given minus spectacle lenses, they become more myopic. It is as if the eye strives to adjust the vergence of the light reaching the retina and change its shape to improve image clarity. In fact, evidence exists that chick eyes are capable of altering scleral growth and choroidal thickness; this is due in part to regulation by central nervous system processes that are triggered by defocused images on the retina and mediated by dopamine and vasoactive intestinal polypeptide. Yet, despite these intriguing animal models, it is clear that our understanding of the fundamental mechanisms underlying regulation of eye growth in response to changes in the visual environment is far from complete.

Feldkamper M, Schaeffel F. Interactions of genes and environment in myopia. *Dev Ophthalmol.* 2003;37:34–49.

Fisher AJ, McGuire JJ, Schaeffel F, et al. Light- and focus-dependent expression of the transcription factor ZENK in the chick retina. *Nat Neurosci.* 1999;2:706–712.

Lin LL, Shih YF, Tsai CB, et al. Epidemiologic study of ocular refraction among schoolchildren in Taiwan in 1995. *Optom Vis Sci.* 1999;76:275–281.

McCarty CA, Taylor HR. Myopia and vision 2020. *Am J Ophthalmol.* 2000;129:525–527.

Winawer J, Wallman J, et al. Differential responses of ocular length and choroidal thickness in chick eyes to brief periods of plus and minus lens-wear. *Invest Ophthalmol Vis Sci Suppl.* 1999;40:S963.

Zadnik K, Mutti DO. How applicable are animal myopia models to human juvenile onset myopia? *Vis Res.* 1995;35:1283–1288.

Developmental Hyperopia

Less is known about the epidemiology of hyperopia than of myopia. Apart from those who develop nuclear sclerotic cataracts, there appears to be an increase in prevalence of adult hyperopia with age. In Caucasians, the prevalence of hyperopia increases from about 20% among those in their 40s to about 60% among those in their 70s and 80s. A similar pattern of prevalence was seen among African Americans in Baltimore. Nuclear sclerosis is associated with a myopic shift. In contrast to myopia, hyperopia was associated with lower educational achievement.

Attebo K, Ivers RQ, Mitchell P. Refractive errors in an older population: the Blue Mountains Eye Study. *Ophthalmology.* 1999;106:1066–1072.

Katz J, Tielsch JM, Sommer A. Prevalence and risk factors for refractive errors in an adult inner city population. *Invest Ophthalmol Vis Sci.* 1997;38:334–340.

Lee KE, Klein BE, Klein R. Changes in refractive error over a 5-year interval in the Beaver Dam Eye Study. *Invest Ophthalmol Vis Sci.* 1999:40:1645–1649.

Prevention of Refractive Errors

Over the years, many treatments have been proposed to prevent or slow the progression of myopia. Optical correction in the form of bifocal spectacles, multifocal spectacles, or removal of distance spectacles when performing close work has been recommended to reduce accommodation, because accommodation is a postulated mechanism for the progression of myopia. Administration of atropine eyedrops has long been proposed to prevent progression of myopia because it inhibits accommodation, which may exert forces on the eye that result in axial elongation. Lowering intraocular pressure has been suggested as an alternative pharmacologic intervention; this course works presumably by reducing internal pressure on the eye wall. It has long been postulated that rigid contact lens use could slow the progression of myopia in children. Visual training purported to reduce myopia includes exercises such as near–far focusing change activities and convergence exercises. Evidence reported in the peer-reviewed literature, including from recent randomized clinical trials, is currently insufficient to support a recommendation for intervention in any of these proposed treatments.

Saw SM, Shih-Yeh EC, Koh A, et al. Interventions to retard myopia progression in children: an evidence-based update. *Ophthalmology.* 2002;109:415–421.

Treatment of Refractive Errors

The need to correct refractive errors depends on the patient's symptoms and visual needs. Patients with low refractive errors may not require correction, and small changes in refractive corrections in asymptomatic patients are not generally recommended. Correction options include spectacles, contact lenses, or surgery. Various occupational and recreational requirements as well as personal preferences affect the specific choices for any individual patient. Spectacles should be considered before contact lenses or refractive surgery. Spectacle correction is covered in Chapter 4, Clinical Refraction; contact lens correction is covered in Chapter 5, Contact Lenses. Refractive surgery is covered in BCSC Section 13, *Refractive Surgery.*

Clinical Refraction

Objective Refraction: Retinoscopy

The *retinoscope* allows the physician to objectively determine the spherocylindrical refractive error, as well as determine whether astigmatism is regular or irregular, and to evaluate opacities and irregularities.

The majority of retinoscopes in use today employ the streak projection system, as developed by Copeland. The illumination of the retinoscope is provided by a special bulb that has a straight filament that forms a streak in its projection. The light is reflected from a mirror that is either half silvered (Welch-Allyn model) or totally silvered around a small circular unsilvered aperture (Copeland instrument) (Fig 4-1).

The filament can be moved in relation to a convex lens in the system. If the light is slightly divergent, it appears to come from a point behind the retinoscope, as if the light had been reflected off a plano mirror ("plano mirror setting," Fig 4-2).

Alternatively, the distance between the convex lens and the filament can be increased by moving the sleeve on the handle, thus allowing converging light to be emitted. In this

Figure 4-1 Observation system: light path from patient's pupil, through mirror, to observer's retina. *(Modified from Corboy JM.* The Retinoscopy Book: A Manual for Beginners. *Thorofare, NJ: Slack; 1979:13.)*

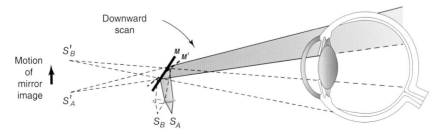

Figure 4-2 Illumination system: position of source with plano mirror effect.

case, the image of the filament would be between the examiner and the patient, as if the light had been reflected off a concave mirror (Fig 4-3).

Retinoscopy is usually performed using the plano mirror setting. Not all retinoscopes employ the same sleeve position for this mirror setting. For example, the original Copeland retinoscope is in plano position with the sleeve up; the Welch-Allyn is in plano position with the sleeve down. The axis of the streak is rotated by rotating the sleeve.

Positioning and Alignment

Ordinarily, the examiner uses the right eye to perform retinoscopy on the patient's right eye, and the left eye for the patient's left eye. If the examiner looks directly through the optical centers of the trial lenses, the reflections from lenses may interfere. If the examiner is too far off-axis, unwanted spherical and cylindrical errors can occur. The optimum alignment is just off-center, where the lens reflections can still be seen between the center of the pupil and the lateral edge of the lens.

Fixation and Fogging

Retinoscopy should be performed with the patient's accommodation relaxed. The patient should fixate at a distance on a nonaccommodative target. For example, the target may be a dim light at the end of the room or a large Snellen letter (20/200 or 20/400 size). (Children may need pharmacologic cycloplegia.)

The Retinal Reflex

The projected streak, forming a blurred image of the filament on the patient's retina, can be considered as a new light source returning to the examiner's eye. By observing characteristics of this reflex, one can determine the refractive status of the eye. If the patient is emmetropic, the light rays will emerge parallel. If the patient is myopic, they will be convergent (Fig 4-4). If the patient is hyperopic, the rays will be divergent. Through the peephole in the retinoscope, these emerging rays are seen as a red reflex in the patient's

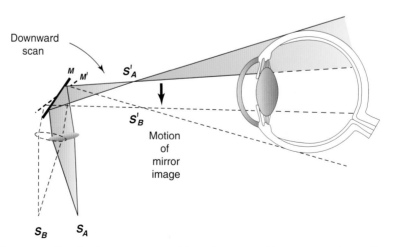

Figure 4-3 Illumination system: position of source with concave mirror effect.

pupil. If the examiner is at the patient's far point, all the light enters the examiner's pupil and illumination is uniform (Fig 4-5). However, if the far point of the patient's eye is not at the peephole of the retinoscope, some rays emanating from the patient's pupil will not enter the peephole and illumination of the pupil is incomplete.

If the far point is between the examiner and the patient (myopia greater than the examiner's dioptric working distance), the rays will have met and will be diverging again. The lighted portion of the pupil will move in a direction opposite to the sweep (known as *against* motion). If the far point is not between the examiner and the patient (hyperopia), the light will move in the same direction as the sweep (so-called *with* motion; Fig 4-6). When the light fills the pupil and does not move—either because the eye is em-

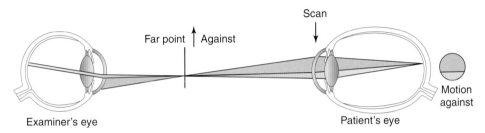

Figure 4-4 Observation system for myopia.

Neutralization

Figure 4-5 Neutrality reflex. Far point of the eye is conjugate with the peephole of the retinoscope. *(Modified from Corboy JM.* The Retinoscopy Book: A Manual for Beginners. *Thorofare, NJ: Slack; 1979:34.)*

Pupil fills

Retinal Reflex Movement

Figure 4-6 Retinal reflex movement. Note movement of the streak from face and from retina in *with* versus *against* motion. *(Modified from Corboy JM.* The Retinoscopy Book. A Manual for Beginners. *Thorofare, NJ: Slack; 1979:32.)*

metropic or because the appropriate correcting lens has been placed before it—the condition is known as *neutrality* (see Fig 4-5).

If, while at the far point of the eye, the examiner moved forward (in front of the far point), *with* motion would be seen; if the examiner moved backward, the light would have reached the far point and begun to diverge again, and *against* motion would be seen.

Characteristics of the reflex

The moving retinoscopic reflex has 3 main characteristics (Fig 4-7):

1. *Speed.* The reflex moves slowest when the examiner is far from the focal point and becomes more rapid as the focal point is approached. In other words, large refractive errors have a slow-moving reflex, whereas small errors have a fast reflex.
2. *Brilliance.* The reflex is dull when the examiner is far from the focal point, becoming brighter as neutrality is approached. *Against* reflexes are usually dimmer than *with* reflexes.
3. *Width.* The streak is narrow when the examiner is far from the focal point. It broadens approaching the focal point and, of course, fills the entire pupil at the focal point itself.

The Correcting Lens

When the examiner uses the appropriate correcting lenses (either with loose lenses or a phoropter), retinoscopic reflexes can be neutralized. In other words, when the examiner brings the patient's far point to the peephole, the patient's entire pupil is illuminated and the reflex will not move (Fig 4-8). The power of the correcting lenses that neutralizes the reflex provides a measure of the patient's refractive error.

It is important to remember that the examiner is determining the refractive error for the distance at which he or she is working. The dioptric equivalent of the working distance should be subtracted from the correcting lens to obtain the patient's actual distance correction. Because a common working distance is 67 cm, many phoropters have a +1.50 D "working-distance" lens that flips in while the examiner chooses the

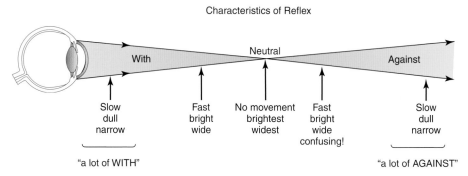

Figure 4-7 Characteristics of the moving retinal reflex on both sides of neutrality. The vertical arrows indicate the position of the retinoscope with regard to the point of neutrality. *(Modified from Corboy JM. The Retinoscopy Book: A Manual for Beginners. Thorofare, NJ: Slack; 1979:38.)*

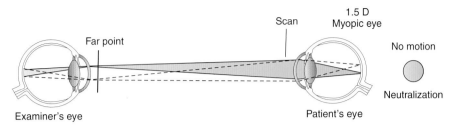

Figure 4-8 Observation system at neutralization.

corrective lenses to neutralize the reflex. This added lens can produce bothersome re-flexes. However, any working distance may be used (the examiner may prefer to move closer for a brighter image, for instance) as long as the appropriate working-distance correction is included in the calculations.

For example, suppose that the examiner obtained neutralization with a total of +4.00 D over the eye (gross retinoscopy) at a working distance of 67 cm. Subtracting 1.50 D for the working distance yields a net retinoscopic refractive correction of +2.50 D. As another example, suppose neutralization was obtained with −6.00 D, using a working distance of 50 cm. The dioptric correction for the working distance is now +2.00 D, yielding a net retinoscopic refraction for a distance correction of −8.00 D.

Finding Neutrality

In *against* movement, the far point is between the examiner and the patient. Therefore, to bring the far point to the examiner's pupil, minus lenses should be placed in front of the patient's eye. Similarly, in the case of *with* movement, plus lenses should be placed in front of the patient's eye. This leads to the simple clinical rule: If you see *with* motion, add plus power (or subtract *minus*); if you see *against* motion, add minus power (or subtract *plus*). Lens power should be added (or subtracted) until neutrality is reached (Fig 4-9).

Because it is considered easier to work with the brighter, sharper *with* image, it is preferable to overminus the eye and obtain a *with* reflex and then reduce the minus (add plus) until neutrality is reached. Be aware that the slow, dull reflexes of high refractive errors may be confused with the pupil-filling neutrality reflex or with dull reflexes (as seen in patients with hazy media). Place a high-power plus and minus lens over the eye and look again.

Retinoscopy of Regular Astigmatism

Most eyes have some regular astigmatism. In these cases, light is refracted differently by the 2 principal astigmatic meridians. Let us consider how the retinoscope works in greater detail.

As we sweep the retinoscope back and forth, we are really measuring the power along only a single axis. If we move the retinoscope from side to side (with the streak oriented at 90°), we are measuring the optical power in the 180° meridian. Power in this meridian is provided by a cylinder at axis 90°. Accordingly, the extremely convenient result is that the streak of the retinoscope is aligned at the same axis as the axis of the correcting cylinder being tested. Thus, in a patient with regular astigmatism, we want to neutralize 2 reflexes, one from each of the principal meridians.

Finding the cylinder axis

Before the retinoscope is used to measure the powers in each of the principal meridians, the axes of the meridians must be determined. Four characteristics of the streak reflex can aid in determining axis:

1. *Break.* A break is seen when the streak is not parallel to one of the meridians. The orientation of the reflex streak in the pupil is not the same as that of the streak we are projecting; the line is discontinuous, or *broken* (Fig 4-10). The break disappears (ie, the line appears continuous) when the streak is rotated onto the correct axis. The correcting cylinder should be placed at this axis.
2. *Width.* The width of the streak varies as it is rotated around the correct axis. It appears narrowest when the streak aligns with the axis (Fig 4-11).

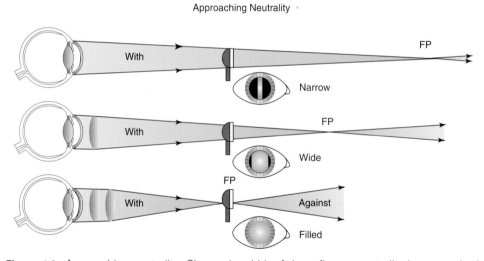

Figure 4-9 Approaching neutrality. Change in width of the reflex as neutrality is approached. Note that working distance remains constant, and the far point *(FP)* is pulled in with plus lenses. *(Modified from Corboy JM.* The Retinoscopy Book: A Manual for Beginners. *Thorofare, NJ: Slack; 1979:41.)*

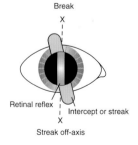

Figure 4-10 Break. The retinal reflex is discontinuous with the intercept when the streak is off the correct axis. *(Modified from Corboy JM.* The Retinoscopy Book: A Manual for Beginners. *Thorofare, NJ: Slack; 1979:90.)*

3. *Intensity.* The intensity of the line is brighter when the streak is on the correct axis. (This is a subtle finding, useful only in small cylinders.)
4. *Skew.* Skew (oblique motion of the streak reflex) may be used to refine the axis in small cylinders. If the streak is off-axis, it will move in a slightly different direction from the pupillary reflex (Fig 4-12). The reflex and streak move in the same direction (both at right angles to the orientation of the streak) when the streak is aligned with one of the principal meridians.

When the streak is aligned at the correct axis, the sleeve may be lowered (in the case of the Copeland instrument) or raised (in the case of the Welch-Allyn instrument) to narrow the streak, allowing the angle to be read more easily from the trial lens apparatus (Fig 4-13).

This axis can be confirmed through a technique known as *straddling,* which is performed with the estimated correcting cylinder in place (Fig 4-14). The retinoscope streak is turned 45° off-axis in both directions, and if the axis is correct, the width of the reflex should be equal in both off-axis positions. If the axis is incorrect, the widths will be

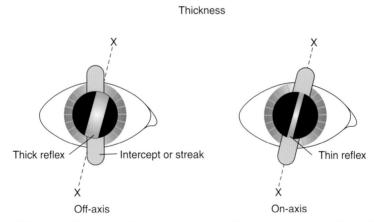

Figure 4-11 Width, or thickness, of the retinal reflex. We locate the axis where the reflex is thinnest. *(Modified from Corboy JM.* The Retinoscopy Book: A Manual for Beginners. *Thorofare, NJ: Slack; 1979:90.)*

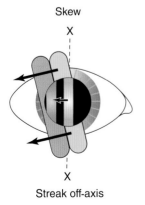

Figure 4-12 Skew (oblique motion). The *arrows* indicate that movements of the reflex and intercept are not parallel. The reflex and intercept do not move in the same direction but are skewed when the streak is off-axis. *(Modified from Corboy JM.* The Retinoscopy Book: A Manual for Beginners. *Thorofare, NJ: Slack; 1979:91.)*

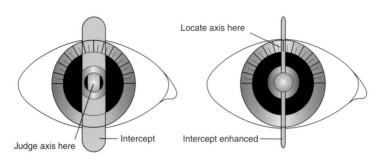

A Axis Determination   **B** Axis Location

Figure 4-13 Locating axis on the protractor. **A,** First determine the astigmatic axis. **B,** Then lower the sleeve to enhance the intercept until the filament is seen as a fine line pinpointing the axis. *(Modified from Corboy JM.* The Retinoscopy Book: A Manual for Beginners. *Thorofare, NJ: Slack; 1979:92.)*

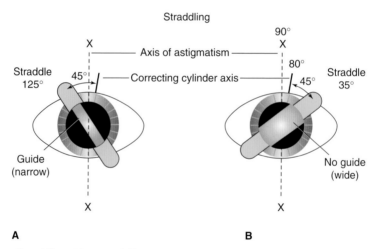

Figure 4-14 Straddling. The straddling meridians are 45° off the correcting cylinder axis, at roughly 35° and 125°. As you move back from the eye while comparing meridians, the reflex at 125° remains narrow **(A)** at the same distance that the reflex at 35° has become wide **(B).** This dissimilarity indicates an axis error; the narrow reflex **(A)** is the guide toward which we must turn the correcting cylinder axis. *(Modified from Corboy JM.* The Retinoscopy Book: A Manual for Beginners. *Thorofare, NJ: Slack; 1979:95.)*

unequal in the 2 positions. The axis of the correcting cylinder should be moved toward the narrower reflex and the straddling performed again until the width is equal.

Finding the cylinder power

Once the 2 principal meridians are identified, we can follow the previously explained spherical techniques, applying them to each axis separately in turn.

With 2 spheres: Neutralize one axis with one spherical lens. If the 90° axis is neutralized with a +1.50 sphere and the 180° axis is neutralized with a +2.25 sphere, the gross retinoscopy would be $+1.50 + 0.75 \times 180$. The examiner's working distance should be subtracted from the sphere to obtain the refractive correction.

With a sphere and cylinder: Neutralize 1 axis with a spherical lens. To continue working using *with* reflexes, neutralize the *less plus* axis first. Then, with this spherical lens in place, neutralize the axis 90° away by adding a plus cylindrical lens at the appropriate orientation. The spherocylindrical gross retinoscopy can be read directly from the trial lens apparatus.

It is also possible to use 2 cylinders at right angles to each other for this gross retinoscopy; however, this variant does not seem to provide any advantages over the other methods.

Aberrations of the Retinoscopic Reflex

With irregular astigmatism, almost any type of aberration may appear in the reflex. Spherical aberrations tend to increase the brightness at the center or periphery of the pupil, depending on whether the aberrations are positive or negative.

As the point of neutrality is approached, one part of the reflex may be myopic, whereas the other is hyperopic relative to the position of the retinoscope. This will produce the so-called *scissors reflex.*

Sometimes a marked irregular astigmatism or optical opacity produces confusing, distorted shadows that can markedly reduce the precision of the retinoscopic result. In such cases, other techniques such as subjective refraction should be used.

All of these aberrant reflexes become more noticeable with larger pupillary diameters. In these cases, considering the central portion of the light reflex yields the best approximation.

Summary of Retinoscopy

The following steps summarize how to perform streak retinoscopy using a plus cylinder phoropter:

1. Set the phoropter to 0 D sphere and 0 D cylinder. Use cycloplegia if necessary. Otherwise, fog the eyes or use a nonaccommodative target.
2. Hold the sleeve of the retinoscope in the position that produces a divergent beam of light. (If the examiner can focus the linear filament of the retinoscope on a wall, the sleeve is in the wrong position.)
3. Sweep the streak of light (the intercept) across the pupil perpendicular to the long axis of the intercept and watch the pupillary light reflex. Sweep in several different meridians. Use the right eye to examine the patient's right eye, and use the left eye to examine the patient's left eye.
4. Add minus sphere (dial up on a phoropter) until the retinoscopic reflex shows *with* motion in all meridians. Add a little extra minus sphere if uncertain. If the reflexes are dim or indistinct, consider high refractive errors and make large changes in sphere (-3 D, -6 D, -9 D, and so on).
5. Add plus sphere (dial down on a phoropter) until the retinoscopic reflex neutralizes or shows a small amount of residual *with* motion in 1 meridian. If all

meridians neutralize simultaneously, the patient's refractive error is spherical. Proceed to step 9.

6. Rotate the streak 90° and set the axis of the correcting plus cylinder parallel to the streak. Sweep this meridian to reveal additional *with* motion. Add plus cylinder power until the remaining *with* motion is neutralized. Now the retinoscopic reflex should be neutralized in all meridians simultaneously.

7. Refine the correcting cylinder axis by sweeping 45° to either side of it. Move in slightly closer to the patient to pick up *with* motion. Rotate the axis of the correcting plus cylinder a couple of degrees toward the "guide" line, the brighter and narrower reflex. Repeat until both reflexes are equal.

8. Refine the cylinder power by moving in closer to the patient to pick up *with* motion in all directions. Back away slowly, observing how the reflexes neutralize. Change sphere or cylinder power as appropriate to make all meridians neutralize simultaneously.

9. Subtract the working distance. If working at 67 cm, subtract 1.5 D. If the examiner's arms are short or the examiner prefers working closer, the appropriate dioptric power for the distance chosen should be subtracted.

10. Record the streak retinoscopy findings and, if possible, check the patient's visual acuity after he or she has had time to wear the prescription and readjust to ambient room light.

Corboy JM. *The Retinoscopy Book: An Introductory Manual for Eye Care Professionals.* 4th ed. Thorofare, NJ: Slack; 1995.

Safir A. Retinoscopy. In: Tasman W, Jaeger EA, eds. *Duane's Clinical Ophthalmology.* Philadelphia: Lippincott-Raven; 1995.

Subjective Refraction Techniques

Subjective refraction techniques rely on the patient's responses to obtain the refractive correction that gives the best visual acuity. If all refractive errors were simply spherical, subjective refraction would be easy. However, determining the astigmatic portion of the correction is more complex, and different subjective refraction techniques are employed. Although the Jackson cross cylinder is the most common instrument for determining the astigmatic correction, we will begin with the astigmatic dial technique because it is easier to understand.

Astigmatic Dial Technique

The pencil of light from every point on the astigmatic dial is imaged by an astigmatic eye as a conoid of Sturm. Those spokes of the dial that are parallel to the principal meridians of the eye's astigmatism will be imaged as sharp lines corresponding to the focal lines of the conoid of Sturm.

Figure 4-15A shows an eye with compound hyperopic astigmatism and how it sees an astigmatic dial. The vertical line of the astigmatic dial is the blackest and sharpest, because the vertical focal line of each conoid of Sturm is closer to the retina than the horizontal focal line. By accommodating, however, the patient might pull both focal lines

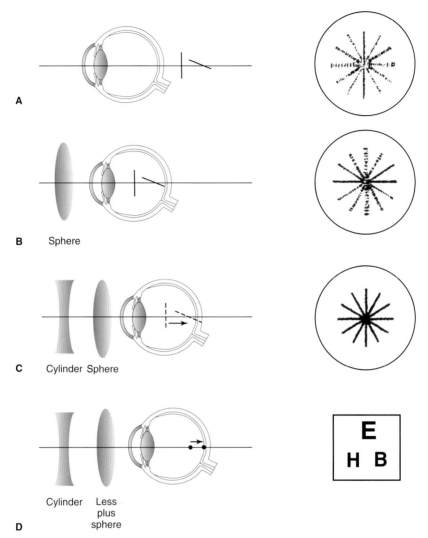

Figure 4-15 Astigmatic dial technique. **A,** Conoid of Sturm and retinal image of an astigmatic dial as viewed by an eye with compound hyperopic astigmatism. **B,** Fogging to produce compound myopic astigmatism. **C,** The conoid of Sturm is collapsed to a single point. **D,** Minus sphere is added (or plus sphere subtracted) to produce a sharp image.

forward, far enough to make even the horizontal line of the astigmatic dial clear. To avoid confusion from accommodation, fogging is used. That is, enough plus sphere is placed before the eye to pull both the focal lines into the vitreous, creating compound myopic astigmatism, as in Figure 4-15B.

With the eye fogged, accommodation can only blur the lines more, and the patient therefore tends to relax accommodation. The focal line closest to the retina can now be identified with certainty as the horizontal line, because it is now the blackest and sharpest line of the astigmatic dial. Note that the terms *blackest* and *sharpest* are more easily understood by patients and should be used instead of the word *clearest*.

After the examiner locates one of the principal meridians of the astigmatism, the interval of Sturm can be collapsed by moving the anterior focal line back toward the posterior focal line, in the direction of the light. This is done by adding a minus cylinder with axis parallel to the anterior focal line. In Figure 4-15C, the vertical focal line has been moved back to the position of the horizontal focal line and collapsed to a point by adding a minus cylinder with axis at 90°. Note that the minus cylinder is placed with its axis *perpendicular* to the blackest meridian on the astigmatic dial. Note further that as the interval of Sturm is collapsed, the focal lines disappear into a point focus.

All of the lines of the astigmatic dial now appear equally black but still are not in perfect focus, because the eye is still slightly fogged to control accommodation. A visual acuity chart is now used as plus sphere is removed until best visual acuity is obtained (Fig 4-15D).

In summary, the following steps are used in astigmatic dial refraction:

1. Obtain best visual acuity using spheres only.
2. Fog the eye to about 20/50 by adding plus sphere.
3. Note the blackest and sharpest line of the astigmatic dial.
4. Add minus cylinder with axis perpendicular to the blackest and sharpest line until all lines appear equal. (A rotatable cross dial aligned with the principal meridians is often used for this step, in order to compare the 2 meridians more easily.)
5. Reduce plus sphere (or add minus) until best acuity is obtained with the visual acuity chart.

Astigmatic dial refraction can also be performed with plus cylinder equipment, but it must be used in a way that simulates minus cylinder effect. All of the above steps remain the same except for step 4, which becomes: Add *plus* cylinder with axis *parallel* to the blackest and sharpest line. As each 0.25 D of plus cylinder power is added, change the sphere simultaneously 0.25 D in the minus direction. This simulates minus cylinder effect exactly, moving the anterior focal line posteriorly without changing the position of the posterior focal line.

An opposite "double-click-stop" technique is used with minus cylinder refracting equipment in retinoscopy to simulate plus cylinder effect. Do not confuse these double-click-stop techniques with the procedure used in cross-cylinder refinement of cylinder power, in which the sphere is adjusted 0.25 D in the opposite direction for every 0.50 D of cylinder power change (see the following section). This latter procedure is designed to keep the circle of least confusion of the conoid of Sturm on the retina.

Michaels DD. *Visual Optics and Refraction: A Clinical Approach.* 3rd ed. St Louis: Mosby; 1985:319–322.

Cross-Cylinder Technique

The Jackson cross cylinder, in Edward Jackson's words, is probably "far more useful, and far more used" than any other lens in clinical refraction. Every ophthalmologist should be familiar with the principles involved in its use. Although the cross cylinder is usually used to *refine* the cylinder axis and power of a refraction already obtained, it can also be used for the entire astigmatic refraction.

The first step in cross-cylinder refraction is adjusting the sphere to yield best visual acuity without accommodation. First, place the prescription the patient is wearing, if any, into a trial frame or phoropter. Fog the eye to be examined with plus sphere while the patient views a visual acuity chart; then decrease the fog until best visual acuity is obtained. The goal, if astigmatism is present, is to place the circle of least confusion of the conoid of Sturm on the retina, thus creating mixed astigmatism. The cross cylinder is then introduced, first for refinement of cylinder axis and then for refinement of cylinder power.

If no cylindrical correction is present initially, the cross cylinder may still be used, placed arbitrarily at 90° and 180°, to check for the presence of astigmatism. If a preferred flip position is found, cylinder is added with axis parallel to the respective plus or minus axis of the cross cylinder until the 2 flip choices are equal. If no preference is found with the cross-cylinder axes at 90° and 180°, then 45° and 135° should always be checked before assuming that no astigmatism is present. Once any cylinder power is found, axis and power are refined in the usual manner.

Although it is more difficult to understand refinement of cylinder axis than of cylinder power, cylinder axis is always refined first. This sequence is necessary because the correct axis can be found in the presence of an incorrect power, but the full cylinder power will not be found in the presence of an incorrect axis.

Refinement of cylinder axis involves the combination of cylinders at oblique axes. When the axis of the correcting cylinder is slightly off, the combination of the correcting cylinder with the eye's cylinder error produces residual astigmatism having principal meridians roughly 45° away from the principal meridians of the 2 cylinders. To refine the axis, therefore, place the cross cylinder with its principal meridians *45° away from* the principal meridians of the correcting cylinder. Present the patient with alternative flip choices, inquiring which is "blackest and sharpest," and rotate the axis of the correcting cylinder toward the corresponding plus or minus axis of the cross cylinder. Low-power cylinders are rotated in large steps; high-power cylinders are rotated in small steps. Repeat this procedure until the flip choices appear equal.

To refine cylinder power, align the cross-cylinder axes with the principal meridians of the correcting lens, as illustrated in Figure 4-16. As the examiner changes cylinder power according to the patient's responses, the spherical equivalent of the refractive correction should remain constant to keep the circle of least confusion on the retina. One achieves this by changing the sphere half as much in the opposite direction as the cylinder power is changed. That is, for every 0.50 D of cylinder power change, the sphere is changed 0.25 D in the opposite direction. If the cylinder power is changed a large amount, however, the sphere power should be readjusted for best visual acuity.

Continue to refine cylinder power until both flip choices appear "about the same" to the patient. This is the correct endpoint, for the 2 flip choices now produce equal and opposite mixed astigmatism, blurring the visual acuity chart equally (Fig 4-17).

Remember always to use the proper-power cross cylinder for the patient's visual acuity level. For example, a ±0.25 D cross cylinder is commonly used with visual acuity levels of 20/30 and better. A high-power cross cylinder (±0.50 D or ±1.00 D) should be used with poorer vision. Otherwise, the patient might not appreciate the difference in the flip choices, and significant astigmatism can be missed.

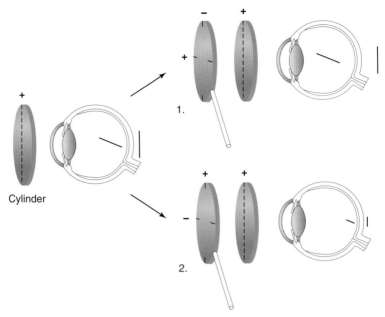

Figure 4-16 Cross-cylinder refinement of cylinder power. The cross cylinder is flipped between positions 1 and 2 as the patient is asked, "Which is better, one or two?" In position 1, the astigmatism is increased; in position 2, it is decreased. Position 2 is chosen because it yields a clearer image. In position 2, the plus axis of the cross cylinder is parallel to the plus cylinder axis, indicating that the plus cylinder should be increased in power.

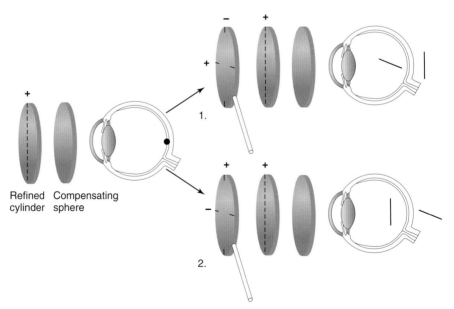

Figure 4-17 Correct endpoint for cross-cylinder refinement of cylinder power. Equal and opposite mixed astigmatism is provided by the 2 flip choices.

Summary of Cross-Cylinder Refraction

1. Adjust sphere to the most plus or least minus that gives best visual acuity.
2. Use test figures 1 or 2 lines larger than the patient's best visual acuity because introduction of the cross cylinder produces blur.
3. If cylindrical correction is not already present, look for astigmatism by testing with the cross cylinder at axes 90° and 180°. If none is found there, test at 45° and 135°.
4. Refine axis first. Position the cross-cylinder axes 45° from the principal meridians of the correcting cylinder. Determine the preferred flip choice and rotate the cylinder axis toward the corresponding axis of the cross cylinder (plus cylinder axis is rotated toward the plus cylinder axis of the cross cylinder, and minus cylinder axis is rotated toward the minus cylinder axis of the cross cylinder). Repeat until the 2 flip choices appear equal.
5. Refine cylinder power. Align the cross-cylinder axes with the principal meridians of the correcting cylinder. Determine the preferred flip choice and add or subtract cylinder power according to the preferred position of the cross cylinder. Keep track of the cylinder power added or subtracted, and compensate for the change in position of the circle of least confusion by adding half as much sphere in the opposite direction.
6. Refine sphere, cylinder axis, and cylinder power until no further change is necessary.

"Tricking" the patient is sometimes helpful in cross-cylinder refinement. Avoid confusion with previous choices by giving different numbers to subsequent choices: "Which is better, one or two, three or four?" and so forth. If the patient persists in always choosing either the first or the second number, reverse the order of presentation to check for consistency.

Guyton DL. *Subjective Refraction: Cross-Cylinder Technique.* Continuing Ophthalmic Video Education [videotape]. San Francisco: American Academy of Ophthalmology; 1987.

Michaels DD. *Visual Optics and Refraction: A Clinical Approach.* 3rd ed. St Louis: Mosby; 1985:322–325.

Wunsh SE. The cross cylinder. In: Tasman W, Jaeger EA, eds. *Duane's Clinical Ophthalmology.* Philadelphia: Lippincott-Raven; 1995.

Refining the Sphere

After cylinder power and axis have been determined using either the astigmatic dial or the cross-cylinder method, the final step in monocular refraction is to refine the sphere. The endpoint in the refraction is the strongest plus, or weakest minus, sphere that yields maximum visual acuity. Following are some of the methods that can be used.

Once the cross-cylinder technique has been used to determine the cylinder power and axis, the conoid of Sturm is presumed to be collapsed to a point on the retina. Add plus sphere, +0.25 at a time, until the patient reports a decrease in vision. If no plus sphere is accepted, add minus sphere, −0.25 D at a time, until the patient reaches maximum acuity.

Because the patient can, by accommodating, compensate for excess minus sphere, it must be emphasized that the endpoint is the *least* minus that permits maximum acuity. Accommodation creates, in effect, a reverse Galilean telescope, with the eye generating more plus as minus is added by lenses in front of the eye. Thus, the test letters will appear to the patient to become smaller and/or move farther away.

The patient should be told what to look for. Before subtracting each 0.25 D increment, tell the patient that the letters on the line being tested may appear smaller, darker, or farther away, and ask the patient to report any such change.

If the astigmatic dial has been used and the astigmatism is neutralized (all of the lines on the astigmatic dial are equally clear or equally blurred), the eye should still be fogged; additional plus will only increase the blur. Therefore, use minus spheres to reduce the sphere power until maximum acuity is reached. Again, be careful not to overminus the patient (wherein the patient describes letters as being "smaller," "darker," and "farther away").

The sphere endpoint can be verified by the *duochrome* (*red-green* or *bichrome*) test, in which a split red-green filter divides the acuity chart vertically into red and green backgrounds. Because the eye is not corrected for chromatic aberration, the shorter wavelengths (green) will be focused in front of the longer red wavelengths of the spectrum. Because the eye generally focuses at some midpoint in the color spectrum, the letters on the red and green halves of the chart will appear equally clear when read through the correct sphere. With the commercial filters used in the duochrome test, the chromatic interval is about 0.50 D between the red and the green. When the image is clearly focused in white light, the eye will, therefore, be 0.25 D myopic for the green symbols and 0.25 D hyperopic for the red symbols.

With the duochrome test, each eye is tested separately. The duochrome test should always be started with the eye slightly fogged (by 0.5 D to relax accommodation). In this situation, the letters on the red side should appear clearer, and minus sphere should be added until the 2 halves are equal. If the patient responds that the symbols on the green side are sharper, the patient is overminused and more plus power must be added to bring the chromatic interval forward.

The patient's first response should be that the red side is clearer if the patient is properly fogged. Add minus sphere in 0.25 D increments until the symbols are equally clear on each side. Some clinicians use the RAM-GAP mnemonic—red add minus—green add plus—to help them with the duochrome test.

Because this test is based on chromatic aberration, not on color discrimination, it can be used even with color-blind patients. The eye with overactive accommodation may still require too much minus sphere in order to balance the red and green. A cycloplegic refraction may be necessary. The duochrome test is not useful for patients with visual acuities worse than 6/9 (20/30), for the 0.50 D difference between the 2 sides is too subtle for them to distinguish.

Binocular Balance

As the final step in subjective refraction, it is important to be sure that accommodation has been relaxed equally in the 2 eyes. Several methods of binocular balance are commonly used. Most require correctable visual acuity to be essentially equal in the 2 eyes.

Fogging

When the endpoint refraction is fogged using a +2.00 sphere before each eye, the visual acuity should be reduced to 6/60–6/30 (20/200–20/100). Place a −0.25 D sphere first before one eye and then the other, and rapidly alternate cover; the patient should then be able to identify the eye with the −0.25 D sphere before it as having the clearer image at the 6/30 (20/100) or 6/20 (20/70) level. If the eyes are not in balance, sphere should be added or subtracted in 0.25 steps until balance is achieved.

In addition to testing for binocular balance, the fogging method also provides information regarding appropriate sphere power. If either eye is overminused or underplussed, the patient will read farther down the chart, as far as 6/20 (20/70), 6/15 (20/50), or even 6/12 (20/40) with the +2.00 fogging spheres in place. In that case, the refraction endpoints should be reconsidered.

Prism dissociation

The most sensitive test of binocular balance is performed by fogging the refractive endpoints with +1.00 spheres and then placing vertical prisms of 4 or 5 prism diopters before 1 eye. A single line, usually 6/12 (20/40), is projected on the chart. The patient is then able to view the same line with both eyes simultaneously. Differences between the fogged image in the 2 eyes of 0.25 D sphere or even less can be identified readily. In practice, +0.25 D sphere is placed before 1 eye and then before the other. In each instance, if the eyes are balanced, the patient will report that the image corresponding to the eye with the additional +0.25 D sphere is more blurred. After a balance is established between the 2 eyes, remove the prism and reduce the fog binocularly until maximum visual acuity is obtained with the highest plus or lowest minus spheres.

Cycloplegia

Binocular balance is determined simply by the monocular findings when cycloplegia has been used, if adequate relaxation of accommodation is verified.

Cycloplegic and Noncycloplegic (Manifest) Refraction

Ideally, refractive error is measured with accommodation relaxed. The amount of habitual accommodative tone varies from person to person, and even within individuals it varies at different times and ages. Because the examiner might not be able to estimate this variable, cycloplegic agents are sometimes used. The indication and appropriate dosage for a specific cycloplegic agent depend on the patient's age, accommodative amplitude, and refractive error.

A practical approach to satisfactory refraction is to perform a careful manifest refraction, relaxing accommodation by fogging or other nonpharmacologic means. If results are inconsistent or variable, a cycloplegic refraction should be performed. If the 2 refractions are similar, the prescription can be based on the initial refraction findings. If they show a disparity, a postcycloplegic evaluation may be necessary.

All cycloplegic agents produce mydriasis as well as cycloplegia; however, not all mydriatic agents produce cycloplegia. For example, the sympathomimetic agents such as phenylephrine produce mydriasis without a significant effect on accommodation. Cycloplegic agents can be classified on the basis of their intensity and duration of action (Table 4-1). In each instance, cycloplegia lasts somewhat longer than mydriasis.

Side effects may occur with any of these agents, occasionally because of an idiosyncratic reaction but more commonly because of rapid systemic absorption through the nasolacrimal mucosa. Atropine can produce dryness, flushing, high fever, and delirium. The most frequent complications of scopolamine are hallucinations and ataxia.

Overrefraction

Phoropters may be used to refract highly ametropic patients, but prescribing directly from the findings can be unreliable. The vertex distance of the refraction is often unknown and variable during the refraction, the pantoscopic tilt of the final glasses is not taken into account, and the lenses in the phoropter do not always add up to exactly the readings on the dials ("additivity error"). For a $+12.00$ D sphere spectacle lens, each millimeter change of vertex distance creates about 0.12 D sphere error, and 10° of pantoscopic tilt introduces about $+0.37$ D of cylinder error at an axis of 180° and increases the sphere by 0.12 D. Even when vertex distance and pantoscopic tilt are controlled by the use of trial frames for the refraction, the trial lenses may have different aberrations from the final spectacle lens; also, there is no guarantee that the optician will heed the vertex distance notation on the prescription.

These problems are avoided if patients with a high refractive error undergo refraction over their current glasses. If the new lenses are prescribed with the same base curve as the old ones and are fitted in the same frames, many potential difficulties can be circumvented, including vertex distance error and pantoscopic tilt error, as well as problems caused by marginal astigmatism or chromatic aberration.

Overrefraction may be performed with loose lenses, with trial lens clips (such as Halberg trial clips) on the glasses, with a standard phoropter in front of the patient's glasses, or with some automated refracting instruments.

Table 4-1 Commonly Used Cycloplegic Agents

Drug	Concentration (%)	Dosage	Onset of Maximum Cycloplegia	Total Duration of Cycloplegia
Atropine sulfate[1]	0.5, 1.0, 2.0	2–3 times/day for 3 days	6–24 hr	10–15 days
Scopolamine HBr[2]	0.25	2 drops separated by 5 min	30–60 min	3–4 days
Homatropine HBr[3]	2.0, 5.0		1 hr	1–2 days
Cyclopentolate[3]	0.5, 1.0, 2.0		20–45 min	12–24 hr
Tropicamide	0.5, 1.0, 2.0		20–30 min	4–10 hr

[1] Usually reserved for young children. May be prescribed in ointment or drop form. Side effects, such as flushing and fever, may be avoided by applying pressure over the puncta and canaliculi for 1–2 minutes after instilling atropine drops. The same precautions should be used for all cycloplegic-mydriatic drops.
[2] Rarely used for refraction but clinically useful in case of atropine allergy.
[3] The concentration needed will vary with the clinical problem. Higher concentrations of the agents are associated with an increased incidence of undesired side effects.

If the patient is wearing spherical lenses, the new prescription is easy to calculate by combining the old spherical correction with the spherocylindrical overrefraction. If the old lenses are spherocylindrical and the cylinder axis of the new refraction is not at 0° or 90° to the old correction, other methods are used to determine the resultant refraction. Such lens combinations were often determined with a lensmeter used to read the resultant lens power through the combinations of the old glasses and the overrefraction correction. This procedure is awkward and prone to error, however, because the lenses may rotate with respect to each other or transfer to the lensmeter. Manual calculation is possible using the formulas discussed in Chapter 2, Geometrical Optics (under "Combining cylinders at oblique axes").

Programmable calculators can be used to perform the trigonometric combination of cylinders at oblique axes, but these may not be readily available in the clinic. The old glasses must still be measured accurately, of course, but the difficult calculations required are accomplished instantly by these calculators.

Overrefraction has other uses. For example, a patient wearing a soft toric contact lens may undergo overrefraction for the purpose of ordering new lenses. Overrefraction can also be used in the retinoscopic examination of children. With the child fixing at distance and fogged by the examiner's working distance, the examiner can quickly judge whether enough refractive change has occurred to warrant a more careful refraction and prescription of new lenses.

Spectacle Correction of Ametropias

An ametropia is a refractive error; it is the absence of emmetropia. The most common method of correcting refractive error is by prescribing spectacle lenses.

Spherical Correcting Lenses and the Far Point Concept

The far point plane of the nonaccommodated eye is conjugate with the retina. For any simple lens, distant objects (those at optical infinity) come into sharp focus at the secondary focal point (f_2) of the lens. To compensate for the refractive error of an ametropic eye, a correcting lens must place the image it forms (or its f_2) at the eye's far point. The image at the far point plane becomes the object that is focused onto the retina. For example, in a myopic eye, the far point lies somewhere in front of the eye, between the eye and optical infinity. In this case, the correct *diverging* lens forms a virtual image of distant objects at its secondary focal point, coincident with the far point of the eye (Fig 4-18).

The same principle holds for the correction of hyperopia. However, because the far point plane of a hyperopic eye is behind the retina, a *converging* lens must be chosen in the appropriate power to focus parallel rays of light to the far point plane.

Vertex Distance

It is apparent that, for any spherical correcting lens, the distance from the lens to its focal point is constant. Changing the position of the correcting lens relative to the cornea will also change the relationship between the secondary focal point of the correcting lens and the far point plane of the eye. With high-power lenses, as used in the spectacle correction of aphakia or high myopia, a small change in the placement of the lens produces considerable blurring of vision unless the lens power is changed to compensate for the altered position.

The distance from the back surface of the lens to the cornea is called the lens *vertex distance*. With refractive errors greater than ±5 D, the vertex distance must be accounted for in prescribing the power of the spectacle lens. The opposite is true for minus lenses. Moving a plus correcting lens closer to the eye reduces its effective plus power, whereas moving it farther from the eye increases its effective power.

For example, in Figure 4-19, the +10 D lens placed 10 mm from the cornea (assumed to be at the cornea) provides sharp retinal imagery. Because, by definition, the secondary focal plane of the correcting lens is identical to the far point plane of the eye and because this lens is placed 1 cm in front of the eye, the far point plane of the eye must be 9 cm behind the cornea. If the correcting lens is moved to a new position 20 mm in front of the eye and the far point plane of the eye is 9 cm, the secondary focal plane of the new lens must be 11 cm, requiring a +9.1 D lens for correction. This example demonstrates the significance of vertex distance in spectacle correction of large refractive errors. Thus, the prescription must indicate not only the lens power but also

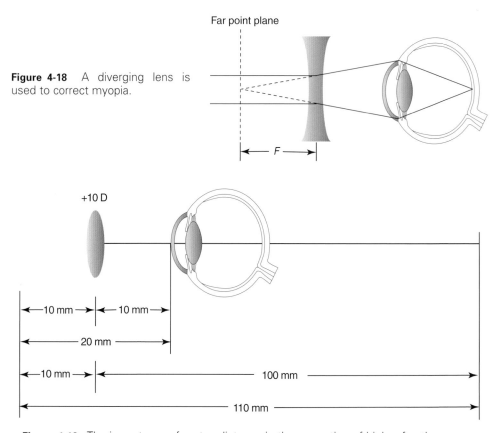

Figure 4-18 A diverging lens is used to correct myopia.

Figure 4-19 The importance of vertex distance in the correction of high refractive errors.

the vertex distance at which the refraction was performed. The optician must, in turn, recalculate the lens power as necessary for the actual vertex distance of the chosen spectacle–frame combination.

Cylindrical Correcting Lenses and the Far Point Concept

The correction of astigmatism with spectacle lenses follows the same basic principles of far point conjugacy as hyperopia and myopia. However, in astigmatism, the required lens power must be determined separately for each of the 2 principal meridians. When an appropriate spherocylindrical combination is used to correct an astigmatic refractive error, the conoid of Sturm is collapsed to a point focus on the retina. If, instead of the correct spherocylindrical combination, an equivalent sphere were used, the result would be a somewhat blurred retinal image representing the circle of least confusion.

Cylinders in spectacle lenses produce both monocular and binocular distortion. The primary cause is *meridional aniseikonia*—that is, unequal magnification of retinal images from the various meridians. Although aniseikonia may be corrected by iseikonic spectacles, such corrections may be complicated and expensive; and most practitioners prefer to prescribe cylinders according to their "clinical judgment." Clinical experience also suggests that adult patients vary in their ability to tolerate distortion; younger children always adapt to their cylindrical corrections. The following guidelines may prove helpful in prescribing astigmatic spectacle corrections.

- For *children,* prescribe the full astigmatic correction at the correct axis.
- For *adults,* try the full correction initially. Give the patient a "walking-around" trial with trial frames before prescribing, if appropriate. Inform the patient about the need for adaptation.
- To reduce distortion, use minus cylinder lenses (most lenses dispensed today are minus cylinder) and minimize vertex distance.
- Spatial distortion from astigmatic spectacles is a binocular phenomenon. Occlude one eye to verify that this is the cause of the patient's difficulty.
- If necessary, reduce distortion by rotating the axis of the cylinder axis toward 180° or 90° (or toward the old axis) and/or reduce the cylinder power. Adjust the sphere to maintain spherical equivalent but rely on a final subjective check to obtain the most satisfactory visual result.
- If distortion cannot be reduced sufficiently, consider contact lenses or iseikonic corrections.

For a more detailed discussion of the problem of, and solutions for, spectacle correction of astigmatism, see Appendix: Common Guidelines for Prescribing Cylinders.

Prescribing for Children

The correction of ametropia in children presents several special and challenging problems. In adults, the correction of refractive errors has one measurable endpoint: the best-corrected visual acuity. Prescribing visual correction for children often has 2 goals: providing a focused retinal image and achieving the optimal balance between accommodation and convergence.

In some patients, *subjective refraction* may be impossible or inappropriate, often because of the child's inability to cooperate with subjective refraction techniques. In addition, the optimal refraction in an infant or a small child (particularly with esotropia) requires the *paralysis of accommodation* with complete cycloplegia. (In such cases, objective techniques such as retinoscopy are the best way to determine the refractive correction.) Moreover, the presence of *strabismus* may modify normal prescribing guidelines.

Myopia

Childhood myopia falls into 2 groups: *congenital* (usually high) myopia and *developmental* myopia, usually manifesting itself between ages 7 and 10 years. The latter type of myopia is less severe and easier to manage, as the patients are older and refraction is less difficult. However, both forms of myopia are progressive; frequent refractions (every 6–12 months) and periodic prescription changes are necessary. The following are general guidelines for correction of significant childhood myopia.

- Cycloplegic refractions are mandatory. In infants, esotropic children, and children with very high myopia (>10 D), atropine refraction may be necessary if tropicamide (Mydriacyl) or cyclopentolate fails to paralyze accommodation in the office.
- In general, the full refractive error, including cylinder, should be corrected. Young children tolerate cylinder well.
- Some ophthalmologists undercorrect myopia, and others may even use bifocals with or without atropine, on the theory that prolonged accommodation hastens or increases the development of myopia. Studies are under way to settle this long-standing controversy.
- Intentional undercorrection of a child with myopic esotropia to decrease the angle of deviation is rarely tolerated.
- Intentional overcorrection of a myopic error (or undercorrection of a hyperopic error) can be of some value in controlling an intermittent exodeviation.
- Parents should be educated about the natural progression of myopia and the need for frequent refractions and possible prescription changes.
- Contact lenses may be desirable in older children to avoid the problem of image minification found with high-minus lenses.

Hyperopia

The appropriate correction of childhood hyperopia is more complex than that of myopia. First, children who are significantly hyperopic (>5 D) are more visually impaired than their myopic counterparts, who can at least see clearly at near. Second, childhood hyperopia is more frequently associated with strabismus and abnormalities of the accommodative convergence/accommodation (AC/A) ratio. The following are general guidelines for correcting childhood hyperopia:

- Unless there is esodeviation or evidence of reduced vision, it is not necessary to correct low hyperopia. As with myopia, significant astigmatic errors should be fully corrected.

- When hyperopia and esotropia coexist, initial management includes full correction of the cycloplegic refractive error. Later, reductions in the amount of correction may be appropriate, based on the amount of esotropia and level of stereopsis at near and at distance with the full cycloplegic correction in place.
- In a school-age child, the full refractive correction may cause blurring of distance vision because of the inability to relax accommodation fully. The amount of correction may have to be reduced for the child to accept the glasses. A short course of cycloplegia may help a child to accept the hyperopic correction.

Anisometropia

An anisometropic child or infant should be given the full cycloplegic refractive difference between the 2 eyes, regardless of age, presence or amount of strabismus, or degree of anisometropia.

Anisometropic amblyopia is frequently present and may require occlusion therapy. Amblyopia is more common in conjunction with anisohyperopia than with either anisomyopia or antimetropia.

Clinical Accommodative Problems

See also Chapter 3, Optics of the Human Eye, for a discussion of the terminology and mechanisms of accommodation.

Presbyopia

Presbyopia is the gradual loss of accommodative response resulting from loss of elasticity of the lens. Accommodative amplitude diminishes with age. It becomes a clinical problem when the remaining accommodative amplitude is insufficient for the patient to read and carry out near-vision tasks. Fortunately, appropriate convex lenses can compensate for the waning of accommodative power.

Symptoms of presbyopia usually begin after age 40 years. The age of onset depends on preexisting refractive error, depth of focus (pupil size), the patient's visual tasks, and other variables. Table 4-2 presents a simplified overview of age norms.

Accommodative Insufficiency

Accommodative insufficiency is the *premature* loss of accommodative amplitude. This problem may manifest itself by blurring of near visual objects (as in presbyopia) or by the inability to sustain accommodative effort. The onset may be heralded by the development of asthenopic symptoms, with the ultimate development of blurred near vision. Such "premature presbyopia" may signify concurrent or past debilitating illness, or it may be induced by medications such as the parasympatholytics used in treating some gastrointestinal disorders or tranquilizing drugs. In both cases, the condition may be reversible; however, permanent accommodative insufficiency may be associated with neurogenic disorders such as encephalitis or closed head trauma. In some cases, the etiology may never be determined. These patients require reading add for near vision.

Table 4-2 Average Accommodative Amplitudes for Different Ages

Age	Average Accommodative Amplitude*
8	14.0 (±2 D)
12	13.0 (±2 D)
16	12.0 (±2 D)
20	11.0 (±2 D)
24	10.0 (±2 D)
28	9.0 (±2 D)
32	8.0 (±2 D)
36	7.0 (±2 D)
40	6.0 (±2 D)
44	4.5 (±1.5 D)
48	3.0 (±1.5 D)
52	2.5 (±1.5 D)
56	2.0 (±1.0 D)
60	1.5 (±1.0 D)
64	1.0 (±0.5 D)
68	0.5 (±0.5 D)

* Under age 40, accommodation decreases by 1 D for each 4 years. Over age 40, accommodation decreases more rapidly. From age 48 on, 0.5 D is lost every 4 years. Thus, one can recall the entire table by remembering the amplitudes at age 40 and age 48.

Accommodative Excess

Ciliary muscle spasm, often incorrectly termed *spasm of accommodation,* causes accommodative excess. A ciliary spasm has characteristic symptoms: headache, brow ache, variable blurring of distance vision, and an abnormally close near point. Ciliary spasm may occur as a manifestation of local disease such as iridocyclitis; it may be caused by medications such as the anticholinesterases used in the treatment of glaucoma; or it may be associated with uncorrected refractive errors, usually hyperopia but also astigmatism. In some patients, ciliary spasm exacerbates preexisting myopia. It also occurs after prolonged and intense periods of near work. *Spasm of the near reflex* is a characteristic clinical syndrome often seen in tense or anxious persons presenting with (1) excess accommodation, (2) excess convergence, and (3) miosis.

Accommodative Convergence/Accommodation Ratio

Normally, accommodative effort is accompanied by a corresponding convergence effort (expressed in terms of meter angles). Thus, 1 D of accommodation would be accompanied by a 1-m angle of convergence. For practical purposes, the AC/A ratio is ordinarily expressed in terms of prism diopters of deviation per diopter of accommodation. Using this type of expression, the normal AC/A ratio is 3:1–5:1.

The AC/A ratio is relatively constant for each person, but fortunately there can be some variability among individuals. For example, a patient with an uncorrected 1 D of hyperopia may accommodate 1 D for clear distance vision without exercising a convergence effort. Conversely, a patient with uncorrected myopia must converge without accommodative effort in order to see clearly at the far point of the eye.

The AC/A ratio can be measured by varying the stimulus to accommodation in several ways.

Heterophoria method (moving the fixation target)

The heterophoria is measured at 6 m and again at 0.33 m.

$$AC/A = PD + \frac{\Delta n - \Delta d}{D}$$

where

PD = interpupillary distance in centimeters
Δn = near deviation in prism diopters
Δd = distance deviation in prism diopters
D = diopters of accommodation

Sign convention:
  Esodeviations +
  Exodeviations −

Gradient method

The AC/A ratio can be measured in 1 of 2 ways using the gradient method. The first way is by *stimulating accommodation*. Measure the heterophoria with the target distance fixed at 6 m. Then remeasure the induced phoria after interposing a − 1 D sphere in front of both eyes. The AC/A ratio is the difference between the 2 measurements.

The second way is by *relaxing accommodation*. With the target distance fixed at 0.33 m, measure the phoria before and after interposing + 3 D spheres. The phoria difference divided by 3 is the AC/A ratio.

An abnormal AC/A ratio can place stress on the patient's fusional mechanisms at one distance or another, leading to asthenopia or manifest strabismus. Abnormal AC/A ratios should be accounted for when prescribing corrective lenses.

Parks MM. Vergences. In: Tasman W, Jaeger EA, eds. *Duane's Clinical Ophthalmology.* Philadelphia: Lippincott-Raven; 1995.

Effect of Spectacle and Contact Lens Correction on Accommodation and Convergence

Both accommodation and convergence requirements differ between contact lenses and spectacle lenses. The effects become more noticeable as the power of the correction increases.

Let us consider accommodative requirements first. Remember that because of vertex distance considerations, particularly with high-power corrections, the dioptric power of the distance correction in the spectacle plane is different from that at the contact lens plane: For a near object held at a constant distance, the amount that an eye needs to accommodate depends on the location of the refractive correction relative to the cornea. Patients with myopia must accommodate more for a given near object when wearing contact lenses than when wearing glasses. For example, those with myopia in their early

40s who switch from single-vision glasses to contact lenses may suddenly experience presbyopic symptoms. The reverse is true with patients with hyperopia; the spectacle correction requires more accommodation for a given near object than the contact lens correction. Patients with spectacle-corrected high myopia, when presbyopic, need only weak bifocal adds or none at all. For example, a highly myopic patient wearing -20 D glasses needs to accommodate only about 1 D to see an object at 33 cm.

Now let us consider convergence requirements and refractive correction. Because contact lenses move with the eyes and glasses do not, different amounts of convergence are required for viewing near objects. Spectacle correction gives a myopic patient a base-in prism effect when converging and thus reduces the person's requirement for convergence. (Fortunately, this reduction parallels the lessened requirement for accommodation.) In contrast, the patient with spectacle-corrected hyperopia encounters a base-out prism effect that increases the requirement for convergence. These effects may be the source of a patient's symptoms on switching between glasses and contact lenses. (See also Chapter 5, Contact Lenses.)

Prescribing Multifocal Lenses

A multifocal lens has 2 or more refractive elements. The power of each segment is prescribed separately.

Determining the Power of a Bifocal Add

The information necessary to prescribe bifocals includes: (1) an accurate baseline refraction, (2) the accommodative amplitude, and (3) the patient's social or occupational activities that require near-vision correction (eg, reading, sewing, or computer use).

Measuring accommodative amplitude

Any of the following tests can provide useful information for determining the accommodative amplitude: (1) the near point of accommodation with accurate refractive correction in place, (2) the accommodative rule (for example, with a Prince rule), or (3) plus and minus spheres at near distance until the fixation target blurs. *Binocular amplitude of accommodation* is normally greater than the measurement for either eye alone by 0.5–1.0 D.

Near point of accommodation The simplest practical method of measuring the near point of accommodation is to have the patient fixate on a near target (most commonly, small print such as 5-point or Jaeger 2 type print, although a single sharp vertical line or two slightly separated vertical lines may also be used) and move the test card toward the eye until the print blurs. If the eye is emmetropic (or rendered emmetropic by proper refractive correction), the far point of the eye will be at infinity, and the near point can be converted into diopters of amplitude.

This method is subject to certain errors, one of which is the apparent increased amplitude resulting from angular magnification of the letters as they approach the eye. In addition, if the eye is ametropic and not corrected for distance, the near point of accommodation cannot be converted into diopters of amplitude. In the following examples, each eye has 3 D of amplitude.

- An person with emmetropia will have a near point of 33 cm and a far point at optical infinity.
- A patient with an uncorrected 3 D of myopia will have a near point at 16.7 cm, because at the far point of 33 cm no accommodation is needed.
- A patient with an uncorrected 3 D of hyperopia will have a near point at infinity, because all of the available accommodation is needed to overcome the hyperopia.

Accommodative rule Amplitude of accommodation can be measured with a device such as a Prince rule, which combines a reading card with a ruler calibrated in centimeters and diopters. Placing a $+3$ D lens before the emmetropic (or accurately corrected ametropic) eye places the far point of accommodation at 33 cm, and the near point will also be brought a corresponding 3 D closer. The amplitude is then determined by subtracting the far point (in diopters) from the near point (in diopters).

Method of spheres Amplitude of accommodation may also be measured by having the patient fixate on a reading target at 40 cm. Accommodation is stimulated by placing successively stronger minus spheres before the eye until the print blurs; accommodation is then relaxed by using successively stronger plus lenses until blurring begins. The difference between the 2 lenses is a measure of accommodative amplitude. For example, if the patient accepted -3 D to blur (stimulus to accommodation) and $+2.5$ D to blur (relaxation of accommodation), the amplitude would be 5.5 D.

Range of accommodation

In addition to measuring the amplitude of accommodation, determining the range of accommodation is valuable in ensuring that a prescribed bifocal add meets the patient's visual needs. The range of accommodation measures the useful range of clear vision when a given lens is employed. For this purpose, a measuring tape, meter stick, or accommodation rule may be used.

Selecting an add

Determine the amount of accommodation required for the patient's near-vision tasks. For example, reading at 40 cm would require 2.5 D of accommodation. From the patient's measured accommodative amplitude, allow one half to be held in reserve. For instance, if the patient has 2.0 D of accommodation, 1.0 may be comfortably contributed by the patient. (Some patients may use more than one half of their available accommodation with comfort.) Subtract the patient's available accommodation (1.0 D) from the total amount of accommodation required (2.5 D); the difference (1.5 D) is the approximate additional plus lens power (add) needed.

  Place this add in front of the distance refractive correction and measure the accommodative *range* (near point to far point of accommodation in centimeters). Does this range adequately meet the requirements of the patient's near-vision activities? If the accommodative range is too close, reduce the add in steps of 0.25 D until the range is appropriate for the patient's requirement.

Because binocular accommodative amplitude is usually 0.50–1.0 D greater than the monocular measurement, using the binocular measurement generally guards against prescribing too high an add.

Types of Bifocal Lenses

Most bifocals dispensed today are 1-piece bifocals, made by generating the different refracting surfaces on a single lens blank (Fig 4-20). *Round segment* 1-piece bifocals have their segment on the concave surface. One-piece molded *plastic bifocals* are available in various shapes, including (1) round top with button on convex surface, (2) flat top with button on convex surface, and (3) Franklin style with split bifocal.

With *fused bifocals,* the increased refracting power of the bifocal segment is produced by fusing a button of glass that has a higher refractive index than the basic crown glass lens into a countersink in the crown glass lens blank. With all such bifocals, the add segment is fused into the convex surface of the lens; astigmatic corrections, when necessary, are ground on the concave surface.

Trifocal Lenses

A bifocal lens may not fully satisfy all the visual needs of an older patient with limited accommodation. Even when near and distant ranges are corrected appropriately, vision will not be clear in the intermediate range, approximately at arm's length. This problem can be solved with trifocal spectacles, which incorporate a third segment of intermediate strength (typically one half the power of the reading add) between the distance correction and reading segment. The intermediate segment allows the patient to focus on objects beyond the reading distance but closer than 1 m. (See Clinical Example 4-1.)

Progressive Addition Lenses

Both bifocals and trifocals have an abrupt change in power as the line of sight passes across the boundary between one portion of the lens and the next; image jump and diplopia can occur at the segment lines. Progressive addition lenses (PALs) avoid these difficulties by supplying power gradually as the line of sight is depressed toward the reading level (Fig 4-21). Unlike bifocals and trifocals, PALs offer clear vision at all focal distances (Fig 4-22). Other advantages of PALs include lack of intermediate blur and absence of any visible segment lines.

The progressive addition lens form has 4 optical zones on the convex surface: a spherical distance zone, a reading zone, a transition zone (or "corridor"), and zones of peripheral distortion. The progressive change in lens power is generated on the convex surface of the lens by progressive aspheric changes in curvature from the top to the bottom of the lens. The concave surface is reserved for the sphere and cylinder of the patient's distance lens prescription.

However, there are certain drawbacks to PALs. Most notably, some degree of peripheral distortion is inherent in the design of all PALs. This peripheral aberration is caused by astigmatism resulting from the changing aspheric curves, most pronounced in the lower inner and outer quadrants of the lens. These distortions produce a "swimming" sensation with head movement.

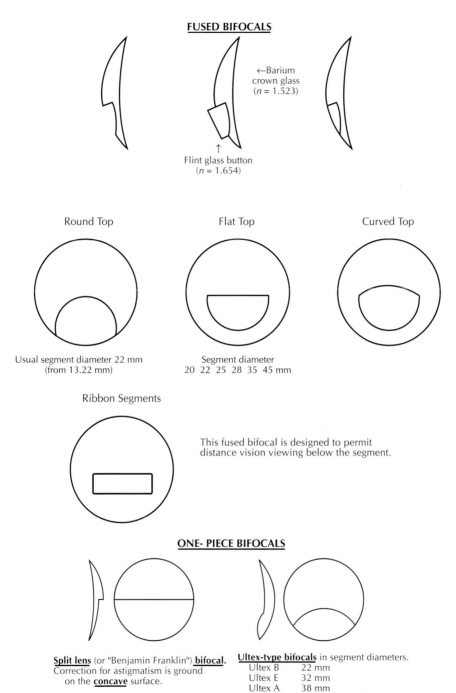

FUSED BIFOCALS

←Barium
crown glass
(n = 1.523)

↑
Flint glass button
(n = 1.654)

Round Top

Usual segment diameter 22 mm
(from 13.22 mm)

Flat Top

Segment diameter
20 22 25 28 35 45 mm

Curved Top

Ribbon Segments

This fused bifocal is designed to permit
distance vision viewing below the segment.

ONE- PIECE BIFOCALS

Split lens (or "Benjamin Franklin") **bifocal**.
Correction for astigmatism is ground
on the **concave** surface.

Ultex-type bifocals in segment diameters.
Ultex B   22 mm
Ultex E   32 mm
Ultex A   38 mm
Ultex AL   38 mm (up to 33 mm high)

Astigmatism correction is ground on
the **convex** surface.

Figure 4-20 Bifocal lens styles.

CLINICAL EXAMPLE 4-1

Consider a patient with 1 D of available accommodation. He wears a bifocal with a +2.00 add. His accommodative range for each part of the spectacle lens is:

> *Distance segment:* Infinity to 100 cm
> *Bifocal segment:* 50–33 cm

He now has a blurred zone between 50 and 100 cm. An intermediate segment, in this case +1.00 D (half the power of the reading segment), would provide sharp vision from 50 cm (using all of his available accommodation plus the +1.00 D add) to 100 cm (using the add only). This trifocal combination therefore provides the following ranges:

> *Distance segment:* Infinity to 100 cm
> *Intermediate segment:* 100–50 cm
> *Near segment:* 50–33 cm

Bifocal

A

Trifocal

B

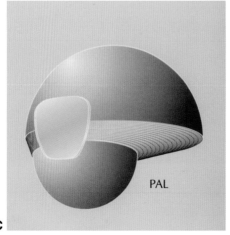

PAL

C

Figure 4-21 Bifocal, trifocal, and progressive addition lens designs compared. **A,** In a bifocal lens, the distance vision sphere is above the near vision sphere; they are linked by a single "step" that is seen as a single line. **B,** In a trifocal lens, an intermediate vision sphere is added between the distance and near vision spheres, producing 2 visible lines. **C,** In a PAL, an uninterrupted series of curves links distance, intermediate, and near vision parts of the lens with no visible separations. *(From Wisnicki HJ. Bifocals, trifocals, and progressive-addition lenses.* Focal Points: Clinical Modules for Ophthalmologists. *San Francisco: American Academy of Ophthalmology; 1999, module 6.)*

The vertical meridian joining the distance and reading optical centers is free of surface astigmatism and affords maximum visual acuity. To either side of this distortion-free vertical meridian, induced astigmatism and a concomitant degradation of acuity occur. If the lens is designed so that the peripheral distortions are spread out over a relatively wide portion of the lens, there is a concomitant decrease in the distortion-free principal zones. This is the basis of soft-design PALs (Fig 4-23). Conversely, a wider distortion-free zone for distance and reading means a more intense deformity laterally. This is the basis of hard-design PALs. If the transition corridor is lengthened, the distortions are less pronounced, but problems arise because of the greater vertical separation between the distance optical center and the reading zone. Therefore, each PAL design represents a series of compromises. Some manufacturers prefer less distortion at the expense of less useful aberration-free distance and near acuity; others opt for maximum acuity over a wider usable area, with smaller but more pronounced lateral distortion zones.

PALs are readily available from −8.00 to +7.50 D spheres and up to 4.00 D cylinders, with adds from +1.50 to +3.50 D. Some vendors also make custom lenses with parameters outside these limits. Prism can be incorporated into PALs.

The best candidates for PALs are patients with early presbyopia who have not previously worn bifocals, patients who do not require wide near-vision fields, and highly motivated patients. The patient who changes from conventional multifocals to PALs should be advised that distortion will be present and that adaptation will be necessary. The key to successful prescribing is careful patient selection.

Prentice's Rule and Bifocal Design

There are special considerations when prescribing lenses for patients with significant anisometropias.

Prismatic effects of lenses

All lenses act as prisms when one looks through the lens at any point other than the optical center. The amount of the induced prismatic effect depends on the power of the lens and the distance from the optical center. Specifically, the amount of prismatic effect (measured in prism diopters) is equal to the distance (in centimeters) from the optical center multiplied by the lens power (in diopters). This is known as *Prentice's rule.*

$$\Delta = hD$$

where

Δ = prism diopters
h = distance from optical center in cm
D = diopters

Image displacement

When reading at near through a point below the optical center, a patient may induce an anisophoria if there is anisometropia. With a bifocal segment, the gaze is usually directed

Figure 4-22 Fields of clear vision with bifocals, trifocals, and progressive addition lenses for a patient with 1.5 D of accommodative ability. **A,** Bifocal with a 2.00 D add. **B,** Trifocal with a 1.00 D intermediate add and 2.00 D reading add. **C,** PAL with a 2.00 add. *(From Wisnicki HJ. Bifocals, trifocals, and progressive-addition lenses.* Focal Points: Clinical Modules for Ophthalmologists. *San Francisco: American Academy of Ophthalmology; 1999, module 6.)*

Figure 4-23 Comparison of hard-design and soft-design PALs. These illustrations compare the power progression and peripheral aberration of these 2 PAL designs. *(From Wisnicki HJ. Bifocals, trifocals, and progressive-addition lenses.* Focal Points: Clinical Modules for Ophthalmologists. *San Francisco: American Academy of Ophthalmology; 1999, module 6.)*

8–10 mm below and 1.5–3.0 mm nasal to the distance optical center of the distance lens (in the following examples, we assume the usual 8 mm down and 2 mm nasal). As long as the bifocal segments are of the same power and type, the prismatic displacement is determined by the power of the distance lens alone.

If the lens powers are the same for the 2 eyes, the displacement will be the same (Figs 4-24 and 4-25). However, if the patient is anisometropic, a phoria will be induced by the unequal prism displacement of the 2 lenses (Figs 4-26 and 4-27). The amount of *vertical* phoria is determined by subtracting the smaller prismatic displacement from the larger if the lenses are both myopic or both hyperopic (see Fig 4-26) or by adding the two if the patient is antimetropic—that is, hyperopic in 1 eye and myopic in the other (see Fig 4-27).

To determine the induced *horizontal* phoria, the induced prisms for the 2 eyes are added together if they are in the same direction (see Fig 4-26) and subtracted if they are in opposite directions (see Fig 4-27).

Image displacement is minimized when round-top segment bifocals are used with plus lenses and flat-top segment bifocals are used with minus lenses (Fig 4-28).

Image jump

The usual position of the top of a bifocal segment is 5 mm below the optical center of the distance lens. As the eyes are directed downward through a lens, the prismatic displacement of the image increases (downward in plus lenses, upward in minus lenses).

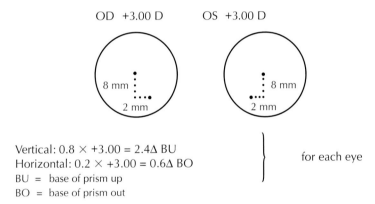

OD +3.00 D   OS +3.00 D

8 mm   8 mm

2 mm   2 mm

Vertical: 0.8 × +3.00 = 2.4Δ BU
Horizontal: 0.2 × +3.00 = 0.6Δ BO
BU = base of prism up
BO = base of prism out

for each eye

Figure 4-24 Prismatic effect of bifocals in isometropic hyperopia.

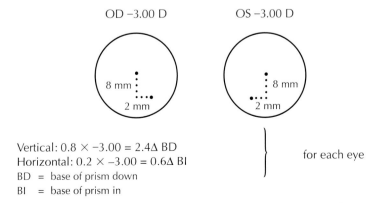

OD −3.00 D   OS −3.00 D

8 mm   8 mm

2 mm   2 mm

Vertical: 0.8 × −3.00 = 2.4Δ BD
Horizontal: 0.2 × −3.00 = 0.6Δ BI
BD = base of prism down
BI   = base of prism in

for each eye

Figure 4-25 Prismatic effect of bifocals in isometropic myopia.

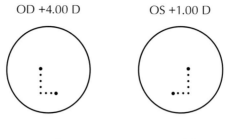

OD +4.00 D   OS +1.00 D

Vertical: OD 0.8 × 4 = 3.2Δ BU   OS 0.8 × 1 = 0.8Δ BU
Horizontal: OD 0.2 × 4 = 0.8Δ BO   OS 0.2 × 1 = 0.2Δ BO
Induced phoria: OD 3.2Δ − 0.8Δ = 2.4Δ BU
                OD 0.8Δ BO + 0.2Δ BO = 1.0Δ BO

Figure 4-26 Prismatic effect of bifocals in anisometropic hyperopia.

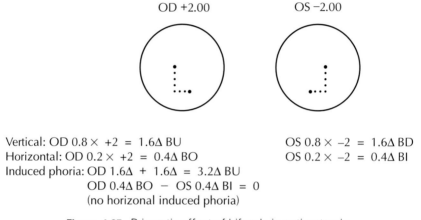

OD +2.00   OS −2.00

Vertical: OD 0.8 × +2 = 1.6Δ BU   OS 0.8 × −2 = 1.6Δ BD
Horizontal: OD 0.2 × +2 = 0.4Δ BO   OS 0.2 × −2 = 0.4Δ BI
Induced phoria: OD 1.6Δ + 1.6Δ = 3.2Δ BU
                OD 0.4Δ BO − OS 0.4Δ BI = 0
                (no horizonal induced phoria)

Figure 4-27 Prismatic effect of bifocals in antimetropia.

When the eyes encounter the top of a bifocal segment, they meet a new plus lens with a different optical center, and the object appears to jump upward unless the optical center of the add is at the very top of the segment (Fig 4-29). Executive-style segments have their optical centers at the top of the segment. The optical center of a typical flat-top segment is located 3 mm below the top of the segment. It is apparent that the closer the optical center of the segment approaches the top edge of the segment, the less the image jump. Thus, flat-top segments produce less image jump than round-top segments because the latter have much lower optical centers.

Patients with myopia who wear round-top bifocals would be more bothered by image jump than patients with hyperopia because it occurs in the direction of image displacement. Thus, it is good practice to avoid prescribing round-top bifocal segments to those with myopia.

Compensating for induced anisophoria

When anisometropia is corrected with spectacle lenses, anisophoria is induced in all secondary positions of gaze. The spectacle correction of anisometropia can cause an

With plus lenses:

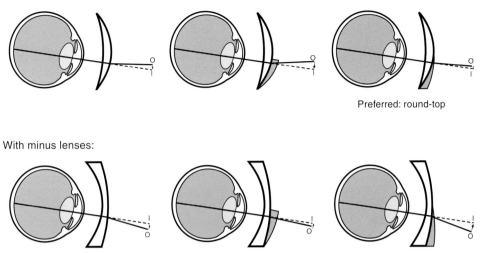

Preferred: round-top

With minus lenses:

Preferred: flat-top

Figure 4-28 Image displacement through bifocal segments. *(From Wisnicki HJ. Bifocals, trifocals, and progressive-addition lenses.* Focal Points: Clinical Modules for Ophthalmologists. *San Francisco: American Academy of Ophthalmology; 1999, module 6. Reprinted with permission from Guyton DL.* Ophthalmic Optics and Clinical Refraction. *Baltimore: Prism Press; 1998. Redrawn by C. H. Wooley.)*

Round-top segment: maximum image jump

Flat-top segment: minimal image jump

Executive-style segment: no image jump

Figure 4-29 Image jump through bifocal segments. If the optical center of a segment is at its top, no image jump occurs. *(From Wisnicki HJ. Bifocals, trifocals, and progressive-addition lenses.* Focal Points: Clinical Modules for Ophthalmologists. *San Francisco: American Academy of Ophthalmology; 1999, module 6. Reprinted with permission from Guyton DL.* Ophthalmic Optics and Clinical Refraction. *Baltimore: Prism Press; 1998. Redrawn by C. H. Wooley.)*

anisophoria with or without a bifocal add. This induced anisophoria may be the source of symptoms, even diplopia, especially when the anisometropia is of recent and/or sudden origin. Acquired symptomatic anisophoria may have its onset with the first pair of bifocals in a patient with early presbyopia, with spectacle correction following retinal detachment surgery, with gradual asymmetrical progression of cataracts, or after unilateral intraocular lens implantation. The patient usually adapts to horizontal imbalance by increasing head rotation but may have symptoms when looking down, in the reading position. Remember that horizontal vergence amplitudes are large compared to vertical fusional amplitudes, which are typically less than 2Δ. The amount of induced phoria can be calculated using Prentice's rule (Fig 4-30).

At the reading point, 8 mm below distance optical center:

OD	4.0 × 0.8	=	3.2Δ BU
OS	1.0 × 0.8	=	0.8Δ BU
Net difference			2.4Δ BU

In this example, there is an induced right hyperdeviation of 2.4Δ. Conforming to the usual practice in the management of heterophorias, approximately two thirds to three fourths of the vertical phoria should be corrected—in this case, 1.75Δ. This correction may be accomplished in several ways.

Press-On Prisms With Press-On Prisms, 2Δ BD may be added to the right segment (in the preceding example) or 2Δ BU to the left segment.

Bicentric grinding ("slabbing off") The most satisfactory method of compensating for the induced vertical phoria in anisometropia is the technique of bicentric grinding *(slab-off)* (Fig 4-31). In this method, 2 optical centers are created in the lens having the greater minus (or less plus) power, counteracting the base-down effect of the greater minus lens in the reading position.

In the bicentric grinding technique, a dummy lens is cemented to the convex front surface of a semifinished lens blank. This combined lens blank is resurfaced employing the same front curve, with optical center displaced upward. When the remaining portion of the dummy lens is removed, the resulting front surface has 2 optical centers, each with

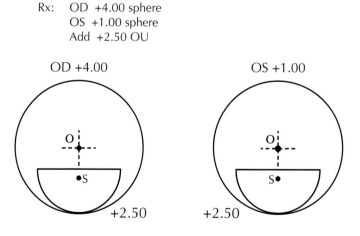

Rx: OD +4.00 sphere
     OS +1.00 sphere
     Add +2.50 OU

O = optical center, distance
S = optical center of seg
R (= S): Reading position 8 mm below distance optical center.

Figure 4-30 Calculating induced anisophoria.

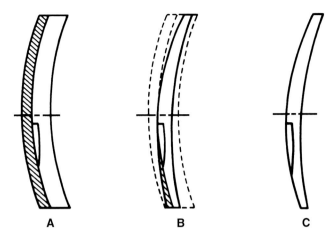

Figure 4-31 Bicentric grinding. **A,** Lens form with a dummy lens cemented to the front surface. **B,** Both surfaces of the lens are reground with the same curvatures but removing base-up prism from the top segment of the front surface and removing base-down prism from the entire rear surface. **C,** The effect is a lens that has had base-down prism removed from the lower segment only.

the same curvature. In this way, base-down prism has been created in the upper part of the lens. Actually, it is more convenient to think of the slab-off process as creating *base-up* prism over the reading area of the lens.

Bicentric grinding can be used for single-vision lenses as well as multifocals. By increasing the distance between the 2 optical centers, this method can achieve as much as 4Δ of prism compensation at the reading position.

Reverse slab-off As the preceding discussion suggests, prism correction in the reading position can be achieved not only by removing base-down prism from the lower part of the more minus lens (slabbing off) but also just as well by adding base-down prism to the lower half of the more plus lens. This technique is known as *reverse slab-off*.

Historically, it was easy to *remove* material from a standard lens. Today, with plastic lenses fabricated by molding, it is more convenient to *add* material so as to create a base-down prism in the lower half of what will be the more plus lens. Because plastic lenses account for a majority of the lenses dispensed, reverse slab-off is now the most common method of correcting anisometropically induced anisophoria. Special molds are required for specific amounts of prism, but with them, the fabrication of a reverse slab-off lens is no more expensive than any other type and is free of the considerable shop difficulties associated with bicentric grinding.

In ordering a lens that requires prism correction for an anisophoria in downgaze, it is often appropriate to leave the choice of slab-off versus reverse slab-off to the optician by including a statement in the prescription such as, "Slab-off right lens 3Δ (or reverse slab-off left lens)." In either case, the prescribed prism should be measured in the reading position, not calculated, because the patient may have partially adapted to the anisophoria.

Dissimilar segments In anisometropic bifocal lens prescriptions, vertical prism compensation can also be achieved by the use of dissimilar segments with their optical centers at 2 different heights. The segment with the lower optical center should be placed in front of the more hyperopic (or less myopic) eye to provide base-down prism. (This method contrasts with the bicentric grinding method, which produces base-up prism and is therefore employed on the lesser plus or greater minus lens.)

In the example shown (Fig 4-32), a 22-mm round segment has been chosen for the right eye, and the top of its segment is at the usual 5 mm below the distance optical center. For the left eye, a 22-mm flat-top segment is used, again with the top of the segment 5 mm below the optical center.

Because the optical center of the flat-top segment is 3 mm below the top of the segment, it is at the patient's reading position and that segment will introduce no prismatic effect. However, the optical center of the OD round segment is 8 mm below the patient's reading position, and, by Prentice's rule, this 2.5 D segment will produce $2.5 \times 0.8 = 2.0\Delta$ base-down prism.

Single-vision reading glasses with lowered optical centers Partial compensation for the induced vertical phoria at the reading position can be obtained with single-vision reading glasses, with the optical centers placed 3–4 mm below the pupillary centers in primary gaze. The patient's gaze will be directed much closer to the optical centers of the lenses when reading.

Contact lenses Contact lenses can be prescribed for patients with significant anisometropia that causes a symptomatic anisophoria in downgaze. Reading glasses can be worn over the contacts if the patient is presbyopic.

Refractive surgery Refractive surgery may be an option for some patients with symptomatic anisometropia.

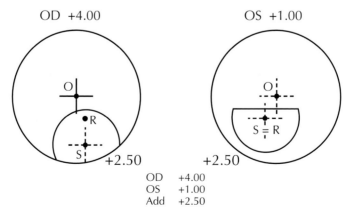

Figure **4-32** Dissimilar segments used to compensate for anisophoria in anisometropic bifocal prescriptions.

Occupation and Bifocal Segment

The *dioptric power* of a segment depends on the patient's accommodative reserve and the working distance required for each specific job. It must be emphasized that such focal length determinations are a characteristic not of the job but of the individual patient's adaptation to that job. If the patient is allowed to use half of his or her available accommodation (which must be *measured*), the remainder of the dioptric requirement will be met by the bifocal add. For example, if the job is proofreading at 40 cm, the dioptric requirement for that focal length is 2.5 D. If the patient's accommodative amplitude is 2.0 D, and half of that (1.0 D) is used for the job, the balance of 1.5 D becomes the necessary bifocal add.

It is essential that the *accommodative range* (near point to far point) be *measured* and be adequate for the job.

Lens design

The most important characteristic of the bifocal segment is the segment *height* in relation to the patient's pupillary center. The lenses will be unsuitable if the segment is placed too high or too low for the specific occupational need.

Segment *width* is substantially less important. The popular impression that very large bifocals mean better reading capability is not supported by projection measurements. At a 40-cm reading distance, a 25-mm flat-top segment provides a horizontal reading field of 50–55 cm.

At a 40-cm distance, an individual habitually uses face rotation to increase his or her fixation field when it exceeds 45 cm (30° of arc); therefore, a 25-mm-wide segment is more than adequate for all but a few special occupations, such as a graphic artist or an architectural drafter using a drawing board. Furthermore, with a 35-mm segment producing a horizontal field 75 cm wide, the focal length at the extremes of the fixation field would be 55 cm, not 40 cm! Therefore, the split bifocal is useful not because it is a wider bifocal but because of its monocentric construction.

The *shape* of the segment must be considered. For example, round-top segments (Kryptok, Ultex type) require the user to look well down in the segment in order to employ their maximum horizontal dimension. In addition, they exaggerate image jump, especially in myopic corrections.

Segment decentration To avoid inducing a base-out prism effect when the bifocal-wearing patient converges for near-vision tasks, the reading segment is generally decentered inward. The following are some considerations for proper decentration:

- *Working distance.* Because the convergence requirement increases as the focal length decreases, additional inward decentration of the bifocal segment is required.
- *Interpupillary distance.* The wider the interpupillary distance, the greater the convergence requirement and, correspondingly, the need for inward decentration of the segments.
- *Lens power.* If the distance lens is a high-plus lens, it will create a greater base-out prism effect (ie, induced exophoria) as the viewer converges. Additional inward decentration of the segments may be helpful. The reverse would be true for high-minus lenses.

- *Existing heterophoria.* As with lens-induced phorias, the presence of an existing exophoria suggests increasing the inward decentration; an esophoria would call for the opposite approach.

Prescribing Special Lenses

Some patients require special prescription lenses.

Aphakic Lenses

The problems of correcting aphakia with high-plus power spectacle lenses are well known and have been described eloquently by Alan C. Woods (1952). They include

- magnification of approximately 20%–35%
- altered depth perception resulting from the magnification
- pincushion distortion; for example, doors appear to bow inward
- difficulty with hand–eye coordination
- ring scotoma generated by prismatic effects at the edge of the lens (causing the "jack-in-the-box" phenomenon)
- extreme sensitivity of the lenses to minor misadjustment in vertex distance, pantoscopic tilt, and height
- in monocular aphakia, loss of useful binocular vision because of differential magnification

In addition, aphakic spectacles create cosmetic problems. The patient's eyes appear magnified and, if viewed obliquely, may seem grotesquely displaced because of prismatic effects. The high-power lenticular lens is itself somewhat unattractive with its "fried-egg" appearance.

For all these reasons, intraocular lenses and aphakic contact lenses now account for the great majority of aphakic corrections. Nevertheless, spectacle correction of aphakia is sometimes appropriate, as in pediatric aphakia. Correct lens selection, frame selection and adjustment, and refraction technique can make a great deal of difference to the aphakic patient.

Refracting technique

Because of the sensitivity of aphakic glasses to vertex distance and pantoscopic tilt, it is nearly impossible to refract an aphakic eye reliably using a phoropter. The vertex distance and the pantoscopic tilt are not well controlled, nor are they necessarily close to the values for the final spectacles. Rather than a phoropter, trial frames or lens clips should be used.

The trial frame allows the refractionist to control vertex distance and pantoscopic tilt. It should be adjusted for minimal vertex distance and for the same pantoscopic tilt planned for the actual spectacles (about 5°–7°, not the larger values appropriate for conventional glasses).

Another good technique is to refract with clip-on trial lens holders placed over the patient's existing aphakic glasses (overrefraction). Care should be taken that the center of the clip coincides with the optical center of the existing lens. Even if the present lens contains a cylinder at an axis different from what is needed, it is possible to calculate resultant spherocylindrical correction with an electronic calculator, manually, or by measuring the combination in a lensmeter.

Guyton DL. *Retinoscopy. Minus Cylinder Technique.* Continuing Ophthalmic Video Education [videotape]. San Francisco: American Academy of Ophthalmology; 1986.

Guyton DL. *Retinoscopy. Plus Cylinder Technique.* Continuing Ophthalmic Video Education [videotape]. San Francisco: American Academy of Ophthalmology; 1986.

Woods AC. Adjustment to aphakia. *Am J Ophthalmol.* 1952;35:118–122. [Editorial originally published anonymously. The author was later acknowledged to be Woods.]

Absorptive Lenses

In certain high-illumination situations, sunglasses allow better visual function in a number of ways.

Improvement of contrast sensitivity

On a bright, sunny day, irradiance from the sun will range from 10,000 to 30,000 foot-lamberts. These high light levels tend to saturate the retina and therefore decrease finer levels of contrast sensitivity. The major function of dark sunglasses (gray, green, or brown) is to allow the retina to remain at its normal level of contrast sensitivity. Most dark sunglasses absorb 70%–80% of the incident light of all wavelengths.

Improvement of dark adaptation

A full day at the beach or on the ski slopes on a sunny day (without dark sunglasses) can impair dark adaptation for more than 2 days. Thus, dark sunglasses (absorption of 70%–80% of incident light) are recommended for prolonged periods in bright sun.

Reduction of glare sensitivity

Various types of sunglasses can reduce glare sensitivity. Because light reflecting off a horizontal surface becomes polarized in the horizontal plane, properly oriented *polarized* (Polaroid) lenses reduce the intensity of dazzle glare from road surfaces, glass windows, lake and river surfaces, and metal surfaces. *Graded-density sunglasses* are deeply tinted at the top and gradually become lighter toward the lens center. They are effective in removing dazzle glare sources above the line of sight, such as the sun. Wide-temple sunglasses work by reducing temporal glare sources.

Improvement of contrast

The range of filters in yellow-orange sunglasses efficiently absorbs wavelengths in the purple through blue-green range, making these colors appear as different shades of dark gray. On the other hand, the wearer clearly sees the spectrum from green through yellow to orange to red. Accordingly, although colors appear slightly unreal, the color contrast is increased (Fig 4-33). Therefore, patients with conditions that decrease color sensitivity, such as cataracts or corneal edema, report improvements in color contrast with such sunglasses.

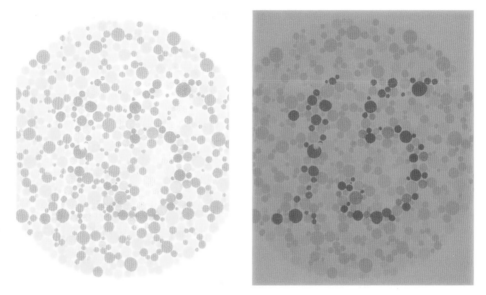

Figure 4-33 Photograph illustrates the color-contrast-enhancing properties of an orange-yellow filter. Although this filter distorts the color, it increases the contrast of the Ishihara plate.

Use of photochromic lenses

When short-wavelength light (300–400+ nm) interacts with photochromic lenses, they darken by means of a chemical reaction that converts silver ions to elemental silver. This process is similar to the reaction that occurs when photographic film is exposed to light. Unlike with photographic film, however, the chemical reaction in photochromic lenses is reversible. Photochromic lenses can darken enough to absorb about 80% of the incident light; when the amount of illumination falls, they can lighten until they absorb about 20% of the incident light. It should be noted that these lenses take longer to lighten than to darken. When darkened, these lenses are also excellent ultraviolet absorbers.

Ultraviolet-absorbing lenses

The spectrum of ultraviolet light is divided into 3 classifications: UVA contains wavelengths from 400 to 320 nm, UVB contains wavelengths from 320 to 290 nm, and UVC contains wavelengths below 290 nm.

The ozone layer of the atmosphere absorbs almost all UVC coming from the sun. Most exposure to UVC is from manufactured sources, including welding arcs, germicidal lamps, and excimer lasers. Of the total solar radiation falling on the earth, about 5% is ultraviolet light, of which 90% is UVA and 10% UVB.

The amount of ultraviolet light striking the earth varies with season (greatest in the summer), latitude (greatest near the equator), time of day (greatest at noon), and elevation (increases with higher elevation). Ultraviolet light can also strike the eye by reflection. Fresh snow reflects between 60% and 80% of incident light; sand (beach, desert) reflects about 15% of incident light; and water reflects about 5% of incident light.

Laboratory experiments have shown that ultraviolet light damages living tissue in 2 ways. First, chemicals such as proteins, enzymes, nucleic acids, and cell membrane components absorb ultraviolet light. In so doing, their molecular bonds (primarily the double bonds) may become disrupted. Second, these essential biochemicals may become disrupted by the action of free radicals (such as the superoxide radical). Free radicals can often be produced by ultraviolet light in the presence of oxygen and a photosensitizing pigment. For a fuller discussion of free radicals, see the biochemistry chapters in BCSC Section 2, *Fundamentals and Principles of Ophthalmology.*

Because it may take many years for ultraviolet light to damage eye tissue, a tight linkage between cause and effect is difficult to prove. Therefore, proof that ultraviolet light damages the eye comes primarily from acute animal experiments and epidemiologic studies covering large numbers of patients.

Actinic (Labrador) keratopathy is probably produced by ultraviolet exposure. The relation between pterygium and ultraviolet light is more controversial. Because the onset of presbyopia is significantly earlier in populations living closer to the equator, increased light exposure is felt to contribute to presbyopia. Some epidemiologic and laboratory studies suggest that ultraviolet light contributes to cataract production. Other epidemiologic studies suggest that light exposure is related to the development of age-related macular degeneration in the white population. This work is also supported by animal studies.

The available data on the effects of exposure to ultraviolet light have suggested that it might be beneficial to protect patients from ultraviolet light after cataract surgery. Some surgeons routinely prescribe UV-absorbing glasses after surgery. Today, intraocular lenses incorporating UV-absorbing chromophores are in general use.

For further information regarding the effects of ultraviolet radiation on various ocular structures, see BCSC Section 8, *External Disease and Cornea;* Section 11, *Lens and Cataract;* and Section 12, *Retina and Vitreous.*

Almost all dark sunglasses absorb most of the incident ultraviolet light. This is also true for certain coated clear glass lenses and the clear plastic lenses made of CR-39 or polycarbonate.

It has been suggested that, ironically, certain sunglasses (primarily light blue) produce light damage to the eye. The argument contends that the pupil dilates behind dark glasses and that if the sunglasses then do not absorb significant amounts of ultraviolet light, they will actually allow more ultraviolet light to enter the eye than if no sunglasses were worn. In fact, dark sunglasses (which absorb 80% of incident light) reduce light levels striking the eye on a bright, sunny day to the range of 2000–6000 footlamberts. Such levels are about 10 times higher than those of an average lighted room. At such light levels, the pupil is significantly constricted. Thus, contrary to the preceding argument, a dark pair of sunglasses used on a bright day will allow pupillary dilation of only a fraction of a millimeter and thus will not lead to light injury of the eye.

Miller D. *Clinical Light Toxicity to the Eye.* New York: Springer-Verlag; 1987.

Miranda MN. The environmental factor in the onset of presbyopia. In: Stark L, Obrecht G, eds. *Presbyopia: Recent Research and Reviews from the Third International Symposium.* New York: Professional; 1987.

Special Lens Materials

It is important for the ophthalmologist to be aware of the variety of special spectacle lens materials now available.

Plastic lenses

Plastic lenses are increasingly used because of their lighter weight and reduced susceptibility to breakage compared to glass. Large frames require plastic lenses, although warpage can be a problem with these large, thinner lenses. Plastic lenses are available in practically all of the same lens forms as glass: bifocals, trifocals, aphakic lenses, and tints. A scratch-resistant coating is usually advisable because of the ease with which plastic lenses can be scratched.

Impact-resistant lenses

By government regulation, all prescription lenses, glass or plastic, must meet impact-resistance specifications (unless the refractionist designates in the written prescription that the lenses are not hardened and the patient is so advised).

All lenses must be at least 2.0 mm thick; glass lenses must be hardened by either a heat-tempering process or a chemical hardening method. The finished lens must withstand the impact of a 5/8-inch steel ball dropped from a height of 50 inches. Industrial safety lenses must be at least 3.0 mm thick and withstand the impact of a 1⅛-inch steel ball dropped from the 50-inch height.

High-index glass lenses

High-index glass lenses (refractive index of 1.70 or more) are cosmetically useful in spectacles for highly myopic patients. They reduce the edge thickness by some 30% compared to the usual barium crown glass (refractive index 1.523). Unfortunately, their increased chromatic aberration and the altered spatial perception caused by changes in base curve and lens thickness may be bothersome, especially for patients wearing higher-power lenses.

An aphakic Ultra Thin lens (Optical Systems International) is made of a glass having a refractive index of 1.80, which allows the lens to be much thinner. It reduces magnification from about 30% for common aphakic lenses to about 18% and provides somewhat improved cosmesis. The reduction in magnification, however, is still not sufficient to allow binocular vision in most spectacle-corrected, monocularly aphakic patients. Because this glass is much denser than plastic, a lens made from it is somewhat heavier than a plastic lens, even though it is thinner.

Polycarbonate lenses

Polycarbonate (Lexan) plastic, discovered in the 1950s, was the first of the engineering plastics, so-called because of its then unprecedented mechanical strength and heat resistance. Polycarbonate is extremely impact resistant, and it is tough—that is, it will undergo considerable and repeated deformation before breaking.

Polycarbonate has a higher refractive index (1.586) than many other lens materials, nearly as high as barium flint glass and high-index plastic. Furthermore, even though it has great strength and shatter resistance, its density is lower than that of the other plastic lens materials and, of course, much lower than that of any glass.

Thus, polycarbonate is an excellent material for spectacle lenses, with its combination of low density and high index making possible a very light lens that is also very safe. In spectacles designed for eye protection in sports or industrial environments, polycarbonate lenses are many times more impact and shatter resistant than any other commonly available material.

There are also disadvantages. Polycarbonate is generally more expensive than other plastics. Furthermore, its toughness creates a problem in optical manufacture: polycarbonate cannot be shaped by the abrasive grinding wheels used for glass and CR-39 plastic. It requires special small-toothed cutters, and the machining process adds somewhat to the expense.

In addition, polycarbonate has an optical disadvantage. Its low Abbe number of 30 indicates a high degree of chromatic dispersion. Thus, color fringing can be an annoyance, particularly in strong prescriptions.

> Stephens GL, Davis JK. Spectacle lenses. In: Tasman W, Jaeger EA, eds. *Duane's Clinical Ophthalmology*. Philadelphia: Lippincott-Raven; 1995.

Therapeutic Use of Prisms

Small horizontal and vertical deviations can be corrected conveniently in spectacle lenses by adding prisms.

Horizontal heterophorias

Patients (usually adults) may develop asthenopic symptoms if fusion is disrupted by inadequate vergence amplitudes; if fusion cannot be maintained, diplopia results. Thus, patients with an exophoria at near develop symptoms when their convergence reserve is inadequate for the task. In some patients, this fusional inadequacy can be compensated for by improving fusional amplitudes. Younger patients may be able to accomplish this through orthoptic exercises, sometimes used in conjunction with prisms that further stimulate their fusional capability (base-out prisms to enhance convergence reserve).

Some patients may have symptoms because of abnormally high accommodative convergence. Thus, an esophoria at near may be improved by full hyperopic correction for distance and/or by using bifocals to decrease accommodative demand. In adult patients, orthoptic training and maximum refractive correction may be inadequate, and prisms or surgery may be necessary to restore binocularity.

Prisms are especially useful if a patient experiences an *abrupt* onset of symptoms secondary to a basic heterophoria or heterotropia. The prisms may be needed only temporarily, and the minimum amount of prism necessary to reestablish and maintain binocularity should be used.

Vertical heterophorias

Vertical fusional amplitudes are small ($<2\Delta$). Thus, if a vertical muscle imbalance is sufficient to cause asthenopic symptoms or diplopia, it should be compensated for by the incorporation of prisms into the refractive correction. Once again, the minimum amount of prism needed to eliminate symptoms is prescribed. In a noncomitant vertical heterophoria, the prism should be sufficient to correct the imbalance in primary gaze, and, if necessary, a different prism should be used for the most frequent secondary position of gaze (usually the reading position). With combined vertical and horizontal muscle imbalance, correcting only the vertical deviation may help improve control of the horizontal deviation as well. If the horizontal deviation is not adequately corrected, an oblique Fresnel prism may be helpful. The brief period usually allowed for clinical heterophoria testing may be insufficient to unmask a latent muscle imbalance completely. Often, after prisms have been worn for a time, the phoria appears to increase, and the prism correction must be correspondingly increased.

Methods of prism correction

The potential effect of prisms should be evaluated by having the patient test the indicated prism in trial frames or trial lens clips over the current refractive correction.

Temporary prisms in the form of clip-on lenses or Fresnel Press-On Prisms can be used to evaluate and alter the final prism requirement. The Fresnel prisms have several advantages: They are lighter in weight (1 mm thick) and more acceptable cosmetically because they are affixed to the concave surface of the spectacle lens. In addition, they allow much larger prism corrections (up to 40Δ). With higher prism powers, however, it is not unusual to note a decrease in the visual acuity of the corrected eye. Patients may also note chromatic fringes.

Prisms can be incorporated into spectacle lenses within the limits of cost, appearance, weight, and technical skill of the optician. Prisms should be incorporated into the spectacle lens prescription only after an adequate trial of temporary prisms has established that the correction is appropriate and the deviation is stable.

Prism correction may also be achieved by decentering the optical center of the lens relative to the visual axis, although substantial prism effect by means of this method is possible only with higher-power lenses. Aspheric lens designs are not suitable for decentration. (See earlier discussion of lens decentration and Prentice's rule.) Bifocal segments may be decentered *in* more than the customary amount to give a modest additional base-in effect to help patients with convergence insufficiency.

Monocular Diplopia

Monocular diplopia is a frequent and confusing complaint in general ophthalmic practice. Under certain conditions, up to 40% of normal eyes can experience this phenomenon. White letters or lines on a dark background, such as chalk marks on a blackboard, or neon signs at night are most likely to elicit monocular diplopia, often manifested as a ghost image overlapping the true image.

The usual cause of monocular diplopia is optical irregularity in either the cornea or the lens. In some cases, the corneal irregularity may be transient, such as after contact lens wear or from lid pressure during reading in a sustained gaze position. Chalazia may induce irregular astigmatism that lasts weeks to months. Such irregularities of the optical system may be lumped together under the term *irregular astigmatism,* which indicates any irregular refractive property of the eye (eg, scissors movement noted on retinoscopy). If the cross section of each bundle of light rays approaching the retina contains 2 areas of concentration of light rays, the result will be monocular diplopia.

Other causes of monocular diplopia, usually obvious, include a decentered contact lens, double reflection in spectacle lenses, or transient sensory adaptation after strabismus surgery. Retinal lesions may produce metamorphopsia that the patient occasionally interprets as diplopia.

Optical irregularity as the cause of monocular diplopia may be confirmed by evaluating the retinoscopic reflex, eliminating the diplopia with a pinhole, or eliminating the diplopia with a trial rigid contact lens. (About 40% of monocular diplopia is caused by corneal pathology.) Because irregular astigmatism causes confusion with retinoscopy and with astigmatic dial methods of refracting, use of the Jackson cross cylinder is probably the best refractive technique in cases of monocular diplopia.

Treatment of monocular diplopia includes trying a different refractive correction, contact lenses, miotics (such as pilocarpine), or simply more light (to constrict the pupil). Sometimes the best approach to monocular diplopia is explanation, demonstration that it can be eliminated by optical techniques, and reassurance that it does not indicate a serious health problem such as a brain tumor. Once reassured, most patients can tolerate monocular diplopia and can often learn to ignore it entirely.

Guyton DL. Diagnosis and treatment of monocular diplopia. *Focal Points: Clinical Modules for Ophthalmologists.* San Francisco: American Academy of Ophthalmology; 1984, module 2.

CHAPTER 5

Contact Lenses

Introduction

Contact lenses are another device used for correcting refractive errors. One description of contact lens–type devices goes back to the Renaissance, but their first documented use occurred in the 1880s. These lenses were large and made of glass, and they extended to the sclera. Corneal lenses were introduced in the 1940s; they were made of a plastic, polymethylmethacrylate (PMMA), and became a popular alternative to spectacles for refractive correction. Soft hydrogel lenses were introduced in the United States in the 1950s and led to the widespread use of contact lenses. Today, it is estimated that 51% of US adults use some kind of vision correction; a quarter of these use contact lenses. This means that over 30 million Americans use contact lenses (Fig 5-1). As a result, all ophthalmologists will, at some time, interact with contact lens users—for fitting, follow-up care, and/or treating complications. Some knowledge of contact lenses, therefore, is essential for all practitioners.

Figure 5-1 Contact lens use over time in the United States. *(HPR Consumer Survey 2003. Used with permission from Health Products Research, Inc.)*

Contact Lens Glossary

It is important that ophthalmologists know the vocabulary of contact lenses. The 3 most important terms in this vocabulary are base curve, diameter, and power (Fig 5-2):

Base curve The curvature of the central posterior surface of the lens, which is adjacent to the cornea; it is measured by its radius of curvature (mm) or is sometimes converted to diopters (D) by taking the reciprocal of the radius.

Diameter (chord diameter) The width of the contact lens, which typically varies with the lens material; the diameter of soft contact lenses, for example, ranges from 13 to 15 mm, whereas that of rigid gas-permeable (RGP) lenses ranges from 9 to 10 mm.

Power Determined by its shape and calculated indirectly by Snell's law:

$$D = [n_2 - n_1]/r$$

The posterior vertex power is measured (as with spectacles) by placing the lens (convex surface facing the observer) on a lensmeter.

The following terms are also important to know:

Apical zone The steep part of the cornea, generally including its geometric center; usually 3 to 4 mm in diameter.

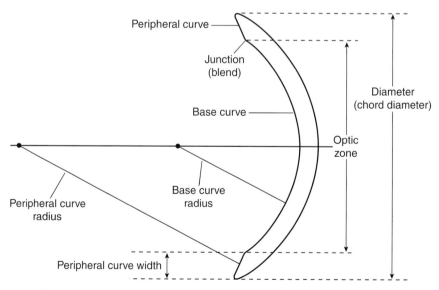

Figure 5-2 Contact lens. Note the relationship among the parts. *(Used with permission from Stein HA, Freeman MI, Stein RM. CLAO Residents Contact Lens Curriculum Manual. New Orleans: Contact Lens Association of Ophthalmologists; 1996. Redrawn by Christine Gralapp.)*

Corneal apex The steepest part of the cornea.

Dk A term describing the oxygen permeability of a lens material, where D is the diffusion coefficient for oxygen movement in the material and k is the solubility constant of oxygen in the material.

Dk/L A term describing the oxygen transmissibility of the lens; dependent on the lens material and the central thickness (L).

Edge lift Description of the peripheral lens and its position in relation to the underlying cornea. Adequate edge lift (as documented by the presence of a ring of fluorescein under the lens periphery) prevents edges from digging into the flatter corneal periphery.

Fluorescein pattern The color intensity of fluorescein dye in the tear lens beneath a rigid contact lens. Areas of contact appear black; green reflects clearance between the lens and the cornea. (Use of a No. 12 yellow Wratten filter in front of the slit lamp enhances the intensity of the pattern.)

K reading Keratometry reading; determined by a manual or an automated keratometer.

Lenticular contact lens A lens with a central optical zone and a nonoptical peripheral zone known as the carrier; designed to improve lens comfort.

Optic zone The area of the front surface of the contact lens that has the refractive power of the lens.

Peripheral curves Secondary curves just outside the base curve at the edge of a contact lens. They are typically flatter to approximate the normal flattening of the peripheral cornea. Typically, junctions between posterior curves (base curve and peripheral curve, for example) are smooth or "blended" to enhance lens comfort.

Polymethylmethacrylate (PMMA) The first plastic used in the manufacture of contact lenses.

Radiuscope A device that measures radius of curvature, such as the base curve of an RGP lens. Flatter surfaces have larger radii of curvature, and steeper surfaces have smaller radii of curvature.

Sagittal depth, or vault A term describing the depth, or vault, of a lens (Fig 5-3); determined by measuring the distance between the center of the posterior surface (or center of the base curve) to the plane connecting the edges of the lens. In general, if the diameter is held constant, the sagittal depth decreases as the base curve increases. Although sagittal depth is critical for determining good fit, designation of the base curve for a particular lens type typically ensures the appropriate sagittal depth.

Tear lens The optical lens formed by the tear film layer between the posterior surface of a contact lens and the anterior surface of the cornea (Fig 5-4). In general, with soft lenses, the tear lens has plano power; with rigid lenses, the power varies, depending on the shape of the lens and the cornea.

Wetting angle The wettability of a lens surface: a low wetting angle means water will spread over the surface, increasing surface wettability, whereas a high wetting angle means that water will bead up, decreasing surface wettability (Fig 5-5). A smaller wetting angle (ie, greater wettability) generally translates into greater lens comfort and better lens optics.

Figure 5-3 Changing the base curve of a contact lens changes the sagittal depth. *(Used with permission from Stein HA, Freeman MI, Stein RM. CLAO Residents Contact Lens Curriculum Manual. New Orleans: Contact Lens Association of Ophthalmologists; 1996. Redrawn by Christine Gralapp.)*

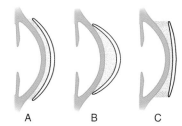

Figure 5-4 The tear film layer between the posterior surface of a contact lens and the anterior surface of the cornea forms **(A)** a plano lens, **(B)** a plus lens, **(C)** a minus lens. *(Used with permission from Key JE II, ed. The CLAO Pocket Guide to Contact Lens Fitting. 2nd ed. Metairie, LA: Contact Lens Association of Ophthalmologists; 1998. Redrawn by Christine Gralapp.)*

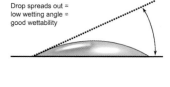

Figure 5-5 The wettability of a lens surface determines whether a wetting angle will be low (greater wettability, greater comfort) or high (less wettability, less comfort). *(Used with permission from Stein HA, Freeman MI, Stein RM. CLAO Residents Contact Lens Curriculum Manual. New Orleans: Contact Lens Association of Ophthalmologists; 1996. Redrawn by Christine Gralapp.)*

Clinically Important Features of Contact Lens Optics

Contact lenses have 4 parameters in common with all conventional lenses: posterior surface curvature *(base curve)*, anterior surface curvature *(power curve)*, diameter, and power (see Fig 5-2). However, unlike with spectacle lenses, the shape of their posterior surface is designed to have certain fitting relationships with the anterior surface of the eye.

The refractive performance of contact lenses differs from that of spectacle lenses for 2 primary reasons: (1) contact lenses have a shorter vertex distance and (2) tears, rather than air, form the interface between the lens and the cornea.

Key optical considerations resulting from contact lens use are as follows:

- field of vision
- image size
- accommodation
- convergence demands
- tear lens
- correcting astigmatism
- correcting presbyopia

Field of Vision

Because they are closer to the entrance pupils and lack frames (spectacle frames reduce the field of corrected vision by about 20°), contact lenses provide a larger field of corrected vision and avoid much of the peripheral distortion, such as spherical aberration, created by high-power spectacle lenses.

Image Size

Retinal image size is influenced by the vertex distance of a corrective lens. Contact lenses have shorter vertex distances than do spectacles, so image size is changed less with contact lenses than with spectacles. For example, minus spectacles and contact lenses both reduce the image size, but contact lenses reduce image size to a lesser extent. Conversely, plus spectacles and contact lenses both increase the image size, but contact lenses do so to a lesser extent.

Anisometropia and image size

The ametropias of eyes with greater (non–surgically induced) refractive errors are predominantly axial. Theoretically, the anisometropic aniseikonia of these eyes is minimized by placing the corrective lens in the eye's anterior focal plane (see discussion of Knapp's law in Chapter 2), on average, about 15.7 mm anterior to the cornea. In axial myopia, moving the corrective lens posterior to the eye's focal plane (closer to the cornea) increases the size of the retinal image compared with that of an emmetropic eye. The reverse is true in axial hyperopia. In practice, however, anisometropic aniseikonia is usually managed best by correcting the refractive error of the eyes with contact lenses, regardless of the dominant type of refractive error present, because this avoids the anisophoria that would be induced by off-axis gaze through a unilateral high-power spectacle lens. In addition, the greater separation of the percipient elements in the stretched retinas of larger myopic eyes may explain the less-than-perceived magnification observed with contact lenses.

Monocular aphakia and aniseikonia

Minimizing aniseikonia in monocular aphakia improves the functional level of binocular vision. An optical model of surgical aphakia can be represented by inserting a neutralizing lens in the location of the crystalline lens and correcting the resulting ametropia with a forward-placed plus-power lens. This creates a Galilean telescope within the optical system of the eye. Accordingly, magnification is reduced as the effective plus-power corrective lens (corrected for vertex distance) is moved closer to the neutralizing minus lens (the former site of the crystalline lens). This model illustrates why contact lens correction of aphakia creates significantly less magnification than a spectacle lens correction, whereas a posterior chamber intraocular lens creates the least magnification of all.

Although the ametropia of an aphakic eye is predominantly refractive, it can also have a significant preexisting axial component. For example, the coexistence of axial myopia would further increase the magnification of a contact lens–corrected aphakic eye (compared with the image size of the spectacle-corrected fellow phakic myopic eye). Even if the image size of the fellow myopic eye were to be increased by fitting it with a contact lens, the residual aniseikonia might still exceed the limits of fusion and lead to diplopia (Clinical Example 5-1). Divergent strabismus can develop in the aphakic eye of adults (and esotropia in children) if fusion is interrupted for a significant period of time. If diplopia does not resolve within several weeks, excessive aniseikonia should be suspected and confirmed by demonstration of the patient's inability to fuse images superimposed with the aid of prisms. These patients are usually aware that the retinal image in their aphakic eye is larger than that of the fellow phakic eye.

When the fellow phakic eye is significantly myopic, correcting it with a contact lens will increase its image size and often reduce the aniseikonia sufficiently to resolve the diplopia. If excessive aniseikonia persists, efforts should be directed at further reducing the image size of the contact lens–corrected aphakic eye. This can be done by overcor-

---

CLINICAL EXAMPLE 5-1

Fitting a unilateral aphakic eye results in diplopia that persists in the presence of prisms that superimpose the two images. The refractive error of the fellow eye is − 5.00 D and the image of the aphakic eye is described as being larger than that of the fellow myopic eye. How can the diplopia be resolved?

The goal is to reduce the aniseikonia of the 2 eyes by magnifying the image size of the phakic eye and/or reducing the image size of the contact lens–corrected aphakic eye. The former can be achieved by correcting the myopic phakic eye with a contact lens to increase its image size. If this is inadequate, we can overcorrect the contact lens by 5.00 D and prescribe a spectacle lens for that eye of − 5.00 D, thereby introducing a reverse Galilean telescope into the optical system of the eye. (If, however, the phakic eye is hyperopic, its image size would be increased by correcting its refractive error with a *spectacle* rather than a contact lens.)

recting the aphakic contact lens and neutralizing the resulting induced myopia with a forward-placed spectacle lens of appropriate minus power. In effect, this introduces a *reverse* Galilean telescope into the optical system of that eye. Empirically, increasing the power of the distance aphakic contact lens power by +3 D and prescribing a −3 D spectacle lens for that eye usually suffices. Alternatively, if it is impractical to fit the fellow myopic eye with a contact lens, the clinician can elect to add plus power to the aphakic contact lens by an amount equal to the spherical equivalent of the refractive error of the fellow eye, in effect equalizing the myopia of the 2 eyes.

The resulting decrease in the residual aniseikonia usually improves fusional potential and facilitates the recovery of fusion of even large amounts of aniseikonic exotropia over several weeks. However, the resolution of aphakic esotropia or cyclotropia is less certain.

In contrast with axial myopia, coexisting axial hyperopia *reduces* the magnification of a contact lens–corrected aphakic eye; residual aniseikonia can be further mitigated by correcting the fellow hyperopic eye with a *spectacle lens* (rather than a contact lens) to *maximize* its image size.

Accommodation

Accommodation is defined as the difference in the vergence at the first principal point of the eye (1.35 mm behind the cornea) between rays originating at infinity and those originating at a near point. This creates different accommodative demands for spectacle and contact lenses. Compared with spectacles, contact lenses *increase* the accommodative requirements of myopic eyes and *decrease* those of hyperopic eyes in proportion to the size of the refractive error. The difference in the accommodative efficiency of spectacle and contact lenses results from the effect of these 2 modalities on the vergence of light rays as they pass through the respective lenses. Contact lens correction requires an accommodative effort equal to that of emmetropic eyes. In other words, contact lenses eliminate the accommodative *advantage* enjoyed by those with spectacle-corrected myopia and the *disadvantage* experienced by those with spectacle-wearing hyperopia. This explains the clinical observation that patients with spectacle-corrected high myopia can read through their distance correction at older ages than those with emmetropia, whereas the opposite is true of patients with spectacle-corrected hyperopia.

> *Example:* The myopic refractive error of an eye is −7.00 D at a vertex distance of 15.00 mm, and the object distance is 33.33 mm.
> The vergence of rays exiting the spectacle lens and originating at infinity is −7.00 D.
> The vergence of these rays at the front surface of the cornea (which is approximately the location of the first principal point) is −1000/[15 + (1000/7)] = −6.33 D.
> The vergence of rays exiting the spectacle lens originating at a distance of 33.33 mm is −10.00 D (−3.00 − 7.00).
> Therefore, the vergence of these rays at the first principal point is approximately −1000/[15 + (1000/10)] = −8.70 D.

Accommodation is the difference in the vergence at the first principal point between rays originating at infinity and those originating at a distance of 33.33 mm, which in this case is 2.37 D (8.70 − 6.33 = 2.37). In contrast, the accommodation required with a contact lens correction is approximately 3.00 D. Therefore, this myopic eye would need 0.63 D more accommodation to focus an object at 33.33 mm when wearing a contact lens compared with correction with spectacles.

Similarly, the accommodative demands of an eye corrected with a +7.00 D spectacle lens would be 4.21 D compared with approximately 3 D for a contact lens.

Convergence Demands

Depending on their power, spectacle lenses (optically centered for distance) and contact lenses require different convergences. Myopic spectacle lenses induce base-in prisms for near objects. This benefit is eliminated with contact lenses. Conversely, hyperopic spectacles increase the convergence demands by inducing base-out prisms. In this case, contact lenses provide a benefit by eliminating this incremental convergence requirement.

In summary, compared with that of spectacle lenses, contact lens correction of myopia increases the accommodative *and* convergence demands of focusing near objects proportional to the size of the refractive error. The reverse is true in hyperopia.

Tear Lens

The presence of fluid, rather than air, between a contact lens and the corneal surface is responsible for another major difference in the optical performance of contact and spectacle lenses (see Fig 5-4). The tear layer between a contact lens and the corneal surface is an optical lens in its own right. As with all lenses, the power of this *tear*, or *fluid*, lens is determined by the curvatures of its anterior surface (formed by the back surface of the contact lens) and its posterior surface (formed by the front surface of the cornea). Because flexible (soft) contact lenses conform to the shape of the cornea and the curvatures of the anterior and posterior surfaces of the intervening tear layer are identical, the power of their fluid lenses is always plano. This is not generally true of rigid contact lenses: the shape of the posterior surface (which defines the anterior surface of the tear lens) can differ from the shape of the underlying cornea (which forms the posterior surface of the tear lenses). Under these circumstances, the tear layer introduces power that is added to the eyes' optical system.

As a rule of thumb, the power of the fluid lens is 0.25 D for every 0.05-mm radius of curvature difference between the base curve of the contact lens and the central curvature of the cornea (K), becoming somewhat greater for corneas steeper than 7.00 mm. Obviously, tear lenses created by rigid contact lenses having base curves steeper (smaller radius of curvature) than K (central keratometry) have plus power, whereas tear lenses formed by base curves flatter than K (larger radius of curvature) have minus power (see Fig 5-4; Fig 5-6). Therefore, the power of a rigid contact lens must account for both the eye's refractive error and the power introduced by the fluid lens. An easy way of remembering this is to use the rules of *steeper add minus (SAM)* and *flatter add plus (FAP)* (Clinical Example 5-2).

Because the refractive index of tears (1.336) is almost identical to that of a cornea (1.3765), the anterior surface of the fluid lens virtually masks the optical effect of the corneal surface. If the back surface of a contact lens is spherical, the anterior surface of

Figure 5-6 A rigid contact lens creates a tear, or fluid, lens, whose power is determined by the difference in curvature between the cornea and the base curve of the contact lens (K). *(Courtesy of Perry Rosenthal, MD. Redrawn by Christine Gralapp.)*

CLINICAL EXAMPLE 5-2

The refractive error of an eye is −3.00 D, the K measurement is 7.80 mm, and the base curve chosen for the rigid contact lens is 7.95 mm. What is the anticipated power of the contact lens?

The power of the resulting fluid lens is −0.75 D. This corrects −0.75 D of the refractive error. Therefore, the remaining refractive error that the contact lens is required to correct is −2.25 D (FAP). (Conversely, with a hyperopic eye, the plus power of the rigid contact lens would have to be *increased* in order to correct for both the hyperopic refractive error and the minus power introduced by the tear lens.) A rigid contact lens that does not provide the expected correction despite verification of its power suggests that its base curve differs from that which was ordered, thereby introducing an unanticipated tear lens power.

---

the fluid lens will also be spherical, regardless of the corneal topography. In other words, the tear layer created by a spherical rigid contact lens neutralizes more than 90% of regular and irregular corneal astigmatism. This principle simplifies the calculation of the tear lens power on astigmatic corneas: Because the powers of the steeper corneal meridians are effectively neutralized, they can be ignored and only the flattest meridians need to be considered. The refractive error along the flattest meridian is represented by the spherical component of refractive errors expressed in *minus cylinder form*. For this reason, *only the minus cylinder format should be used when dealing with contact lenses* (Clinical Example 5-3).

Correcting Astigmatism

Because rigid (and toric soft) contact lenses neutralize astigmatism at the corneal surface, the meridional aniseikonia created by the 2 different powers incorporated within each spectacle lens is avoided. This explains why contact lens–wearing patients with significant corneal astigmatism often experience an annoying change in spatial orientation when they switch to spectacles. However, refractive astigmatism is the sum of corneal and

> ## CLINICAL EXAMPLE 5-3
>
> *The refractive correction is $-3.50+0.75\times90$ and the K measurements along the 2 principal meridians are 7.80 mm horizontal (43.25 D @ 180°) by 7.65 mm vertical (43.12 D @ 90°). The contact lens base curve is chosen to be 7.65 mm. What is the anticipated power of the contact lens?*
>
> The refractive correction along the flattest corneal meridian (7.80) is -2.75 D (don't forget to convert the refractive error to minus cylinder form), and the lens has been fitted steeper than flat K (7.80 − 7.65 = 0.15 mm), creating a tear lens of +0.75 D. Thus, a corresponding amount of minus power must be added (SAM). Accordingly, the power of the contact lens should be −3.50 D [(−2.75) + (−0.75)].

lenticular astigmatism. Lenticular astigmatism, if present, is not corrected by spherical contact lenses. Because lenticular astigmatism usually has an against-the-rule orientation (vertical axis minus cylinder), it persists as residual astigmatism when the corneal astigmatism component is neutralized by rigid contact lenses. This finding is more common among older patients and often explains why their hard contact lenses fail to provide the anticipated vision correction. These cases can be identified via spherocylinder refraction over the contact lens. However, the presence of against-the-rule lenticular astigmatism can be inferred when the against-the-rule *refractive* astigmatism (adjusted to reflect the power at the corneal surface) exceeds the keratometric corneal astigmatism. Such eyes may have less residual astigmatism when the refractive error is corrected with soft rather than rigid spherical contact lenses.

For example, a patient's refraction is $-3.50-0.50\times180$ and the K measurements of the eye are 42.5 D (7.94 mm) horizontal and 44.0 D (7.67 mm) vertical. Would a soft or rigid contact lens provide better vision (less residual astigmatism)? The disparity between the corneal astigmatism of 1.50 D and the refractive astigmatism of 0.50 D reveals the presence of 1.00 D of against-the-rule lenticular astigmatism that neutralizes a similar amount of with-the-rule corneal astigmatism. Neutralizing the corneal component of the refractive astigmatism with a rigid contact lens exposes the lenticular residual astigmatism. Therefore, a spherical soft contact lens would provide better vision, because the residual astigmatism is 0.50 D compared with 1.00 D for a rigid contact lens.

Correcting Presbyopia

Correcting presbyopia with contact lenses can be done in several different ways:

- reading glasses over contact lenses
- alternating vision contact lenses (segmented or annular)
- simultaneous vision contact lenses (aspheric [multifocal] or diffractive)
- monovision
- modified monovision

From an optical point of view, using reading glasses or alternating vision contact lenses is most like standard spectacle correction for presbyopia. Simultaneous vision contact lenses direct light from 2 points in space—one near, one far—to the retina, resulting in a loss of contrast. Distant targets are "washed out" by light coming in through the near segment(s). Near objects are "washed out" by light coming in through the distance segment(s). Monovision allows one eye to have better distance vision and the other to have better near vision, but this arrangement interferes with binocular function, and the patient may have reduced stereopsis.

Contact Lens Materials and Manufacturing

A variety of materials has been used to fashion contact lenses. The choice of material can affect contact lens parameters, such as wettability, oxygen permeability, and lens deposits. In addition, material choice will affect flexibility, contact lens comfort, and stability and quality of vision. Manufacturing techniques primarily address the ability to make reproducible lenses in a cost-effective manner.

Materials

Contact lens materials can be described by flexibility (hard, rigid gas-permeable, soft, or hybrid) (Tables 5-1, 5-2). The first popular corneal contact lenses were made of polymethylmethacrylate (PMMA), a plastic that is durable but is not very oxygen permeable. Gas-permeable materials are rigid but usually more flexible than PMMA. Rigid gas-permeable (RGP) lenses allow some oxygen permeability; this can vary from Dk 15 to over Dk 100, which has allowed some RGP lenses to be approved for overnight or extended wear. Some of the original RGP lenses were made of cellulose acetate butyrate (CAB); CAB, however, has poor wettability, so it is now rarely used for RGP lenses. Most RGP lenses today are made of silicone acrylate, which provides the hardness needed for

Table 5-1 Monomers and USAN for Common Hydrogel Contact Lens Materials

Commercial Name	Manufacturer	USAN	Water Content	Monomers	FDA Group
Frequency 38	CooperVision	polymacon	38.0	HEMA	I
Optima FW	B&L	polymacon	38.0	HEMA	I
Preference	CooperVision	tetrafilcon	42.5	HEMA, MMA, NVP	I
Biomedics 55	Ocular Sciences	ocufilcon D	55.0	HEMA, MA	IV
Focus (1–2 wks)	CIBA Vision	vifilcon	55.0	HEMA, PVP, MA	IV
1-Day Acuvue	Vistakon	etafilcon	58.0	HEMA, MA	IV
Acuvue 2	Vistakon	etafilcon	58.0	HEMA, MA	IV
Proclear Compatibles	CooperVision	omafilcon	62.0	HEMA, PC	II
Soflens 66	B&L	alphafilcon	66.0	HEMA, NVP	II
Focus Dailies	CIBA Vision	nelfilcon	69.0	Modified PVA	II
Soflens One Day	B&L	hilafilcon	70.0	HEMA, NVP	II
Precision UV	CIBA Vision	vasurfilcon	74.0	MMA, NVP	II

Key: HEMA (2-hydroxyethyl methacrylate), MA (methacrylic acid), MMA (methyl methacrylate), NVP (*N*-vinyl pyrrolidone), PC (phosphorylcholine), PVA (polyvinyl alcohol), PVP (polyvinyl pyrrolidone), USAN (United States Adopted Names).

(Jones L, Tighe B. Silicone hydrogel contact lens materials update—part 1. *Silicone Hydrogels* [editorial online]. July 2004.)

Table 5-2 Silicone-Hydrogel Lens Materials

Proprietary name (United States)	PureVision	Focus Night&Day	Acuvue Advance
Adopted name	Balafilcon A	Lotrafilcon A	Galyfilcon A
Manufacturer	Bausch & Lomb	CIBA-Vision	Vistakon
Center thickness (@ −3.00 D) mm	0.09	0.08	0.07
Water content	36%	24%	47%
Oxygen permeability ($\times 10^{-11}$)	99	140	60
Oxygen transmissibility ($\times 10^{-9}$)	110	175	86
Modulus (psi)*	148	238	65
Surface treatment	Plasma oxidation, producing glassy islands	25 nm plasma coating with high refractive index	No surface treatment; internal wetting agent (PVP)
FDA group	3	1	1
Principal monomers	NVP + TPVC + NCVE + PBVC	DMA + TRIS + siloxane macromer	Unpublished

Key: DMA (*N,N*-dimethylacrylamide), NVP (*N*-vinyl pyrrolidone), TPVC (tris-(trimethylsiloxysilyl) propylvinyl carbamate), NCVE (*N*-carboxyvinyl ester), PBVC (poly[dimethysiloxy] di [silylbutanol] bis[vinyl carbamate]), PVP (polyvinyl pyrrolidone).
* Modulus data provided by Johnson & Johnson.

(Jones L, Tighe B. Silicone hydrogel contact lens materials update—part 1. *Silicone Hydrogels* [editorial online]. July 2004.)

sharp vision that was associated with PMMA lenses and the oxygen permeability associated with silicone material; however, wettability is still an issue.

The newest lenses are made of fluoropolymer, which provides greater oxygen permeability. The gas permeability of a material is related to (1) the size of the intermolecular voids that allow the transmission of gas molecules and (2) its gas solubility. Silicon monomers are used most commonly because their characteristic bulky molecular structure creates a more open polymer architecture. Adding fluorine increases the gas solubility of polymers and somewhat counteracts the tendency of silicon to bind hydrophobic debris (such as lipid-containing mucus) to the contact lens surfaces. In general, polymers that incorporate more silicon offer greater gas permeability at the expense of surface biocompatibility.

Soft contact lenses are typically made of a soft hydrogel polymer, hydroxyethylmethacrylate (HEMA) and have significant water content, which adds to their comfort and oxygen permeability. Newer soft lenses are made of silicone acrylate, which provides very high Dk; they are flexible and soft and have been approved for 30-day extended wear.

The surface characteristics of hydrogels can change instantaneously, depending on their external environment. When they are exposed to water, the hydrophilic elements are attracted to (and the hydrophobic components are repelled away from) the surface, which becomes more wettable. On the other hand, drying of the surface repels the hydrophilic elements inward, making the lens surfaces less wettable. The hydrophobic surface elements have a strong affinity for nonpolar lipid tear components through forces known as hydrophobic interaction. This process further reduces surface wettability, accelerates evaporative drying, and compromises the clinical properties of these lenses.

The oxygen and carbon dioxide permeability (Dk) of traditional hydrogel polymers is directly related to their water content. Because tear exchange under soft lenses is minimal, corneal respiration is almost totally dependent on the transmission of oxygen and carbon dioxide through the polymer matrix. Although the oxygen permeability of hydrogel polymers increases with their water content, so does their tendency to dehydrate. Thus, their oxygen transmissibility is limited by the need to make these lenses thicker in order to maintain the integrity of the tear compartment and avoid corneal epithelial desiccation in dry environments.

A new generation of high-Dk, low-water-content silicone hydrogels has been introduced for extended wear. The oxygen transmission of these lenses is a function of their silicon (rather than water) content and is sufficient to meet the oxygen needs of most corneas during sleep. The surfaces of these lenses require special coatings to mask their hydrophobic properties.

Other clinically important properties of contact lens hydrogels include light transmission, modulus (resistance to flexure), rate of recovery from deformation, elasticity, tear resistance, dimensional sensitivity to pH and the osmolality in the soaking solution and tears, chemical stability, deposit resistance, and surface water-binding properties.

Manufacturing

Several methods are used to manufacture contact lenses. Some contact lenses are spin-cast, a technique popularized with the first soft contact lenses. With this technique, the liquid plastic polymer is placed in a mold that is spun on a centrifuge; the shape of the mold and the rate of spin determine the final shape of the contact lens. Soft contact lenses can also be made on a lathe, starting with a hard dry plastic button; this is similar to how RGP lenses are made. Once the soft lens lathe process is complete, the lens is hydrated in saline solution to create the "softness" associated with these lenses. Lathes are manually operated or automated. In either case, very complex, variable shapes can be made that provide correction for many different types of refractive error; lenses can even be customized to meet individual needs.

With the introduction of disposable contact lenses—and thus the need to manufacture large quantities of lenses—cast molding was introduced. With this technique, different metal dies, or molds, are used for specific refractive corrections. Liquid polymer is injected into the mold and then polymerized to create a soft contact lens of the desired dimensions. This process is completely automated from start to finish, enabling cost-effective production of large quantities of lenses.

Scleral contact lenses have very large diameters and touch the sclera 2 to 4 mm beyond the limbus. They have been available for years but, because they were originally made of PMMA—and thus oxygen impermeable—the lenses were not comfortable. Now, with newer RGP materials, interest in these lenses has resurfaced, especially for fitting abnormal corneas. These lenses are made from a mold taken of the anterior surface of the eye using an alginate mix that hardens in the shape of the ocular surface. This alginate mold is then used to make a plaster mold, which, in turn, is used to make the actual scleral lens.

Patient Examination and Contact Lens Selection

As in all patient care, a complete history and eye examination are needed to rule out serious ocular problems such as glaucoma, macular degeneration, and so on.

Patient Examination

Specific information is needed to select a contact lens for a particular patient. This includes the patient's daily activities (desk work, driving, and so on) and reason for using contact lenses (full-time vision, sports only, social events only, changing eye color, avoiding use of reading glasses, and so on). If a patient is already a lens user, the fitter must also determine how many years the patient has worn contact lenses, the current type of lens worn, the wear schedule, the care system used, and if the patient has any past or present problems with lens use.

Patient history that could suggest an increased risk for contact lens use includes diabetes mellitus, especially if uncontrolled; immunosuppression—for example, from AIDS; use of systemic medications, such as oral contraceptives, antihistamines, antidepressants, immunosuppressants (for example, prednisone); chronic use of topical medications such as corticosteroids; or environmental exposure to dust, vapors, or chemicals. Other relative contraindications to contact lens use include an inability to handle and/ or care for contact lenses; monocularity; abnormal lid function, such as with Bell's palsy; severe dry eye; and corneal neovascularization.

Key areas to note during the slit-lamp examination include the eyelids (to rule out blepharitis), lid movement and blink, tear film, the ocular surface (to rule out dry eye), corneal neovascularization, allergy, and so on. Through refraction and keratometry, the ophthalmologist can determine if there is significant corneal and/or lenticular astigmatism or irregular astigmatism, which could suggest other pathologies, such as keratoconus, that would require further evaluation.

Contact Lens Selection

Soft contact lenses are currently the most frequently prescribed and worn lenses in the United States (see Fig 5-1). They can be classified according to a variety of characteristics (Table 5-3). With this variety, selecting the appropriate lens for each patient may be difficult. Typically, an experienced fitter knows the characteristics of several lenses that cover the needs of most patients.

The main advantages of soft contact lenses are their shorter period of adaptation and high level of comfort. They are available with many parameters so that all regular refractive errors are covered. Also, the ease of fitting soft lenses makes them the first choice of many practitioners. See Figure 5-7.

Table 5-3 Soft Lens Characteristics

Wear schedule	Daily wear (DW), extended wear (EW), flexible
Replacement schedule	Conventional, daily disposable, disposable (1 to 2 weeks), frequent replacement (1 to 3 months)
Manufacturing method	Cast-molded, lathe-cut, spin-cast
Water content	Low (under 45%), medium (46%–58%), high (59%–79%)
Oxygen transmissibility	Dk/L: greater with higher water and/or silicone content
FDA classification (Table 5-4)	4 groups based on ionic characteristics and water content
Lens parameters	Base curve, diameter, thickness
Refractive correction	Spherical, toric, bifocal
Color	Handling tint, or enhancing or changing eye color
UV blocking	With or without UV blocker

Table 5-4 FDA Contact Lens Classification

Group 1	Low water content (<50%), nonionic polymers
Group 2	High water content (>50%), nonionic polymers
Group 3	Low water content (<50%), ionic polymers
Group 4	High water content (>50%), ionic polymers

The decision about a replacement schedule may be made on a cost basis. Conventional lenses (changed every 6 to 12 months) are often the least expensive, but disposable lenses and conventional lenses that are replaced more frequently are typically associated with less irritation, such as red eyes, and more consistent quality of vision. One-day daily disposable lenses offer the least need for contact lens care, and thus less expense is involved for care solutions.

Daily wear is the most favored wear pattern in the United States. Extended wear—that is, leaving the lens in while sleeping—is less popular, primarily because of reports from the 1980s of the increased incidence of keratitis with EW lenses. However, new materials have been approved for EW that have far greater oxygen permeability (Dk = 60 to 140), which may decrease the risk of infection (although it is difficult to document the incidence because serious infections are rare with all lenses used today). Patients who want EW should understand the risks and benefits of this modality and the need for careful contact lens care and replacement; they should also know the signs and symptoms of eye problems that require the attention of their physician.

Poggio EC, Glynn RJ, Schein OD, et al. The incidence of ulcerative keratitis among users of daily-wear and extended-wear soft contact lenses. *N Eng J Med.* 1989;321:779–783.

Schein OD, Glynn RJ, Poggio EC, et al. The relative risk of ulcerativekeratitis among users of daily-wear and extended-wear soft contact lenses. A case-control study. Microbial Keratitis Study Group. *N Eng J Med.* 1989;321:773–778.

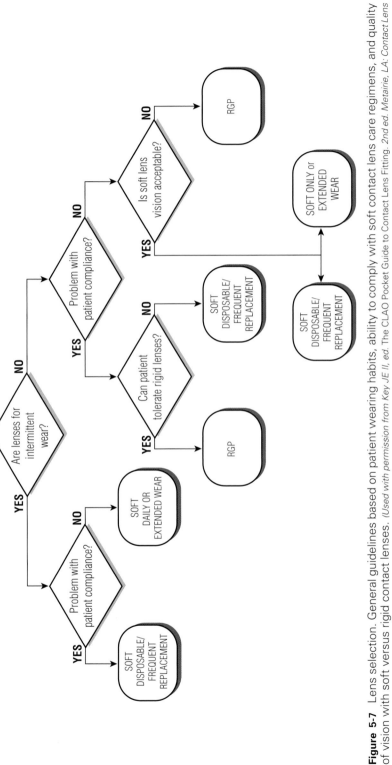

Figure 5-7 Lens selection. General guidelines based on patient wearing habits, ability to comply with soft contact lens care regimens, and quality of vision with soft versus rigid contact lenses. *(Used with permission from Key JE II, ed. The CLAO Pocket Guide to Contact Lens Fitting. 2nd ed. Metairie, LA: Contact Lens Association of Ophthalmologists; 1998. Redrawn by Christine Gralapp.)*

Rigid contact lenses continue to be used today, but by a small percentage of lens wearers in the United States (<20%). The original hard contact lenses, made of PMMA, are rarely used now due to their oxygen impermeability. Today, commonly used RGP materials include fluoronated silicone acrylate with Dks from the 20s to over 250 and manufactured with a great variety of parameters. Modern RGP lenses are approved for daily wear—and some even for extended, overnight wear. Because of the manufacturing costs and the many parameters available, RGP lenses are not usually offered in disposable packs, but yearly replacement is recommended. The main advantages of RGP lenses are the quality of vision they offer and the ease with which they correct astigmatism (Fig 5-8). The main disadvantages are initial discomfort, a longer period of adaptation, and greater difficulty in fitting. Today, RGP lenses are more likely to be provided by individual practitioners with experience and an interest in fitting more challenging patients and not by chain optical stores.

Table 5-5 lists the comparative advantages of soft contact lenses and RGP lenses.

Contact Lens Fitting

The goals of lens fitting include patient satisfaction—good vision that does not fluctuate with blinking or eye movement—and good fit—the lens is centered and moves slightly with each blink. The specifics of what constitutes a good fit vary between soft and RGP lenses and involve the "art" of contact lens fitting. For example, a patient who wants contact lenses only for skiing or tennis is probably best fitted with soft contact lenses because of the rapid adaptation possible with these lenses. On the other hand, a patient with 3 D of astigmatism will likely get the best vision with RGP contact lenses.

Soft Contact Lenses

Soft contact lenses are comfortable primarily because the material is soft and the diameter is large, extending beyond the cornea to the sclera. Most manufacturers make a specific style lens that varies in only 1 parameter, such as a lens that comes in 3 base curves, with all other parameters being the same. The first lens is fit empirically; often the lens chosen is one that the manufacturer reports "will fit 80% of patients." Then, based on the patient's comfort and vision and the slit-lamp evaluation of the fit, the lens may be changed for another base curve and then reevaluated.

A good soft contact lens fit is often described as having "3-point touch," meaning the lens touches the surface of the eye at the corneal apex and at the limbus on either side of the cornea. (In cross section, the lens would touch the limbus at 2 places.) To find a light 3-point touch and reach this goal, one may need to choose a lens with a different sagittal depth. The sagittal depth of a lens can be altered by changing the lens diameter and/or changing the base curve. If the base curve is kept unchanged, as the diameter is increased, the sagittal depth increases and the lens will fit more tightly—that is, there will be less lens movement. If the diameter is kept constant and the base curve is decreased, the sagittal depth increases and, again, the fit is tightened (Table 5-6).

In evaluating the soft lens fit, note the lens movement and centration. In a good fit, the lens will move about 0.5 to 1.0 mm with upward gaze or blink or with gentle pressure

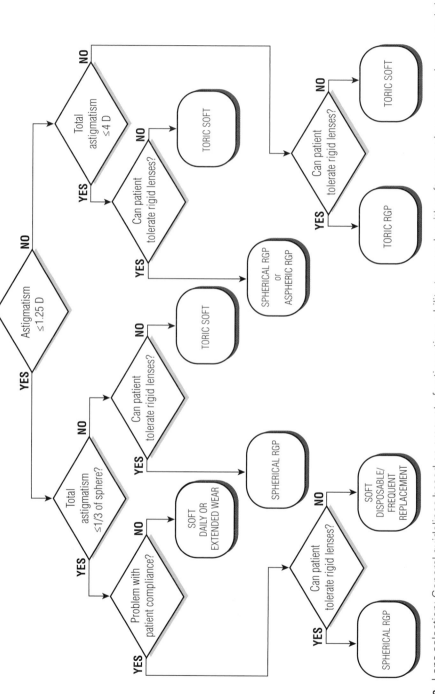

Figure 5-8 Lens selection: General guidelines based on amount of astigmatism, ability to comply with soft contact lens care regimens, and ability to tolerate rigid contact lenses. *(Used with permission from Key JE II, ed. The CLAO Pocket Guide to Contact Lens Fitting. 2nd ed. Metairie, LA: Contact Lens Association of Ophthalmologists; 1998. Redrawn by Christine Gralapp.)*

Table 5-5 Comparative Advantages of Soft and RGP Contact Lenses

Soft Contact Lenses Advantages	RGP Contact Lenses Advantages
Immediately comfortable	Clear and sharp quality of vision
Shorter period of adaptation	Correct small and large amounts of astigmatism
Flexible wear schedule	Ease of handling
Less sensitivity to environmental foreign bodies, dust	Acceptable for dry eye patients, ocular surface disease abnormalities, and so on
Available as disposable and for frequent lens replacement use	Stability and durability
Can change eye color	Ease of contact lens care
	Correct irregular astigmatism

Table 5-6 Adjusting Soft Contact Lens Fit

To create a looser fit	To create a tighter fit
• Decrease the sagittal depth	• Increase the sagittal depth
• Choose a flatter base curve	• Choose a steeper base curve
• Choose a smaller diameter	• Choose a larger diameter

on the lower eyelid to move the lens. A tight lens will not move at all and a loose lens will move too much. By evaluating a patient's vision and comfort, slit-lamp findings (lens movement, lens edge, limbal injection), and keratometry mires, one can determine if the fit is adequate, too loose, or too tight (Table 5-7).

Once a fit is deemed adequate, an overrefraction is performed to check the contact lens power. The power is changed if necessary while other parameters are kept the same.

When the initial fitting process is complete, the patient needs to be taught how to insert and remove the contact lenses, instructed in their use and care, and taught the signs and symptoms of eye emergencies. Follow-up care includes assessing symptoms and vision and performing a slit-lamp examination. The follow-up appointment is usually scheduled for 1 week after the initial fitting (for extended wear, an additional visit is usually scheduled for 24 to 48 hours after the first use of the lens); a second office visit is often scheduled for 1 to 6 months later, depending on the type of lens, the patient's experience with contact lenses, and the patient's ocular status.

At the end of the soft contact lens fitting process, the final lens parameters should be clearly identified (Table 5-8). Also, the chart should note any signs and symptoms of eye infection, any recommendation for lens wear (eg, DW, EW) and lens care, and any follow-up plans.

RGP Contact Lenses

RGP lenses, with their small overall diameter, should center over the cornea but move freely with each blink to allow tear exchange. Unlike with soft contact lenses, the lens parameters are often not determined by the manufacturer but are individualized for each

Table 5-7 Evaluating Soft Contact Lens Fit

Loose Fit	Tight Fit
Excessive movement	No lens movement
Poor centration, lens easily dislocates off the cornea	Centered
Lens edge standoff	Lens edge "digs in"
Blurred mires after a blink	Mires clear with blink
Fluctuating vision	Good vision initially
Continuing lens awareness	Initially lens comfortable, but increasing awareness with continued use
Air bubbles under the lens	Limbal–scleral injection at lens edge

Table 5-8 Soft Lens Parameters

Parameter	Common Abbreviation	Typical Range of Values
Overall diameter	OAD	12.5 to 16.0 mm
Base curve	BC	8.0 to 9.5 mm
Center thickness	CT	0.04 to 0.20 mm (varies with the power of the lens and is set by the manufacturer)
Prescription	RX	Sphere and astigmatism, if any, in D
Manufacturer		Company name and lens style

patient—this makes RGP fitting more challenging. However, for a normal eye, standard parameters are typically used and, as with soft lenses, a patient is fit from trial lenses. The fit is optimized first; then the vision is optimized by overrefraction (Table 5-9).

Some of the key issues in RGP fitting are briefly reviewed in the following sections, but a complete coverage of the topic is beyond the scope of this chapter.

Base curve

Because RGP lenses maintain their shape when placed on a cornea (unlike soft contact lenses), a tear layer is formed between the cornea and the RGP lens that varies in shape, depending on the base curve and whether or not there is corneal astigmatism. The tear layer, usually called the *tear lens*, is one of the parameters used to determine best contact lens fit as well as needed contact lens power.

The type of fit is determined by the relationship of the base curve to the cornea's curvature (K; see Fig 5-6). In selecting the initial base curve, the following options are available:

- Apical alignment (on K): The base curve matches that of the cornea (see Fig 5-6B).
- Apical clearance (steeper than K): The base curve has a steeper fit (smaller radius of curvature, smaller number in millimeters, and thus more curved) than the cornea (see Fig 5-6A).

- Apical bearing (flatter than K): The base curve has a flatter fit (larger radius of curvature, larger number in millimeters, and thus less curved) than the cornea (see Fig 5-6C).

Position

The most common type of RGP fit is the apical alignment fit (see Fig 5-6B), where the upper edge of the lens fits under the upper eyelid (Fig 5-9), thus allowing the lens to move with each blink, enhancing tear exchange, and decreasing lens sensation because the lid does not "hit" the lens edge with each blink.

A central or interpalpebral fit is achieved when the lens rests between the upper and lower eyelids. To achieve this fit, the lens is given a steeper fit than K (apical clearance; see Fig 5-6A) to try to minimize lens movement and keep the lens centered over the cornea. Typically with this type of fit, the diameter of the lens is smaller than in an apical alignment fit, the base curve is steeper than K, and the lens has a thin edge. There is also greater lens sensation because the lid "hits" the lens with each blink. The resulting sensation discourages normal blinking and often leads to an unconscious incomplete blinking pattern and reduced blink rate. Peripheral corneal staining at the 3 o'clock and 9 o'clock positions may be a consequence of poor wetting. This type of fit is best if a patient has a very large interpalpebral opening and/or astigmatism greater than about 1.75 D, and/or against-the-rule astigmatism.

A flatter than K fit (apical bearing) is not typically used with normal eyes.

Table 5-9 RGP Lens Parameters

Parameter	Common Abbreviation	Range of Normal Values
Overall diameter	OAD	8.0–11.5 mm
Optic zone diameter	OZD	7.0–8.5 mm
Peripheral curve width	PCW	0.1–1.0 mm
Base curve	BC	7.0–8.5 mm
Center thickness	CT	0.08–0.30 mm
Prescription	RX	Any power required

Figure 5-9 The most common and most comfortable type of RGP fit is apical alignment, where the upper edge of the lens fits under the upper eyelid. *(Reprinted from Albert DM, Jakobiec FA, eds.* Principles and Practice of Ophthalmology. *Philadelphia: Saunders; 1994;5:3630. Redrawn by Christine Gralapp.)*

Other lens parameters

With an RGP lens, the diameter needs to be chosen so that when the lens moves, it does not ride off the cornea; typically the diameter is about 2 mm less than the corneal diameter. Central thickness and peripheral curves can also be selected, but often the lens laboratory will put in standard parameters. The lens edge is important in enhancing tear exchange and maintaining lens position, as well as providing comfort. A thicker edge helps maintain the lens position under the upper lid in apical alignment fitting; a thin edge maintains centration and comfort for an interpalpebral fit.

Power

The tear lens, as previously noted, is the lens formed by the posterior surface of the RGP and the anterior surface of the cornea. Its "power" is determined by the base curve:

- on K: The tear lens has plano power.
- steeper than K: The tear lens has + power.
- flatter than K: The tear lens has − power.

This leads to the rule of thumb for calculating the needed contact lens power from the spectacle sphere power and the base curve of the RGP:

- SAM = steeper add minus
- FAP = flatter add plus

For example, if the spectacle prescription is $-3.25 - 0.75 \times 180$, and the Ks are 42.25/43.00 @ 90, and the base curve is slightly flatter than K at 41.75 D (ie, 0.50 D flatter), then, per the FAP rule, the contact lens power should be: $-3.75 + 0.50 = -3.25$ D.

The lens power can also be determined empirically by placing a trial lens of known power on the eye, determining the overrefraction, and then adding the lens power and the overrefraction power.

Fit

Three criteria are used to determine a good fit:

1. quality of vision
2. lens movement
3. fluorescein evaluation

Overrefraction determines if a power change is needed. Vision should be stable before and immediately after a blink. Stable vision ensures that the lens is covering the optical axis, even when it moves with normal blinking.

Because the peripheral zone of the cornea flattens toward the limbus, the central vault of a contact lens is determined by its base curve and diameter. Steepening the base curve (ie, decreasing its radius of curvature) obviously increases the vault of a contact lens. However, increasing the diameter of a lens also increases its central vault (see Fig 5-3).

Lens position in the alignment fitting should be such that the lens rides high, with the upper one third or so of the contact lens under the upper lid (see Fig 5-9). With each blink, the lens should move as the lid moves. Insufficient movement means the lens is too tight, so the base curve should be flattened (larger number [in mm]) or the diameter made smaller. Excessive movement means the lens is too loose, so the base curve should be steepened (smaller number [in mm]) or the lens diameter made larger.

Evaluating the fluorescein pattern with a cobalt blue light at the slit lamp can help in evaluating RGP fit (Fig 5-10). If there is apical clearing of the cornea, pooling or a bright green area will be noted; if the RGP lens is touching the cornea, dark areas will be observed (Fig 5-11).

Once the lens parameters are determined, the information is given to a laboratory that typically makes the lens on a lathe to the specific specifications. When the lens is received, the major parameters must be checked: base curve (use an optic spherometer, such as Radiuscope), lens diameter, and lens power (use a lensmeter).

Although RGP lens fitting can be more challenging than soft lens fitting, the use of trial lenses and consultation with the laboratory that will make the lens can lead to a good fit on most patients with a normal anterior segment.

Toric Soft Contact Lenses

It is estimated that 20% of the US population has significant astigmatism, but with today's contact lenses, the astigmatism can be corrected.

When considering a contact lens for a patient with astigmatism, the first question to ask is whether a toric lens is needed. The type of lens usually depends on the amount of astigmatism (Table 5-10).

Soft toric contact lenses are now readily available in several fitting designs. The astigmatic correction can be on the front lens surface—*front toric contact lenses*—or on the back surface—*back toric contact lenses.* To prevent lens rotation, several manufacturing techniques are used: adding prism ballast—that is, placing extra lens material on the bottom edge of the lens; truncating or removing the bottom of the lens to form a straight edge that will align with the lower lid; or creating thin zones—that is, making lenses with a thin zone on the top and bottom so that eyelid pressure can keep the lens in the appropriate position. Most toric soft lenses use either prism ballast or thin zones to provide stabilization and comfort.

Fitting soft toric lenses is similar to fitting other soft lenses, except that lens rotation must also be evaluated. Toric lenses typically have a mark to note the 6 o'clock position. If the lens fits properly, the lens will be in that position. Note that the mark does not indicate the astigmatic axis; it is used only to determine proper fit. If slit-lamp examination shows that the lens mark is rotated away from the 6 o'clock axis, the amount of rotation should be noted, in degrees (1 clock-hour equals 30°) (Fig 5-12). The rule of thumb for adjusting for lens rotation is LARS (left add, right subtract). When ordering a lens, use the adjusted axis (using LARS—that is, adding or subtracting from the spectacle refraction axis), instead of the cylinder axis of the refraction. (See Clinical Example 5-4.)

Fluorescein pattern of a good fit with minimal apical clearance.

Fluorescein pattern demonstrating a flat fit.

Fluorescein pattern showing a steep fit.

Against-the-rule astigmatic band.

Figure 5-10 Examples of fluorescein patterns in contact lens fitting. *(Photographs courtesy of Perry Rosenthal, MD.)*

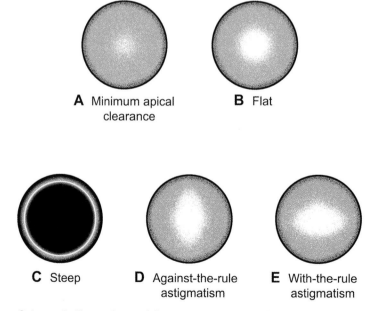

A Minimum apical clearance

B Flat

C Steep

D Against-the-rule astigmatism

E With-the-rule astigmatism

Figure 5-11 Schematic illustrations of fluorescein patterns. See also Figure 5-10. *(Courtesy of Perry Rosenthal, MD.)*

Table 5-10 Astigmatism and Lens Fitting

Amount of Astigmatism	First Choice of Lens
Under 1 D	Spherical soft or RGP
1 D to 2 D	Toric soft contact lens or spherical RGP
2 D to 3 D	Custom soft toric or spherical RGP
Over 3 D	Toric RGP or custom soft toric

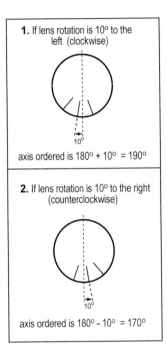

1. If lens rotation is 10° to the left (clockwise)

10°

axis ordered is 180° + 10° = 190°

2. If lens rotation is 10° to the right (counterclockwise)

10°

axis ordered is 180° – 10° = 170°

Figure 5-12 Evaluating lens rotation in fitting soft toric contact lenses using the LARS rule of thumb (*left add, right subtract*). The spectacle prescription in this example is −2.00 −1.00 × 180°. (*Used with permission from Key JE II, ed. The CLAO Pocket Guide to Contact Lens Fitting. 2nd ed. Metairie, LA: Contact Lens Association of Ophthalmologists; 1998. Redrawn by Christine Gralapp.*)

CLINICAL EXAMPLE 5-4

A patient with a refraction of −3.00 −1.00 × 180 is fitted with a toric contact lens with astigmatic axis given as 180°. Slit-lamp examination shows the lens is well centered, but lens markings show that the "6 o'clock mark" is located at the 7 o'clock position. What axis should be ordered for this eye?

Because the trial contact lens rotated 1 clock-hour, or 30°, to the left, using LARS, the contact lens ordered should be 180° + 30° = 210° or 30°: −3.00 −1.00 × 30°.

Bifocal Contact Lenses

Presbyopia affects everyone over age 40. Thus, as contact lens wearers age, their accommodation needs must be considered as well. Three options are available for these patients:

- use of reading glasses with contact lenses
- monovision
- bifocal contact lenses (both soft and RGP)

The first option of using reading glasses over the contact lenses has the advantages of being simple and inexpensive. The second option, monovision, involves correcting one eye for distance and the other eye for near. Many patients tolerate this without difficulty, although some note monocular blurring initially. To work well, adaptation requires interocular suppression, which is easier to achieve with patients who have only 1.00 or 1.50 D difference between their eyes. Typically, the dominant eye is corrected for distance, although often trial and error is needed to determine which eye is best for distance correction. For most tasks, no overcorrection is needed, but for driving and other critical functions, overcorrection is recommended to provide the best-corrected vision in each eye.

The third option for patients with presbyopia is to use bifocal contact lenses. There are 2 types of bifocal lenses:

- alternating vision lenses (segmented or concentric)
- simultaneous vision lenses (aspheric or diffractive)

Alternating vision bifocal contact lenses are similar in function to bifocal spectacles in that there are separate areas for distance and near, and the retina receives light from only 1 image location at a time (Fig 5-13) *Segmented contact lenses* have 2 areas, top and bottom, like bifocal spectacles, whereas *concentric contact lenses* have 2 rings, or tines, one for far and one for near. For segmented contact lenses, the position on the eye is critical and must change as the patient switches from distance to near viewing. The lower

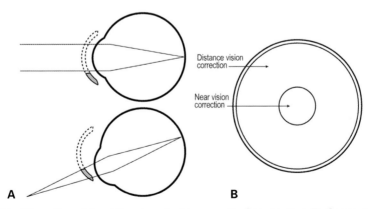

Figure 5-13 Alternating vision bifocal contact lenses. **A,** Segmented. **B,** Concentric (annular). *(Used with permission from Key JE II, ed. The CLAO Pocket Guide to Contact Lens Fitting. 2nd ed. Metairie, LA: Contact Lens Association of Ophthalmologists; 1998. Redrawn by Christine Gralapp.)*

eyelid controls the lens position so that as a person looks down, the lens stays up and the visual axis moves into the reading portion of the lens. Maintenance of the proper lens position is critical, and therefore such lens designs do not work for all patients.

Simultaneous vision bifocal contact lenses provide the retina with light from both distance and near points in space at the same time, which requires the patient's brain to ignore the reduction in contrast (Fig 5-14; see also Fig 5-13B). Usually there is some compromise, either of the distance or near; the compromise is greater for higher adds.

The optical design of 1 type of simultaneous vision contact lens is *aspheric*, or *multifocal*, as with IOLs. Aspheric surfaces change power from the center to the periphery—minus lenses decrease in power from the center to the periphery, whereas plus lenses increase (see Fig 5-14A).

Another type of simultaneous vision lens has a *diffractive* design (Fig 5-14B). This lens has concentric grooves on its back surface, such that the light rays are split into 2 focal packages: near and far. The diffractive surfaces reduce incoming light by 20% or more, which reduces vision in dim lighting. These lenses are less sensitive to pupil size than aspheric multifocal designs, but they must be well centered for best vision.

No one style works for all patients, and most require highly motivated patients and fitters for success. Most fitters must be experienced with at least 2 styles in order to offer alternatives for the best vision and comfort for their patients. Despite the availability of presbyopia contact lenses, however, monovision is still the most common approach, probably because of the ease of fitting and the high acceptance among patients with presbyopia.

Keratoconus and the Abnormal Cornea

Contact lenses often provide better vision than spectacles by masking irregular astigmatism (higher orders of aberration). For mild or moderate irregularities, soft, soft toric, or custom soft toric contact lenses are used. Large irregularities typically require RGP lenses to "cover" the abnormal surface. As with nonastigmatic eyes, fitters should first find the best alignment fit and then determine the optimal power. Three-point touch can

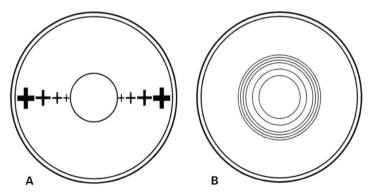

Figure 5-14 Simultaneous vision bifocal contact lenses. **A,** Aspheric, or multifocal. **B,** Diffractive. *(Used with permission from Key JE II, ed.* The CLAO Pocket Guide to Contact Lens Fitting. *2nd ed. Metairie, LA: Contact Lens Association of Ophthalmologists; 1998. Redrawn by Christine Gralapp.)*

be successfully used for larger cones to ensure lens centration and stability: slight apical and paracentral touch or bearing (dark areas on the fluorescein evaluation; Fig 5-15). To have a lens vault slightly over the cone, the apical clearance fitting technique can also be tried. Fitting the abnormal cornea takes an experienced fitter, an understanding patient, and willingness on the part of both the patient and fitter to spend the time needed to optimize the fit. When ordering these lenses, it is best to request a warranty or exchange option, because typically several lenses will be tried before the final lens parameters are found.

Some specialized RGP lenses have been developed specifically for keratoconus. Most provide a steep central posterior curve to vault over the cone and flatter peripheral curves to approximate the more normal peripheral curvature. Among these style lenses are the Soper cone lens, Menicon lens, McGuire lens, NiCone lens, and Rose-K lens. Larger RGP contact lenses with larger optical zones (diameters >11 mm) are now available for keratoconus and posttransplant fitting (intralimbic contact lenses). An alternative approach is to have a hard central lens with a skirt of soft lens; this provides the good vision of an RGP lens and the comfort of a soft lens. The SoftPerm lens is an example of this approach, but it often ends up too tight (little lens movement and tear exchange) for long-term use. Another alternative is piggyback lenses, where a soft lens is fitted to the cornea and an RGP lens is placed on top of it; the 2 lenses are used together in each eye. For a very abnormal cornea that is unable to accommodate any of these designs, scleral contact lenses made of gas-permeable materials have come back into use and, for some patients, provide good vision and comfort and preclude the need for transplant or other eye surgery (see the following section).

Gas-Permeable Scleral Contact Lenses

Scleral lenses have unique advantages over other types of contact lenses in rehabilitating the vision of eyes with damaged corneas: Because they are entirely supported by the sclera, their centration and positional stability are independent of distorted corneal topography, and they avoid contact with a damaged corneal surface. Moreover, these lenses create an artificial tear-filled space over the cornea, thereby providing a protective function for corneas suffering from ocular surface disease.

Scleral lenses consist of a central optic that vaults the cornea and a peripheral haptic that rests on the scleral surface (Fig 5-16). The shape of the back-surface optic is chosen so as to minimize the volume of the fluid compartment while avoiding corneal contact

Figure 5-15 Three-point touch in keratoconus. *(Photograph courtesy of Perry Rosenthal, MD.)*

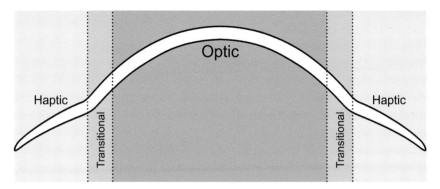

Figure 5-16 Scleral contact lens. *(Reprinted from Albert DM, Jakobiec FA, eds.* Principles and Practice of Oph-thalmology. *Philadelphia: Saunders; 1994;5:3643. Redrawn by Christine Gralapp.)*

after the lenses have settled. The posterior haptic surface is configured to minimize lo-calized scleral compression; the transitional zone that joins the optic and haptic surfaces is designed to vault the limbus.

Unfortunately, the advantages of PMMA scleral lenses as a vision rehabilitating mo-dality were outweighed by the damage they caused through corneal asphyxiation. The introduction of highly oxygen-permeable rigid polymers provided an opportunity to overcome this limitation. However, a second obstacle to safe use of scleral lenses is their propensity to become sucked onto the eye. This occurs when some of the fluid behind the lens is squeezed out during eye movement and forceful blinking, thereby generating negative pressure that pulls the lens into the eye. Unless it is immediately relieved, this process becomes self-perpetuating and leads to massive chemosis and corneal edema.

Traditional scleral lenses avoided suction through holes drilled in the periphery of the optic. These holes permit the aspiration of air bubbles that replace the volume of fluid lost by lens compression and thereby prevent suction. These lenses are known as *air-ventilated lenses.* However, air bubbles desiccate the underlying corneal epithelium, which is especially damaging to corneas suffering from ocular surface disease. Further-more, air-ventilated scleral lenses require a more precise lens–cornea relationship to avoid the intrusion of air bubbles in the visual axis.

Fluid-ventilated gas-permeable scleral lenses depend on tear–fluid interchange to prevent suction. Their posterior haptic surfaces are designed to create channels large enough to allow tears to be aspirated into the fluid compartment of the lens between the haptic and scleral surfaces but small enough to exclude air. The requisite tear–fluid in-terchange must be confirmed in every case via observation of fluorescein dye placed outside the lens seeping under the haptic into the fluid compartment after the lenses have been worn for at least 2 hours. The fitting method for these lenses uses a series of diagnostic lenses with known vaults, diameters, powers, and haptic design.

Indications

Gas-permeable scleral lenses have 2 primary indications: (1) correcting abnormal regular and irregular astigmatism in eyes that preclude the use of rigid corneal contact lenses and (2) managing ocular surface diseases that benefit from the constant presence of a protective, lubricating layer of oxygenated artificial tears.

Whenever possible, it is more convenient and less costly to correct irregular astigmatism with rigid corneal contact lenses. However, the abnormal corneal topography of many eyes may preclude adequate corneal centration, stability, or tolerance. Conditions under which this may occur include pellucid degeneration, Terrien marginal degeneration, keratoconus, Ehlers-Danlos syndrome, elevated corneal scars, and astigmatism following penetrating keratoplasty.

Fluid-ventilated gas-permeable scleral contact lenses are especially useful in managing ocular surface diseases, many of which have no other definitive treatment options. These include complications of neurotrophic corneas, ocular complications of Stevens-Johnson syndrome, tear layer disorders, and ocular cicatricial pemphigoid. The improvement in the quality of life that these lenses offer is most dramatic for patients suffering from Stevens-Johnson syndrome. Through protection of the fragile epithelium of diseased corneas from the abrasive effects of the keratinized lid margins associated with distichiasis and trichiasis and from exposure to air, the disabling photophobia is remarkably attenuated. Moreover, these lenses have proved to be especially valuable in accelerating the healing of persistent epithelial defects that are refractory to all other available treatment strategies. For these unfortunate victims, the accompanying improvement in vision is a bonus.

Therapeutic Lens Usage

Therapeutic, or bandage, contact lenses are used to enhance epithelial healing, prevent epithelial erosions, or control surface-generated pain; they are not used for their optical properties. Usually, soft contact lenses with plano power are used. They are worn on an extended basis without removal to decrease irritation to the ocular surface. Because the lenses are used on an EW basis and fit on abnormal corneas, Dk is high to prevent hypoxia. Fitting principles are similar to those of other soft lenses, although for therapeutic use, a tighter fit is usually sought—any lens movement could injure the healing epithelium further. Some fitters prefer high-water-content lenses, but probably high Dk is the critical factor in lens selection. The use of disposable lenses allows for easy lens replacement, such as during follow-up examinations.

Conditions and circumstances where bandage contact lenses might be useful include

- bullous keratopathy (for pain control)
- recurrent erosions
- Bell's palsy
- keratitis, such as filamentary, post–chemical exposure, and so on
- corneal dystrophy with erosions
- postsurgery (corneal transplant, LASIK, PRK, and so on)
- nonhealing epithelial defect, such as geographic herpes keratitis, slow-healing ulcer, or abrasion
- lid abnormalities (entropion, eyelid lag, trichiasis, and so on)
- bleb leak posttrabeculectomy

At with the bandage contact lens fitting, patients should be made aware of the signs and symptoms of infection, because the risk of infection will be increased given the abnormal surface covered by a foreign body, the lens.

Collagen shields are a special type of therapeutic lens that are biodegradable. They are typically made of collagen extracted from pig sclera and processed in soft-type lens configurations. Shields can last for 12, 24, or 72 hours, depending on the cross-linking of the collagen, but actual resident times will vary from patient to patient. Because they are biodegradable, they do not have to be removed and of course cannot be reused. Collagen shields offer no refractive power and can decrease best vision slightly because, once hydrated, they are translucent. Fitting these shields is a straightforward process: once the dry shield is hydrated in an aqueous solution, "one size fits all." When placed on the eye, it will conform to the anterior surface shape and usually does not move with eye blinking. Which solution is used to hydrate the shield—normal saline, BSS, or antibiotics—depends on its use. Collagen shields hydrated with antibiotics, for example, are sometimes used after cataract surgery. Being biodegradable, they are helpful only for short-term therapeutic treatments.

Orthokeratology and Corneal Reshaping

Orthokeratology generally refers to the process of reshaping the cornea and thus reducing myopia by wearing hard contact lenses designed to flatten the central cornea for a period of time after the lenses are removed. The shape change is similar to that resulting from laser procedures for myopia. Orthokeratology, however, is reversible and noninvasive and no tissue is removed. Experience in the 1970s with this procedure was disappointing: it was unpredictable, the amount of correction that resulted (up to 1.5 D) was small, it induced irregular astigmatism, the lenses were difficult to fit, multiple lenses were needed per patient per eye, and extensive follow-up was required. These problems led to unfavorable publicity about this procedure, and it was only rarely used.

However, advances in the 1990s in lens design and material have led to a resurgence of interest in orthokeratology, and the FDA has approved lenses for myopia correction. The introduction of the so-called *reverse geometry designs* and the strategy of overnight wear have improved results. The shape of the central zone (molding surface) of these lenses is calculated to be somewhat flatter than is needed for the cornea to correct the eye's myopia. The intermediate zones are steeper to provide a peripheral bearing platform, and the peripheral zones are designed to create the necessary clearance and edge lift (Fig 5-17).

Lens centration is key to the effectiveness of these lenses (Fig 5-18). It requires them to be supported by circumferential peripheral bearing at the junction of the intermediate and peripheral zones. It also requires that the lenses incorporate a design mechanism that enables the fitter to adjust the molding pressure independently of the central shape of the molding surfaces. Because the lenses are worn overnight, their oxygen transmissibility must be high; consequently, they are generally made of very high Dk materials (100 or greater).

Figure 5-17 Cross section of a CRT lens, showing lens centration. *(Used with permission from Paragon Vision Sciences, Mesa, Arizona.)*

Figure 5-18 Typical fluorescein pattern of a well-fitting CRT lens. *(Used with permission from Paragon Vision Sciences, Mesa, Arizona.)*

The FDA has approved the corneal refractive lens (CRT, Paragon Vision Sciences) for overnight wear to correct myopia up to 6.00 D ± 0.75 D of astigmatism. The fitting is simple and is based on the manifest refraction and keratometry readings and a nomogram. Typically, once a good fit is achieved—that is, centered, with a bull's-eye fluorescing pattern—that lens is the right one for the patient (Fig 5-19). Refractive change is rapid, usually occurring after less than 2 weeks of wear. The lens is worn only during sleep and provides good vision at night, if needed, and good vision all day without correction. It is not entirely clear how the CRT lens works, but central corneal thinning is noted with epithelial thinning or compression.

Although the CRT lens is approved for all ages, and FDA data show a high safety and efficacy record, corneal ulcers have been reported with other overnight orthokeratology lenses. However, nearly all of these cases are poorly documented in terms of contact lens–fitting technique, lens material, and follow-up care; in addition, most have occurred in Asia, where the education of practitioners and patients may be suboptimal. Nonetheless, CRT and other orthokeratology lenses offer an alternative to permanent laser correction that is less invasive and reversible and may appeal to risk-adverse patients and young people whose refractive errors may not have stabilized yet. There is also

Figure 5-19 Typical topography post–CRT use demonstrating ring pattern. *(Used with permission from Paragon Vision Sciences, Mesa, Arizona.)*

ongoing research to see if correcting myopia in children with these lenses may decrease the progression of myopia; clearly, well-designed clinical trails are needed to address this use.

Custom Contact Lenses and Wavefront Technology

A normal cornea is generally steepest near its geometric center; beyond this, the surface flattens. The steep area is known as the *apical zone* (or *optic cap*), and its center is the *corneal apex.* Outside the apical zone, which is approximately 3 to 4 mm in diameter, the rate of peripheral flattening can vary significantly in the different corneal meridians of the same eye, between the eyes of the same patient, and in the eyes of different patients. This variation is important because peripheral corneal topography significantly affects the position, blink-induced excursion patterns, and, therefore, wearing comfort of corneal contact lenses, especially gas-permeable lenses.

In addition to addressing contact lens fitting in relation to corneal shape, custom contact lenses can also address the correction of optical aberrations, especially higher-order aberrations, in much the same way that custom laser surgery attempts to improve the optics of the eye.

The availability of corneal topographers and wavefront aberrometers, together with desktop graphics programs, allows contact lenses to be designed that are unique for each eye. (For greater discussion of wavefront technology, see Chapters 7 and 9 in this volume and BCSC Section 13, *Refractive Surgery.*) Combining these unique designs with computerized lathes that can create custom, nonsymmetrical shapes has opened the possibility of creating contact lenses that are individualized to each specific cornea, thus offering patients better vision and increased comfort.

However, before this can happen, significant obstacles need to be overcome:

- *Vertical lens movement.* Some contact lens movement is considered integral to good lens fit; it also allows tear fluid exchange under the lens. With each blink, though, this movement may negate or even worsen custom optics. Because movement is typically less with soft as opposed to rigid lenses, soft contact lenses may be better for creating custom contact lenses.
- *Rotational movement.* A wavefront-designed contact lens needs rotational stability to maintain the benefit of aberration correction, but even toric contact lenses rotate about 5° with each blink.
- *Variability of the optical aberration.* Variations in aberrations occur based on pupil size, accommodation, lens changes, age, and probably other factors as well. Deciding which aberrations to correct may be yet another challenge.
- *Maintenance of corneal health.* Tear film exchange is important for good, long-lasting contact lens health; yet it is contrary to the requirements for stability and nonmovement needed for optimal correction of optical aberrations.
- *Manufacturing issues.* Even with custom lathes and the ability to make nonsymmetric curves, challenges remain in creating lens shapes that will correct aberrations, provide comfortable lenses, and allow identical copies to be made on demand.

Despite these challenges, there is now significant interest in using new technology to evaluate aberrations and new methods of lens manufacturing and design to deliver custom contact lenses—perhaps first for abnormal eyes, such as those with keratoconus, and then for the patient with standard refractive errors who wants to reach for "super-vision."

Contact Lens Care and Solutions

Most contact lenses are removed after use, cleaned, stored, and used again (1-day disposable lenses are the exception). Lens care systems have been developed to remove deposits and microorganisms from lenses, enhance their comfort, and decrease the risk of eye infection and irritation associated with lens use. Although the specific components of these systems vary with the type of lens to be cleaned (soft or RGP), most include a lens cleaner, rinsing solution, and disinfecting and storing solution. Multipurpose solutions, which perform several of these functions, are popular because of their ease of use and convenience. Enzymatic cleaners, which remove protein deposits from the lens surface, provide additional cleaning. These cleaners typically include papain, an enzyme derived from papaya; pancreatin, an enzyme derived from pancreatic tissue; or enzymes derived from bacteria. In addition, lubricating drops can be used when the lenses are on the eye.

Several methods have been developed for disinfecting lenses, including the use of

- heat
- chemicals
- hydrogen peroxide
- UV exposure

The care system selected depends on the personal preference of the fitter and patient, the simplicity and convenience of use, cost, and possible allergies to solution components. Today, multipurpose solutions are the most popular care systems in the United States, probably because they are the easiest to use and the least expensive.

The fitter needs to instruct the patient in the care of contact lenses. The following are important guidelines:

- Clean and disinfect a lens whenever it is removed.
- Follow the advice included with the lens care system that is selected—do not "mix and match" solutions.
- Do not use tap water for storing or cleaning lenses because it is not sterile.
- Do not use homemade salt solutions, which also are not sterile.
- Do not use saliva to wet a lens.
- Do not reuse contact lens care solutions.
- Clean and/or replace the contact lens case regularly; it can be a source of contaminants.

In addition to teaching appropriate contact lens and case care, the fitter should instruct the patient in inserting and removing the lens, determine a wear schedule (DW or EW), and decide if and when the lens should be disposed of or replaced. The insertion and handling of lenses vary significantly between soft and RGP lenses, and many manufacturers provide information, both written and videos, to instruct professional staff and patients in appropriate insertion and removal techniques.

Contact Lens–Related Problems and Complications

Cornea

Corneal infections secondary to lens use are rare today, but, when they occur, they are potentially serious and vision threatening. To reduce risk, contact lenses should be fitted properly, contact lens care systems used regularly, and follow-up care provided. In addition, patients should understand the signs and symptoms of serious eye problems and know where to seek medical assistance, if needed. Today, with the increased use of disposable lenses, better patient education, more convenient care systems, and the use of more oxygen-permeable lens materials, serious eye infections from lens use are unusual. However, practitioners should be aware of unusual infections that can occur, such as acanthamoeba keratitis. Diagnosis and treatment of corneal infections are covered in BSCS Section 8, *External Disease and Cornea.*

Following is a list of corneal changes that can occur with contact lens use:

- *Corneal abrasions.* These can result from foreign bodies under a lens, a poor insertion/removal technique, or a damaged contact lens. Because contact lens use can increase the risk of infection, most clinicians treat abrasions with antibiotic eyedrops and no patching.
- *Punctate keratitis.* This finding can be related to a poor lens fit, a toxic reaction to lens solutions, or dry eyes.
- *3 o'clock and 9 o'clock staining.* This specific superficial punctate keratitis (SPK) staining pattern can be seen in RGP contact lens users and is probably related to poor wetting in the horizontal axis (Fig 5-20). The paralimbal staining is characteristic of low-riding lenses and is associated with an abortive reflex blink pattern, insufficient lens movement, inadequate tear meniscus, and a thick peripheral lens profile. Sometimes refitting the lens and/or initiating regular use of wetting drops can decrease the finding.
- *Sterile infiltrates.* Typically these are seen in the peripheral cornea; often there is more than one spot, and the epithelium over the spots is intact. Resolution can be achieved by discontinuing lens use, but often an antibiotic is added, although cultures tend to show no growth.
- *Contact lens superior limbic keratoconjunctivitis (CLSLK).* This finding is similar to SLK, with injection of the superior bulbar conjunctiva and papillary changes in the overlying upper lid. Discontinuing lens use leads to resolution.
- *Dendritic keratitis.* The slit-lamp appearance is like that of herpes simplex virus (HSV) keratitis, but the fluorescein staining is typically less intense. A follow-up examination, after discontinuing lens use, usually confirms its rapid resolution and noninfectious cause.
- *Corneal neovascularization.* This is usually a sign of hypoxia. Refitting with lenses of higher Dk material and/or a looser fit and/or fewer hours of lens wear per day

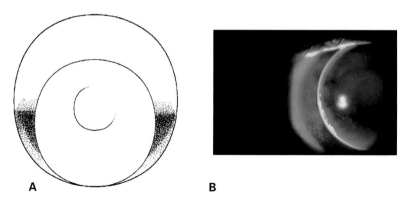

A   B

Figure 5-20 Three o'clock and 9 o'clock corneal staining. **A,** Schematic illustration showing inferior corneal desiccation of the tear film. **B,** Peripheral corneal desiccation. *(Part B courtesy of Perry Rosenthal, MD.)*

and/or switching to disposable lenses can prevent further progression. If neovascularization is extensive, it can lead to corneal scarring and lipid deposition or intracorneal hemorrhage.

- *Corneal warpage.* Change in corneal shape from contact lens use has been reported with both soft and RGP lenses, but it is more commonly associated with hard lenses. Most warpage will resolve after discontinuing lens wear. To evaluate corneal shape on an ongoing basis, part of the contact lens follow-up examination should include a regular evaluation by keratometry or corneal topography and manifest refraction, and the findings should be compared with previous ones.
- *Spectacle blur.* Corneal warpage and more temporary changes in corneal shape can change the normal spectacle-corrected vision immediately after lens removal. If patients complain of spectacle blur, the contact lens fit should be reevaluated and discontinuing lens use for a period of time should be considered.
- *Ptosis.* This problem is related not to corneal changes but possibly to dehiscence of the levator aponeurosis secondary to chronic use of RGP lenses.

Most of these problems can be treated by discontinuing lens use or refitting at a later date after changing lens parameters, material, and Dk or by switching to disposable lenses or decreasing lens wear.

The Red Eye

Red eye in contact lens wearers can have multiple etiologies, including poor contact lens fit and eye infection. Understanding the differential diagnosis is important to determining the correct etiology and appropriate treatment and management. Also, because contact lenses can be associated with vision-threatening infections, patient reports of "red eye" should include recommendations for discontinuing contact lens use and an eye examination if symptoms persist or are associated with loss of vision and if symptoms recur. Red eye can be caused by a number of conditions, including the following:

- *Poor fit.* Both tight and loose fits can cause red eye. With a *tight fit,* inadequate lens movement is noted on slit-lamp examination. Typically, when a lens is first inserted, the patient experiences a good degree of comfort, but this declines over hours of use. With continued use of a tight lens, a "tight lens syndrome" can develop, where the soft lens becomes dehydrated and fits even more tightly on the eye; hypoxia sets in because of poor tear exchange; and severe eye redness, pain, and corneal edema are noted.

    With a *loose fit,* too much lens movement is noted on slit-lamp examination, along with possible lens decentration, and—if soft lenses—edge standoff. The patient complains of varying vision with each blink and increased lens awareness.
- *Hypoxia.* The sequelae of inadequate oxygen reaching the anterior cornea are less common today because of the higher Dk (greater oxygen permeability) of both soft and RGP materials. However, patients who do not replace lenses and/or use them beyond the recommended wearing time may present with red eyes, eye irritation, and slit-lamp findings of punctate staining, epithelial microcysts, corneal

edema, and/or corneal neovascularization. Treatment can include discontinuing lens use and/or refitting with higher Dk lens and reducing hours of lens use.

- *Deposits on contact lenses.* Lens deposits can usually be noted at the slit lamp. With the increased use of disposable lenses, as well as an increase in the rate of lens replacement, deposits are less of an issue; nevertheless, they are seen and can be the cause of red eyes, discomfort with lens use, and allergic reactions such as *giant papillary conjunctivitis (GPC).* In terms of treatment, dry eyes, ocular allergies, and poor lens care should first be ruled out as possible causes of lens deposit formation. Increasing the rate of contact lens replacement, improving lens care, and/or switching to another lens material (lower water content) may all help decrease lens deposit formation.

- *Damaged contact lenses.* Damaged lenses are problematic. For example, a damaged edge (torn if a soft lens, chipped if an RGP lens) can cause pain upon insertion. Inspection at the slit lamp can help in diagnosing such problems.

- *Toxicity or allergy to ingredients in the lens care solutions.* This type of toxicity or allergy may be hard to diagnose. Typically, reactions to lens care products are a degree of redness and discomfort when lenses are inserted that decreases over the time the lens remains in the eye. Conjunctivitis with possible sterile corneal infiltrates can be seen that resolve when lens use is discontinued. Switching lens care products can confirm the diagnosis if the reactions disappear.

- *Preexisting history of systemic and/or ocular allergies.* Patients with this history may have increased symptoms of the red eye with lens use. The symptoms can be reduced with the use of disposable lenses or an increase in the rate of lens replacement, because deposits on the surface may be a source of allergens that stimulate the reaction. GPC typically occurs in an established lens user with no history of problems who now has red and itchy eyes, increased lens awareness, and mucus discharge. Slit-lamp examination of the upper tarsus will demonstrate papillae, reminiscent of findings in vernal keratoconjunctivitis. With GPC, immediate resolution of symptoms comes with discontinuing lens use. If a patient prefers to continue lens wear, disposable contact lenses, an improved lens care regimen, and the use of mast cell stabilizers and topical nonsteroidal anti-inflammatory drops may be considered.

- *Dry eye.* Evaluating a patient for dry eyes should be part of the prefitting eye examination. If a patient has severe dry eyes, he or she is probably not a candidate for lens use; a properly fitting lens rides on the tear film, which is essential for comfort and allows fluid exchange under the lens to remove debris and bring in oxygen. Patients with moderate to mild dry eyes, however, may do well with lenses. Some soft lenses are marketed for dry eye patients; these lenses often have lower water content and/or better wettability and/or are made of material that is less prone to lens deposit formation. Some patients may respond to placement of punctal plugs. Sometimes the signs and symptoms of dry eyes result from incomplete or infrequent blinking (less than 12 times per minute). This condition may be diagnosed by simply observing patients during the examination. Some fitters feel that it is helpful to instruct the patient on how to blink.

HIV Transmission in Contact Lens Care

HIV has been isolated from ocular tissues, tears, and soft contact lenses used by patients with AIDS. However, no documented case of HIV transmission through contact with human tears or contaminated contact lenses has been reported. Nonetheless, proper disinfection of trial lenses is appropriate to minimize the risk of transmitting HIV and all other pathogenic organisms.

The CDC advisory of 1985 recommended the following disinfection methods for trial contact lenses:

- *Hard lenses.* Use a commercially available hydrogen peroxide contact lens disinfecting kit (the type used for soft lenses); other hydrogen peroxide preparations may cause lens discoloration. Heat disinfection (78°–80°C for 10 minutes), as used for soft lens care, can also be used but may damage a lens.
- *RGP lenses.* Same as above, but heat disinfection is not recommended because it can cause lens warpage.
- *Soft lenses.* Same as above, although heat should be used only if the lens is approved for such a care system.

The most commonly used disinfection systems for contact lenses today are chemical. Published studies suggest that chemical disinfection is effectve against HIV-contaminated contact lenses, but these studies have not been reviewed by the FDA. As a result, although the FDA requires demonstration of virucidal activity in treatments for herpes simplex virus, there is no such requirement for HIV.

American Academy of Ophthalmology. Minimizing transmission of bloodborne pathogens and surface infectious agents in ophthalmic offices and operating rooms. Information Statement. San Francisco: AAO; 2002.

Centers for Disease Control Morbidity and Mortality Weekly Report. Recommendations for preventing possible transmission of human T-lymphotropic virus type III/lymphadenopathy-associated virus from tears. Atlanta, GA: Centers for Disease Control; 1985;34:533–534. (www.cdc.gov/mmwr/preview/mmwrhtml/00000602.htm) (Additional information on CDC guidelines can be obtained by viewing the CDC website for the Division of Healthcare Promotion (http://www.cdc.gov/ncidod/hip/).

Slonim CB. AIDS and the contact lens practice. *CLAO J.* 1995;21:233–235.

Federal Law and Contact Lenses

The Federal Fairness to Contact Lens Consumers Act (PL 108-164) was passed by Congress and became effective on February 4, 2004. The law is intended to make it easier for consumers to obtain contact lenses from providers other than the individual who actually fitted the lenses. Once the fitting process is complete, the patient must automatically be provided with a free copy of the prescription, regardless of whether the patient has requested it. In addition, the provider must verify the prescription information—within a reasonable period of time (typically defined as 8 hours during the normal business day)—to anyone designated to act on behalf of the patient, such as an Internet contact lens seller. The Federal Trade Commission (FTC) can impose sanctions for noncompliance on both prescribers and sellers of up to $11,000 per offense. Further details of this law can be obtained at the FTC Internet site: www.ftc.gov.

Aquavella JV, Rao GN. *Contact Lenses*. Philadelphia: Lippincott; 1987.

CLAO Patient Information Brochures. New Orleans, Contact Lens Association of Ophthalmologists, 1993–1995.

Continuous wear contact lenses for the new millennium, challenges, controversies, and new opportunities. *Eye & Contact Lens: Science and Clinical Practice*. Suppl. 2003;29.

Cornea: The Journal of Cornea and External Disease. Philadelphia: Lippincott Williams & Wilkins. Published 8 times per year.

Donshik PC, ed. Contact lenses. *Ophthalmol Clin N Am*. 2003;16.

Eye & Contact Lens: Science and Clinical Practice. Philadelphia: Lippincott Williams & Wilkins. Published quarterly.

Jain S, Arora I, Azar DT. Success of monovision in presbyopes: review of the literature and potential applications to refractive surgery. *Surv Ophthalmol*. 1996;40:491–499.

Kastl PR, ed. *Contact Lenses: The CLAO Guide to Basic Science and Clinical Practice*. 4 vols. Dubuque, Iowa: Kendall-Hunt; 1995.

Kastl PR. Contact lens fitting for regular astigmatism. *Focal Points: Clinical Modules for Ophthalmologists*. San Francisco: American Academy of Ophthalmology; 1997, module 11.

Key JE II, ed. *The CLAO Pocket Guide to Contact Lens Fitting*. 2nd ed. New York: CLAO; 1998.

Laibson PR, Cohen EJ, Rajpal RK. Conrad Berens Lecture. Corneal ulcers related to contact lenses. *CLAO J*. 1993;19:73–78.

McDermott ML, Chandler JW. Therapeutic uses of contact lenses. *Surv Ophthalmol*. 1989; 33:381–394.

Refojo MF. Polymers, Dk, and contact lenses: now and in the future. *CLAO J*. 1996;22:38–40.

Rosenthal P, Cotter JM. Contact lenses. In: Albert DM, Jakobiec FA, eds. *Principles and Practice of Ophthalmology*. Philadelphia: Saunders; 1994;5:3621–3648.

Roth H-W. *Contact Lens Complications: Etiology, Pathogenesis, Prevention, Therapy*. New York: Thieme; 2003.

Ruben M. *A Color Atlas of Contact Lenses & Prosthetics*. 2nd ed. St. Louis: Mosby-Year Book; 1990.

Stein HA, Freeman MI, Stein RM. *CLAO Residents Contact Lens Curriculum Manual*. New York: CLAO; 1996.

Tyler's Quarterly Soft Contact Lens Parameter Guide. PO Box 250406, Little Rock, AR 72225-0406. Published quarterly.

CHAPTER 6

Intraocular Lenses

The history of the modern intraocular lens (IOL) began in 1949, when Harold Ridley, an English ophthalmologist, implanted a polymethylmethacrylate (PMMA) IOL following an extracapsular cataract extraction. Although this event was originally greeted with less than full enthusiasm by his peers, the use of IOLs has now become the standard in modern cataract surgery. In 2000, Harold Ridley was knighted by Queen Elizabeth. Although early IOLs were associated with a high rate of complications, including uveitis, glaucoma, and dislocation, recent improvements in lens design and surgical techniques have greatly reduced the incidence of postoperative problems. IOLs are now used in 98% of cataract extractions in the United States. This chapter discusses optical considerations relevant to IOLs. For surgical and historical information and illustrations, see BCSC Section 11, *Lens and Cataract.*

Types of IOLs

In the 1990s, most IOLs were made with PMMA optics and polypropylene or PMMA-supporting haptics. However, recent improvements in microsurgical techniques, allowing removal of a cataractous lens through an incision smaller than 3.5 mm, have led to the development of foldable IOLs manufactured from materials such as silicone, acrylic, and hydrogels. Such foldable lenses are becoming increasingly popular because smaller incisions allow more rapid wound stabilization, earlier visual rehabilitation, and increased surgical safety. Although the role of ultraviolet light in contributing to retinal damage is still unclear, ultraviolet filters are now routinely included in IOLs without apparent chemical toxicity and without effect on optical performance. Lenses are available that filter out higher-frequency (blue) visible light, with the hope that this will reduce phototoxicity and/or later macular degeneration.

The role of lens material on other factors, such as posterior capsular opacification (PCO), is being investigated. Some papers have suggested that acrylic and hydrogel are associated with lower rates of PCO than IOLs made from silicone or PMMA. However, more recent studies suggest that lens edge design is a more important factor in PCO than lens material. Lenses with square, truncated edges create a barrier effect at the optic edge that reduces cell migration behind the optic, and thus PCO. (However, square-edged IOLs may increase the frequency of undesirable optical phenomena; see Lens-Related Visual Disturbances, later in the chapter.) Lens material may also play a role in condensation on the posterior surface of an IOL (usually after a capsulotomy) during vitrectomy. Acrylic material is associated with less condensation and better visibility than silicone.

Silicone IOLs may be contraindicated for eyes in which silicone oil will be used. Some authors suggest that, for patients who may be at risk for later vitrectomy (ie, patients with diabetes or possibly those with high myopia), IOL choice should be slanted toward those IOL styles and materials that may make later vitrectomy less dangerous.

Abhilakh Missier KA, Nuijts RM, Tjia KF. Posterior capsule opacification: silicone plate-haptic verus AcrySof intraocular lenses. *J Cataract Refract Surg.* 2003;29:1569–1574.

Apple DJ. Influence of intraocular lens material and design on postoperative intracapsular cellular reactivity. *Trans Am Ophthalmol Soc.* 2000;98:257–283.

Ernest PH. Posterior capsule opacification and neodymium:YAG capsulotomy rates with AcrySof acrylic and PhacoFlex II silicone intraocular lenses. *J Cataract Refract Surg.* 2003; 29:1546–1550.

Hainsworth DP, Chen SN, Cox TA, et al. Condensation on polymethylmethacrylate, acrylic polymer, and silicone intraocular lenses after fluid–air exchange in rabbits. *Ophthalmology.* 1996;103:1410–1418.

Kim NJ, Lee JH. Effect of an acrylic posterior chamber intraocular lens on posterior capsule opacification in cataract patients with associated risk factors. *J Cataract Refract Surg.* 2003;29:1575–1578.

Nagamoto T, Fujiwara T. Inhibition of lens epithelial cell migration at the intraocular lens optic edge: role of capsule bending and contact pressure. *J Cataract Refract Surg.* 2003;29: 1605–1612.

Prosdocimo G, Tassinari G, Sala M, et al. Posterior capsule opacification after phacoemulsification: silicone CeeOn Edge versus acrylate AcrySof intraocular lens. *J Cataract Surg.* 2003;29:1551–1555.

Two basic lens designs are currently in use, differentiated by the plane in which the lens is placed (anterior chamber or posterior chamber) and the tissue supporting the lens (Fig 6-1). An early IOL design, the *iris clip lens,* which was attached or sutured to the iris, is very rarely used anymore in the United States. However, some IOLs designed to be inserted in phakic eyes (phakic IOLs) have reintroduced iris clip lenses to the surgical armamentarium. Phakic IOLs are expected to be most useful for patients with high degrees of ametropia. Techniques of "piggyback" lenses, in which 2 IOLs are inserted in one eye either at the same time or sequentially, have become available. These may be useful in 2 situations: when the actual postoperative refraction is very different from what was desired and expected and when the required IOL power is higher than what is commercially available. Minus-power IOLs are available for use in extreme myopia and as piggybacks.

Anterior Chamber Lenses

Anterior chamber lenses are placed entirely within the anterior chamber, with the optical portion of the lens supported by solid "feet" or loops wedged into the chamber angle. Such lenses may be inserted following intracapsular or extracapsular cataract extraction and are a popular style for secondary lens insertion when capsular support is absent. A particular problem with the use of rigid anterior chamber lenses is inaccurate estimation of the size of the lens required to span the anterior chamber. The haptics must rest lightly in the chamber angle without tucking the iris or "propellering" in the anterior chamber from unstable fixation. Unstable fixation can lead to persistent uveitis, hyphema, iris

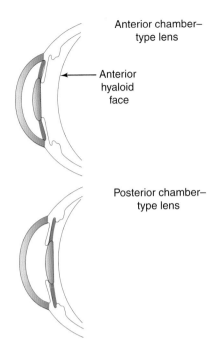

Anterior chamber–
type lens

Anterior
hyaloid
face

Figure 6-1 The 2 major types of intra-ocular lenses. *(Redrawn by C. H. Wooley.)*

Posterior chamber–
type lens

atrophy, corneal decompensation, and glaucoma. The term *UGH syndrome,* from *u*veitis, *g*laucoma, *h*yphema, was coined for such cases. More recently, solid, or closed-loop, anterior chamber IOLs have been replaced by flexible, or open-loop, lenses. Sizing of these lenses is still important, but UGH syndrome has virtually disappeared.

Posterior Chamber Lenses

Posterior chamber lenses are by far the most widely used IOLs in the United States and are generally employed following extracapsular procedures with an intact posterior capsule. With a posterior chamber lens, the optic and supporting haptics are placed behind the iris. The lens is supported by loops placed either in the capsular bag or in the ciliary sulcus. In certain special circumstances, a posterior chamber IOL may be used with a torn or an absent posterior capsule (it may be placed in front of an intact anterior capsule with a good capsulorrhexis). It may even be used in cases with no remaining capsule at all—this is done by suturing the haptics into the ciliary sulcus with *nonabsorbable* suture material.

Optical Considerations for IOLs

A number of factors must be taken into consideration when selecting IOLs, including image magnification, power selection, piggyback IOLs, and power after corneal refractive surgery.

Image Magnification

Theoretically, replacing a clear or cataractous crystalline lens with an artificial lens is the optimal form of aphakic correction. The majority of aberrations and distortions produced by aphakic spectacles derive from their placement anterior to the pupillary plane. These include image magnification, ring scotomata, peripheral distortion, the jack-in-the-box phenomenon, and decreased useful peripheral field.

Image magnification—as much as 20%–35%—is the major disadvantage of aphakic spectacles. Contact lens correction of aphakia magnifies the image 7%–12%; IOLs magnify by 4% or less. Naturally, a lens located in the posterior chamber produces less image magnification than a lens in the anterior chamber. However, the issue of magnification is further complicated by the correction of residual postsurgical refractive errors. A Galilean telescope is constructed by the combination of spectacles worn over pseudophakic eyes. Clinically, each diopter of spectacle overcorrection at a vertex of 12 mm causes a 2% magnification or minification (for plus or minus lenses, respectively). Thus, a pseudophakic patient with a posterior chamber lens and a residual refractive error of −1 D will have 2% magnification from the IOL and 2% minification from the spectacle lens, resulting in no change in image size.

In patients with monocular aphakia, aniseikonia often leads to disturbances in stereopsis. Generally, a person can tolerate spherical aniseikonia of 5%–8%. However, a patient with preexisting abnormalities in sensory fusion may find even 5% aniseikonia intolerable. Although the effect of small amounts of aniseikonia on stereopsis is unclear, some studies of monocular aphakia have found slightly better stereoacuity and less aniseikonia in pseudophakic patients than in aphakic patients whose vision is corrected with contact lenses. In clinical practice, however, aniseikonia with contact lenses is rarely significant.

IOL Power Selection

Nontoric IOLs provide spherical correction of the refractive error without any cylindrical component; this spherical correction should be calculated for each eye as accurately as possible. The optimal postoperative refraction depends on the situation and visual needs of the patient. For example, if a unilateral cataract is present and the fellow eye is more than 1.5–2.0 D hyperopic, the surgeon can consider making the operated eye slightly hyperopic as well. This strategy avoids inducing aniseikonia and anisophoria. In most settings, however, it is desirable to produce emmetropia or slight myopia. The advantages of selecting a lens power to produce 1.0–1.5 D of myopia are threefold:

- Spectacle overcorrection of −1.0 to −1.5 D reduces image magnification essentially to zero.
- If an error occurs in power calculation, the surgeon is less likely to produce significant hyperopia, which is more poorly tolerated than an equal degree of myopia.
- Most significantly, overcorrection (with its resultant mild myopia) allows the patient some degree of function at near unaided by spectacles.

There are 2 major types of IOL formulas. The first is theoretical, derived from a mathematical consideration of the optics of the eye. The second is empirically derived from linear regression analysis of a large number of cases. The best known of the latter type is the modified SRK formula, or SRK II (named after the initials of its originators, Sanders, Retzlaff, and Kraff).

Biometric assumptions in IOL selection

Whatever formula is used, the calculation of IOL power is based on certain clinical measurements that involve approximations and uncertainties. For example, we assume certain values for the index of refraction of the tear film, cornea, aqueous, and vitreous. When ultrasound is used to measure axial length, we assume a certain constant speed of ultrasound through the various ocular structures. *A-scan ultrasonography* can be used to measure axial length prior to cataract surgery in order to help determine the needed power of the IOL to be implanted. However, A-scans do not actually measure axial length. Rather, they measure the time required for a sound pulse to travel through the ocular media, reflect from the retina, and return through the media. Sound moves faster through the crystalline lens than through the cornea, aqueous, and vitreous. Even within the lens itself, the speed of sound can vary according to the hardness of the cataract. The assumptions used in converting time to axial length in an A-scan tend to underestimate the axial length of short eyes and overestimate long ones—and a 1-mm error in the measurement of axial length results in a refractive error of approximately 2.5–3.0 D. Further, the 2 primary A-scan techniques—applanation (contact) and immersion—give different readings. The applanation method may give a shorter axial length measurement, perhaps due to corneal indentation. In addition, for certain theoretical formulas, the question has been raised as to whether the axial length should be used as measured or whether it should be somehow corrected for a slightly greater distance to the photoreceptor layer.

Tehrani M, Krummenauer F, Kumar R, et al. Comparison of biometric measurements using partial coherence interferometry and applanation ultrasound. *J Cataract Refract Surg.* 2003;29:747–752.

A nonultrasonic method of measuring axial length has now been introduced that uses partial coherence interferometry. In a manner analogous to ultrasound, this technique measures the time required for infrared light to travel to the retina. Because light travels at too high a speed to measure directly, light interference methodology is used to determine the transit time and thus the axial length. This technique does not require contact with the globe, so corneal compression artifacts are eliminated. In addition, the patient must fixate a target; thus, the length measured is the path the light takes to the fovea, the "physiological" axial length (rather than some possibly different anatomically determined axial length). However, the media must be clear enough to allow fixation and light transmission; in dense cataracts, ultrasound axial length measurements may still be necessary. The partial coherence interferometry technique is probably more accurate and reproducible than the ultrasound method, although some cases will still require ultrasound biometry.

Drexler W, Findl O, Menapace R, et al. Partial coherence interferometry: a novel approach to biometry in cataract surgery. *Am J Ophthalmol.* 1998;126:524–534.

Tehrani M, Krummenauer F, Blom E, et al. Evaluation of the practicality of optical biometry and applanation ultrasound in 253 eyes. *J Cataract Refract Surg.* 2003;29:741–746.

Similarly, *keratometry,* or *corneal topography,* does not measure corneal power directly. The keratometer measures only a small portion of the central cornea, viewing the cornea as a convex mirror. From this measurement, the corneal curvature is calculated. Both front and back corneal surfaces contribute to corneal power, and a keratometer measures only the front surface. The keratometer does not measure the corneal curvature at just 4 points, as is often stated in the literature; rather, it measures the size of a reflected image. From this, the corneal power is estimated using assumptions. The validity of these assumptions—and, thus, the accuracy of keratometry—varies from patient to patient. In patients who have had previous corneal refractive surgery, just what corneal power to use—and how to measure it—remains an evolving field.

The formulas based on geometrical optics generally require a third parameter as well: *anterior chamber depth* or *optical chamber depth* (OCD). (These 2 measures are not exactly the same.)

Power prediction formulas

The following example represents the first type of IOL formula, based on geometrical optics. The pseudophakic eye can be modeled as a 2-element optical system (Fig 6-2). Using Gaussian reduction equations, the IOL power that produces emmetropia is given by

$$P_{IOL} = \frac{n_{vit}}{AL - acd} - \frac{K}{1 - [K(acd)/n_{aq}]}$$

where

P_{IOL} = power of the IOL
K = dioptric power of the cornea
AL = axial length
acd = anterior chamber depth
n_{vit} = index of refraction of the vitreous
n_{aq} = index of refraction of the aqueous

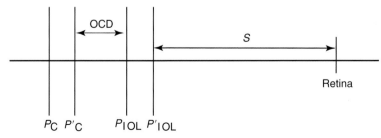

Figure 6-2 Schematic eye. P_C and P'_C are the front and back principal planes of the cornea, respectively. Similarly, P_{IOL} and P'_{IOL} are the front and back principal planes of the IOL. S is the distance between the back principal plane of the IOL and the retina. (The drawing is not to scale.) *(Redrawn by C. H. Wooley.)*

Several problems hinder the application of this and other power formulas based on geometrical optics. As discussed, biometry itself is fraught with uncertainties and assumptions. In addition, the variables in the equation are not the same as the parameters in the theoretical optical model. For example, in the equation, the anterior chamber depth is used instead of the distance from the cornea's back principal plane to the front principal plane of the IOL. The quantity AL − acd, the distance from the IOL plane to the fovea, should, strictly speaking, be the distance from the back principal plane of the IOL to the retina. Also, we are ignoring any effects due to the thickness of the cornea and/or the fact that the index of refraction of the cornea is not identical to that of the aqueous. Usually we approximate a single index of refraction for the cornea/aqueous/vitreous, although each is slightly different. We measure the anterior chamber depth for the formula—but what we really want is not the preoperative anterior chamber depth but rather the position of the intraocular lens in the postoperative eye. In the past, some authorities did not even measure the acd, but used an acd value specific for the particular IOL to be used. In addition, we should reduce the axial length by the distance between the principal planes of the IOL, a quantity that differs from lens to lens. In spite of these theoretical inaccuracies, in practice, formulas based on this reasoning constituted the basis of the early so-called theoretical IOL formulas and were reasonably accurate for many eyes (eg, the Binkhorst formula, the Colenbrander formula).

In the 1980s, Sanders, Retzlaff, and Kraff took a different approach. They analyzed clinical data using regression analysis and calculated what their data suggested would be the optimal formula for IOL calculation. The formula turned out to be a simple linear equation, which was introduced as the SRK formula, after the initials of its originators. According to their analysis, lens power could be predicted with measurements of the axial length and corneal curvature only. Specifically, no additional accuracy was obtained by adding measurements of the anterior chamber depth or by using any of the variables in other than linear fashion (eg, as axial length squared). However, the formula required a third element, the so-called *A constant*.

$$P = A - (2.5 \times \text{axial length in mm}) - (0.9 \times \text{average keratometry in diopters})$$

It was later noted that this formula was less accurate for long or short eyes. The power was too low in short eyes and too high in longer eyes (Fig 6-3). The formula was later modified as the SRK II formula, as follows:

Axial Length (AL)	Modified A Constant
20 > AL	A = A + 3
21 > AL ≥ 20	A = A + 2
22 > AL ≥ 21	A = A + 1
24.5 > AL ≥ 22	A = A (no change)
24.5 ≤ AL	A = A − 0.5

The *A* constant, which is provided by manufacturers for their lenses, is specific to each lens type. Factors related to *A* constants are the lens position in the eye, haptic angulation, and lens shape. In general, the more anterior the placement of an IOL, the

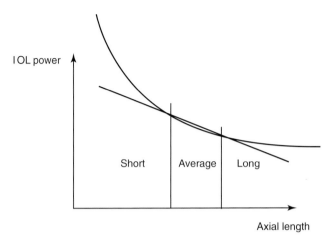

Figure 6-3 Comparison between the SRK formula and the theoretical formula. The formula assumes a linear relationship between IOL power and axial length; however, because the relationship is not truly linear, the equation becomes inaccurate for short and long eyes. *(Redrawn by C. H. Wooley.)*

lower its *A* constant. Surgeons should come into the operating room knowing the power of the equivalent anterior chamber lens to use in case a surgical mishap precludes insertion of a posterior chamber lens. The larger the lens–retina distance, the weaker the lens needed to focus the light. An anterior chamber lens will always be of lower power than a posterior chamber lens in the same patient. In fact, simply placing a posterior chamber lens in the sulcus rather than in the capsular bag may call for a power reduction of approximately 0.5–1.0 D in average eyes. In some cases, surgeons may wish to modify the formula, based on patient outcomes, to compensate for their particular surgical techniques. Alternatively, the surgeon planning for postoperative ametropia (rather than emmetropia) can modify the formula as appropriate.

> Suto C, Hori S, Fukuyama E, et al. Adjusting intraocular lens power for sulcus fixation. *J Cataract Refract Surg.* 2003;29;1913–1917.

Use of the *A* constant also makes it easy to switch the power calculation for one lens to another. The difference in required IOL powers is simply the difference between the *A* constants. For example, suppose that a lens with an *A* constant of 118.2 is calculated to require 20.0 D power. If, at the last minute, the surgeon must switch to a different IOL, the power can easily be calculated for the new lens. If the new IOL has an *A* constant of 116.7, we see that the *A* constant is 1.5 less. Thus, the required power of the new IOL is also 1.5 less, or 18.5 D. (Unfortunately, this simple relationship no longer holds true for the more accurate SRK/T formula, discussed below.)

Newer theoretical formulas were developed that also tried to correct for discrepancies in unusually short or long eyes. Whether the SRK formulas are inherently more accurate than theoretical formulas has not been settled, but the SRK has the advantage of being much simpler to calculate.

Second-generation formulas added modifications based on axial length for short or long eyes. Third- and fourth-generation formulas added modifications for other factors, such as corneal curvature, anterior chamber diameter, and so on. These newer formulas are thought to be more accurate than those of the first and second generation, although the differences between these and the earlier formulas are most pronounced in "non-average" eyes. Some of these newer formulas include the SRK/T formula and the Hoffer Q formula. These formulas are too complex for convenient hand calculation; fortunately, however, the widespread availability of programmable calculators today obviates this disadvantage.

Hoffer KJ. The Hoffer Q formula: a comparison of theoretic and regression formulas. *J Cataract Refract Surg.* 1993;19:700–712.

Retzlaff JA, Sanders DR, Kraff MC. Development of the SRK/T intraocular lens implant power calculation formula [corrections appear in *J Cataract Refract Surg.* 1990;16:528; *J Cataract Refract Surg.* 1993;19:442–446]. *J Cataract Refract Surg.* 1990;16:333–340.

The choice of formula is, of course, up to the surgeon, but whatever the method, every effort should be made to ensure that the biometry is as accurate as possible. Preoperative axial lengths and K readings should be reviewed by the operating surgeon. Readings that are suspicious because they lie outside normal limits should be repeated. The surgeon should also exercise clinical judgment in considering these values. For example, an axial length of 28 mm would be suspicious if the patient were not highly myopic. Similarly, both eyes should be measured and the readings rechecked if there is a large discrepancy between the 2 eyes.

Piggyback IOLs

Sometimes an IOL may be inserted in an eye that already has an IOL, usually to correct a postoperative refractive error (piggyback IOL). In this case, theoretically, there is no change in any of the optical parameters of the eye, so calculation of the needed second IOL power is straightforward geometrical optics (although the postoperative position of the piggyback IOL—its distance from the cornea—must be known). Because the powers are often relatively low, differences in this distance may be less clinically important. In practice, these calculations are sometimes made less accurate by factors such as a posterior displacement of the original IOL by the piggyback IOL and/or compression or adhesion of the 2 convex surfaces of the touching IOL pair and thus modification of their refractive properties. (Note that displacement of the higher-power original IOL is much more significant than displacement of the usually lower-power secondary, "piggybacked," IOL.) There may even be some increased depth of focus with these IOL pairs due to flattening of the area of contact. This may reduce the optical power in the center region while leaving the steeper peripheral curves unaffected.

Findl O, Menapace R. Piggyback intraocular lenses [letter]. *J Cataract Refract Surg.* 2000;26: 308–309.

Findl O, Menapace R, Rainer G, et al. Contact zone of piggyback acrylic intraocular lenses. *J Cataract Refract Surg.* 1999;25:860–862.

IOL Power After Corneal Refractive Surgery

Corneal refractive procedures, such as LASIK and PRK, are becoming increasingly popular. When patients who have undergone these procedures require cataract surgery, the needed IOL calculations have been disappointingly inaccurate. The manipulation of the cornea by these refractive procedures changes measured corneal power and, thus, its contribution to the refractive status of the eye. Standard keratometers measure the corneal refractive power in an indirect way. They measure the reflection from the central cornea, treating it as a convex mirror. From this measurement of the corneal *reflective* power, the cornea's *refractive* power is calculated.

Corneal refractive surgery alters the usual relationship of the corneal structure. The prolate shape of the cornea may be changed into an oblate shape. The thickness of the central cornea is altered, which also alters the relationship between the anterior surface of the cornea and its posterior surface. (Refraction does occur at the posterior surface/aqueous interface!)

Several methods are available for calculating IOL power in these patients, none of them completely satisfactory. One method is based on the patient's history (if it is available). With this method, the measured change in refraction (at the corneal plane) is subtracted from the original K reading; that result is then used as the current K measurement for IOL calculation. For example, suppose the original K reading was 45 D and the patient had a refraction of −6. Now, after a corneal refractive procedure, his refracted power is −1. We can assume from this that the cornea has been weakened by 5 D, and thus the patient has a K reading of 40 D.

A second method involves the use of an overrefracting hard contact lens. Consider the previous patient, who this time presents with no history available. He has a refraction of −1. We insert a hard contact lens of, say, base curve 45 D, and power of, say, −2. Now, with this lens on, his refraction is −4. The hard lens we used had a power of −2. That means that if we had used a plano lens, his refraction would have been −6. We have thus added −5 to his refraction, which means that the contact lens has added +5 to his previous optical status. Because the contact lens is 45 D, we can assume that his corneal power is 40 D and use that for our IOL calculations.

Perhaps in the future a more satisfactory method using newer corneal measuring techniques and topography will more accurately measure the effects of the curves of the front and rear corneal surfaces and the corneal thickness, as well as changes in the prerefractive surgery prolate shape of the cornea. At the present time, however, the ideal method of handling such patients is still undetermined.

Lens-Related Visual Disturbances

The presence of IOLs may lead to the occurrence of a number of optical phenomena. Various light-related visual phenomena encountered by pseudophakic (and phakic) patients have been termed *dysphotopsias*. These have been further subdivided into positive and negative dysphotopsias. Positive dysphotopsias are characterized by brightness, streaks, and rays emanating from a central point source of light, sometimes with a diffuse hazy glare. Negative dysphotopsias are characterized by subjective darkness or shadowing. Such optical phenomena may be related to light reflection and refraction along the edges of the lens. Lenses with square or truncated edges produce a more intense edge glare (Fig 6-4). These phenomena may also be due to internal re-reflection within the IOL itself, which may be more likely to occur with materials with a higher index of refraction, such as acrylic (Fig 6-5). The curvature of the anterior IOL surface may be a factor as well. Lenses in which the anterior curvature is lower may be more likely to have internal reflections directed toward the fovea and thus be more distracting (Fig 6-6).

Davison JA. Positive and negative dysphotopsia in patients with acrylic intraocular lenses. *J Cataract Refract Surg.* 2000;26:1346–1355.

Erie JC, Bandhauer MH. Intraocular lens surfaces and their relationship to postoperative glare. *J Cataract Refract Surg.* 2003;29:336–341.

Farbowitz MA, Zabriskie NA, Crandall AS, et al. Visual complaints associated with the AcrySof acrylic intraocular lens (1). *J Cataract Refract Surg.* 2000;26:1339–1345.

Franchini A, Gallarati BZ, Vaccri E. Computerized analysis of the effects of intraocular lens edge design on the quality of vision in pseudophakic patients. *J Cataract Refract Surg.* 2003;29:342–347.

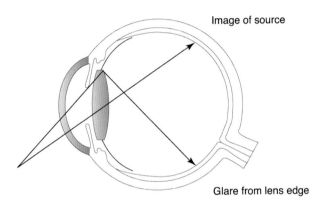

Figure 6-4 Light striking the edge of the IOL may be reflected to another site on the retina, resulting in undesirable dysphotopsias. This occurs less with smoother-edged IOLs. *(Redrawn by C. H. Wooley.)*

Figure 6-5 Light may be internally re-reflected within an IOL, producing an undesirable second image or halo. This may be more likely to occur as the index of refraction of the IOL increases. *(Redrawn by C. H. Wooley.)*

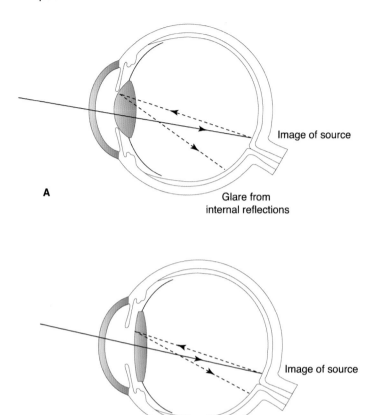

Figure 6-6 Light may reflect back from the surface of the retina and reach the IOL's anterior surface. This acts as a concave mirror, reflecting back an undesirable dysphotopsic image. **A,** With a more curved anterior surface, the annoying image is displaced relatively far from the fovea. **B,** With a less steeply curved anterior IOL surface, the annoying image appears closer to the true image and is likely to be more distracting. *(Redrawn by C. H. Wooley.)*

Holladay JT, Lang A, Portney V. Analysis of edge glare phenomena in intraocular lens edge designs. *J Cataract Refract Surg.* 1999;25:748–752.

Tester R, Pace NL, Samore M, et al. Dysphotopsia in phakic and pseudophakic patients: incidence and relation to intraocular lens type. *J Cataract Refract Surg.* 2000;26:810–816.

Nonspherical Optics

IOLs with more complex optical parameters may come into increasing use as experience with them grows. It may be possible, for example, to correct for the positive spherical aberration of the cornea in pseudophakic patients by putting the appropriate negative spherical aberration into the anterior surface of the IOL. To correct astigmatism, IOLs with toric optics are useful. Rotational stability continues to be of concern in plate haptic toric lenses. As a lens rotates from the optimum desired angular orientation, the benefit of the toric correction diminishes. A toric IOL that is more than 31° off-axis increases the residual astigmatism of an eye. Fortunately, some benefit remains with lesser degrees of axis error, although the axis of residual cylinder will change.

Mester U, Dillinger P, Anterist N. Impact of a modified optic design on visual function: clinical comparative study. *J Cataract Refract Surg.* 2003;29:652–660.

Ruhswurm I, Scholz U, Zehetmayer M, et al. Astigmatism correction with a foldable toric intraocular lens in cataract patients. *J Cataract Refract Surg.* 2000;26:1022–1027.

Sun XY, Vicary D, Montgomery P, et al. Toric intraocular lenses for correcting astigmatism in 130 eyes. *Ophthalmology.* 2000;107:1776–1781.

IOL Standards

The American National Standards Institute (ANSI) and the International Standards Organization (ISO) set standards for IOLs. Among these standards is one for IOL power labeling, which requires that the IOL be within 0.50 D of the labeled power and have no axial power variations of more than 0.25 D. A mislabeled IOL power is quite rare. In addition, ANSI, the ISO, and the FDA have set various other standards for *optical performance,* a term used to refer roughly to the image quality produced by an IOL. Lenses are also tested for biocompatibility, for the absence of cytotoxicity for the lens and possible additives (such as UV filters), for genotoxicity, and for photostability and safety with YAG lasers. The resolution efficiency of an IOL is tested, relative to the diffraction-limited, cut-off spatial frequency or by testing with the modulation transfer function. There are also standards for spectral transmission. Physical standards exist to ensure adherence to the labeled optic diameter, angulation, strength, and mechanical fatiguability of the components, as well as to ensure sterility, safety if injected, and so on. In the early days of IOL use, explanted IOLs were sometimes found with significant optical distortions or incorrect powers. The quality of modern IOLs is much better. In general, an IOL itself does not limit a patient's postoperative acuity.

Multifocal IOLs

Conventional IOLs correct the refractive ametropia associated with removal of the crystalline lens. However, an IOL has no accommodative power, and its focus is essentially for a single distance only. Of course, the improved visual acuity resulting from IOL implantation may allow a patient to see with acceptable clarity over a range of distances. This ability may be further augmented if the patient is left with a residual refractive cylinder such as a myopic astigmatism. If one endpoint of the conoid of Sturm corresponds to distance focus while the other represents several diopters of myopia and, thus, a near focus, satisfactory visual clarity may be possible if the object in view is focused between these two endpoints. Thus, even standard IOLs may provide some degree of depth of focus and "bifocal" capabilities. An alternative approach to this problem is to correct one eye for distance and the other for near vision, so-called *monovision.*

Nevertheless, most patients who receive IOLs are corrected for distance vision and require overcorrection for near vision. Multifocal IOLs are designed to provide patients with both near and distance vision without additional spectacle correction. Multifocal IOLs differ from spectacles in the way they attempt to correct presbyopic symptoms. Bifocal spectacles provide (in effect) 2 different lenses in the same frame. The patient chooses which segment to look through, depending on the visual task. At any time, either the near or the distance correction is used, but not both at the same time.

However, with a multifocal IOL, the correcting lens is placed in a fixed location within the eye and the patient cannot voluntarily change the focus. Depending on the type of multifocal IOL and the viewing situation, both near and far foci may be presented to the eye at the same time.

Two factors that need particular consideration with multifocal IOLs are lens centration and pupil size. The performance of certain types of lenses is greatly impaired by decentration if the visual axis does not pass through the center of the IOL. However, in general, modern surgical techniques result in adequate lens centration. Pupil size, on the other hand, is an active variable, but it can actually be employed in some situations to improve IOL function.

Accuracy of IOL power calculation is important for multifocal IOLs (because their purpose is to reduce or eliminate the need for spectacle overcorrection). Preoperative and postoperative astigmatism should be low. The surgeon should be careful to select only those patients for whom the benefits of multifocal IOLs outweigh the disadvantages.

Types of Multifocal IOLs

Several types of multifocal IOLs are available, including bifocal, multiple-zone, and diffractive multifocal IOLs.

Bifocal IOL

The bifocal IOL is conceptually the simplest of the various designs. A central zone corresponding to the desired near power is surrounded by a zone corresponding to the desired distance power. When the pupil constricts for near vision, its smaller size reduces or eliminates the contribution from the distance portion of the IOL. For viewing distant objects, when the pupil dilates, more of the distance portion of the IOL is exposed and contributes to the final image. (Obviously, lens decentration can have disastrous effects on the IOL's optical performance.)

One problem with this design is that the patient's pupil size does not always correspond to the desired visual task. For example, if the patient is viewing a distant object in bright light, the pupil constricts, and much of the distance portion of the lens is blocked. In compensation, however, the depth of focus increases as the pupil constricts—thus, fairly satisfactory vision may persist even though the IOL power is off by several diopters. This lens performs most poorly for near vision in low-light situations, in which the pupil dilates. In this case, the pupillary dilation exposes the distance portion of the IOL and the large pupil creates a poor depth of focus.

Multiple-zone IOL

To overcome the problems associated with pupil size, other designs incorporate 3 zones (Fig 6-7). The central and outer zones are for distance; the inner annulus is for near. The diameters were selected to provide near correction for moderately small pupils and distance correction for both large and small pupils.

Another design uses several annular zones, each of which varies continuously in power from 20 D to 23.5 D. The advantage is that whatever the size, shape, or location of the pupil, all the focal distances are represented (Fig 6-8; the undulations in this lens profile have been exaggerated).

Diffractive multifocal IOL

The diffractive multifocal IOL design (Fig 6-9) uses geometrical optics and diffraction optics to achieve a multifocal effect. The overall spherical shape of the surfaces produces a geometrical optics image for distance vision (ie, it provides the +20.0 D power). The posterior surface has a stepped structure. Diffraction from these multiple rings produces a second image, with an effective add power of 3.5 D. The principle involved is that of the Fresnel zone plate.

At a particular point along the axis, waves diffracted by the various zones add in phase, giving a focus for that wavelength. Optical aberrations with diffractive IOLs can be particularly troublesome. Different wavelengths have different foci. This chromatic aberration is in the opposite direction from that produced by the cornea and the spherical surface of the IOL, so there is partial compensation for the eye's usual chromatic aberration.

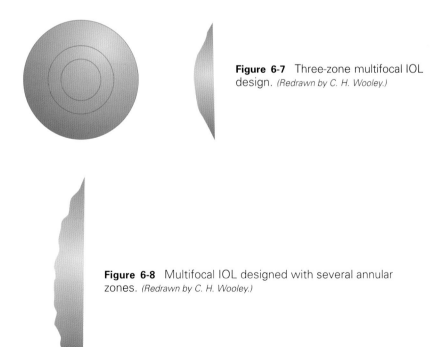

Figure 6-7 Three-zone multifocal IOL design. *(Redrawn by C. H. Wooley.)*

Figure 6-8 Multifocal IOL designed with several annular zones. *(Redrawn by C. H. Wooley.)*

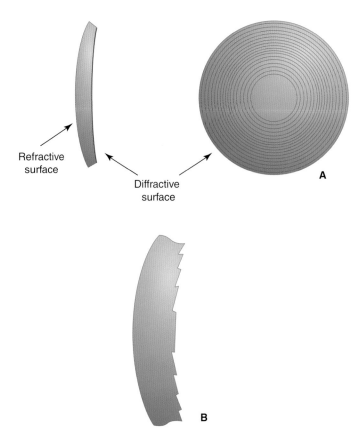

Refractive
surface

Diffractive
surface

A

B

Figure 6-9 **A,** Diffractive multifocal IOL. **B,** Magnified cross section of central portion (the depth of the grooves is exaggerated). *(Redrawn by C. H. Wooley.)*

Clinical Results of Multifocal IOLs

Multifocal IOLs involve some trade-offs. Multifocal spectacles or contact lenses offer different refractive powers to the patient, and in one way or another the patient's gaze is directed through the appropriate power for the appropriate visual task. Multifocal IOLs are different because they do not move (at least laterally) as the eye changes direction or exercises accommodative effort. In effect, both distance and near foci are present from a given object at the same time. The eye, or the brain, can, in effect, choose which image to process and achieve better uncorrected near vision than would be possible with mono-focal IOLs focused for distance vision. The disadvantages of this system are that it results in image degradation, "ghost" images (or *monocular diplopia*), a decrease in contrast sensitivity and lower-light performance (eg, trouble with night vision), and so on.

The best-corrected visual acuity may be less with a multifocal IOL than with a mono-focal IOL; this difference increases in low-light situations. However, the need for addi-tional spectacle correction for near vision is greatly reduced in patients with multifocal IOLs. Some patients are quite pleased with multifocal IOLs; others have requested their removal and replacement with monofocal IOLs. Interestingly, patients with a multifocal

IOL in one eye and a monofocal in the other seem to be less tolerant of the multifocal, and some surgeons will not insert this combination.

Patients must be made aware of the trade-offs with multifocal lenses and be willing to accept their disadvantages. Thus, patient selection is crucial for successful adaptation. Patients must be willing to accept the trade-off of decreased performance at distance (and at near, compared with that of a monofocal IOL and reading glasses)—particularly in low-light situations—in exchange for the ability to see well enough at all distances to be able to dispense with spectacles altogether. Indications for multifocal IOL use are still evolving.

Ford JG, Karp CL. *Cataract Surgery and Intraocular Lenses: A 21st-Century Perspective.* 2nd ed. Ophthalmology Monograph 7. San Francisco: American Academy of Ophthalmology; 2001.

Sanders DR, Retzlaff, JA, Kraff MA. A-scan biometry and IOL implant power calculations. *Focal Points: Clinical Modules for Ophthalmologists.* San Francisco: American Academy of Ophthalmology; 1995, module 10.

Accommodating IOLs

Most IOLs have a fixed focus with a single focal length and lens power. Multifocal IOLs may have multiple focal lengths and lens powers, but they are still fixed and unchanging. Accommodating IOLs may allow some degree of improved near vision with accommodative effort. The mechanism usually involves accommodative effort being linked to an anterior movement of the IOL, thus increasing its effective power in the eye. Note that this mechanism may be more efficacious with higher-power IOLs, because their effective powers are more sensitive to small changes in position than are lower-power IOLs. Investigators are exploring various ways to develop IOLs in which the power may be modified after insertion.

Cummings JS, Slade SG, Chayer A. AT-45 Study Group. Clinical evaluation of the model AT-45 silicone accommodating intraocular lens: results of feasibility and the initial phase of a Food and Drug Administration clinical trial. *Ophthalmology.* 2001;108:2005–2009.

Findl O, Kiss B, Petternel V, et al. Intraocular lens movement caused by ciliary muscle contraction. *J Cataract Refract Surg.* 2003;29:669–676.

Kuchle M, Seitz B, Langenbucher A, et al. Erlangen Accommodative Intraocular Lens Study Group. Stability of refraction, accommodation, and lens position after implantation of the 1CU accommodating posterior chamber intraocular lens. *J Cataract Refract Surg.* 2003; 29:2324–2329.

Langenbucher A, Huber S, Nguyen NX, et al. Measurement of accommodation after implantation of an accommodating posterior chamber intraocular lens. *J Cataract Refract Surg.* 2003;29:677–685.

Matthews MW, Eggleston HC, Hilmas GE. Development of a repeatedly adjustable intraocular lens. *J Cataract Refract Surg.* 2003;29:2204–2210.

Matthews MW, Eggleston HC, Pekarek SD, et al. Magnetically adjustable intraocular lens. *J Cataract Refract Surg.* 2003;29:2211–2216.

CHAPTER 7

Optical Considerations in Refractive Surgery

This chapter provides an overview of the issues and optical considerations specific to refractive surgery. Refractive surgical procedures performed with the intent to reduce or eliminate refractive errors can generally be categorized as *corneal* or *lenticular*. Kerato-refractive procedures include radial keratotomy (RK), astigmatic keratotomy (AK), photorefractive keratectomy (PRK), laser in situ keratomileusis (LASIK), implantation of plastic ring segments (eg, Intacs), laser thermal keratoplasty (LTK), and radiofrequency conductive keratoplasty (CK). Lenticular refractive procedures include cataract and clear lens extraction with intraocular lens implantation, phakic intraocular lens implantation, and piggyback lens implantation. Although all of these refractive surgical techniques alter the optical properties of the eye in some way, keratorefractive surgery (KRS) is generally more likely than lenticular refractive surgery to produce unwanted optical aberrations. This chapter deals only with KRS and its optical considerations. See BCSC Section 13, *Refractive Surgery*, for more information on KRS.

Various optical considerations are relevant to refractive surgery, in both screening patients for candidacy and evaluating those with visual complaints after surgery. In the following sections, we discuss optical considerations related to the change in corneal shape following KRS, issues related to angle kappa and pupil size, and the various causes of irregular astigmatism.

Corneal Shape

The normal human cornea has a prolate shape (Fig 7-1), similar to the pole of an egg. In the human eye, the central cornea is steepest, and there is a gradual flattening of curvature toward the periphery. In contrast, a simple spherical refracting surface produces a nearer point of focus for marginal rays than for paraxial rays, a refractive condition known as *spherical aberration*. Factor Q is the relative difference between pericentral and central cornea. Note that this is different from the Q factor that characterizes a resonator such as a laser cavity. In an ideal visual system, asphericity factor Q has a value of -0.50, indicating that the center curvature is steeper than the periphery (prolateness). At this value of Q, spherical aberration equals zero. However, this is not anatomically possible in the human eye due to the junction between the cornea and the sclera. The Q factor for the human cornea has an average value of -0.26, allowing for a smooth transition

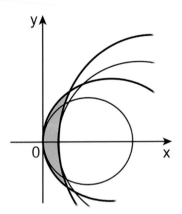

Figure 7-1 Diagram of the cornea's natural prolate shape *(in gray)*, which minimizes spherical aberration, and the oblate shape created by refractive techniques designed to treat myopia. *(Used with permission from Gatinel D, Malet J, Hoang-Xuan T, et al. Analysis of customized corneal ablations: theoretical limitations of increasing negative asphericity.* Invest Ophthalmol Vis Sci. *2002;43:941–948. Redrawn by Christine Gralapp.)*

at the limbus. The human visual system, therefore, suffers from a small amount of spherical aberration, which increases with increasing pupil size.

Myopic KRS results in an oblate cornea, which is like an egg on its side. The central cornea becomes flatter than the periphery (see Fig 7-1). This results in an increase in spherical aberration.

To demonstrate this, consider the point spread function produced by all rays from a single object point that traverse the pupil. Generally, KRS reduces spherical refractive error and regular astigmatism, but it does so at the expense of increasing spherical aberration and irregular astigmatism (Fig 7-2). KRS moves the location of the best focus closer to the retina but, at the same time, makes the focus less stigmatic. It is such irregular astigmatism that causes many visual complaints following refractive surgery.

A basic premise of refractive surgery is that the cornea's optical properties are intimately related to its shape. Consequently, manipulating corneal shape changes the eye's refractive status. Although this assumption is true, the relationship between corneal shape and corneal optical properties is more complex than generally appreciated.

Ablative procedures, incisional procedures, and intracorneal rings change the natural shape of the cornea to effect a reduction in refractive error. Keratometry readings in eyes prior to KRS typically range from 38 D to 48 D. When considering refractive surgical procedures, it is important to avoid changes that may result in excessively flat (less than 35 D) or excessively steep (greater than 52 D) corneas. An 0.8 D change in K corresponds to about a 1.0 D change of refraction. The following equation is often used to predict corneal curvature after KRS:

$$K_{postop} = K_{preop} + (0.8 \times RE)$$

where K_{preop} and K_{postop} are pre- and postoperative K readings, respectively, and RE is the refractive error to be corrected at the corneal plane. For example, if a patient's preoperative keratometry readings are 45/43, the average K is 44. If the amount of refractive correction at the corneal plane is -8.50 D, the predicted average postoperative K reading is $44 + (-8.50 \times 0.8) = 37.2$, which is acceptable.

The ratio of dioptric change in refractive error to dioptric change in keratometry approximates 0.8 due to the change in posterior corneal surface power after excimer

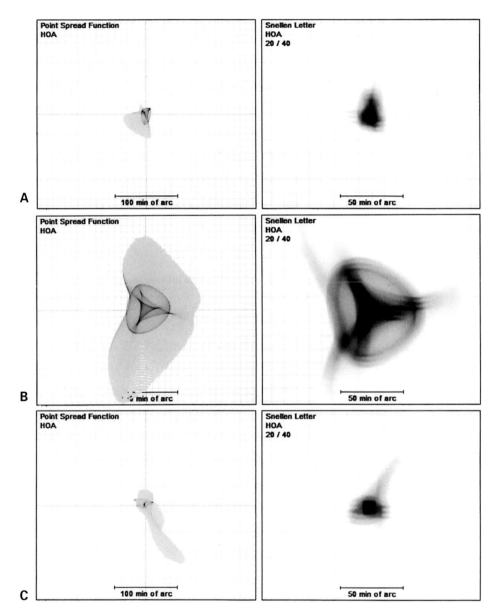

Figure 7-2 Examples of the effects of **(A)** coma, **(B)** spherical aberration, and **(C)** trefoil on the point spread function (PSF) and Snellen letter E. *(Photographs courtesy of Ming Wang, MD.)*

ablation. The anterior corneal surface produces most of the eye's refractive power. In Gullstrand's model eye, the anterior corneal surface has a power of +48.8 D and the posterior corneal surface has a power of −5.8 D, for an overall corneal refractive power of +43.0 D. It is important to recognize that standard corneal topography instruments and keratometers do not precisely measure corneal power because they do not assess the back corneal surface. These instruments estimate total corneal power by assuming a constant relationship between the anterior and posterior corneal surfaces. This constancy is disrupted by keratorefractive surgery. For example, after myopic excimer surgery, the anterior corneal curvature is reduced. At the same time, due to the reduction in corneal pachymetry and weakening of corneal strength, the posterior corneal surface bulges forward, increasing its negative power. The reduction in positive anterior corneal power and increase in negative posterior corneal power results in an increase in the relative contribution to overall corneal refractive power of the posterior surface. When the change of posterior corneal power is included, the ratio of total corneal power to refractive correction at the corneal plane after KRS is unity.

It is important to appreciate the fact that a small amount of tissue removal (in micrometers, µm) in KRS can result in a significant change in refraction (in diopters) (Fig 7-3). Munnerlyn's formula relates these 2 parameters:

$$t = S^2D/3$$

where t is the central ablation depth in micrometers, S is the diameter of the optical zone in millimeters, and D is the amount of refractive correction.

An ideal LASIK ablation removes a convex positive meniscus in myopic ablations. A concave positive meniscus is removed in simple hyperopic corrections. A toric positive meniscus is removed in astigmatic corrections. In toric corrections, the specific shape of the ablation depends on the spherical component of the refractive error (Fig 7-4).

Klyce S. Night vision after LASIK: the pupil proclaims innocence. *Ophthalmology.* 2004;111: 1–2.

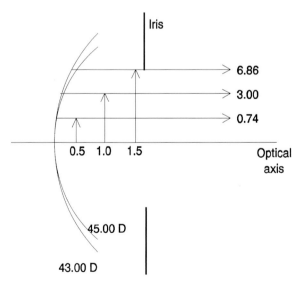

Figure 7-3 Comparison between a 43 D cornea and a 45 D cornea. Numbers below the vertical arrows indicate distance from the optical axis in millimeters; numbers to the right of the horizontal arrows indicate the separation between the corneas in micrometers (µm). A typical pupil size of 3.0 mm is indicated. A typical red blood cell has a diameter of 7 µm. Within the pupillary space (ie, the optical zone of the cornea), the separation between the corneas is less than the diameter of a red blood cell. *(Courtesy of Edmond H. Thall, MD.)*

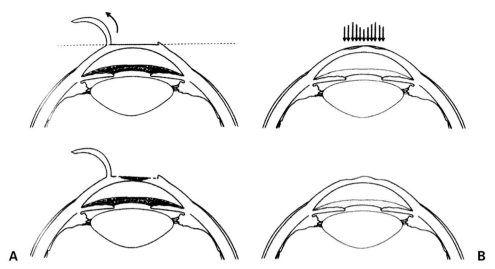

Figure 7-4 An illustration of the tissue removed during excimer ablative procedures. **A,** LASIK myopic treatment. **B,** PRK hyperopic treatment. *(Used with permission from Azar DT. Refractive Surgery. Stamford, CT: Appleton and Lange; 1997.)*

Munnerlyn CR, Koons SJ, Marshall J. Photorefractive keratectomy: a technique for laser refractive surgery. *J Cataract Refract Surg.* 1988;14:46–52.

Angle Kappa

The pupillary axis is the line perpendicular to the corneal surface through the midpoint of the entrance pupil. The visual axis is the line connecting the point of fixation to the fovea. *Angle kappa* is defined as the angle between the pupillary axis and the visual axis. A large angle kappa results if the pupillary axis differs significantly from the central corneal apex. If angle kappa is large, centering an excimer ablation over the geometric center of the cornea will effectively result in a decentered ablation. This can be particularly problematic in a hyperopic correction, in which a large angle kappa can result in a refractively significant "second corneal apex," causing monocular diplopia and decreased visual quality. A large angle kappa needs to be identified prior to surgery to avoid a poor visual outcome.

Freedman KA, Brown SM, Mathews SM, et al. Pupil size and the ablation zone in laser refractive surgery: considerations based on geometric optics. *J Cataract Refract Surg.* 2003;29:1924–1931.

Pupil Size

Pupil size measurement became the standard of care in the late 1990s, when it was observed that patients with large pupils (greater than 6 mm) had poor night vision after KRS. Typical symptoms included glare, starbursts, halos, decreased contrast sensitivity, and poor overall visual quality. Night vision problems tend to occur in patients with large pupils and small treatment zones (6.0 mm or less). The algorithms used in third-generation lasers incorporate larger optical and transition zones, enabling surgeons to perform refractive procedures on patients with larger pupils. These algorithms decrease the incidence and severity of night vision problems dramatically.

Many surgeons use default ablation zones during excimer procedures. The accepted standard transition zone between ablated and unablated cornea is 0.5 to 1.0 mm larger than the pupil to minimize night vision problems. Smaller optical zones are typically used in higher myopic corrections to conserve corneal tissue. In these patients, the incidence of night vision problems increases because of the mismatch between pupil size and optical zone size.

Although pupil size does not impact surgical outcome as it once did, pupil size measurement continues to be the standard of care in the preoperative evaluation. Patients with extremely large pupils (8 mm or more) should be identified. Spherical aberration may be increased in these patients. Clinical management of night vision problems postoperatively includes the use of miotics such as brimonidine 0.2% or pilocarpine (0.5%–1%).

Freedman KA, Brown SM, Mathews SM, et al. Pupil size and the ablation zone in laser refractive surgery: considerations based on geometric optics. *J Cataract Refract Surg.* 2003; 29:1924–1931.

Klyce S. Night vision after LASIK: the pupil proclaims innocence. *Ophthalmology.* 2004;111: 1–2.

Lee YC, Hu FR, Wang IJ. Quality of vision after laser in situ keratomileusis: influence of dioptric correction and pupil size on visual function. *J Cataract Refract Surg.* 2003;29:769–777.

Schallhorn SC, Kaupp SE, Tanzer DJ, et al. Pupil size and quality of vision after LASIK. *Ophthalmology.* 2003;110:1606–1614.

Irregular Astigmatism

The treatment of postoperative irregular corneal astigmatism is one of the great challenges of refractive surgery today. The diagnosis of irregular astigmatism is made by clinical and imaging criteria: loss of spectacle best-corrected vision but preservation of vision using a gas-permeable contact lens, coupled with topographic corneal irregularity. One important sign of postsurgical irregular astigmatism is a refraction inconsistent with the uncorrected acuity. For example, consider a patient who has -3.50 D myopia with essentially no astigmatism before the operation. Following KRS, the patient has uncorrected acuity of 20/25 but a refraction of $+2.00 - 3.00 \times 060$. Ordinarily, this refraction would be inconsistent with an uncorrected acuity of 20/25, but such results can occur in patients who have irregular astigmatism after KRS.

Another important sign is difficulty in determining axis location during manifest refraction in a patient with a large amount of astigmatism. Normally, it is easy to accurately determine the correcting cylinder axis in a patient with significant cylinder. However, a patient with irregular astigmatism following KRS often has difficulty choosing an axis. Automated refractors may identify significant amounts of astigmatism that are rejected by patients on manifest refraction. Because the astigmatism is irregular (and thus has no definite axis), patients may achieve nearly the same acuity with large powers of cylinder at markedly different axes. Streak retinoscopy often demonstrates irregular scissoring in patients with irregular astigmatism.

Astigmatic enhancements (ie, astigmatic keratotomy, LASIK) are unpredictable in patients with irregular astigmatism. Avoid "chasing your tail" in KRS. For instance, it may be tempting to perform an astigmatic enhancement on a patient who had little preexisting astigmatism but has significant postoperative astigmatism. However, if the patient is happy with the uncorrected acuity (despite irregular astigmatism), it may be preferable to avoid further intervention. Astigmatic enhancement in such cases can cause the axis to change dramatically without much reduction in cylinder power.

It is, in fact, possible to quantify irregular astigmatism in much the same way that we quantify regular astigmatism. We think of regular astigmatism as a cylinder superimposed on a sphere. Similarly, irregular astigmatism can be thought of as additional shapes superimposed on cylinders and spheres. This approach is widely used in optical engineering.

Wavefront Analysis

Ophthalmologists should understand irregular astigmatism for 2 important reasons. First, KRS produces visually significant irregular astigmatism in many cases. Second, KRS may also be able to treat it. To study irregular astigmatism effectively, it is necessary to describe it quantitatively. The most effective method developed to date for describing irregular astigmatism is wavefront analysis.

To understand irregular astigmatism and wavefront analysis, it is best to begin with stigmatic imaging. A stigmatic imaging system brings all rays from a single object point to a perfect point focus (Fig 7-5). According to Fermat's principle, a stigmatic focus is possible only when the amount of time required for light to travel from an object point to an image point is identical for all possible paths the light might take.

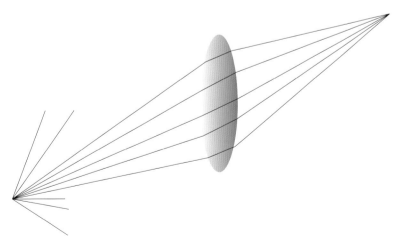

Figure 7-5 If all rays from an object point converge to a single image point, the focus is stigmatic.

An analogy to a foot race is helpful. Suppose that several runners simultaneously depart from an object point *(A)*. Each runner follows a different path represented by a ray. The runners all travel at the same speed in air and all run at the same (but slower) speed in glass. If all the runners reach the image point *(B)* simultaneously, the image is stigmatic. If not, the rays do not meet at a single point and the image is astigmatic.

Fermat's principle explains how a lens works. Rays going through the center of a lens travel a short distance in air, but moving through the thickest part of the glass slows them down. Rays going through the edge of the lens travel a longer distance in air but slow down only briefly when they traverse the thin section of glass. The shape of the ideal lens precisely balances each path so that no matter what path the light travels, it reaches point *B* at the same time. If the lens shape is not ideal, some rays miss point *B*, and the focus is astigmatic.

Wavefront analysis is based on Fermat's principle. Construct a circular arc centered on the image point with a radius approximately equal to the image distance (Fig 7-6). This arc is called the *reference sphere*. Again, consider the analogy of a foot race, but now think of the reference sphere as the finish line (instead of point *B*). If the image is stigmatic, all runners (from point *A*) will cross the reference sphere simultaneously. If the image is astigmatic, the runners will cross the reference sphere at slightly different times (Fig 7-7). The *geometric wavefront* is like a photo finish of the race. It represents the position of each runner shortly after the fastest runner crosses the finish line. The *wavefront aberration* is the time each runner finishes minus the time of the fastest runner. In other words, it's the difference between the reference sphere and the wavefront. When the focus is stigmatic, the reference sphere and the wavefront coincide so the wavefront aberration is zero.

Wavefront aberration is a function of pupil position. Figure 7-8 shows some typical wavefront aberrations. Myopia, hyperopia, and regular astigmatism can be expressed as wavefront aberrations. Myopia produces an aberration that optical engineers call *positive defocus*. Hyperopia is called *negative defocus*. Not surprisingly, regular (cylindrical) astigmatism produces a wavefront aberration that looks like a cylinder.

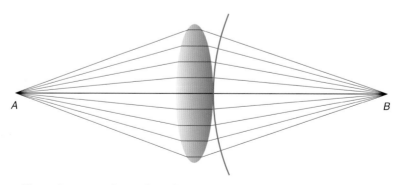

A   *B*

Figure 7-6 The reference sphere *(in red)* is represented in 2 dimensions by a circular arc centered on point B and drawn through the center of the exit pupil of the lens. If the image is stigmatic, all light from point A crosses the reference sphere simultaneously.

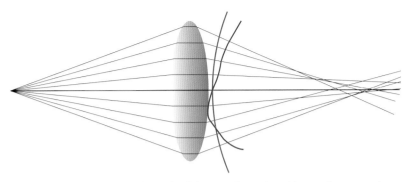

Figure 7-7 When the image is astigmatic, light rays from the object point cross the wavefront *(in blue)*, not the reference sphere, simultaneously.

When peripheral rays focus in front of more central rays, the effect is called *spherical aberration.* Clinically, this is the cause of night myopia and is commonly seen after LASIK and PRK.

Another common wavefront aberration is called *coma.* In this case, rays at one edge of the pupil cross the finish line first; rays at the opposite edge of the pupil cross the finish line last. The effect is that the image of each object point resembles a comet with a tail. The word *coma* means "comet." Coma is common in patients with decentered keratorefractive ablation. Coma is commonly seen in the aiming beam during retinal laser photocoagulation. If you tilt the lens too far off-axis, the aiming beam spot becomes coma-shaped.

Higher-order aberrations tend to be less significant than low-order aberrations but may increase in diseased or surgically altered eyes. For example, if interrupted sutures are used to sew in a corneal graft during corneal transplantation, they will produce higher-order "clover-shaped" aberrations. Also, in the manufacture of IOLs, the lens blank is sometimes improperly positioned on the lathe; this too can produce higher-order aberrations.

Optical engineers have found about 18 basic types of astigmatism, of which only a few—perhaps as few as 5—are of clinical interest. As you might expect, most patients probably have a combination of all 5.

Wavefront aberrations can be represented in different ways. One approach is to represent them as 3-dimensional shapes. Another is to represent them as contour plots. Irregular astigmatism is a combination of a few basic shapes, just as conventional refractive error is a combination of sphere and cylinder. We do not use graphs or contour plots to represent conventional refractive errors, although we could. We simply specify the amount of sphere and cylinder that make up the refractive error. Similarly, once we are comfortable with the basic forms of irregular astigmatism, there is little need for 3-dimensional graphs or 2-dimensional contour plots. We simply specify the amount of each basic form of astigmatism present in a given patient. The prescription of the future may consist of 8 or so numbers. The first 3 will be sphere, cylinder, and axis. The rest of the numbers will specify the irregular astigmatism as quantitated by higher-order aberration.

Figure 7-8 The Zernicke expansion pyramid displaying the first 15 Zernicke modes. The weighted Zernicke modes added together, form a representation of the measured wavefront error **(A)**. Second-, third-, and fourth-order aberrations are most pertinent to refractive surgery **(B)**. *(Reproduced with permission from Applegate RA. Glenn Fry Award Lecture 2002: wavefront sensing, ideal corrections, and visual performance. Optom Vis Sci. 2004;81:169.)*

Currently, wavefront aberrations are specified by Zernicke polynomials, which are the mathematical formulas used to describe wavefront surfaces. Wavefront aberration surfaces are simply graphs generated using Zernicke polynomials. There are several techniques for measuring wavefront aberrations clinically, but the most popular is based on the Hartmann-Shack wavefront sensor. In this device, a low-power laser beam is focused on the retina. A point on the retina then acts as a point source. In a perfect eye, all the rays emerge in parallel and the wavefront is a flat plane. In reality, the wavefront is not flat. An array of lenses sample parts of the wavefront and focus light on a detector. The wavefront shape can be determined from the position of the focus on each detector (Fig 7-9).

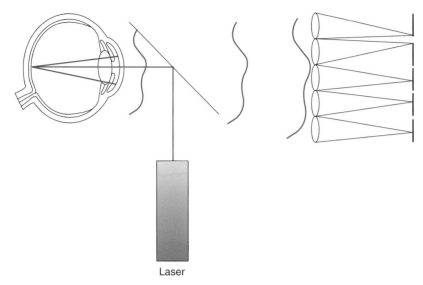

Laser

Figure 7-9 Schematic of a Hartmann-Shack wavefront sensor.

Another method of measuring wavefront is a raytracing method that projects detecting light beams in a sequential manner rather than simultaneously, as in a Hartmann-Shack device, further improving the resolution of wavefront aberration measurement. Zernicke polynomials are less than perfect in their mathematical description of aberrations, however, and alternative methods, such as Fourier transforms, are now being considered.

To normalize wavefront and improve postoperative visual quality in KRS, technologies are being developed today to improve the accuracy of higher-order aberration measurements and treatment using "flying spot" excimer lasers. Such lasers use small spot sizes (<1 mm diameter) to create smooth ablations, addressing the minute topographic changes associated with aberration errors.

Causes of Irregular Astigmatism

Irregular astigmatism may exist before KRS, it may be caused by surgery, or it may develop postoperatively. Preoperative causes include keratoconus, pellucid marginal degeneration, contact lens warpage, dry eye, and anterior basement membrane dystrophy (ABMD). All of these conditions should be identified prior to surgery (Fig 7-10). Common intraoperative causes include decentered ablations and central islands, and, less commonly, poor laser optics, nonuniform stromal bed hydration, and flap complications (thin, torn, irregular, incomplete, or buttonhole flaps; folds or striae of the flap; and epithelial defects). Postoperatively, flap displacement, diffuse lamellar keratitis and its sequelae, flap striae, posterior corneal ectasia, dry eye, and flap edema may contribute to irregular astigmatism.

Figure 7-10 Irregular astigmatism in a patient with significant anterior basement membrane dystrophy (ABMD). The patient complained of glare and overall loss of visual quality. *(Photograph courtesy of Ming Wang, MD.)*

Conclusion

Optical considerations are important in treating patients who undergo keratorefractive surgery. A good understanding of key parameters such as corneal shape, pupil size, the ocular surface, spherical and astigmatic errors, higher-order aberrations, laser centration and angle kappa, and irregular corneal astigmatism can help optimize visual outcomes after KRS. Most patient complaints after surgery are based on subjective loss of visual quality, which can most often be explained by a sound understanding of how refractive surgery changes the optics of the eye.

CHAPTER 8

Vision Rehabilitation

The goal of examining and treating patients in ophthalmology is twofold. The first goal is to prevent, recognize, and treat disease in order to preserve ocular and adnexal function. The second goal is to alleviate patients' symptoms or complaints.

Regarding the first goal, much of the eye examination is aimed at identifying normal and abnormal anatomical structures and physiologic processes. With respect to the second goal, the patient assessment must be approached somewhat differently. The central question in our mind during the history and examination should be, "Why is this patient complaining?" A patient with diabetes, for example, may complain of poor night vision and difficulty reading despite visual acuity of 20/25. These complaints are probably due to extensive panretinal photocoagulation and central photoreceptor damage from macular edema. Conversely, a patient with a nuclear sclerotic cataract may not complain at all, despite visual acuity of 20/70. This situation may be due to preserved near acuity from a myopic shift and minimal demand for distance viewing.

Patients present for help if their visual *function* is impaired, not their visual acuity. The goal of alleviating patient symptoms and complaints can be accomplished only by employing a *functional* approach to patient assessment and treatment in order to improve visual performance and patient function.

The assessment and treatment of pediatric patients is even more complex. Children do not voice their difficulties as adults do, especially those with visual impairment since birth. In addition, several levels of complexity, including developmental and educational issues and the frequent presence of multiple handicaps, are added to the mix.

Vision rehabilitation aims to reduce the functional impact of visual impairment so that patients can effectively maintain their independence, productivity, and quality of life. It should not be thought of as a separate entity from comprehensive ophthalmologic care. All ophthalmologists treat glaucoma patients, retina patients, and external disease patients even if they may not be subspecialists in those fields. Vision rehabilitation is the same.

Any patient with a complaint that cannot be remedied by standard optical, medical, or surgical means is a "low vision" patient who requires "rehabilitation." It may be as simple as completing an accurate refraction and prescribing single-vision reading spectacles or as complicated as prescribing spectacle-mounted telescopes and eccentric viewing training.

A thorough understanding of the principles and practice of vision rehabilitation allows one to address patient complaints more effectively on a day-to-day basis and to recognize when appropriate referral to a vision rehabilitation specialist is required. Much can be done to help patients maximize their remaining visual function in the face of irreversible deficits.

Figure 8-1 presents a useful framework that demonstrates both the overlapping areas of low vision management and how anatomic changes lead ultimately to socioeconomic consequences. For example, a patient with macular degeneration (disorder) who has decreased visual acuity (impairment) may not be able to read road signs (disability) and may ultimately lose his or her driving license (handicap).

Epidemiology of Vision Impairment

It is estimated that 13.5 million Americans over the age of 45 have visual impairments, and more than two thirds of them are over the age of 65. The over-65 age group is expected to rise from 33.2 million in 1994 to 80 million by 2050. Thus, the number of individuals with vision impairment will increase as well. Vision loss is ranked third after arthritis and heart disease as the most common chronic condition requiring aid in activities of daily living (ADL) among people over age 70.

Age-related macular degeneration (AMD) accounts for 45% of low vision patients in the United States, and every year 200,000 Americans lose significant vision from neovascular complications of AMD and require rehabilitation assistance. Glaucoma and diabetic retinopathy are the next most frequent causes. Before these patients become legally blind, they may suffer significant functional visual impairment for many years. Identifying impaired patients and addressing their needs is as important as preventive and therapeutic medical and surgical treatment.

Important Definitions in Low Vision

It is important to define certain terms in order to appreciate the scope of vision rehabilitation in ophthalmic practice.

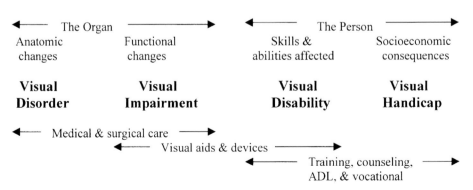

Figure 8-1 Overlapping areas of management for patients with ocular disease. *(Courtesy of Mathias Fellenz, MD.)*

Legal Blindness

The World Health Organization (WHO) defines legal blindness as best-corrected Snellen visual acuity of 20/200 or worse in the better eye or a visual field of 20° or worse in the better eye. Although widely quoted, this definition is not clinically useful, but it is one that was adopted by the federal government to determine eligibility for income tax benefits and federal and state assistance in the United States. It is interesting to note that, because visual field testing is not required in all states to obtain a driver's license, one can be "legally blind" and still drive in some states.

Low Vision

The traditional definitions of low vision rely on quantitative measures of visual acuity and visual field. For example, the WHO defined *low vision* in 1992 as follows:

> A person with low vision is one who has an impairment of visual functioning even after treatment and/or standard refractive correction, and has a visual acuity of less than 6/18 (20/60) to light perception or a visual field of less than 10° from the point of fixation, but who uses or is potentially able to use, vision for the planning and/or execution of a task.

The International Classification of Diseases, 9th Revision, Clinical Modification (ICD-9-CM) divides low vision into 5 categories, as follows:

1. *Moderate visual impairment.* Best-corrected visual acuity of less than 20/60 to 20/160
2. *Severe visual impairment.* Best-corrected visual acuity of less than 20/160 to 20/400, or visual field diameter of 20° or less (largest field diameter for Goldmann isopter III4e, 3/100 white test object or equivalent)
3. *Profound visual impairment.* Best-corrected visual acuity of less than 20/400 to 20/1000, or visual field diameter of 10° or less (largest field diameter for Goldmann isopter III4e, 3/100 white test object or equivalent)
4. *Near-total vision loss.* Best-corrected visual acuity of 20/1250 or less
5. *Total blindness.* No light perception

More recent definitions of low vision include measures of contrast sensitivity and central or paracentral scotomata. The trend to include measures of visual function in addition to visual acuity and visual field reflects an evolving understanding of the complex nature of vision and the factors that lead to functional visual impairment as opposed to visual impairment alone.

The weakness inherent in these definitions of legal blindness and low vision is that the emphasis is placed on only a few objective, quantitative measures that do not fully characterize the visual system's capabilities and do not directly address patients' difficulties.

Visual Function

The term *visual function* is defined simply as the ability to perform important tasks that require vision. It is not synonymous with *visual acuity.* In fact, visual acuity is only 1 measure of visual function. Other measures of visual function include visual field, contrast sensitivity, electroretinography (ERG), glare sensitivity, preferred retinal locus ability, color vision, binocularity, and stereopsis. In order to improve visual performance and patient function, an organized approach to patient assessment and treatment is required. Low vision can better be defined as *reduced visual function resulting from any disorder of the eye or visual system.*

Classification of Functional Visual Deficits

The way in which various eye diseases affect visual performance can be better understood by using an important classification of visual deficits pioneered by Eleanor E. Faye. Three predictable patterns of visual deficits emerge from this classification that clearly relate the pathologic process to the patient's functional status: cloudy media, central field deficit, and peripheral field deficit. These categories help predict patient difficulties and complaints and help the practitioner choose and implement rehabilitation strategies.

Cloudy Media

For a clear overall image to be formed on the retina, light rays must travel through the tear film, cornea, anterior chamber, pupil, lens, and vitreous. Diseases affecting these structures usually impair overall image clarity, causing blurred vision, decreased detailed vision, and significant glare. Contrast sensitivity is typically reduced uniformly at all spatial frequencies. Variable performance on visual function tests often depends on illumination; this is reflected by patient complaints of poor function in sunlight or with strong direct lighting.

Examples of diseases in this category include uncorrected refractive errors, corneal epithelial and stromal disease (dry eyes, dystrophies, keratoconus, scarring from herpes simplex), traumatic mydriasis, cataracts, vitreous hemorrhage, and posterior uveitis.

Central Field Deficit

A clear central image depends on an intact macula and the nerve pathways subserving central vision. Diseases affecting these structures exert their influence via relative or absolute scotomata (blind spots) at or near fixation and/or decreased retinal sensitivity.

Symptoms depend on the number, size, location, and density of the scotomata and on the ability of the patient to reliably use an alternate (eccentric) point of fixation, called a *preferred retinal locus (PRL)*. In the same way that normally sighted people do not perceive their own blind spot as a dark area in their visual field, patients with central and paracentral scotomata usually do not complain of black spots or missing areas in their visual field. This is due to the extraretinal phenomenon of *perceptual completion,* where the brain fills in the missing information using surround information from the edges of the scotoma.

The scanning laser ophthalmoscope (SLO) can be used to accurately map the size, location, and depth of scotomata in the macular region, while directly observing and quantifying patient fixation and eye movement patterns. A great deal of information regarding patient function can be learned from results of SLO testing and studies (Fig 8-2).

Figure 8-2 Patient with a complex scotoma. The *cross* and *circle* indicate preferred retinal locus (PRL) location; *ds,* dense scotoma. **A,** Right eye with a small inferior retinal (superior field) scotoma. **B,** Left eye with a ring scotoma. Even though these eyes have the same acuity, the right eye functions better. For reading, the right eye will not encounter scotomata (which would slow reading speed) to the right or left of fixation. The left eye has only a small functioning central island surrounded by large dense scotomata. *(From Colenbrander A, Schuchard RA, Fletcher DC. Evaluating visual function. In: Fletcher DC, ed. Low Vision Rehabilitation: Caring for the Whole Person. Ophthalmology Monograph 12. San Francisco: American Academy of Ophthalmology; 1999:45.)*

Usual symptoms in patients with central field deficits include difficulty in reading and recognizing people's faces and any task that requires fine-detailed vision. Common descriptions of reading difficulties include blurred or distorted vision, letters popping in and out of view, or the need for more light. Because the highest concentration of cones is found in the macula, color vision deficits can also occur.

Mobility is not affected because the peripheral field is spared. It is for this reason that patients with central vision loss are often misunderstood by their friends, family, and even by their doctors. Their disability is not visible—they can navigate with ease in their environment, do not require a white cane, and yet may be labeled as legally blind. They can spot small items in their normal peripheral field and yet may not be able to recognize a friend or read a bus number. They often continue to drive despite not meeting legal requirements because good visual acuity is generally required only to read street signs in unfamiliar areas.

Visual acuity tests that use single letters or numbers (Snellen, ETDRS) often result in better estimates of visual function than do visual acuity tests that use continuous text, because reading text involves more than looking at each letter one at a time.

Contrast sensitivity is variably affected. Performance for tasks such as reading can be greatly diminished in the presence of a reduction in contrast sensitivity, even when high-contrast visual acuity is apparently good.

Examples of diseases in this category include macular degeneration (age-related or other), macular hole, diabetic macular edema and ischemia, myopic degeneration, toxoplasmosis, histoplasmosis, phototoxicity, drug toxicity, and optic nerve disorders. Focal and grid laser treatment for clinically significant macular edema and photocoagulation [with or without photodynamic therapy (PDT)] of choroidal neovascular membranes cause iatrogenic central and paracentral scotomata with similar symptoms and problems.

Peripheral Field Deficit

The peripheral visual field is crucial for successful mobility and orientation. Variable patterns of field loss can result from diseases of the retina, optic nerve, and central nervous system. The functional implications for the patient are very different from those of the other 2 categories of deficits and, as such, rehabilitation strategies take a different approach.

Typical symptoms include bumping into objects or people and difficulty navigating through unfamiliar territory, especially under poor illumination or at night. A great deal of the peripheral field must be lost before symptoms become apparent to the patient, especially with asymmetric involvement. In advanced cases, reading performance can suffer despite good visual acuity because the peripheral field is involved in tracking and repositioning fixation.

Visual acuity is not affected until very advanced stages; therefore, acuity testing will completely miss early objective findings. Automated or manual field testing is necessary to quantify deficits that occur in this category. Central contrast sensitivity testing will likewise be normal unless the central field is affected.

Examples of diseases in this category include retinitis pigmentosa, retinal dystrophies, retinal detachment, proliferative diabetic retinopathy, glaucoma, ischemic optic neuropathy, stroke, trauma, and tumor. Panretinal laser photocoagulation causes iatrogenic peripheral field loss and reduced contrast sensitivity function that can significantly limit a patient's performance at night.

Patient Assessment

Taking a functional history and measuring visual function are important aspects of patient assessment.

Functional History

The goal of history taking in general is to collect information from the patient that guides the investigation and leads to a diagnosis and treatment plan. This same approach is used for patients who require vision rehabilitation. A shift in emphasis to the patient's functional deficits is required, but a few specific questions can easily elicit this information. Patients usually welcome this approach because, from their point of view, only function matters—how can they more easily accomplish the task they are having difficulty with? The following information is a useful guide to completing a functional history.

Ocular history

Correlate the patient's functional complaints to progression of the disease and to any medical and surgical interventions. Miotic therapy and panretinal photocoagulation are 2 examples of treatments that may adversely affect visual function while having a positive effect on ocular disease.

General medical history

Systemic diseases indirectly affect patient functioning in the completion of visual tasks, in addition to their own direct effects on the visual system. Physical weakness, tremors, or paralysis from a stroke can impair a patient's ability to hold a book or a handheld magnifier and thus interfere with reading. For a patient with cognitive dysfunction, it may be necessary to alter the approach to low vision device prescription and training in order to simplify the information.

Task analysis

Determine what tasks the patient is finding difficult or impossible to accomplish. Doing so allows both the physician and patient to focus on important areas and set realistic goals that can be accomplished.

- *General level of functioning.* What restricted activities are most important for the patient to continue or resume? What adaptations has the patient already made? What are the conditions at home or at work under which the patient is functioning? These are usually not the same as conditions in the ophthalmologist's office, where testing is done. What is the impact of vision loss on the patient and his or her significant others? Are they depressed? Is the patient working? Answers to these questions are best obtained during an open-ended discussion and not necessarily when asked as a list of questions.
- *Near.* Do you have trouble . . . reading books, mail, newspapers, or food or medication labels? Writing, signing your name, paying bills, or managing checks? Seeing the time on your watch, grooming, sewing, or engaging in your hobbies?
- *Intermediate.* Do you have trouble . . . shopping, cooking, or housekeeping? Reading appliance displays, dialing a phone number, or using a computer? Seeing your food or shaving or combing your hair in the mirror?
- *Distance.* Do you have trouble . . . recognizing people's faces, reading signs or traffic signals? Watching television, theater, or sporting events? Driving, and if so under what conditions?
- *Mobility.* Do you have trouble . . . seeing curbs and stairs? Walking in a crowded location? Leaving the house on your own to travel or shop?
- *Lighting/Illumination.* Do you have trouble . . . seeing or reading in dim light? Tolerating bright sunlight or coming in from outdoors? Traveling or walking outdoors at night?

Not all questions need to be asked of every patient. The relevant information can be ascertained in just a few minutes. Appreciate that different patients have different needs and be specific in order to identify reasonable objectives. Asking the patient what he or she would like the most help with is a useful tactic to make this point clear.

Measuring Visual Function

The following tests are useful in quantifying functional losses and adding important information to guide clinical decisions. One should not endeavor to perform all tests on all patients in a clinical ophthalmology setting. However, knowledge of their use, application, and common patterns of deficit allows one to selectively employ the appropriate test and enhance the understanding of patient complaints.

Distance visual acuity

Obtaining an accurate measure of visual acuity is important for the following reasons:

- to follow disease progression and the effects of treatment
- to measure improvement during refraction
- to determine the power of spectacles or optical aids needed for reading and near work
- to estimate a person's ability to perform specific tasks such as reading and driving
- to categorize patients for the purpose of obtaining government, insurance, and other benefits or exemptions

The single-letter Snellen visual acuity chart is the most commonly used test of visual function. Although Snellen acuity provides useful information, it measures only a narrow range of the visual system's capabilities (see Chapter 3, Optics of the Human Eye). It consists of high-contrast black letters on a white background under near ideal illumination conditions. A patient's performance on this test does not characterize typical function, especially under low light or poor contrast conditions, which may be important for many common activities at night or twilight or in dimly lit areas. The effects of glare from extraneous light sources, the presence of central field scotomata, and the intactness of the peripheral field are also not taken into account.

Common acuity charts are not ideal for obtaining accurate visual acuity measurements in patients with reduced vision. Most were essentially designed to measure vision in patients with normal or near normal vision. There are too few lines and too few letters per line on most charts below acuities of 20/70. This can underestimate a patient's ability and makes an accurate refraction almost impossible. The distance between the chart and patient cannot be easily shortened, contrast and illumination may vary over time, and it can be psychologically discouraging for the patient, who may be able to make out only "the big E."

The Lighthouse Distance Visual Acuity Test (a modified ETDRS chart) overcomes many of these disadvantages and is widely used to assess patients with reduced visual acuity (see Fig 3-6 in Chapter 3, Optics of the Human Eye). It uses metric notation and has equal line difficulty, proportional interletter and interline spacing, and geometric progression of optotype sizes from line to line. There are more lines at lower levels of acuity and 5 letters on each line, making assessment and measurement of change more accurate. This is especially important during refraction so that the patient and physician can correctly perceive and measure improvement on the visual acuity chart. The chart is commonly used at a distance of 2 m, which covers visual acuities from 20/20 to 20/400. At 1 m, it covers visual acuities from 20/40 to 20/800. Other charts with similar properties are also commercially available.

If only standard visual acuity charts are available, the patient can be moved closer and the resulting acuity corrected by measuring the new distance from the patient to the chart.

Near visual acuity

The task of reading words and sentences is more complex than recognizing single letters at a time. Testing near "reading" acuity with text samples better estimates a patient's functional reading ability than doing so with single-letter acuity charts. Reading speed is also of practical importance to the reader, who might find it frustrating or even pointless if information cannot be acquired at a reasonable rate.

When recording near visual acuity, using metric notation is simpler and more informative than using Snellen equivalents, Jaeger numbers (J) or points (p). The metric unit for letter size is the M unit. A 1-M symbol subtends 5 minutes of arc at 1 meter (m). It is roughly equal in size to regular newsprint, which can be read with a visual acuity of approximately 20/50. Any visual acuity result can be recorded simply as the distance of the chart or reading material (in meters) over the letter size (in M units). For example, reading 2-M letters at 40 cm would result in a visual acuity of 0.4 meter/2 M, or 0.4/2. This can be easily converted to Snellen acuity: $0.4/2 = 20/x$ ($x = 100$); therefore, the Snellen acuity is 20/100.

Several commercial reading tests are available, including the Lighthouse Continuous Text Card, the Minnesota Low Vision Reading Test (MNRead), the Colenbrander 1-m chart, and the Pepper Visual Skills for Reading Test.

Contrast sensitivity

The visual system's ability to resolve detail depends not only on the size or separation of the objects in question but also on the contrast or luminance difference between the object and its surroundings. Research has demonstrated that visual spatial processing is organized as a series of independent, parallel channels. Each channel is sensitive to different frequencies or separations between lines, and each channel has a different threshold or contrast level at which it functions. A contrast sensitivity function curve can be constructed that, like an audiogram, records a wider range of visual sensitivity than can visual acuity testing (see Chapter 3, Optics of the Human Eye).

Many activities are difficult for patients with reduced contrast sensitivity. Reading gray or colored text on a colored background, walking in foggy or cloudy conditions or in dim light, and pouring milk into a white cup are just a few examples.

Contrast sensitivity testing has several important uses when evaluating patients with reduced visual function:

- *Magnification need.* Patients with poor contrast sensitivity usually require more magnification than would otherwise be expected by their level of visual acuity. Knowing this saves time, allows for realistic recommendations to be made regarding device prescription, and helps explain why patients may not be functioning at an expected level.
- *Ability to use optical aids.* Patients with extremely poor contrast sensitivity may require additional contrast enhancement to be able to read using magnification. These patients may require a closed-circuit television (CCTV), which can significantly enhance contrast and enlarge the field of view enough to see more than 1 or 2 letters at a time.
- *Lighting.* Patients with poor contrast often benefit from better illumination for certain tasks. Although this can be determined clinically, confirmation is helpful.
- *Dominant eye.* By testing contrast monocularly and binocularly, one can determine if the patient will perform better or worse with binocular optical aids (glasses,

CCTV). Superior monocular performance suggests interference from a poorer functioning dominant eye and supports the use of monocular aids such as magnifiers and monocular spectacles.

- *Overall function.* Keeping all the preceding in mind, we see how contrast sensitivity testing can better characterize a patient's functional ability and guide rehabilitative strategies in a directed manner. Specific measures to improve contrast can be employed when testing reveals a significant deficit.
- *Longitudinal parameter.* Following contrast sensitivity over time may reveal deterioration in function that might not otherwise have been detected by visual acuity testing alone. This can corroborate a patient's subjective deterioration in function.

Several contrast sensitivity charts are available commercially, with different features and advantages, including the Vision Contrast Test System (VCTS), the Functional Acuity Contrast Test (FACT), the Pelli-Robson chart, the Regan chart, the LEA Low-Contrast Test, and the Lighthouse Letter Contrast Sensitivity Test. It is not necessary to test contrast sensitivity in all patients; however, it is especially useful in patients who appear to be functioning at a lower level than expected and in patients with deteriorating vision despite stable acuity.

Contrast sensitivity tests may not always be available or practical, but contrast function can also be assessed in other ways (Clinical Pearl 8-1).

Peripheral visual field testing

Kinetic (Goldmann) and static (Humphrey, Octopus) perimetry are the standard tests for peripheral field assessment. Early peripheral visual field loss is usually asymptomatic, and even moderate to advanced loss does not affect function for tasks such as reading. Patients generally present with orientation and mobility difficulties, especially in unfamiliar surroundings. Severe peripheral field loss, as in advanced glaucoma or retinitis pigmentosa, that leaves a residual central field of less than 20° is one of the criteria for *legal blindness* in the United States and Canada.

Central visual field testing

Goldmann kinetic perimetry and static macular perimetry (eg, 10-2 test on the Humphrey Field Analyzer) depend on stable, foveal fixation and have no way of accurately monitoring or compensating for small eye movements. Central tangent screening and Amsler grid testing also depend on foveal fixation and are inadequate for detecting small

---

CLINICAL PEARL 8-1

Contrast sensitivity function can often be assessed by asking a few relevant questions. For example, patients are usually aware that their reading ability is greatly enhanced under better illumination. If a contrast sensitivity chart is unavailable, visual acuity can be retested under low room illumination. Patients with poor contrast sensitivity function will have a greater reduction in visual acuity under these circumstances. However, this only works with non-illuminated and nonprojector charts.

scotomata. Some of these methods work well for peripheral field testing but present problems for accurate central field testing in the presence of macular disease, where fixation is often unstable or extrafoveal. In fact, both problems often coexist.

If fixation is unstable, the patient will show significant eye movement, and the size of measured scotomata will be inaccurate. If fixation is extrafoveal, then all points will be shifted with respect to their true foveal location, and a correct map of the defects will be impossible. In addition, perceptual filling in of scotomata may render some tests, such as the Amsler grid, useless because the patient may not perceive the scotomata at all.

Macular perimetry is best accomplished with a *scanning laser ophthalmoscope (SLO)*. The SLO is a fundus perimeter that allows simultaneous visualization of the retina and stimulus presentation so that one can observe the exact retinal site being tested. This permits a precise correlation between field defects and their true retinal location. In addition, one can determine the specific retinal location employed by a patient for a visual task, such as reading. Simpler methods to map scotomata also exist, such as performing a tangent field at near using a laser pointer as a stimulus on a white sheet of paper.

Most patients with central scotomata reliably develop an eccentric "pseudofovea" called the *preferred retinal locus (PRL)*. The PRL may change over time as the disease progresses, and there may be multiple loci of eccentric fixation. Knowing the location and ability of the PRL in a patient with a scotoma helps the clinician to understand the specific difficulties the patient has in carrying out visual tasks.

The presence of central and paracentral scotomata in diseases that affect macular function, such as macular degeneration and macular edema, is more common than once thought. In addition, the presence of scotomata may or may not correlate with the visible retinal changes of atrophy, scarring, or pigment alteration. Scotomata may be single, multiple, irregularly shaped, or ring-shaped surrounding the macula. They greatly affect function and lead to many of the common complaints heard from patients with macular degeneration (see Fig 8-2).

Eccentric fixation and PRL training can sometimes help patients improve coordination, tracking, and scanning and thereby facilitate function for tasks such as reading.

Glare testing

Many patients suffer from glare or light sensitivity, which interferes with visual performance under certain lighting conditions. Common conditions resulting in glare include corneal edema and scarring, iris defects and abnormalities, posterior subcapsular cataracts, and retinal diseases such as retinitis pigmentosa, cone–rod dystrophy, and albinism. The simplest way to assess glare is by getting the history or performing visual acuity and contrast sensitivity testing with and without a direct source of light pointed toward the patient. Commercially available tests include the Brightness Acuity Test (BAT) and the Miller-Nadler Glare Tester, which reflect light into the patient's eye off a diffusing surface.

Because many patients with reduced visual function require increased illumination in the face of poor contrast sensitivity function, determining whether patients experience glare is important. A balance sometimes exists between too much light and too little light.

Color vision

Acquired color vision deficits may occur in patients with reduced visual function. Poor color vision can affect performance in tasks involving color identification or matching at work, home, or school. It is important to ask patients if they are having any color perception problems that need to be addressed.

Most acquired color vision defects in low vision patients are blue-yellow defects. However, the commonly used pseudoisochromatic plate tests (Ishihara) do not allow assessment of blue-yellow defects; rather, they detect hereditary color vision deficits.

The Farnsworth Dichotomous Test for Color Blindness (Panel D-15) jumbo version is probably the most convenient color vision test for low vision patients, although it can miss mild deficits.

Helping Patients Function Better

Ophthalmologists can help patients function better through a careful refraction and by providing them with the appropriate optical or nonoptical aid.

Refraction

A careful refraction is important for patients with permanent vision loss. A careful refraction helps to determine the appropriate best spectacle prescription, optimize distance vision, and determine the correct reading add. It also helps ophthalmologists advise patients properly in the use of optical and electronic aids with respect to their spectacles and incorporate the correct cylindrical and/or asymmetric corrections into glasses or optical devices.

The following key points will help in obtaining a quick and accurate refraction:

- Use an appropriate acuity chart with sufficient lines and optotypes at the low acuity range.
- Use a trial frame instead of a phoropter to allow for an abnormal head position, nystagmus, and maximal light transmittance during retinoscopy, and to allow for a sufficiently large dioptric interval, or *just noticeable difference,* to be displayed during subjective refraction. In order for patients with reduced visual function to perceive a change between the 2 choices shown during manifest refraction, the dioptric interval between the lenses must be increased. As a starting point, increase the interval from the usual 0.50 D $(+0.25$ D$/-0.25$ D$)$ to 1.00 D $(+0.50$ D$/-0.50$ D$)$ for patients with visual acuity from 20/50 to 20/100 and to 2.00 D $(+1.00$ D$/-1.00$ D$)$ for patients with visual acuity worse than 20/100.

Distance Spectacles

New distance glasses should be prescribed if a patient perceives an improvement in distance vision with the new manifest refraction compared to his or her current glasses.

Optical Aids Providing Magnification

Optical aids include spectacles and magnifiers.

Spectacles

A number of lens types are available in spectacles.

Near (reading) spectacles The simplest way to obtain a larger retinal image is to bring the object closer to the eye. This requires either accommodation or a lens (add) that focuses at the appropriate, shortened distance. The amount of add needed depends on the patient's accommodative amplitude (which decreases with age) and the required reading distance.

The reading add can be predicted by using *Kestenbaum's rule* (Clinical Pearl 8-2). The result is, however, only a starting point. Patients with poor contrast sensitivity or macular scotomata or those who must read print that is smaller than 1 M invariably require greater magnification than predicted by Kestenbaum's rule.

How to prescribe low vision reading spectacles:

1. Determine the best distance refraction and resulting best distance acuity.
2. Place this prescription in a trial frame and add to it the predicted add (determined using Kestenbaum's Rule). Increase the near addition until the patient can comfortably read the target size print (at least 1 M letter size) at a reasonable reading speed. Be sure to reduce the reading distance (1/add, in meters) as the add is increased. Keep in mind that the patient's reading material may be of poorer contrast and quality than standard text reading cards.
3. Introduce additional lighting to determine if this helps the patient read better.
4. Have the patient read his or her own or similar material—newspapers, bills, and so on.
5. Determine if base-in prism is required to assist accommodative convergence. Base-in prism should be considered when binocular function is better than monocular function. This usually occurs when visual acuities are similar in the 2 eyes or if there are complementary bilateral scotomata (Clinical Pearl 8-3).
6. If the patient is functionally monocular, try occluding the poorer seeing eye to determine if reading improves. Consider occluding or frosting the fellow lens if this helps performance.

The near (reading) add may be provided in several ways, depending on the power and needs of the patient.

Progressive addition lenses Although progressive adds up to $+3.50$ are available, patients cannot easily accept this power for prolonged use because the maximum add is only at the very bottom of the lens. It may still be reasonable (after taking cost into account) to prescribe a new pair of progressive addition lenses with the best distance correction and the maximum possible reading add, as well as a separate pair of single-vision readers. Patients can be told, for example, that they will see better for distance and better for near with their bifocals, but they will still need to wear a separate pair of low vision reading glasses to see small print.

Bifocals Bifocal segment adds can be prescribed in strengths greater than $+3.00$ D as long as the shortened working distance is explained to the patient. Such adds are usually

> **CLINICAL PEARL 8-2**
>
> *Kestenbaum's Rule.* The add required to read 1 M print can be quickly esti-
> mated from the measured visual acuity. This *predicted add* in diopters is sim-
> ply the inverse of the visual acuity fraction. For example, a 20/200 patient
> (200/20 = 10) would benefit from a +10 D lens, with the material held at the
> focal point of the lens, 1/10 m (ie, 10 cm, or 4 inches). This, however, is only
> a starting point, and a stronger addition may be needed for some patients,
> especially those with reduced contrast sensitivity function.

> **CLINICAL PEARL 8-3**
>
> Base-in prism should be incorporated into high-plus, single-vision reading
> spectacles for patients who function better binocularly. The ideal range for
> the use of such prisms is usually between +4 and +10 add. The amount of
> prism required is 2Δ (prism diopters) more base-in than the add, in each eye.
> For example, if the distance prescription is plano OU and the appropriate add
> for reading is 8 D, then the prescription should read: OD +8 with 10Δ BI; OS
> +8 with 10Δ BI.

well tolerated binocularly up to the +4.50 range, and, in some cases, an even stronger add can be prescribed monocularly for the better seeing eye. In binocular patients, the optical centers of the segments should be decentered more than required by the near pupillary distance (PD), as this will induce base-in prism and assist accommodative convergence for patients with binocular function.

Single-vision readers A separate pair of reading glasses affords several advantages over bifocals or progressive lenses for patients who are already having difficulty at near.

- The wider field of view facilitates eccentric viewing, abnormal head positions, and the positioning of the illumination source and reading material.
- There is full lens power throughout the spectacle lens.
- If a high-powered add required for reading is placed in a bifocal, the patient will have difficulty with intermediate tasks (such as eating and preparing food) and distance tasks (such as walking and seeing steps) viewed inferiorly through the bifocal.
- Task-specific glasses can be purchased less expensively for more than 1 activity. For example, a patient may have a pair of glasses for reading small print, a stronger pair for loading insulin syringes, and a weaker pair for signing his or her name, looking at photographs, or reading larger-print books.

In patients with predominantly monocular function, always consider the appropriate spectacle strength in the worse eye to avoid the negative effects of prescribing a "balance" lens (Clinical Pearl 8-4). In patients with mild visual impairment, an accurate refraction and the prescription of single-vision readers may be the only intervention required to improve reading performance and function.

High-plus prismatic half-eye glasses Prismatic half-eye glasses are commercially available from $+4$ to $+14$ D with the appropriate base-in prism already incorporated. Fusion may be difficult for some patients above $+8$ D, however, in which case a monocular aid may be more appropriate. These glasses are inexpensive and suitable for patients with low ametropia, with minimal astigmatism and better binocular than monocular function. High-index "thin lenses" with fashionable frames are now available that address past cosmetic concerns. These can also be custom made with the appropriate power and astigmatic correction for each eye and the necessary prism (see Clinical Pearl 8-3). Half-eye spectacle frames are convenient for patients with low ametropia, as they can perform distance tasks above their readers and near tasks through the reader (Fig 8-3).

High-plus aspheric lenses Aspheric spectacles reduce lenticular distortion when higher-power addition is required for near tasks. They are commercially available from $+6$ D to $+20$ D and are essentially a monocular aid. The added cost for an aspheric lens is usually justified above $+10$ D. The short working distance of these lenses makes them more difficult to use, and patients require proper instruction and training.

CLINICAL PEARL 8-4

Patients with greatly asymmetric visual acuity and/or function are often pre-scribed a balance lens in the poorly seeing eye, because it is thought that they "will not use this eye." This logic and practice are flawed. If a central field defect exists, as in macular degeneration, the entire peripheral field im-age will be blurred without the correct prescription. If the eye with the more advanced disease is the patient's dominant eye, interference with the current "better" eye may be increased by the blurred image perceived through a balance lens. If an accurate manifest refraction cannot be obtained, retinos-copy can be used to determine the correct prescription.

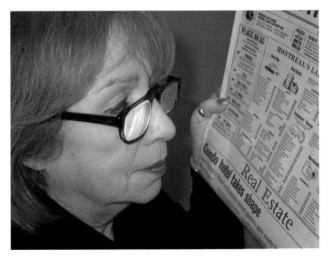

Figure 8-3 Prismatic, half-eye glasses allow binocular, hands-free function at a shortened working distance. *(Photograph courtesy of Darren L. Albert, MD.)*

ADVANTAGES Spectacle aids are familiar and cosmetically acceptable, and they provide hands-free functioning for a wide range of tasks. They provide the largest field of vision and allow for greater reading speed than devices from other categories. Binocular vision is possible up to approximately +10 D of add.

DISADVANTAGES High-add spectacles require a shortened working distance that can obstruct lighting and make tasks such as writing difficult. They are inconvenient for spot reading tasks (eg, seeing price tags when shopping) because they must be put on and taken off and they cannot be worn for ambulation.

Magnifiers

One can think of a magnifier as simply the add-on lens in a spectacle that is moved away from the eye (spectacle plane). As the object and add-on lens are moved as a unit (constant lens-to-object distance), the virtual image also moves. As the lens and object are moved away, the working distance (eye to object) is increased by the eye-to-lens distance. Because the virtual image moves away also, the retinal image becomes smaller. The effective (retinal) magnification of a magnifier is less than that of the corresponding reading add. With handheld magnifiers, the lens-to-object distance can be changed to bring the plane of the virtual image to the posterior focal plane of the eye. Thus, a patient with emmetropic presbyopia can use a +4 magnifier in lieu of reading glasses.

Because the effective field of view is limited by the rim of the lens, the field of view decreases as the lens is moved away from the eye. Hence, spectacle correction gives the widest field of view and the highest magnification for a given lens power.

Continuous text reading is possible with magnifiers for patients with mild to moderate vision loss. When function is more severely affected, magnifiers may allow for only short reading periods or spot reading because of the reduced reading speed associated with a smaller field of view.

Handheld magnifiers Handheld magnifiers are readily accepted by a majority of patients with reduced visual function. The variety found in most regular stores and pharmacies is, however, generally of low quality and low power. Higher-quality lenses, including aspheric models, greatly enhance image quality and function. Once the magnification need is deteremined for a specific task, several models should be demonstrated to patients. The most commonly prescribed powers usually fall between +10 D and +20 D because below +10 D, spectacles can usually be used effectively; above +20 D, the higher magnification necessitates greater image stability and contrast enhancement.

ADVANTAGES Handheld magnifiers are readily accepted, as they are familiar devices that allow a greater working distance than high-plus spectacles. They are relatively inexpensive and portable and can be used with a patient's regular spectacles in place. Illuminated models are available that enhance contrast if needed while limiting glare.

DISADVANTAGES Patients with tremors, arthritis, paralysis, or poor hand–eye coordination have difficulty holding handheld magnifiers steady as they scan along lines of continuous text. Prolonged reading can be tedious because of the reduced field of view, especially with higher-power magnifiers. They must be held at the correct working distance to obtain the maximum effect.

Stand magnifiers Stand magnifiers maintain the correct lens-to-object distance, allowing the device to rest on a flat surface with perfect stability. They can be moved along a page to read or for other near tasks. They are useful for patients who are unable to hold a handheld magnifier steady or for those who need greater magnification than is practical to provide in a handheld magnifier or spectacle. Illuminated stand magnifiers are one of the most useful devices for patients with macular degeneration who have poor contrast sensitivity (Fig 8-4). The added illumination improves contrast and reduces the amount of magnification needed, usually resulting in faster reading speeds.

ADVANTAGES It is easy to maintain a stabilized image at higher magnification; they are hands-free.

DISADVANTAGES Stand magnifiers may be bulky to carry and difficult to use on uneven surfaces. They require proper positioning of reading material and tend to elicit poor posture. The design of stand magnifiers often blocks good lighting unless they are illuminated.

Telescopes Tasks that require magnification for distance viewing are far less common than those for near viewing, especially in older patients. As many patients with low myopia realize, clear distance vision is usually required only for reading street signs while driving, reading a blackboard in school, or reading text or subtitles on television or at the movies. The simplest way to enlarge the image for distance viewing is by "approach

Figure 8-4 An illuminated stand magnifier placed flat against the page combines magnification, illumination, and stability. As with all optical magnifiers, the field of view decreases with increased magnification. *(Photograph courtesy of Darren L. Albert, MD.)*

magnification"—sitting closer to the television or to the blackboard, for example—but this may not always be possible.

Telescopic devices can be prescribed to improve function for specific tasks. For example, monocular, handheld telescopes can be worn around the neck on a cord and used for intermittent distance viewing. The patient stops walking or moving, holds the telescope up to the better-seeing eye, views the material, and then puts down the telescope to resume activities. Binoculars are familiar, are available in different powers, and can be used at sporting events and theaters (Fig 8-5).

Monocular or binocular spectacle-mounted telescopes can allow hands-free use for continuous distance or near viewing, but they cannot be used while ambulating or driving because of the limited field of view and magnified motion. Self-contained, autofocus models are also available. Bioptic telescopes mounted in the top of distance spectacles can be used for driving in many states. The telescopic portion of the spectacles is usually positioned superiorly and temporally to the line of sight and used only briefly to read signs. Proper prescription and training is usually required on an individual basis.

ADVANTAGES Models are available that focus from near through intermediate and distance for a wide range of tasks. They are mostly lightweight and portable and can be mounted on spectacles in some cases.

DISADVANTAGES Telescopes have a restricted field of view and a narrow depth of field, making their use somewhat more difficult. Luminance and contrast are reduced by the multiple-lens system, and they are relatively expensive. They must be held very steady, especially as magnification power increases.

Prisms for special clinical situations: Partial prism for homonymous hemianopia Suppose a patient has a dense or complete left homonymous hemianopia that makes scanning of the left visual field problematic. If a 10Δ base-out prism is placed over the left half of the left spectacle lens and a 10Δ base-in prism over the left half of the right lens (without obstructing the primary position), the patient will be able to scan more quickly through the blind half-field.

Prisms for special clinical situations: Parallel prisms for nystagmus Parallel prisms have been used for patients who assume a head turn because of an eccentric nystagmus null point; however, they are of limited value with small head turns, which are not generally noticeable.

Nonoptical Aids

Many devices are available to facilitate the daily activities of patients with vision loss. It is helpful to provide patients and/or their family members with a catalog or list of stores where these items can be seen and purchased. Many vision rehabilitation programs or centers can identify specific patient needs via a home visit.

Large-print books are printed in a font size 2 to 3 times that of normal newsprint. Patients with moderate vision loss benefit from books, newspapers, magazines, playing cards, and bank checks with larger-than-normal letters. Other useful items include digital

Figure 8-5 **A,** *Top:* Binocular, spectacle-mounted telescopes are available for prolonged distance tasks such as watching a theater play and/or near tasks such as reading. *Bottom left:* A high-power (6×), monocular, handheld Keplerian telescope may be difficult to hold steady and on target due to magnified motion and a narrow field of view. *Bottom right:* A low-power (2.8×) monocular, handheld Galilean telescope is ideal for intermittent distance tasks such as reading a street sign or bus number. **B,** Hand–eye coordination and training are both required for successful use of telescopic and other visual aids. *(Photographs courtesy of Darren L. Albert, MD.)*

clocks, wristwatches, telephones, remote controls, and thermostats with extra-large numbers. Patients should be made aware of useful aids such as needle threaders, dark-lined writing paper, felt-tip pens, and reverse-contrast keyboard stickers.

Nonvisual assistance

As visual loss becomes more profound, vision enhancement may become less effective, and the importance of "visual substitution skills" such as tactile and auditory aids increases.

Tactile aids range from raised dots on a kitchen dial to a white cane for mobility to the use of braille for reading. Scanners that convert standard print directly into braille are available for blind students.

Auditory aids include such information sources as radio and television, talking books, and reader services. Talking wristwatches and voice output computers are also available. Optical character recognition (OCR) and screen-reading software, coupled with a voice synthesizer, are employed to help blind or nearly blind people read.

Electronic magnification

Closed-circuit television (CCTV) systems consist of a camera to capture an image of the object to be viewed (eg, written text, photograph) and a monitor to display the material to the person with a visual impairment. The image can be processed to enlarge it, increase the brightness, improve the contrast, or change the color, in much the same way that the image on a television can be adjusted.

Thanks to the revolution in display technology, a clear image can be rendered on a television or a portable liquid crystal display (LCD) or on goggles that were developed for the computer gaming industry. Flexible organic light-emitting diode (OLED) displays and retinal scanning technology, which projects an image pixel by pixel directly onto the retina, will greatly improve the design possibilities for electronic magnification systems in the coming years.

Improvements in video camera technology and control systems have allowed for CCTVs with autofocus or focus-free zoom lenses, voice-activated controls, automatic scrolling, and simple lightweight designs that make these devices accessible to a greater audience (Fig 8-6).

Miniaturization of electronics now allows complete systems that provide magnification for distance, intermediate, and near viewing to be worn on the head. The development of handheld CCTVs that use a patient's own television has allowed prices to fall from thousands of dollars to a few hundred.

Whereas optical systems suffer from numerous problems that accompany increasing magnification—smaller field of view, closer working distance, critical depth of field, decreased contrast, increased aberrations, and problems with lighting and glare—CCTVs allow for very high magnification without these drawbacks. Objects and text can be viewed at variable magnification, and, with practice, sufficient reading speeds can be attained to allow for useful continuous text reading. Bright, even illumination and contrast enhancement greatly improve function in patients with poor contrast sensitivity. Most systems allow text to be viewed with *reverse contrast* (white letters on a black background), which offers excellent contrast with reduced glare because the normally bright white background of a page is eliminated. Traditional CCTV models and those with a writing stand allow for a sufficient camera-to-object distance such that writing and other tasks can be performed with these devices.

Computers as low vision devices

Years ago, access to computers by people with visual impairment was difficult, if not impossible. Today, not only is computer access easier, but computers allow people with visual impairment to access a world of information in ways that were previously impossible. For someone to use a computer, he or she needs to input information and access information.

Inputting information is made easier by improved keyboard access due to keys with large, reverse contrast characters or *tactile-key* labels placed on a regular keyboard. Special *large-key* keyboards and alternative input devices also exist, including voice recognition systems.

Screen access can be improved by moving the monitor closer, using a larger monitor, fitting an optical magnifier over the screen, or using alternative displays such as those just described. Microsoft Windows and Apple Macintosh operating systems incorporate several accessibility features, including a magnifier, narrator, and on-screen keyboard; these can be very useful for people with mild to moderate vision impairment. Several vendors [eg, ZoomText (www.aisquared.com) and Jaws For Windows (www.freedomscientific.com)] sell excellent screen enlargement software and screen readers that convert information on-screen to audible speech. These third-party software packages have more flexibility and are helpful for people with moderate to severe dysfunction.

Electronic magnification systems and computer technology are merging and will likely provide the most useful and flexible low vision aids in the near future. They may very well replace optical devices completely.

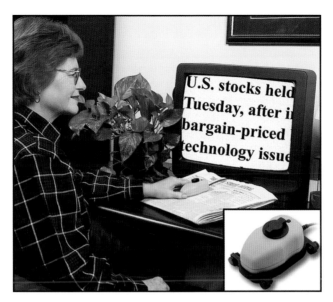

Figure 8-6 A portable, handheld closed-circuit television (CCTV) can be plugged into any monitor or television. It provides magnification as well as contrast enhancement. *(Photograph courtesy of Enhanced Vision, Huntington Beach, CA.)*

Reading device A computer can be thought of as a reading device for people with low vision, because any material that can be scanned, photographed, or retrieved from a compact disc or online can be enlarged on-screen or printed using a larger, darker font. As with CCTVs, the color and contrast can be enhanced at the same time. Conversion to speech and braille output allows those with severe vision loss and blindness to benefit as well.

Writing device A computer is also a writing device, allowing one to record information for later access without the difficulties inherent in writing and reading handwritten text. A laptop computer can be used as a portable electronic notebook, with all the possibilities for access just described.

Contrast Enhancement

Contrast enhancement strategies have already been discussed, but several different approaches can be used simultaneously, such as

- increasing the contrast of the material by reprinting it via a computer or photocopying it with darker print
- using electronic magnification, with its inherent contrast enhancement
- enhancing color contrast between objects and their background—light object on dark background and vice versa
- using contrast-enhancing yellow- or orange-tinted lenses, which have an effect similar to that of lenses in ski goggles.

Lighting and Glare Control

Proper lighting is important for patients with reduced visual function, especially when contrast sensitivity is affected. Depending on the disease process and patient preferences, lighting recommendations can be made that will help patients perfom better.

In the absence of glare, patients with macular degeneration who have poor contrast sensitivity perfom better, read faster, and require less magnification when strong illumination is provided. Many of the drawbacks of high-powered devices can be alleviated by reducing the magnification required. Patients should be shown how to position light sources, such as lamps and overhead lighting, so that glare is not produced by a direct light shining toward the patient's face. Illuminated hand and stand magnifiers often provide the additional boost in function that patients need.

Too much light can also be a problem for some patients. Patients may suffer from glare, both indoors and outdoors. Glare control may be provided via nonoptical solutions such as hats, visors, sunglasses, and tinted lenses of varying color and density, or by reducing indoor lights. Wraparound and fit-over glasses provide additional protection from overhead and side glare sources. Polarizing lenses can be especially useful for reducing reflected light from water or roads.

Instruction and Training

Some instruction, training, and practice are required for patients to be successful at using any of the devices or techniques described. The use of magnifiers, high-add spectacles, and adaptations for activities of daily living are not intuitive, and explanations must be provided by either the physician or a qualified vision rehabilitation therapist. Training sessions should be given to the patient and, preferably, also to a significant other, who can later reinforce the training.

Counseling and Support Groups

Vision loss can have a tremendous impact on patients' quality of life and emotional well-being. Patients with vision loss experience fear, isolation, anger, and depression when dealing with loss of their independence. Seniors with vision loss are at high risk for falls, injuries, medication errors, nutritional decline, social isolation, and depression at far higher rates than reported for any other disease process.

Psychological counseling and support groups may be part of the rehabilitation team approach to helping patients cope and adapt. Keep a list of patients in your practice who would be willing to talk to new patients dealing with the frustration of recent vision loss. Family members, general physicians, social workers, and others may be called upon to contribute to this rehabilitation process.

Visual Rehabilitation Professionals and Services

A number of rehabilitation professionals provide services for low vision patients, including ophthalmologists, optometrists, *occupational therapists (OTs), orientation and mobility*

(O&M) specialists, rehabilitation teachers, assistants in low vision, psychologists, and social workers. The ophthalmologist should know of the availability of local services and must be able to initiate an appropriate referral.

O&M specialists help patients whose movement difficulties are related to vision loss. Through education and skill training, independent movement is encouraged and maintained. O&M specialists have either a bachelor's or a master's degree and may be voluntarily registered by the Association for Education and Rehabilitation of the Blind and Visually Impaired, the national professional organization.

Resource materials should be provided to all patients. Such materials may include information about alternative transportation, free local and national services (like the Library of Congress Talking Books Program and radio reading services), sources of large-print books and music, telephone information and dialing services, and support groups.

Levels of Vision Rehabilitation Services

Vision rehabilitation services span a continuum from a simple refraction and prescription of high-add single-vision readers to a complex bundle of services provided through several rehabilitation professionals. Many of the principles and techniques described in this chapter can easily be incorporated into the armamentarium of the comprehensive ophthalmologist and must become part of everyday practice.

Patients will benefit if ophthalmologists offer any level of service, as described in the following graduated examples.

A *first* level of service might include providing the patient with information regarding better lighting and contrast and glare control, as well as catalogs of nonoptical aids and a referral for low vision and visual rehabilitation services, if they are available in the community. Communicating to an internist that the patient's irreversible vision loss puts him or her at high risk for depression may also be helpful.

A *second* level might include the preceding services, plus the provision of simple optical solutions. For example, high-add prism readers could be offered that would allow access to standard print for many patients with acuities of 20/60 to 20/100 and even less. The only training required would be a demonstration showing the closer working distance necessary when using these devices.

The *third* level would include the preceding services, plus the provision of a basic or comprehensive low vision evaluation, with the rehabilitation component outsourced. This could be accomplished by encouraging the local hospital's rehabilitation department to have a therapist trained in vision rehabilitation.

The *fourth* level would be the provision of comprehensive visual rehabilitation. This would include all of the preceding services, plus an integrated rehabilitation program, including office-based and home-based therapy. Whereas comprehensive visual rehabilitation may have been financially impractical for an ophthalmology practice in the past, new rehabilitation reimbursement guidelines may allow more practices, clinics, and academic departments to develop comprehensive visual rehabilitation centers.

Pediatric Low Vision Issues

The majority of adults with low vision have lost vision due to an ocular disease. As such, they have already acquired many of the vision-aided skills (eg, reading) that are important for functioning in our society. Children with low vision, however, need to learn these skills despite poor or no vision. The majority of these children have coexisting physical and/or mental disabilities that create further challenges to successful integration into society. In addition, skill acquisition is developmentally linked, thus requiring different interventions at different ages. It is important to be aware of the needs of each age group and then to tailor the assistance to those needs. Rehabilitation of infants and children requires a team approach involving therapists, special educators, and physicians working together with the child and family from the earliest possible moments. Ophthalmologists are the most consistent contact for the parent of a visually impaired child and as such need to be aware of and involved in the rehabilitation process. (See BCSC Section 6, *Pediatric Ophthalmology and Strabismus*, Chapter 31.)

Fletcher, DC. *Low Vision Rehabilitation: Caring for the Whole Person.* Ophthalmology Monograph 12. San Francisco: American Academy of Ophthalmology, 1999; ch 7.

Infants

The ophthalmologist plays a key role in the examination and assessment of an infant with suspected low vision. A definite diagnosis, together with a realistic prognosis, helps to guide the rehabilitation plan. Early intervention by a skilled multidisciplinary team is critical during this stage of development. Vision is the primary means by which infants interact with their world, and vision drives motor development as well. Interventions must be individualized, as each child has different capabilities and challenges.

Preschool Children

For preschool children, more sophisticated low vision testing and more precise evaluation are possible. Near visual aids are usually not necessary due to a child's high accommodative amplitude and the relatively large size of toys and images or text in printed books. In order for accommodation to be used effectively, large astigmatic errors, hyperopic errors, and anisometropia must be treated. As children grow, their interests and needs change rapidly and so must the rehabilitation plan.

School-Age Children

The whole spectrum of low vision aids should be made available to school-age children. The introduction of a dome-type magnifier for near tasks may be well accepted. A hand-held monocular telescope can be used for viewing the blackboard. It is a good idea to introduce new devices at home, so the child becomes comfortable with their use before using them among his or her peers. Typing skills and computer use should be taught early, because computers will likely become the children's main portal to the world of information, and many adaptations are possible through their use.

As each child matures, he or she will begin to formulate and express personal goals. Parents and the vision rehabilitation team need to be sensitive to these goals, because the ultimate success of the rehabilitation program depends on the child's continued active participation.

Teenagers

Low vision aids that were used at a younger age may be rejected by teenagers concerned about peer acceptance. Peer pressure, real or perceived, may influence teens so much that they may choose to compromise their visual functioning in order to appear "normal." Good communication and sensitivity to these issues allow the rehabilitation specialist to provide aids that maximize visual function but minimize the cosmetic unacceptability.

American Academy of Ophthalmology, Vision Rehabilitation Committee. *Vision Rehabilitation for Adults.* Preferred Practice Pattern. San Francisco: American Academy of Ophthalmology; 2001.

Faye E, Albert D, Freed B, et al. *The Lighthouse Ophthalmology Resident Training Manual: A New Look at Low Vision Care.* New York: Lighthouse International; 2001.

Fletcher, DC. *Low Vision Rehabilitation: Caring for the Whole Person.* Ophthalmology Monograph 12. San Francisco: American Academy of Ophthalmology; 1999.

Rosenthal BP, Cole RG, London R. *Functional Assessment of Low Vision.* St. Louis: Mosby-Year Book; 1996.

CHAPTER 9

Telescopes and Optical Instruments

The instruments used in clinical ophthalmology are based on the very optical principles discussed in this book. An understanding of the inner working of the instruments we use in everyday practice provides a greater degree of proficiency in their use and a recognition of their limitations.

Direct Ophthalmoscope

The direct ophthalmoscope (Fig 9-1) allows for a highly magnified, monocular image of the retina and optic disc. The optical principles on which this instrument is based are relatively straightforward. Assume that a patient's fundus could somehow be made luminous. If the patient's eye were emmetropic, the patient's retina would be in sharp focus to a clinician looking through the ophthalmoscope, assuming that the clinician too were emmetropic. The patient's crystalline lens and cornea refract light rays emanating from the retina, causing them to exit the patient's eye parallel to one another. These parallel rays then enter the observer's eye and are refracted by the observer's cornea and crystalline lens to a focus on the observer's retina (Fig 9-2A).

A series of auxiliary lenses built into the direct ophthalmoscope serves to compensate for the refractive errors of the patient and observer. When a patient is myopic, light rays

Figure 9-1 Photograph of a direct ophthalmoscope: *a,* opening for illumination and viewing systems; *b,* dial for "correcting" lenses; *c,* handle and battery supply. *(Photograph courtesy of Neal H. Atebara, MD.)*

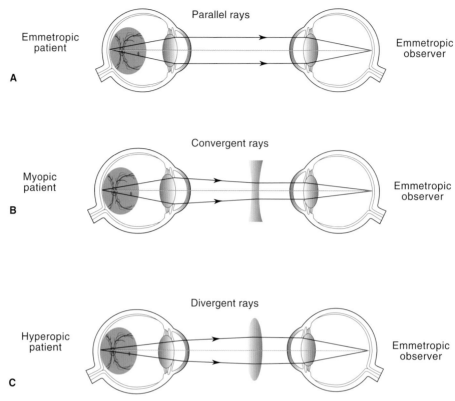

Figure 9-2 Viewing system of a direct ophthalmoscope. **A,** If the retina of an emmetropic patient were self-luminous, an emmetropic observer looking into the patient's eye would see a focused fundus image. This is because light rays from the retina exit the emmetropic patient's eye parallel to one another, and these parallel rays are then focused onto the emmetropic observer's retina. **B,** When a patient is myopic, a minus "correcting" lens must be clicked into place to produce a sharp retinal image. **C,** Conversely, when a patient is hyperopic, a plus lens must be used to compensate for the refractive error. *(Courtesy of Neal H. Atebara, MD. Redrawn by Cyndie C. H. Wooley.)*

emanating from the patient's eye are convergent, and a minus "correcting" lens must be dialed in for the clinician to see a sharp image of the retina (Fig 9-2B). When a patient is hyperopic, divergent rays emanate from the patient's eye and a plus lens is required (Fig 9-2C).

The patient's fundus can be illuminated in several different ways, but they all require that light be passed through the pupil nearly coaxial to the line of sight of the observer. The light rays cannot be exactly coaxial to the observer's line of sight; otherwise, corneal reflection will get in the way. The early direct ophthalmoscopes used a partially reflective mirror. Light rays were reflected by the mirror into the patient's eye. This same mirror allowed some of the returning light rays to pass through it as they traveled from the patient's eye to the observer's eye (Fig 9-3A). This strategy, however, caused light to be lost as it was reflected into the patient's eye and as it passed from the patient's eye to the observer's eye.

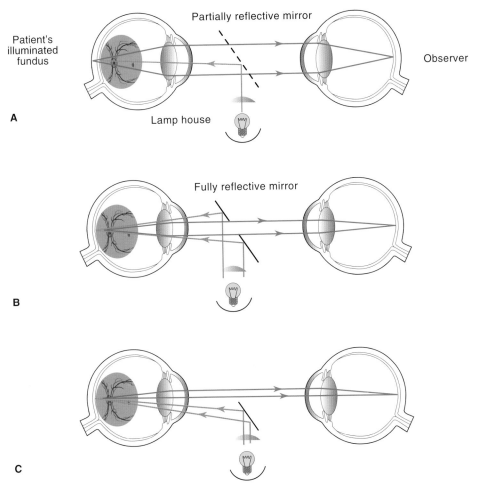

Figure 9-3 Illumination system of a direct ophthalmoscope. There are different ways to illuminate the fundus (using a tungsten or halogen lightbulb). **A,** A partially reflective mirror reflects light into the patient's eye *(orange rays)* but also allows some of the light to pass through it from the patient's eye to the observer's eye *(blue rays)*. **B,** A small circular aperture within a fully reflective mirror allows light to be reflected into the patient's eye while allowing the observer to see the retina through the "peep-hole." **C,** The observer can look above the mirror and view the retina. *(Courtesy of Neal H. Atebara, MD. Redrawn by Cyndie C. H. Wooley.)*

Less light is lost when a fully reflective mirror is used. In this case, the observer views the patient's fundus through a circular aperture in the mirror (Fig 9-3B) or looks just over the edge of the mirror (Fig 9-3C).

Because an eye acts as a simple magnifier, we can calculate its magnification using the "simple magnifier formula," magnification = power/4. An emmetropic schematic eye has a refractive power of about 60 D, so the magnification is about 15×. If the eye is hyperopic by +10 D, its total refractive power is about 50 D and the magnification is only 50/4 = 12.5×. If the eye is myopic by −10 D, its total refractive power is about 70 D, and the magnification is 70/4 = 17.5×.

Indirect Ophthalmoscope

The binocular indirect ophthalmoscope (Fig 9-4A) provides a brightly illuminated and wide-angle view of the retina. This instrument, in conjunction with a condensing lens (Fig 9-4B), works on a principle similar to that of the astronomical telescope. A patient's cornea and crystalline lens act as the astronomical telescope's objective lens, and the condensing lens acts as the astronomical telescope's eyepiece lens. As with all images produced by astronomical telescopes, the image produced by the indirect ophthalmoscope is inverted. The principles on which this instrument works can be broken down into 5 aspects.

Optics of Fundus Image Formation

Fundus illumination is achieved by shining an intense source of light through the pupil. The fundus image is projected out, refracted by the patient's eye. An emmetropic eye projects the fundus image to optical infinity (Fig 9-5A). The parallel light bundles emanating from the eye are captured with a handheld condensing lens (eg, + 20 D lens), and a new image is created at its posterior focal plane (about 5 cm behind the lens) (Fig 9-5B).

Aerial Image

The image floating above the condensing lens is real and inverted and is called an *aerial image*. This image has depth, representing the depth of the 3-dimensional fundus itself. An observer merely focuses on the aerial image to view the fundus. The only lenses required to view the aerial image are those that correct the observer's refractive error and compensate for the near distance of the image, because the aerial image is usually located within arm's length of the observer (Fig 9-6).

Conjugacy of Pupils

In indirect ophthalmoscopy, the pupils of the examiner and patient must be *optically conjugate*—that is, the observer's pupil must project optically to the patient's pupil, and

Figure 9-4 A, Photograph of an indirect ophthalmoscope: *a,* housing for illumination source; *b,* eyepiece; *c,* mirror complex. **B,** Photograph of a + 20 D condensing lens. *(Photograph courtesy of Neal H. Atebara, MD.)*

A

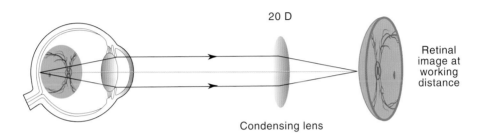

B

Figure 9-5 Indirect ophthalmoscope. **A,** When the fundus of an emmetropic patient is illuminated, light is refracted by the crystalline lens and cornea and is projected out of the eye, forming an image of the retina at optical infinity. **B,** To make it more practical to view this image, a condensing lens is used to focus light to a comfortable working distance. A +20 D condensing lens focuses collimated light 5 cm behind the lens, producing a retinal image at a comfortable working distance in front of the observer *(Courtesy of Neal H. Atebara, MD. Redrawn by Cyndie C. H. Wooley.)*

Figure 9-6 Indirect ophthalmoscope: the "aerial" image. After a condensing lens produces an aerial image, all the observer has to do to see the patient's retina is look at this image. The only optical correction the observer needs is that for refractive error or presbyopia. *(Courtesy of Neal H. Atebara, MD. Redrawn by Cyndie C. H. Wooley.)*

vice versa. When this happens, the maximal amount of light passes from the patient's fundus into the observer's eye (Fig 9-7A). From this position, if the condensing lens is moved closer to the patient's eye, the peripheral fundus is not illuminated. To the observer, the peripheral retina is dark (Fig 9-7B). If the condensing lens is moved farther

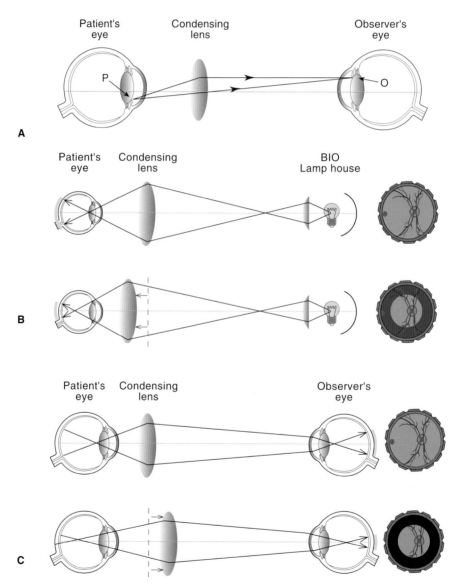

Figure 9-7 Indirect ophthalmoscope: conjugacy of pupils. **A,** In indirect ophthalmoscopy, the pupils must be "in register" with each other—that is, the observer's pupil (O) must project optically to the patient's pupil (P). **B,** If the condensing lens is moved too close to the patient's eye, the peripheral fundus will not be illuminated. **C,** If the condensing lens is moved too far from the patient's eye, light from the peripheral retina will not reach the observer's eye. (Courtesy of Neal H. Atebara, MD. Redrawn by Cyndie C. H. Wooley.)

away from the patient's eye, light from the peripheral retina will not reach the observer's eye and, again, the peripheral retina will appear dark to the observer (Fig 9-7C).

Fundus Illumination

The same condensing lens must also project an image of the illumination source into the patient's eye, and it must do so through an area of the patient's pupil that is not "occupied" by outgoing light; otherwise, reflections will get in the way (Fig 9-8).

Binocular Observation

To appreciate the 3-dimensionality of the aerial image, both of the observer's pupils must receive light from the aerial image. This can occur only if both of the observer's pupils are imaged within the patient's pupil. To "fit" both of the observer's pupils in this small space, the observer's interpupillary distance must be reduced by mirrors (Fig 9-9).

If a patient's pupil does not dilate well, the images of the observer's pupils must be squeezed into an even smaller space. One way this can be accomplished is by retracting the triangular mirror of the indirect ophthalmoscope, causing the path of light from the patient's eye to be reflected nearer to the tip of the triangular mirror and resulting in a narrower path of light (Fig 9-10A). A similar effect can be achieved by widening the interpupillary distance of the indirect ophthalmoscope. This causes light from the patient's eye to be reflected nearer to the tip of the triangular mirror, resulting in a narrower path of light (Fig 9-10B).

Fundus Camera

Fundus cameras capture black-and-white, color, fluorescein angiographic, and indocyanine green angiographic images of the fundus. These cameras employ the same optical principles as the indirect ophthalmoscope, except that the condensing lens is fixed within the camera housing and a flash illumination source is required for the photographic

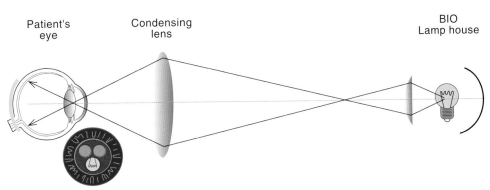

Figure 9-8 Indirect ophthalmoscope: illumination source. Light is projected into the patient's eye using the same condensing lens that creates the aerial image. When incoming light passes through the patient's pupil, it must not coincide with the path taken by outgoing light; otherwise, reflections will interfere with the observer's view. *(Courtesy of Neal H. Atebara, MD. Redrawn by Cyndie C. H. Wooley.)*

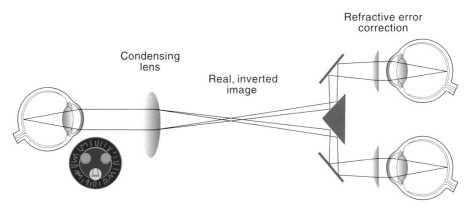

Figure 9-9 Indirect ophthalmoscope: binocular observation. To "fit" both of the observer's pupils *(orange circles)* inside the patient's pupil *(black circle)*, the interpupillary distance must be narrowed using mirrors. *(Courtesy of Neal H. Atebara, MD. Redrawn by Cyndie C. H. Wooley.)*

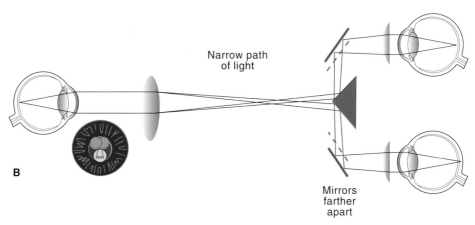

Figure 9-10 A, If a patient's pupil does not dilate well, the observer's interpupillary distance can be narrowed to "squeeze through" a smaller space. This can be accomplished by moving the triangular mirror closer to the observer. **B,** Alternatively, it can be accomplished by moving the viewing lenses farther apart. *(Courtesy of Neal H. Atebara, MD. Redrawn by Cyndie C. H. Wooley.)*

exposure. As a result, these cameras are relatively large; their weight is supported on an adjustable platform similar to that of a slit-lamp biomicroscope (Figs 9-11 and 9-12).

As in indirect ophthalmoscopy, the illumination source is projected through a patient's pupil with a series of condensing lenses and mirrors or beam splitters. In addition, a photography flash lamp is folded into the optical pathway via a beam splitter. This

Figure 9-11 Photograph of a fundus and fluorescein angiography camera: *a*, patient forehead rest; *b*, fixation light; *c*, objective lens; *d*, fixation pointer; *e*, magnification lever; *f*, camera housing and eyepiece; *g*, joystick. *(Photograph courtesy of Neal H. Atebara, MD.)*

Figure 9-12 Schematic view of a Zeiss fundus camera. The incandescent lamp (for observation) and the flash lamp (for photography) are superimposed by means of a beam splitter so that light from the flash travels along exactly the same path as the observation light. The lamp filaments are imaged in the vicinity of the holed mirror, which deflects light toward the eye. The holed mirror is similar to the mirror in many retinoscopes, having a central hole to allow observation. Unlike a retinoscope's mirror, however, the holed mirror in a fundus camera is imaged into the plane of the patient's pupil by the objective lens. The objective lens corresponds to the condensing lens in an indirect ophthalmoscope and, like the condensing lens, it is designed with aspheric surfaces to provide the best possible image quality over a wide field of view. *(Courtesy of Neal H. Atebara, MD.)*

allows light from the flash to travel along exactly the same path as that from the illumination source (Fig 9-13). Optical filters can be positioned within the optical pathway to restrict the wavelengths of light used to illuminate the fundus during photography and angiography. A fixation pointer can be placed in the illumination pathway at a position conjugate to the patient's fundus. The patient sees a sharp outline of the pointer, and the shadow of the pointer on the patient's fundus appears on the photographic film.

With the fundus illuminated, an aerial image of the fundus is formed by the camera's objective lens. This image, like the aerial image in indirect ophthalmoscopy, is inverted. The viewing system is a camera, often employing a single-lens reflex (SLR) 35-mm camera body or digital camera. The camera lens focuses on the image formed by the condensing lens and projects it onto photographic film or a photodetector (Fig 9-14). As in indirect ophthalmoscopy, the optical pathways of illumination and observation/photography must pass through different areas of the patient's pupil; otherwise, reflections from the cornea and crystalline lens will degrade the camera image.

Nonmydriatic cameras have been developed to allow fundus photography without dilation. These cameras use infrared light in conjunction with semiautomatic or automatic focusing systems. Infrared light does not constrict the pupil. After alignment and focusing are completed, a white light flash is triggered, and the photograph is taken before the pupil has a chance to constrict.

Most standard fundus cameras provide a 30° field of view that includes the optic disc and the temporal macula. Special wide-angle fundus cameras have large-diameter, aspheric objective lenses with a field of view of up to 60°. Wide-angle photographs (even up to 148°) are possible, but a contact-type objective lens and a special transscleral illumination source are necessary.

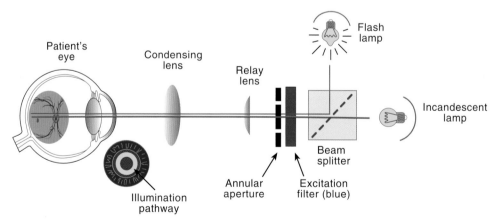

Figure 9-13 Illumination system of a fundus camera. A fundus camera requires 2 separate light sources: (1) an incandescent lamp so a photographer can view the fundus to position and focus the image, and (2) a flash lamp, which produces a bright flash for the photographic exposure. A beam splitter allows the 2 systems to travel along the same optical path. An annular aperture controls the amount of light projected from the flash lamp and incandescent lamp, and a relay lens helps direct the light into the patient's eye. *(Courtesy of Neal H. Atebara, MD. Redrawn by Cyndie C. H. Wooley.)*

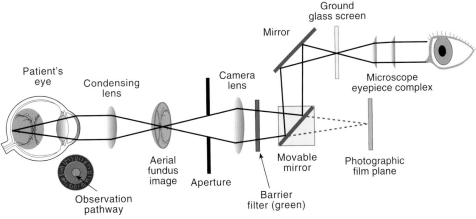

Figure 9-14 Observation system of a fundus camera. The observation system of a fundus camera is similar to that of an indirect ophthalmoscope. The condensing lens takes light rays from the illuminated fundus and creates an "aerial" image. A conventional single-lens reflex camera body, with its microscope eyepiece and ground glass screen, is then used to focus on the aerial image. When the photograph is taken, a movable mirror flips up, exposing the film or photodetector. *(Courtesy of Neal H. Atebara, MD. Redrawn by Cyndie C. H. Wooley.)*

Video ophthalmoscopy has been attempted, but thus far excessive illumination is required and resolution has been poor. Scanning laser ophthalmoscopy is a promising technology. A single spot of laser light is scanned over the fundus, with each point being recorded as it is illuminated. Extremely low levels of total fundus illumination are therefore required.

Slit-Lamp Biomicroscope

A slit-lamp biomicroscope (Fig 9-15) is a high-powered binocular microscope with a slit-shaped illumination source, specially designed for viewing the different optically transparent layers of the eye. The slit lamp is a compound microscope, meaning that it is constructed using multiple lenses carefully arranged to form a more magnified and sharper image than a single lens could produce on its own. Other lenses and mirrors are also incorporated into the instrument to ensure an upright image, provide variable magnification, and deliver the brightest image possible. Each manufacturer has its own proprietary refinements, but the basic design includes the following components:

- astronomical telescope
- inverting prism
- Galilean telescope
- objective lens
- illumination system
- binocular viewing system

Figure 9-15 Photograph of a typical slit-lamp biomicroscope: *a,* patient headrest; *b,* lamp housing; *c,* slit-beam control; *d,* magnification changer; *e,* eyepiece complex. *(Photograph courtesy of Neal H. Atebara, MD.)*

Astronomical Telescope

An astronomical telescope is a system of 2 lenses, one in front of the other, both of which are convex (plus-powered) (Fig 9-16). The image is more magnified and freer from optical aberrations than that which a single convex lens could produce. The telescope's name derives from its common usage in astronomy, where observation and photography of the stars and planets are not hampered by the inverted (reversed top-to-bottom and left-to-right) image it produces. The astronomical telescope, when used as a component of a microscope, is often referred to as "the eyepiece."

Inverting Prism

Because clinicians need to be able to simultaneously observe and manipulate ocular structures, sometimes using fine instruments, an upright image is essential for precise eye–hand coordination. An inverting prism takes the upside-down image formed by the astronomical telescope and inverts it to produce an erect image. There are numerous designs for inverting prisms. One of the common ones used in slit-lamp biomicroscopes is the Porro-Abbe prism, which is essentially 2 triangular prisms arranged to reflect light (using the principle of total internal reflection) several times, ultimately resulting in an optically sharp, inverted image with no magnification and little loss of light (Fig 9-17).

Galilean Telescope

A Galilean telescope, in series with an astronomical telescope, is often employed to produce even higher magnifications. Galilean telescopes have 1 convex lens and 1 concave lens, separated by the sum of their focal lengths (Fig 9-18). The image produced is upright, so no additional inverting prism is necessary. When the object being studied is in front of the convex lens, the image is magnified. If the positions of the lenses are

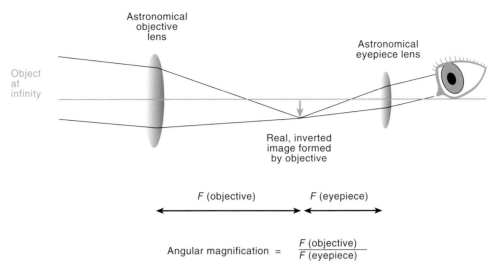

Astronomical
objective
lens

Astronomical
eyepiece lens

Object
at
infinity

Real, inverted
image formed
by objective

F (objective)   F (eyepiece)

$$\text{Angular magnification} = \frac{F\text{ (objective)}}{F\text{ (eyepiece)}}$$

Figure 9-16 Slit-lamp biomicroscope, astronomical telescope. One optical component of the slit-lamp biomicroscope is the astronomical telescope, which consists of 2 plus lenses separated by the sum of their focal distances. This configuration produces a real, inverted image with an angular magnification equal to the focal length of the objective lens (the lens closer to the patient) divided by the focal length of the eyepiece (the lens closer to the observer). *(Courtesy of Neal H. Atebara, MD. Redrawn by Cyndie C. H. Wooley.)*

reversed (with the object now closer to the concave lens), the image is minified. Many microscope designs use this optical "trick" to allow variable magnification. A knob or lever rotates the lenses to reverse their positions. This turns the system into a "reverse" Galilean telescope.

Objective Lens

The astronomical and Galilean telescope systems just discussed are effective at magnifying the image of a distant object—hence their classification as *telescopes*. The slit-lamp instrument, however, requires a working distance of only a few centimeters—hence its classification as a *biomicroscope.* Just as adult patients sometimes require reading spectacles for up-close work, the slit-lamp biomicroscope needs an "objective lens" to move the working distance from infinity to a distance close enough to focus on the eye (Fig 9-19).

Illumination System

The illumination system of the slit-lamp biomicroscope is a unique adaptation that greatly increases the amount and quality of information the clinician is able to glean from observing the eye. An aperture can be introduced to restrict the circular light beam to a slit of variable height, width, and rotation, allowing the light beam to cut a cross section through the optically transparent structures of the eye. Furthermore, illumination and observation systems can be pivoted independently around the eye being viewed (Fig 9-20). This arrangement allows the observer to study the eye from a wide range of angles and vary the angle of incidence of the slit light beam. In this way, a variety of illumination techniques for studying the eye become possible (Fig 9-21).

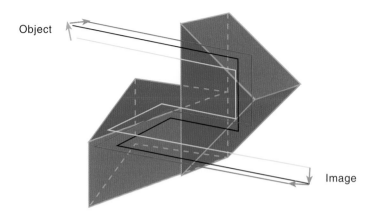

Figure 9-17 Slit-lamp biomicroscope, Porro-Abbe prism. Because the image produced by an astronomical telescope is inverted, a Porro-Abbe prism is added to reinvert the image. A Porro-Abbe prism is essentially the product of 2 triangular prisms arranged to reflect light internally. It produces a sharp, inverted image with no magnification. *(Courtesy of Neal H. Atebara, MD. Redrawn by Cyndie C. H. Wooley.)*

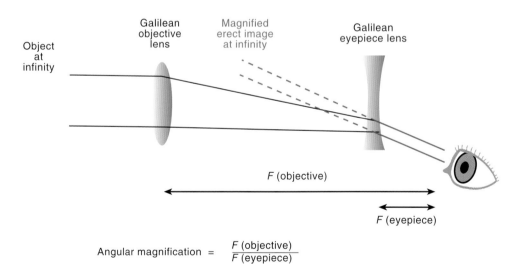

$$\text{Angular magnification} = \frac{F \text{ (objective)}}{F \text{ (eyepiece)}}$$

Figure 9-18 Slit-lamp biomicroscope, Galilean telescope. To produce even greater magnification than an astronomical telescope alone, an additional Galilean system is often used. A plus lens and a minus lens, separated by the difference in their focal lengths, produce an upright, virtual image. The angular magnification is equal to the focal length of the objective lens divided by the focal length of the eyepiece. If the positions of the plus and minus lenses are reversed, the image becomes minified. This optical property is used by the slit-lamp biomicroscope—a quick switch in lens positions allows 2 different magnification powers. *(Courtesy of Neal H. Atebara, MD. Redrawn by Cyndie C. H. Wooley.)*

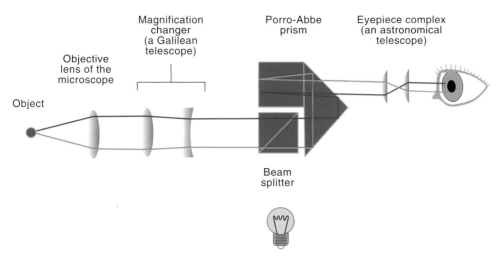

Figure 9-19 Slit-lamp biomicroscope. The final optical element of the observation system is the objective lens. This moves the working distance from optical infinity to approximately 10 cm in front of the microscope. *(Courtesy of Neal H. Atebara, MD. Redrawn by Cyndie C. H. Wooley.)*

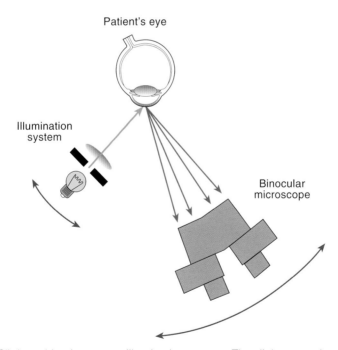

Figure 9-20 Slit-lamp biomicroscope, illumination system. The slit lamp can be pivoted around the same axis as the microscope complex. This unique arrangement allows the observer to vary the angle of incidence of the slit light beam and study the eye from a wide range of angles. *(Courtesy of Neal H. Atebara, MD. Redrawn by Cyndie C. H. Wooley.)*

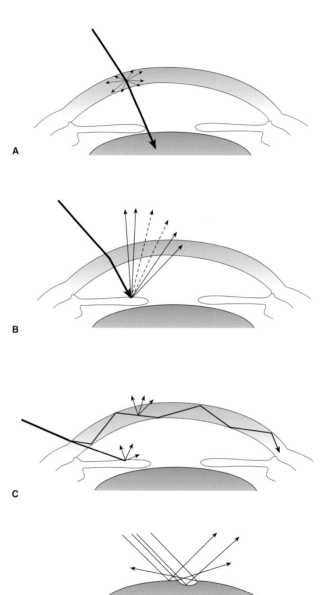

Figure 9-21 Diagram of how light rays interact with the eye in the 4 forms of slit-lamp biomicroscopic examination. **A,** Direct illumination. **B,** Retroillumination. **C,** Sclerotic scatter. **D,** Specular reflection. *(From Tasman W, Jaeger AE, eds. The slit lamp: history, principles, and practice. In: Duane's Clinical Ophthalmology. Philadelphia: Lippincott, 1995–1999:33. Redrawn by Cyndie C. H. Wooley.)*

Binocular Viewing System

In ophthalmology, stereoscopic appreciation of the various layers of the eye is vitally important. The slit-lamp biomicroscope uses 2 lens systems of identical design (one for each eye), each focused on a common point in space, coincident with the point of focus of the slit beam. In this way, the clinician can use both eyes together to get a 3-dimensional appreciation of the magnified eye (Fig 9-22).

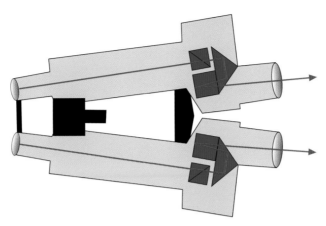

Figure 9-22 Slit-lamp biomicroscope, binocular microscope system. The slit-lamp biomicroscope uses 2 lens systems of identical design, each focused on a common point in space (also coincident with the slit beam). This allows the clinician to obtain a stereoscopic view. *(Courtesy of Neal H. Atebara, MD. Redrawn by Cyndie C. H. Wooley.)*

Slit-Lamp Fundus Lenses

Because the cornea has such high refractive power, it is possible to see only about one third of the way into the eye using a slit-lamp biomicroscope. Special lenses, however, can be placed in front of the slit-lamp objective lens to view the vitreous and posterior pole of the eye. There are 2 approaches to getting around the high corneal refractive power: (1) nullifying the corneal power and (2) using the power of the cornea as a component of an astronomical telescope, in a manner similar to that exploited by the indirect ophthalmoscope.

The Goldmann contact lens (Fig 9-23) and other fundus lenses work by nullifying the dioptric power of the cornea, thereby bringing the retina into the depth of field of the slit-lamp biomicroscope. These lenses are plano-concave contact lenses. Placed on the cornea, they form a virtual, erect, and minified image of the illuminated retina near the pupillary plane and within the range of view of the slit-lamp biomicroscope (Fig 9-24).

The Hruby lens is a powerful plano-concave lens, −58.6 D in power. It is held immediately in front of the cornea, forming a virtual, erect, and minified image of the illuminated retina. The image formed lies near the pupillary plane and is therefore within the focal range of the slit-lamp biomicroscope (Fig 9-25).

The 60 D, 78 D, and 90 D funduscopic lenses (Fig 9-26) allow the vitreous and posterior pole to be viewed by a different mechanism. These lenses act as high-powered biconvex condensing lenses, which project an inverted, real image in front of the lens, within the focal range of the slit-lamp biomicroscope (Fig 9-27). The optical principle is the same as that used in indirect ophthalmoscopy. The higher the power of the lens, the lower the magnification.

The Goldmann 3-mirror contact lens (Fig 9-28), as its name implies, incorporates 3 internal mirrors. The contact lens nullifies the refractive power of the cornea. The 3

Figure 9-23 Photograph of a Goldmann fundus contact lens. *(Photograph courtesy of Neal H. Atebara, MD.)*

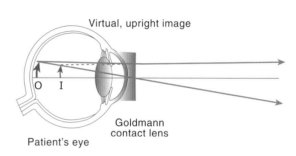

Figure 9-24 A Goldmann fundus contact lens, or any similar plano-concave contact lens, essentially nullifies the refractive power of the cornea, thereby moving the retinal image to a point near the pupillary plane, within the focal range of the slit-lamp biomicroscope. The image formed is virtual, erect, and diminished in size. *I* = image; *O* = object. *(Courtesy of Neal H. Atebara, MD. Redrawn by Cyndie C. H. Wooley.)*

Virtual, upright image

Goldmann contact lens

Patient's eye

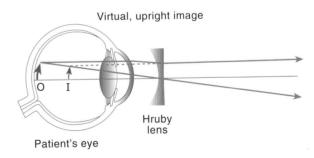

Figure 9-25 A concave Hruby lens, when placed close to a patient's eye, forms a virtual, erect image of the illuminated retina within the focal range of the slit-lamp biomicroscope. *I* = image; *O* = object. *(Courtesy of Neal H. Atebara, MD. Redrawn by Cyndie C. H. Wooley.)*

Virtual, upright image

Hruby lens

Patient's eye

Figure 9-26 Photograph of 60 D and 90 D fundus lenses. *(Photographs courtesy of Neal H. Atebara, MD.)*

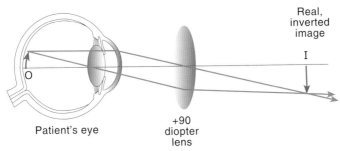

Figure 9-27 The 60 D, 78 D, and 90 D lenses produce real, inverted images of the retina within the focal range of a slit-lamp biomicroscope in a fashion similar to that used by an indirect ophthalmoscope. *I* = image; *O* = object. *(Courtesy of Neal H. Atebara, MD. Redrawn by Cyndie C. H. Wooley.)*

Figure 9-28 Photographs of a Goldmann 3-mirror contact lens. Side view **(A)** and observer's view **(B),** showing the 3 mirrors and a circular contact lens. *(Photographs courtesy of Neal H. Atebara, MD.)*

Figure 9-29 Schematic diagram of the part of the eye that can be seen with the central contact lens *(1)*, midperipheral fundus mirror *(2)*, peripheral fundus mirror *(3)*, and iridocorneal angle mirror *(4)*. *(Courtesy of Neal H. Atebara, MD. Redrawn by Cyndie C. H. Wooley.)*

mirrors then reflect light from the midperipheral retina, peripheral retina, and iridocorneal angle, respectively (Figs 9-29 and 9-30). The posterior pole of the fundus can also be visualized in a manner similar to that of a fundus contact lens.

View of equator

View of posterior pole

View of interior retina

Figure 9-30 The contact lens of a Goldmann lens nullifies the refractive power of a patient's cornea; the 3 mirrors then reflect light from the patient's peripheral retina *(orange ray)* and iridocorneal angle *(green ray)*. The posterior pole of the fundus can be visualized in a way similar to that of a Goldmann posterior pole contact lens *(blue ray)*. *(Courtesy of Neal H. Atebara, MD. Redrawn by Cyndie C. H. Wooley.)*

Figure 9-31 Photograph of the Zeiss 4-mirror goniolens. *(Photograph courtesy of Neal H. Atebara, MD.)*

The Zeiss 4-mirror goniolens (Fig 9-31) consists of a contact lens that allows for visualization of the posterior pole and 4 mirrors, each of which enables visualization of the iridocorneal angle. (See Chapter 2, Geometrical Optics.)

The panfundoscope contact lens and the Rodenstock contact lens consist of corneal contact lenses and high-powered, spherical condensing lenses (Figs 9-32 and 9-33). A real, inverted image of the fundus is formed within the spherical glass element, which is within the focal range of the slit-lamp biomicroscope. Because the condensing lens is so close to the eye and has such a high power, the field of view is very wide. This makes these lenses especially suited for a wide-angle view of the posterior pole and midperipheral fundus.

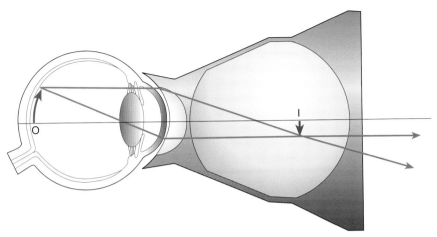

Figure 9-32 A panfundoscope lens consists of a corneal contact lens and a high-powered, spherical condensing lens. A real, inverted image of the fundus is formed within the spherical glass element, which is within the focal range of a slit-lamp biomicroscope. *(Courtesy of Neal H. Atebara, MD. Redrawn by Cyndie C. H. Wooley.)*

Figure 9-33 Photograph of the panfundoscope lens. *(Photograph courtesy of Neal H. Atebara, MD.)*

Goldmann Applanation Tonometer

The applanation tonometer (Fig 9-34) is used to measure intraocular pressure. This instrument relies on an interesting physical principle: For an ideal, dry, thin-walled sphere, the pressure inside is proportional to the force applied to its surface. Unlike an ideal sphere, however, the human eye is not thin-walled and it is not dry. This produces 2 confounding forces: (1) a force produced by the eye's scleral rigidity (because the eye is not thin-walled), which is directed away from the globe, and (2) a force produced by the surface tension of the tear film (because the eye is not dry), which is directed toward the globe (Fig 9-35). Goldmann determined empirically that if enough force is applied to produce a circular area of flattening 3.06 mm in diameter, the scleral rigidity exactly cancels out the force caused by surface tension. Therefore, the applanating force required to flatten a circular area of cornea exactly 3.06 mm in diameter is directly proportional to the intraocular pressure. Specifically, the force (measured in dynes) multiplied by 10 is equal to the intraocular pressure (measured in millimeters of mercury).

Figure 9-34 Photograph of a Goldmann applanation tonometer in the working position on a slit-lamp biomicroscope. *(Photograph courtesy of Neal H. Atebara, MD.)*

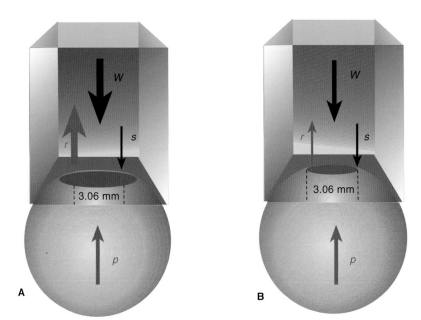

A

B

Figure 9-35 A, When a flat surface is applied to a cornea with enough force *(w)* to produce a circular area of flattening greater than 3.06 mm in diameter, the force caused by scleral rigidity *(r)* is greater than that caused by the tear film surface tension *(s)*. **B,** When the force of the flat surface produces a circular area of flattening exactly 3.06 mm in diameter, the opposing forces of scleral rigidity and tear film surface tension cancel each other out, and the applied force *(w)* then becomes directly proportional to the intraocular pressure *(p)*. *(Courtesy of Neal H. Atebara, MD. Redrawn by Cyndie C. H. Wooley.)*

How, then, does an observer know when the area of applanation is exactly 3.06 mm in diameter? First, the applanation tonometer is mounted on a biomicroscope to produce a magnified image. When the cornea is applanated, the tear film—which rims the circular area of applanated cornea—appears as a circle to the observer. The tear film is often stained with fluorescein dye and viewed under a cobalt blue light to enhance the visibility of the tear film ring. Higher pressure from the tonometer head causes the circle to have a larger diameter because a larger area of cornea is applanated (Fig 9-36). Split prisms—each mounted with its bases in opposite directions—are mounted in the applanation

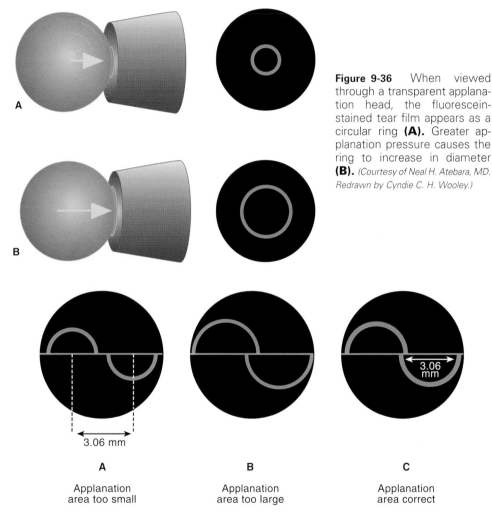

Figure 9-36 When viewed through a transparent applanation head, the fluorescein-stained tear film appears as a circular ring **(A)**. Greater applanation pressure causes the ring to increase in diameter **(B).** *(Courtesy of Neal H. Atebara, MD. Redrawn by Cyndie C. H. Wooley.)*

A

B

3.06 mm

A

Applanation
area too small

B

Applanation
area too large

C

3.06
mm

Applanation
area correct

Figure 9-37 The split prism in the applanation head creates 2 images offset by 3.06 mm. This allows greater ease in determining when the circular ring is exactly 3.06 mm in diameter. When the area of applanation is smaller than 3.06 mm, the arms of the semicircles do not reach each other **(A).** When the area of applanation is greater than 3.06 mm, the arms of the semicircles reach past each other **(B).** When the area of applanation is exactly 3.06 mm, the arms of the semicircles just touch each other **(C).** This is the endpoint for measuring intraocular pressure. *(Courtesy of Neal H. Atebara, MD. Redrawn by Cyndie C. H. Wooley.)*

head, and they create 2 images offset by exactly 3.06 mm. The clinician looks through the applanation head and adjusts the applanation pressure until the half circles just overlap one another (Fig 9-37). At this point, the circle is exactly 3.06 millimeters in diameter, and the reading on the tonometer (multiplied by a factor of 10) represents the intraocular pressure in millimeters of mercury (Fig 9-38).

A

Figure 9-38 When the applanation pressure is too low (1.0 dyne in this illustration), the circular ring is smaller than 3.06 mm in diameter, and the arms of the ring do not reach each other in the split image **(A).** When the applanation pressure is too high (3.0 dynes in the illustration), the circular ring is larger than 3.06 mm in diameter, and the arms of the ring stretch past each other in the split image **(B).** When the applanation pressure creates a circular ring exactly 3.06 mm in diameter, the arms of the ring just reach each other in the split image **(C).** In this illustration, the endpoint is reached at 2.0 dynes of applanation pressure, which corresponds to an intraocular pressure of 20 mm Hg. *(Courtesy of Neal H. Atebara, MD. Redrawn by Cyndie C. H. Wooley.)*

B

C

Pachymeter

Pachymeters are used to measure corneal thickness. These values are especially important in refractive surgery and in monitoring corneal edema. The 3 main methods for measuring corneal thickness are

- optical doubling
- optical focusing
- ultrasonography

In optical doubling, an image-doubling prism (similar to that used in keratometers and applanation tonometers) is used in conjunction with a slit-lamp biomicroscope. The pachymeter is designed to measure the distance between the Purkinje-Sanson images formed by the anterior and posterior corneal surfaces, a value that represents the corneal thickness. The endpoint is reached when the images are superimposed; the corneal thickness can then be directly read off a scale (Fig 9-39).

In the optical focusing technique, a specular microscope is calibrated so that when the endothelium is in focus, the thickness of the cornea is automatically displayed. The zero is established by focusing on the interface between the contact element and the epithelial layer.

Ultrasound techniques can also be used to measure corneal thickness, similar to the way ultrasound is used to measure the axial length of the globe. If the velocity of sound

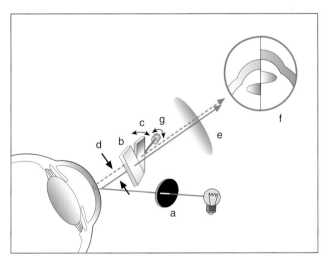

Figure 9-39 In the most common type of optical pachymeter, the cornea is illuminated with a slit beam *(a)*. The image is viewed through a biomicroscope, half through a glass plate orthogonal to the path of light *(b)* and half through a glass plate rotated through an angle *(c)*. The beam path through the plate is displaced laterally for a distance *(d)* that varies depending on the angle of rotation. Through the eyepiece *(e)*, a split image is seen *(f)*, wherein half the image comes from the fixed plate and the other half from the rotatable plate. The endothelial surface of 1 image and the epithelial surface of the other image are aligned by the observer by carefully adjusting the rotatable plate *(c)*, and the corneal thickness is read off a calibrated scale *(g)*. *(Courtesy of Neal H. Atebara, MD. Redrawn by Cyndie C. H. Wooley.)*

in the cornea is known and if the precise time required for sound waves to pass through the cornea can be measured, the thickness of the cornea can be calculated. Multiple measurements allow construction of a 2-dimensional map of corneal thickness (Fig 9-40).

Specular Microscope

Specular microscopy is a modality for examining endothelial cells that uses specular reflection from the interface between the endothelial cells and the aqueous humor. The technique can be performed using contact or noncontact methods. In both methods, the instruments are designed to separate the illumination and viewing paths so that reflections from the anterior corneal surface do not obscure the very weak reflection arising from the endothelial cell surface.

Endothelial cells can also be visualized through a slit lamp biomicroscope if the illumination and viewing axes are symmetrically displaced on either side of the normal line to the cornea (Fig 9-41). A narrow illumination slit must be used; hence, the field of view is narrow. Photographic recording has been made possible by adding a long-working-distance microscope system on the viewing axis and flash capability to the illumination system. Patient eye motion is the chief problem with this technique.

In contact specular microscopy, the illumination and viewing paths are through opposite sides of a special microscope objective, the front element of which touches the cornea. This reduces eye rotation and effectively eliminates longitudinal motion that interferes with focus. Contact specular microscopy allows for higher magnifications than slit-lamp biomicroscopy, making cellular detail and endothelial abnormalities more discernible.

Figure 9-40 Two-dimensional map of corneal thickness, with the corneal thickness ranging from 300 μm centrally *(pink)* to 660 μm peripherally *(light blue)*. *(Courtesy of Neal H. Atebara, MD.)*

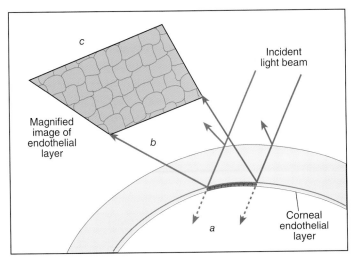

Figure 9-41 Specular reflection microscopy. When a beam of light passes through the transparent corneal structures, most of the light is transmitted *(a)*. However, at each optical interface, such as the corneal endothelium, a proportion of light is reflected *(b)*. This light (called *specular reflection*) can be collected to form a relatively dim image of the corneal endothelium *(c)*, where individual endothelial cells can be counted. *(Courtesy of Neal H. Atebara, MD. Redrawn by Cyndie C. H. Wooley.)*

Video recording of endothelial layer images makes it possible to document larger, overlapping areas of the endothelial layer. Also, it allows the recording of high-magnification images, despite patient eye motion.

Wide-field specular microscopy employs special techniques to ensure that reflections from the interface between the cornea and contact element do not overlap the image of the endothelial cell layer. Because scattered light from edema in the epithelium and stroma can degrade the endothelial image, variable slit widths are sometimes provided to reduce this problem.

Analysis of specular micrographs may consist simply of assessment of cell appearance together with notation of abnormalities such as guttata or keratic precipitates. Frequently, cell counts are desired; these are often obtained by superimposing a transparent grid of specific dimensions on the endothelial image (photograph or video image) and simply counting the cells in a known area. Cell size distribution can be determined by computer analysis after cell boundaries have been determined digitally. The normal cell density in young people exceeds 3000 cells/mm^2; the average density in the cataract age group is 2250 cells/mm^2, which suggests a gradual decrease with age.

Specular microscopy has been important in studying the morphology of the endothelium and in quantifying damage to the endothelium produced by various surgical procedures and intraocular devices. This in turn has led to refined surgical procedures and new device designs.

Operating Microscope

The operating microscope (Fig 9-42) works on principles similar to those of the slit-lamp biomicroscope. Like the slit-lamp biomicroscope, the operating microscope has the following optical components: (a) an astronomical telescope, (b) an inverting prism, (c) a Galilean telescope, (d) an objective lens, (e) a light source, and (f) a binocular viewing system (Figs 9-43 and 9-44). Unlike that of the slit-lamp biomicroscope, the operating microscope's illumination source is not slit-shaped, and the working distance for the operating microscope is longer to accommodate the specific requirements of ocular surgery. Also, most operating microscopes contain a zoom lens that smoothly varies magnification without changing focus.

The working distance of the microscope (the distance from the objective lens to the patient's eye) is equal to the focal length of the objective lens. Common focal lengths for objective lenses in ophthalmic surgery are 150, 175, and 200 mm. Use of the proper working distance can greatly lessen surgeon back and neck strain, especially during lengthy operations. A difference as small as 25 mm can affect body comfort and the positioning of the surgeon's arms and hands.

The total magnification provided by an operating microscope is the product of the magnifications of its various optical components. Because various lenses are available for the objective and eyepiece, magnification can be controlled. Smoothly variable magnification changers (zoom Galilean telescopes) are now incorporated into many operating microscopes. The 12.5× eyepiece is the most popular choice for ophthalmic surgery, and the total resultant magnification varies from 6× to 40×.

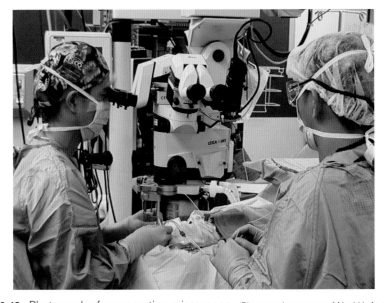

Figure 9-42 Photograph of an operating microscope. *(Photograph courtesy of Neal H. Atebara, MD.)*

Figure 9-43 Schematic diagram of an operating microscope. The major components include *(a)* an eyepiece, an astronomical telescope, which provides most of the magnification; *(b)* an inverting prism, such as a Porro-Abbe prism, which compensates for the inverted image produced by the eyepiece; *(c)* a magnification changer, such as a Galilean telescope system, in which different lenses can be introduced to change the magnification; and *(d)* an objective lens, which adjusts the working distance. Two parallel optical systems, each a mirror image of the other, provide a stereoptic view of the patient's eye. *(Courtesy of Neal H. Atebara, MD. Redrawn by Cyndie C. H. Wooley.)*

Figure 9-44 Schematic diagram of an operating microscope: *a,* the eyepiece; *b,* an inverting prism; *c,* a magnification changer; *d,* the objective lens; and *e,* the illumination source. *(Courtesy of Neal H. Atebara, MD. Redrawn by Cyndie C. H. Wooley.)*

Various illumination systems are also available, but the most important system for ophthalmic surgery is known as *coaxial illumination.* This type is especially useful for visualization of the posterior capsule and for vitreous surgery. Fiber-optic delivery systems reduce heat near the microscope and allow easier change of bulbs during surgery.

Keratometer

The keratometer is used to approximate the refracting power of the cornea (Figs 9-45 and 9-46). It does this by measuring the radius of curvature of the central cornea (by assuming the cornea to be a convex mirror) and using a mathematical approximation to convert this radius of curvature to corneal refractive power. In essence, a keratometer measures reflecting power and infers refracting power.

The central cornea can be thought of as a convex spherical mirror. If an illuminated object of known size is placed at a fixed distance from the cornea, and we are able to measure the size of the greatly minified reflected image, we can deduce the radius of curvature of the mirror using the following formula: $r = 2u(I/O)$, where r is the radius of curvature of the reflective cornea, u is the distance from the object to the cornea, I is the size of the image, and O is the size of the object (Fig 9-47). Because the cornea is a high-powered mirror (about 250 D), an object does not have to be very far away to be effectively at optical infinity; that is, the distance (u) becomes essentially constant. When this is the case, for all practical purposes, the corneal radius is directly proportional to the size of the reflected image it produces and indirectly proportional to the size of the object (r is directly proportional to I and indirectly proportional to O).

The challenge, then, is to measure the size of the image relative to the object. This is achieved using a microscope to magnify the tiny image. However, because the eye is constantly moving about, it is difficult to measure the image size against a reticule (Fig 9-48). If we place 2 prisms base to base and position them such that the baseline splits

Figure 9-45 Photograph of a keratometer. *(Photograph courtesy of Neal H. Atebara, MD.)*

Figure 9-46 Schematic diagram of a keratometer. The major components include *(a)* the eyepiece, *(b)* doubling prisms, *(c)* objective lens, *(d)* mirror, *(e)* condenser lens, *(f)* mire, *(g)* lamp, *(h)* measurement controls, and *(i)* focus control. *(Courtesy of Neal H. Atebara, MD. Redrawn by Cyndie C. H. Wooley.)*

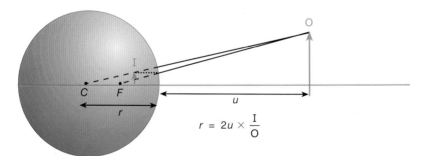

Figure 9-47 Keratometer. The cornea can be thought of as a convex spherical mirror. If an illuminated object *(O)* of known size is placed a known distance *(u)* from the cornea, and the size of the reflected image *(I)* can be measured, then the radius of curvature *(r)* of the sphere can be deduced using the formula $r = 2u(I/O)$. *C* is the center of the sphere, and *F* is the focal point of the convex spherical mirror. *(Courtesy of Neal H. Atebara, MD. Redrawn by Cyndie C. H. Wooley.)*

the pupil, the observer will see 2 images separated by a fixed amount (depending on the power of the prisms). Thus, any oscillation of the cornea during measurement will affect both doubled images equally—that is, motion of the eye will not cause the separation between the doubled images to change. This allows the observer to adjust knobs on the keratometer to arrive at the "contact" position despite small eye movements. This technique is commonly employed in other ophthalmic instruments and is called the *doubling principle.*

In practice, keratometers either vary object size to achieve a known image size (Javal-Schiøtz keratometers, Figs 9-49 and 9-50), or they vary the image size to achieve a known object size (von Helmholtz keratometers, Figs 9-51, 9-52; see also 9-45 and 9-46).

The final step is to convert radius of curvature into an estimate of the cornea's dioptric refractive power. This is performed using the following formula:

$$P = (n' - n)/r$$

where P is the refractive power of the cornea, n' is the refractive index of the cornea, n is the refractive index of air (which is close to 1.0), and r is the measured radius of curvature of the cornea. Because different layers of the cornea have slightly different refractive indices and because the posterior surface of the cornea, which is not measured, contributes -5 to -6 D of power on average, instrument manufacturers and clinicians have adopted an "averaged" corneal refractive index of 1.3375. Therefore, if we measure

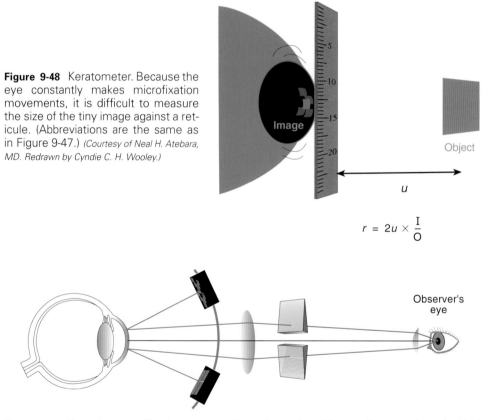

Figure 9-48 Keratometer. Because the eye constantly makes microfixation movements, it is difficult to measure the size of the tiny image against a reticule. (Abbreviations are the same as in Figure 9-47.) *(Courtesy of Neal H. Atebara, MD. Redrawn by Cyndie C. H. Wooley.)*

Figure 9-49 Keratometer split prism system. Two prisms placed base to base produce doubled images separated by a fixed distance that are not affected by small movements of the eye. The observer varies the object size (ie, the distance between the red and green objects) until the doubled images touch. At this point, the images are a known distance from each other, and the object size can be measured to calculate the corneal radius of curvature. Keratometers that vary object size to achieve a known image size are called Javal-Schiøtz keratometers. *(Courtesy of Neal H. Atebara, MD. Redrawn by Cyndie C. H. Wooley.)*

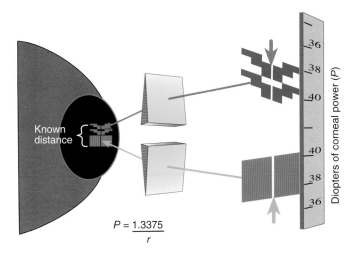

Figure 9-50 On most Javal-Schiøtz keratometers, the scale that measures the size of the object has already been converted to its corresponding estimates in diopters of corneal refractive power using the formula $P = 1.3375/r$, where P is the refractive power of the cornea, r is the radius of corneal curvature, and 1.3375 is an "averaged" corneal refractive index. *(Courtesy of Neal H. Atebara, MD. Redrawn by Cyndie C. H. Wooley.)*

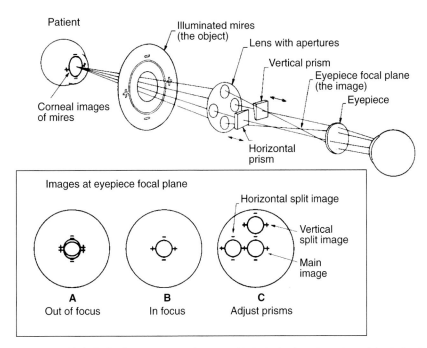

Figure 9-51 von Helmholtz keratometer. In a von Helmholtz keratometer, object size is fixed and image size is measured. In one popular design, the object consists of a large, illuminated ring-shaped mire. A vertical and a horizontal prism are each adjustable to measure the image size in 2 meridians. The image is formed at the eyepiece focal plane *(inset)*. The first step involves focusing the image using the eyepiece (A and B). Next, the vertical prism is adjusted to bring the vertical split image into alignment with the main image (overlap the minus signs; C). The corneal power in this meridian can then be read off the scale. Finally, the horizontal prism is adjusted to bring the horizontal split image into alignment with the main image (overlap the plus signs; C). *(Courtesy of Neal H. Atebara, MD. Redrawn by Cyndie C. H. Wooley.)*

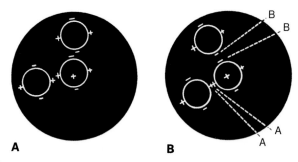

Figure 9-52 In oblique astigmatism, the vertical and horizontal split images are askew from the main image (**A**). The keratometer must be rotated around its optical axis to bring the vertical and horizontal split images into alignment with the main image (**B**). This alignment allows the observer to measure the axis of corneal astigmatism. The plus and minus signs can then be aligned to measure the corneal curvature in each meridian. *(Courtesy of Neal H. Atebara, MD.)*

the corneal curvature (by using the doubling technique) to be 8.5 mm, we can calculate: $P = (1.3375 - 1.0) \div (0.0085 \text{ m}) = 39.7$ D. In most instruments, this calculation is performed automatically, because the conversion is already built into the reading on the keratometer dial. So all the clinician needs to do is line up the targets to reach their "endpoints" and record the reading on the dial. In this fashion, measurements can be made in each of the 2 major meridians of corneal curvature of an astigmatic eye.

Corneal Topographer

Conventional keratometry measures the curvature of only the central 3 mm of the cornea. This is not representative of the entire surface, however, because corneal curvature generally flattens from apex to limbus. A "map" of corneal curvature can be useful in contact lens fitting and corneal refractive surgery.

Methods for ascertaining the topography of the cornea are commonly based on either a circular mire, similar to a Placido disc (Fig 9-53), which consists of many concentric lighted rings, or a standard keratometer directed to different, off-center areas of the cornea. One may consider a series of concentric lighted rings as a series of many different-sized mires, all in the same plane. Thus, the central ring would function very much like the standard mire on a keratometer and act as a target for the central 3 mm of cornea. The next ring can be considered to subtend the zone surrounding the center and produce a reflected ring representative of the curvature of that zone, and so on.

A flat series of illuminated rings held at the usual distance from the cornea can accurately measure only the central 7 mm of the cornea. To measure corneal curvature closer to the limbus, the concentric rings must be presented in the shape of a concave surface (ie, open bowl) so that the distances from rings to cornea remain similar over the whole cornea. If the series of lighted rings is placed in front of a camera (the camera lens placed at an opening in the center of the ring pattern), the device is called a *pho-*

Figure 9-53 A Placido disc consists of many concentric lighted rings. When placed in front of the cornea, the reflected image can be analyzed to qualitatively assess corneal curvature and irregularities of the corneal surface. *(Courtesy of Neal H. Atebara, MD. Redrawn by Cyndie C. H. Wooley.)*

Figure 9-54 Photograph of a computerized corneal topography system. *(Photograph courtesy of Neal H. Atebara, MD.)*

tographic keratoscope, and the picture of the reflected rings may be quantitatively analyzed. With irregular astigmatism (scars, keratoconus), the irregular pattern of reflected rings can be used as a qualitative representation of the corneal map.

The use of computerized videokeratoscopes (Fig 9-54) has grown rapidly in recent years. These devices enable image analysis of multiple rings (often 16 or 32), producing color-coded dioptric maps of the corneal surface. Some of these instruments also calculate the SIM K (simulated keratometry) value, providing the power and location of the steepest and flattest meridians for the 3-mm optical zone (Figs 9-55 and 9-56). Other parameters include the surface asymmetry index (SAI) and the surface regularity index (SRI). The SAI is a centrally weighted summation of differences in corneal power between corresponding points 180° apart on 128 meridians that cross the 4 central mires. The SAI can be used to monitor changes caused by contact lens warpage or keratoplasty or by such progressive alterations as keratoconus, keratoglobus, Terrien marginal degeneration, and pellucid degeneration. The SRI is determined from a summation of local fluctuations in power among 256 hemimeridians in the 10 central mires. (See also BCSC Section 8, *External Disease and Cornea.*)

Figure 9-55 In corneal topography, the image produced by a Placido disc is analyzed by a computer. Calculation of the distance between the circular mires in each clock-hour allows for an accurate 2-dimensional map of corneal curvature. The corneal topographic map of a nearly emmetropic eye reveals minute geographic variations in corneal curvature, ranging from 41.5 D *(light green)* to 44.5 D *(yellow)*. *(Courtesy of Neal H. Atebara, MD.)*

Figure 9-56 Corneal topographic map of an eye with against-the-rule astigmatism. Corneal curvature ranges from relatively flat *(dark blue)* to relatively steep *(orange)*. *(Courtesy of Neal H. Atebara, MD.)*

Manual Lensmeter

The lensmeter (Fig 9-57) (commercially known as a Lensometer, Focimeter, or Vertometer) measures the power of spectacles and contact lenses. This device consists of

- an illuminated target
- a platform for the "unknown" lens (the lens whose power the user intends to measure)
- an eyepiece (an astronomical telescope), which produces a sharp image when parallel light rays enter it
- a standard (or fixed) lens

To understand how a lensmeter works, it is useful to consider first how a simplified version of this instrument works in principle. An illuminated target is moved backward and forward behind the "unknown" lens. At the position where the target is at the unknown lens's focal point, emergent light rays are parallel (by definition of a focal point). These parallel rays, when viewed through the eyepiece, produce a clear image, indicating that the focal length of the unknown lens has been found. Taking the inverse of the focal length gives us the power of the unknown lens (Fig 9-58).

There are 2 major problems with the simple lensmeter. The first is that the instrument would have to be too large to be practical. To measure a +0.25 D lens, the instrument would have to be 4 m long! The second problem is that the scale for measuring the lens power would be nonlinear. Therefore, measurements of more powerful lenses would become very inaccurate.

Figure 9-57 Photograph of a manual lensmeter: *a*, eyepiece; *b*, eyepiece graticule; *c*, support for spectacle; *d*, housing for lamp, adjustable target graticule, and standard lens. *(Photograph courtesy of Neal H. Atebara, MD.)*

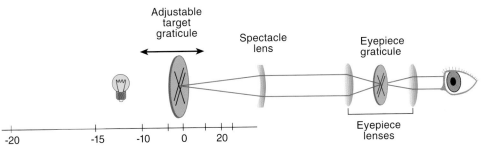

Figure 9-58 In a simplified version of a manual lensmeter, an illuminated target is moved back and forth behind the "unknown" lens. At the position at which the target is at the unknown lens's focal point, emergent light rays are parallel to one another and a clear image is produced by the eyepiece graticule. Taking the inverse of the focal length gives the power of the unknown lens. *(Courtesy of Neal H. Atebara, MD. Redrawn by Cyndie C. H. Wooley.)*

Both of these problems can be solved by introducing another lens to the system, called the *standard* (or *field*) *lens,* and using an optical trick called *Badal's principle.* If the standard lens is placed so that its focal point coincides with the posterior vertex of the unknown lens, then not only is the length of the instrument shortened considerably, but the dioptric scale of the instrument becomes linear (Fig 9-59).

The target usually has a set of lines that permit the observer to determine whether the lens has cylindrical power. To measure cylindrical power, the target is first rotated, as well as moved forward or backward, until 1 set of lines is sharp. The target is then moved forward or backward until the perpendicular set of lines is sharp. The difference in target settings is the cylindrical power. The cylindrical axis is read from the wheel setting.

It should be kept in mind that a lensmeter measures the vertex power of a lens (Fig 9-60); therefore, it is important to note which surface of the lens is placed against the

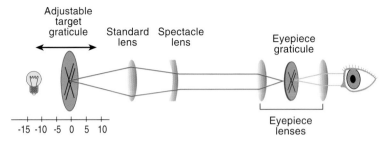

Figure 9-59 Introducing another lens into a simplified lensmeter (called a *standard lens*) shortens the required length of the instrument considerably. It also makes the dioptric scale of the instrument linear (and therefore more accurate at higher dioptric powers). *(Courtesy of Neal H. Atebara, MD. Redrawn by Cyndie C. H. Wooley.)*

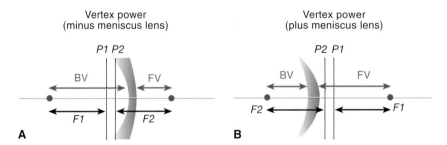

Figure 9-60 The lens power measured by a lensmeter actually represents the back vertex power. With a simple thin lens, a single principal plane goes through the center of the lens perpendicular to the optical axis. Most spectacles, however, are thick, meniscus lenses, which means that there are 2 principal planes (*P1* and *P2*) whose positions are "pushed away" from the concave surface in a minus lens **(A)** and away from the convex surface in a plus lens **(B).** This makes it difficult to measure the actual focal length (distance from a focal plane to its corresponding focal point) and the actual focal power (inverse of the focal distance). In clinical practice, it is more convenient to measure the back vertex distance *(BV)* of a spectacle, which is the distance from the back surface of the optical center of the lens to the focal point. Taking the inverse of the back vertex distance yields the back vertex power of the lens. In clinical practice, the back vertex power is easier to measure and more clinically relevant than the true lens power. *(Courtesy of Neal H. Atebara, MD. Redrawn by Cyndie C. H. Wooley.)*

holder. The instrument can also detect and determine the amount of prism at any given point in a lens. When the optical center of the test lens is not centered on the test aperture, the image of the target is decentered relative to the reticule. The procedure is to use a felt-tip pen to mark the point of interest on the test lens, usually the location of the patient's pupil. With the point of interest centered in the lensmeter aperture, the amount and orientation of the prism are read from the reticule scale.

Measuring the Bifocal Add

When we determine a patient's distance refraction, we usually measure the required back vertex power of the spectacle lens. Back vertex power would seem, therefore, to be the most relevant optical parameter to consider when evaluating spectacle power. However, for a bifocal add, the spectacle is turned around so that the front vertex power is measured.

The bifocal add is different from the rest of the spectacle lens. The distance portion is designed to deal with essentially parallel light, and that is the basis on which the lensmeter is calculated. The bifocal add, however, is designed to work on diverging light, originating, for example, at 40 cm from a +2.50 bifocal add. If one imagines the bifocal add as being an additional lens placed an infinitesimal distance in front of the distance lens, the principle becomes clearer. Diverging light from the near object passes through the bifocal lens and is made parallel. The parallel light then enters the distance lens from its anterior surface and is refracted with the expected optical effect, yielding the back vertex vergence required to give the patient clear vision. In a sense, the bifocal add exerts its effect on the light *before* it passes through the rest of the lens (Fig 9-61).

Thus, the add segment should be measured from the front. The front vertex power of the distance portion is measured, and the difference in front vertex power between the distance and near portions specifies the add. The spectacle power itself is still the back vertex power of the distance portion. With a strongly plus distance lens, there will be a significant difference in the front and back vertex measurements of the add, which will cause errors if the add is not measured from the front. In cases other than a strongly positive distance lens, there is usually little or no clinically significant difference in the measurements.

Automatic Lensmeter

The principles underlying automatic electronic lensmeters (Fig 9-62) are different from those of manual lensmeters. A lens bends or reflects a beam of light passing through it (except at its optical center), and automatic lensmeters use this effect to calculate a lens's power. The deviation of a beam of light passing through a lens is based on 2 factors: the power of the lens and the prismatic effect related to the distance from the lens center (Prentice's rule). Consider the number of variables we need to measure. To calculate the power of a lens, 3 variables must be ascertained: spherical power, cylindrical power, and axis. Because the lens may be placed on the instrument off-center, we must be prepared to determine 2 more variables: the x and y displacements from lens center. Thus, the

Parallel light from distance enters
lens with zero vergence, which
gives desired back vergence power.

Diverging light from
near hits reading add...

...enters distance portion of
lens with zero vergence

Figure 9-61 The effect of a bifocal add segment in measuring lens power with a lensmeter. *(Courtesy of Neal H. Atebara, MD. Redrawn by Cyndie C. H. Wooley.)*

Figure 9-62 Photograph of an automated lensmeter: *a,* support platform for spectacles; *b,* graphical display. *(Photograph courtesy of Neal H. Atebara, MD.)*

automatic lensmeter must somehow obtain at least 5 independent pieces of information to characterize the lens being measured.

By examining a single light beam passing through a test lens, a lensmeter can determine its displacement from a straight path (ie, its x and y displacement). Most commercial lensmeters actually shine 4 beams (in an approximately square pattern, 5×5 mm) through the lens and thus obtain measurements of 4 pairs of x and y displacements. The 4 light beams are projected either simultaneously or sequentially. They pass through various optical devices so that they are made parallel as they approach the test lens. After passing through the test lens, the light beams fall on a detector that determines their respective displacements. Thus, each of the 4 beams produces 2 variables—its x displacement and its y displacement. From these 8 independent variables (3 more than actually needed), lens power and decentration/prism can be determined. The 3 extra variables allow confirmation of the accuracy of the measured power and toricity of the lens—that is, this built-in redundancy confirms that the lens is of a legitimate spherocylindrical form and that the measurements are consistent. Note that with this system, no gross movement of the optical elements is necessary.

Diagnostic Ultrasonography

Ophthalmic ultrasonography is an invaluable diagnostic tool (Fig 9-63). Its primary uses in ophthalmology include detection and differentiation of intraocular and orbital lesions, location of intraocular foreign bodies, biomicroscopy, and biometry (for intraocular lens power calculations and tissue thickness measurements). A brief discussion of specific clinical applications of ultrasonography may be found in BCSC Section 4, *Ophthalmic*

Figure 9-63 Photograph of a diagnostic ultrasound instrument: *a,* echographic probe; *b,* graphical display; *c,* camera; *d,* digital storage device. *(Photograph courtesy of Neal H. Atebara, MD.)*

Pathology and Intraocular Tumor, and Section 7, *Orbit, Eyelids, and Lacrimal System.* It is appropriate to discuss the basic principles of ultrasonography in this section, as sound waves behave in many respects as light waves, obeying many similar laws of physics.

Sound is produced as an oscillating particle collides with a neighboring particle, causing that particle to oscillate at the same frequency. Ultrasound has a frequency greater than 20,000 cycles per second (20 kHz), which is beyond the range of audible sound. Most ophthalmic ultrasonography is performed in the range of 8–15 MHz (8–15 million cycles per second). Ultrasound is produced in the ultrasonographic probe by the oscillation of a piezoelectric crystal, which converts electrical energy into mechanical energy. Ultrasound spreads in advancing wavefronts from the emitting crystal and is attenuated (reduced in amplitude) by 3 factors:

- distance from the probe head
- differential absorption by different media
- acoustic interfaces within a given medium causing reflection, refraction, or scattering of sound

After modification by scattering and differential absorption, the emitted sound waves are reflected to the probe as ultrasonographic signals. These are electronically processed and displayed as ultrasonograms on a display screen. The echoes themselves are produced by acoustic interfaces that reflect sound in characteristic patterns. An acoustic interface occurs where 2 substances with different sonic densities are juxtaposed. The strength of the returned (reflected) signal is greatest when the beam is perpendicular to the reflecting surface. Therefore, to sonically characterize an interface, the probe must be perpendicular to it in order to maximize the signal. Interfaces that are smooth and characterized by significant acoustic differences (in density and in sound velocity) are said to be highly reflective. Both corneal surfaces, both lens surfaces, and the inner scleral surface are all examples of highly reflective interfaces. Irregular interfaces between acoustically similar tissues do not reflect effectively; rather, they weakly scatter sound waves.

The major differences between the 2 most commonly used ultrasound modes (A and B) depend on probe design and mode of signal processing and display. Standardized A-scan ultrasonography uses a parallel nonfocused beam emanating from a stationary 8-MHz piezoelectric crystal that emits and receives pulsed signals. Reflectivity versus time is displayed for the single direction in which the probe is pointing, as shown in Figure 9-64. Biometric determination may be performed using A-scan, measuring the time delay (in microseconds) before a particular signal is displayed (Fig 9-65). This value may then be converted to millimeters. A-scan biometry is used in calculating intraocular lens power, determining extraocular muscle thickness (in thyroid ophthalmopathy), and measuring tumor height (in choroidal melanomas).

B-scan, on the other hand, uses a focused crystal in an oscillating probe that scans a chosen acoustic section. The image is displayed as a 2-dimensional slice, similar in gross appearance to computed tomography, as shown in Figure 9-66. B-scan ultrasonography of the globe can be performed by immersion or contact techniques. Immersion scanners are of particular value in scanning the anterior segment, an area to which the contact scanner is blind (because of superimposition of the probe artifact on anterior segment echoes). Disadvantages of immersion scanners include the cumbersome water-bath setup and the inability to perform kinetic, real-time ultrasonography. Contact B-scan ultrasonography allows kinetic studies and is easier to perform in infants and patients with ruptured globes. In contact scanning, the probe head is placed on the lids or on the globe itself, with methylcellulose as a coupling medium.

Figure 9-64 Normal A-scan ultrasonogram.

Probe artifact

Anterior lens capsule

Posterior lens capsule

Retina

Cornea

Figure 9-65 A-scan ultrasonogram for biometry (at reduced sensitivity).

Optic nerve shadow

Probe artifact

Posterior capsule

Vitreoretinal interface

Figure 9-66 Normal B-scan ultrasonogram.

Standardized A-scan ultrasonography is much less aesthetically attractive to the beginner and is more difficult to perform. However, it potentially conveys much more diagnostic information than the B-scan. (Note that the A-scan displayed on many B-scan instruments is not standardized and has less value in judging reflectivity.) For instance, in evaluation of a choroidal mass lesion, B-scan ultrasonography demonstrates gross topography of the lesion, such as secondary overlying membranes and choroidal excavation. However, A-scan ultrasonography can measure elevation to within 0.5 mm, quantify overlying membranes, and identify the presence of large vascular channels. Most important, based on the lesion's internal reflectivity (acoustic density), it can help differentiate a melanoma from a metastatic lesion, from a choroidal hemangioma, from a choroidal osteoma, and from a disciform lesion.

In practice, the 2 ultrasonographic modes are complementary: the B-scan for general topography and gross reflectivity of the lesion and the A-scan for detailed information regarding measurement, internal structure, and intrinsic vascularity. Ultrasonography may be a useful tool in the following clinical settings:

- opaque media
- previtrectomy evaluation
- choroidal mass lesions
- intraorbital or intraocular foreign bodies
- proptosis
- optic nerve abnormalities
- abnormalities of the extraocular muscles

Automated Refraction

More than 100 automated refractors (Fig 9-67) have been devised during the past century. Most have been based on the optometer principle (Fig 9-68), providing smoothly variable change in vergence for the neutralization of refractive error. Variations of the Scheiner double-pinhole principle (Fig 9-69) have frequently been used to achieve an alignment endpoint of measurement rather than a focus endpoint. The Scheiner principle, however, provides refractive measurement through only small portions of the eye's optics, and alignment of the various measuring apertures with the patient's pupil becomes critical. Furthermore, in the presence of even minor optical irregularities (found in almost all eyes), the refraction obtained through small portions of the eye's optics may not represent the eye's refractive state as a whole. Experience has shown that automatic objective measurements using infrared light must usually be refined subjectively for best results, using the entire pupil.

So-called *instrument myopia*, the tendency to accommodate when looking into instruments, has caused major problems with automated refractors in the past. Various methods of fogging and automatic tracking have been developed to overcome this problem, with some success.

Automated refractors generally fall into 5 categories:

- manual objective refractors

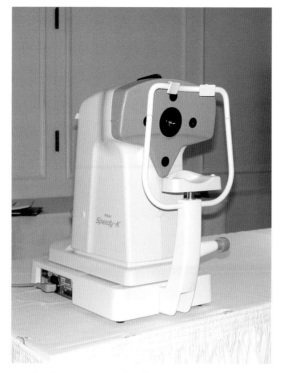

Figure 9-67 Photograph of an automated refractor. *(Photograph courtesy of Neal H. Atebara, MD.)*

- automatic objective refractors (automatic retinoscopes) without visual acuity capability
- automatic objective refractors with visual acuity capability
- automated subjective refractors
- remote-controlled conventional refractors

Manual objective refractors require the operator to align mires formed with infrared light on a patient's retina. Automatic objective refractors obtain the refractive measurements automatically using infrared light, requiring 0.2–10 seconds for the actual measurement. Most of the automatic objective refractors are purely objective, with no visual acuity capability. Some, however, have built-in spherocylindrical optics and visual acuity charts. Most of these same instruments also have subjective refinement capability.

Automated subjective refractors use subjective responses from the patient to arrive at the refractive correction. Instruments with subjective capability require more patient cooperation than the strictly objective instruments but have the advantage of providing subjective refinement and visual acuity as part of the refracting procedure.

Remote-controlled conventional refractors have been introduced. Some are impressive and they ease back strain, but they require the same skill in refracting as a conventional phoropter.

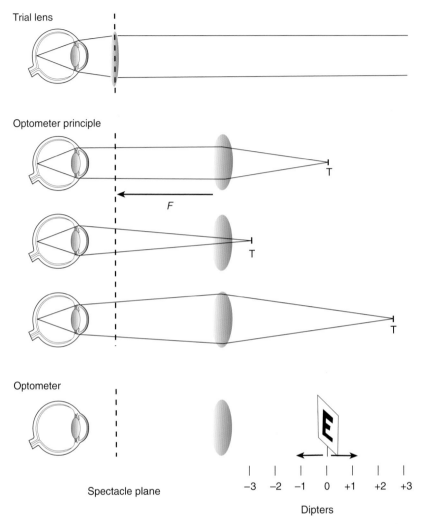

Figure 9-68 The optometer principle. Instead of interchangeable trial lenses, a single converging lens is placed at its focal length from the spectacle plane. Light from a target on the far side of the lens enters the eye with different amounts of vergence (zero, minus, or plus), depending on the position of the target. Vergence in the spectacle plane may thus be changed smoothly and is directly proportional to the axial displacement of the target. This arrangement exactly simulates a spherical trial lens having smoothly variable power. *(From Tasman W, Jaeger AE, eds. Duane's Clinical Ophthalmology. vol 1, chap 67. Hagerstown, MD: Harper & Row; 1983:2.)*

Overrefraction techniques (see Chapter 4, Clinical Refraction) are possible with some instruments. Such techniques are particularly recommended for patients with high refractive errors to avoid problems from vertex distance and pantoscopic tilt.

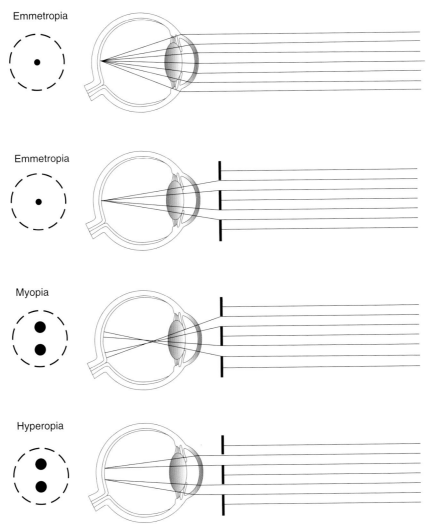

Figure 9-69 The Scheiner principle. Double-pinhole apertures placed before the pupil isolate 2 small bundles of light. An object not conjugate to the retina appears doubled instead of blurred. *(From Tasman W, Jaeger AE, eds.* Duane's Clinical Ophthalmology. *vol 1, chap 67. Hagerstown, MD: Harper & Row; 1983:2.)*

Macular Function Testing

Laser Interferometer

Several instruments are available for evaluating the functional status of the macula in the presence of a visually significant cataract. All are based on the principle that even a cataractous lens may have small, relatively clear regions, which allow a narrow beam of light to reach the retina relatively unaffected by the cataract.

Perhaps the simplest of these devices to understand is the laser interferometer. A beam, usually from a helium-neon laser, is optically split. The 2 beams are then projected at a small angle relative to one another through separate clear areas of the lens. Inside the eye they overlap, and because the laser light is coherent, the beams interfere, forming interference fringes on the retina. The spacing of the fringes can be varied by changing the relative angle between the 2 beams. Retinal function is estimated by the finest fringes that can be identified by the patient.

The laser interferometer has disadvantages: It requires 2 somewhat separated clear areas of lens, the fringes may be difficult for some patients to recognize, and fringe spacing does not correlate directly with visual acuity.

Potential Acuity Meter

The Guyton-Minkowski Potential Acuity Meter (PAM) (Fig 9-70) avoids these problems by imaging a Snellen chart on the retina, using a small-aperture Maxwellian view projector. Although in practice the optics may be folded, consider the following optical arrangement. A light source is positioned anterior to the eye. Posterior to the source is a small aperture. Posterior to the aperture is a screen with Snellen letters, and posterior to the Snellen screen is a positive focusing lens.

From our discussion on image movement (see Chapter 2, Geometrical Optics), we know that if the Snellen screen is imaged onto the patient's retina, and if there is a real image of the aperture, the aperture, which is anterior to the screen, must be imaged anterior to the patient's retina. By appropriate selection of optical parameters, we can arrange for the image of the aperture to be located within the patient's lens. What this means is that all the light reaching the retina passes through a very small aerial opening,

Figure 9-70 Photograph of a Potential Acuity Meter (PAM): *a*, point of attachment to slit-lamp biomicroscope; *b*, small-aperture view projector for imaging a Snellen chart on the retina; *c*, dial for changing the projected image; *d*, dial for adjustment of illumination intensity. *(Photograph courtesy of Neal H. Atebara, MD.)*

approximately 0.1 mm in diameter, somewhere at the anteroposterior position of the patient's lens. By appropriate positioning, we try to select a small clear area of the patient's lens to "shoot through."

The reader familiar with diffraction effects may object that limitation of the beam to a 0.1-mm aerial aperture necessarily reduces retinal image quality far below the 20/20 level routinely measured with this device. This is a subject of considerable complexity. The usual formulas governing diffraction assume a plane electromagnetic wave that is uniform across all space perpendicular to its direction of motion. This plane wave is incident on an aperture. The electromagnetic field is constrained by the aperture to be zero outside the aperture and to be the value of the plane wave within it. One then determines solutions of Maxwell's equations at positions beyond the aperture, subject to the boundary conditions imposed by the aperture.

The PAM does not allow such a procedure to be used at the position of the aerial image. At the position of the actual aperture (just posterior to the light source), the light striking the aperture may indeed be approximately a plane wave, and the field downstream will therefore be governed by the usual diffraction rules. For just this reason, however, the light wave at the position of the aerial image of the aperture is *not* a plane wave, nor is it limited by a physical aperture and thereby constrained to have zero amplitude outside the 0.1-mm diameter mentioned. As a consequence, the usual diffraction formulas do not apply.

A similar situation is also encountered in focusing laser light. The lowest-order spatial mode of a laser, TEM_{00}, is not a plane wave. Rather (in the usual case), it has an amplitude that decreases in a Gaussian exponential manner with distance from the beam center. In passing through an aperture larger than the Gaussian half width, the majority of the beam is unaffected by the aperture, and diffraction is therefore reduced below what one would expect from simple and incorrect application of the usual formulas. Thus is derived the important fact that a TEM_{00} laser beam can be focused to a spot size smaller than that predicted by the formulas derived for plane wave diffraction. This does not mean that the plane wave formulas are wrong; rather, what *is* wrong is the assumption that all beams of light are plane waves.

Glare Testing

As discussed in the section on visual function (see Chapter 3, Optics of the Human Eye), Snellen acuity does not completely characterize the quality of a patient's visual optical system. Some patients may have a disabling media opacity with reduced contrast sensitivity and still have otherwise good Snellen acuity. Modulation transfer function testing (contrast grating) is one approach to testing these patients.

Another approach is to simulate the clinical situations that patients find most disabling. Most of these patients notice that extraneous light markedly degrades their visual performance. For example, headlights from oncoming cars at night may render an individual unable to see any detail of the road ahead. Various glare testers (Fig 9-71) have been devised to simulate this situation. They all shine a bright light into the eye at an

Figure 9-71 Photograph of a glare tester: *a,* eyepiece for viewing the Snellen chart; *b,* illumination source for shining a bright light into the eye from the side. *(Photograph courtesy of Neal H. Atebara, MD.)*

angle or at many angles away from the visual axis. With normal media, the glare source is imaged away from the macula and does not affect central acuity. In the presence of a scattering lesion, light from the glare source reaches the macula, reducing the image contrast of an on-axis target and making it harder to discern.

The major limitation of the various glare testers is that results are qualitative, not quantitative, and not very reproducible. Nevertheless, they do document the problem and alert the physician to problems not detectable with routine Snellen testing.

Wavefront Aberrometers

Small flying spot excimer lasers allow ophthalmologists to correct refractive problems more complex than simple spherocylindrical errors. Although conventional autorefractors are able to measure basic spherical and cylindrical errors, they do not measure irregular astigmatism. Corneal topography is able to measure the shape of the surface of an irregular cornea, but it is not able to measure the actual refractive topography of the entire lens–cornea optical system. For such measurements, instruments traditionally used in astronomy to reduce the complex and continually changing refractive effects of the earth's atmosphere have been applied to the examination of the human eye. These instruments are called *wavefront analyzers.*

Wavefront Analysis

Measurement of higher-order optical aberrations requires a basic understanding of *wavefront analysis.* Wavefront analysis is the study of the shape of light waves as they leave an object point and how they are affected by optical media. In an ideal optical system with no aberrations (Fig 9-72A), an object viewed from optical infinity produces parallel rays of light (red arrows in the figure). The photons emitted or reflected by an object point

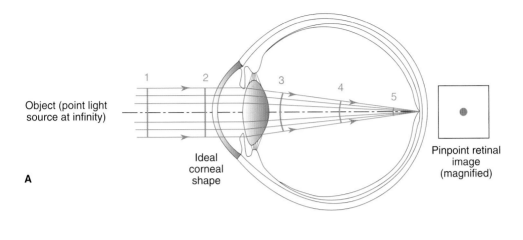

Object (point light source at infinity)

Ideal corneal shape

Pinpoint retinal image (magnified)

A

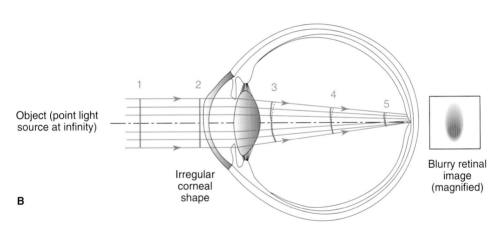

Object (point light source at infinity)

Irregular corneal shape

Blurry retinal image (magnified)

B

Figure 9-72 Wavefronts produced by an ideal optical system **(A)** and those produced by an aberrated optical system **(B).** *(Courtesy of Neal H. Atebara, MD. Redrawn by Cyndie C. H. Wooley.)*

at specific moments in time are called wavefronts (blue lines). Wavefronts are oriented perpendicular to the direction of propagation of the light rays. The wavefront produced at a specific point in time is represented by "moment 1." Parallel light rays from infinity produce planar wavefronts.

At the next moment in time, the wavefront has progressed to moment 2 and is still planar. The wavefront is subsequently refracted by the cornea and lens, resulting in a concave spherical shape (moment 3). In an ideal optical system, this spherical wavefront converges to the macula (moments 4 and 5), producing a pinpoint retinal image point.

In an aberrated eye, where the superior midperipheral cornea is ectatic (Fig 9-72B), the transmitted wavefronts are not perfectly spherical. The solid blue line in the figure at moment 3 demonstrates how the superior aspect of the wavefront is delayed (an ideal sphere is represented by the black dashed line). As the aberrated wavefront converges to the macula (moments 4 and 5), the light rays spread out over the superior macular, and a blurred retinal image is produced.

Hartmann-Shack Aberrometry

Hartmann-Shack aberrometry uses the principle of "optical reversibility." A low-intensity laser beam is directed onto the retina, and this is used as the object for the aberrometer. Light rays from the laser spot diverge as they leave the retina, thereby creating convex spherical wavefronts that travel toward the front of the eye (Fig 9-73A, moments 1–3). In an ideal eye, the lens and cornea would transform the spherical wavefronts into plano wavefronts (moments 4 and 5). A lens array in the aberrometer focuses these light rays onto a photodetector (CCD). An ideal eye produces Hartmann-Shack images with dots of light that are equally spaced from each other. Because the measured wavefronts are those *exiting* the eye, this is considered *outgoing aberrometry.*

In an aberrated eye (Fig 9-73B), the wavefronts are not entirely planar. At moments 4 and 5 in the figure, the dashed black lines represent ideal planar wavefronts, whereas the solid blue lines represent the aberrated wavefronts. The images captured by the photodetector show areas where the spots of light are more closely spaced; these represent areas where the eye's optical aberration of the system is greatest.

The data from the photodetector are then processed in a manner similar to those from an automated lensmeter to arrive at a correction that includes low- and higher-order aberrations. The data further define the amount of photoablation performed at each position on the cornea using a wavefront-guided excimer laser (Fig 9-73C).

Tscherning Aberrometry

Tscherning aberrometry is similar to Hartmann-Shack aberrometry except that the wavefronts measured by the system are those *entering* the eye (Fig 9-74), making this *ingoing aberrometry.* A collimated beam is passed through a mask of holes and a plus lens. Aberrations in the eye distort the spacing between the spots of light imaged onto the retina. A high-magnification camera captures the image on the retina. Areas where the spots of light are more closely spaced represent areas where the aberration of the eye's optical system is greatest.

Retinal Raytracing Technique

Retinal raytracing is another example of ingoing aberrometry. It works on the same principle as Tscherning aberrometry, but instead of using a mask with an array of holes, a laser beam is used to scan across the pupil (Fig 9-75A, B). Normally, the laser beam at each position would focus to a single point on the fovea. Where optical aberrations are present, however, the path of the laser beam is deviated. At each laser beam position, the amount of deviation is measured, and the degree of aberration can thereby be calculated.

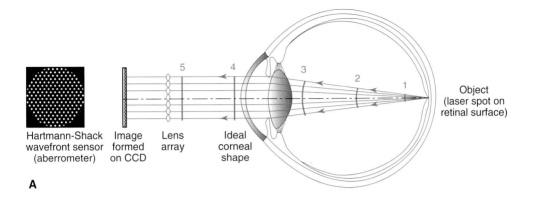

Hartmann-Shack wavefront sensor (aberrometer) | Image formed on CCD | Lens array | Ideal corneal shape

A

Hartmann-Shack wavefront sensor (aberrometer) | Image formed on CCD | Lens array | Irregular corneal shape

B

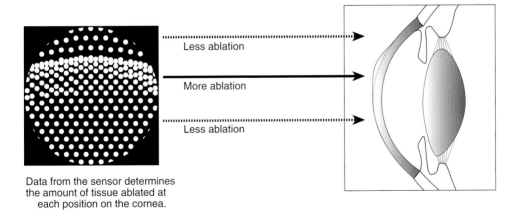

Data from the sensor determines the amount of tissue ablated at each position on the cornea.

C

Figure 9-73 Hartmann-Shack image produced by an ideal optical system **(A)** and by an aberrated optical system **(B).** The Hartmann-Shack image is used to perform corrective corneal ablation **(C).** *(Courtesy of Neal H. Atebara, MD. Redrawn by Cyndie C. H. Wooley.)*

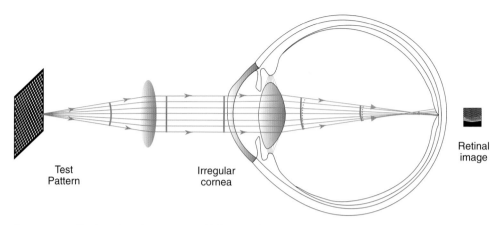

Figure 9-74 Tscherning aberrometry. Light rays from a test pattern are made parallel by a plus lens and directed into the eye. A high-magnification camera captures the retinal image produced. Discrepancies between the test pattern and the retinal image are due to wavefront aberrations. *(Courtesy of Neal H. Atebara, MD. Redrawn by Cyndie C. H. Wooley.)*

Optical Coherence Tomography

Optical coherence tomography (OCT) is used to create a cross-sectional image of the living retina at a resolution of 10 micrometers or less. This technology is increasingly useful in the diagnosis and management of many different macular conditions, such as macular edema and vitreomacular traction. OCT is based on the Michelson interferometer, which takes advantage of the interference properties of temporally coherent light.

When 2 coherent light waves that are fully "in-phase" with one another overlap, their superposition results in a doubling of light intensity. When they are precisely "out-of-phase," they cancel each other out, resulting in darkness. Between the 2 extremes, the intensity varies as a function of how closely in-phase the waves are.

The major components of an OCT include a light source (usually a superluminescent diode), a light detector, a beam splitter, and a movable mirror, arranged as in Figure 9-76. Light from the diode is split by the beam splitter, with half the light directed to the movable mirror (called the *reference beam* [blue waves]) and half to the retina (called the *object beam* [red waves]). These 2 beams are superimposed by the beam splitter and transmitted together to the light detector.

The principle of the Michelson interferometer tells us that light reflected from the movable mirror (reference beam) will cancel out almost all light from the retina (objective beam) except light from the level of the retina corresponding to the position of the movable mirror. That is, if the movable mirror is positioned "6 units" from the beam splitter, only light from the retina at a distance of "6 units" from the beam splitter will be seen by the light detector; light from all other layers of the retina will be canceled out by destructive interference. Likewise, when the mirror is moved up and down, it will allow only light from the corresponding retinal distance.

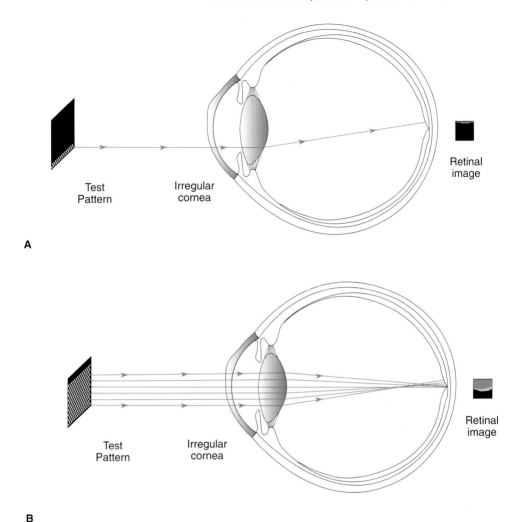

Figure 9-75 Retinal raytracing aberrometry. Similar to that of Tscherning aberrometry, the test pattern is projected by a laser beam scanning across the retina line by line. *(Courtesy of Neal H. Atebara, MD. Redrawn by Cyndie C. H. Wooley.)*

The various layers of the retina reflect light to different degrees, with the highest reflection occurring in layers with cell surfaces and membranes, such as the RPE layer, the inner and outer nuclear layers, and the internal limiting membrane. If light intensity as measured by the detector is plotted against the position of the movable mirror, an "A-scan" image of the retina cross section can be generated (see Fig 9-76). A tilting mirror positioned between the beam splitter and the retina can be used to scan the retina to generate a 2-dimensional B-scan cross-sectional image of the retina (see Fig 9-76).

Figure 9-76 Optical coherence tomography (OCT). Based on the principle of the Michelson interferometer, the OCT analyzes the interference patterns between a reference beam and the object beam to create a precise cross-sectional reflectivity map of the internal retina. *(Courtesy of Neal H. Atebara, MD. Redrawn by Cyndie C. H. Wooley.)*

Common Guidelines for Prescribing Cylinders

[The material in this appendix is reprinted from Guyton DL. Prescribing cylinders: the problem of distortion. *Surv Ophthalmol.* 1977;22:177–188. Copyright © 1977, *Survey of Ophthalmology.*]

Commonly taught guidelines are the following:

1. Children accept the full astigmatic correction.
2. If an adult cannot tolerate the full astigmatic correction, rotate the cylinder axis toward 90° or 180° and/or reduce the cylinder power to decrease distortion. When reducing the cylinder power, keep the spherical equivalent constant by appropriate adjustment of sphere.
3. With older patients, beware of changing the cylinder axis.

The Problem: Distortion

Why have such guidelines developed? Why can some patients not tolerate the full astigmatic correction in the first place? One text on clinical refraction states that full correction of a high astigmatic error may initially result in considerable blurring of vision. Another teaching is that with the full astigmatic correction the image is too sharp—the patient is not used to seeing so clearly. Statements such as these are not only misleading; they are incorrect.

The reason for intolerance of astigmatic spectacle corrections is distortion caused by meridional magnification. Unequal magnification of the retinal image in the various meridians produces monocular distortion manifested by tilting lines or altered shapes of objects (Fig A-1). But monocular distortion by itself is rarely a problem; the effect is too small. Maximum tilting of vertical lines (declination error) in the retinal image will occur when the correcting cylinder axis is at 45° or 135°, but even under these conditions each diopter of correcting cylinder power produces only about 0.4° of tilt.

The clinically significant problem occurs only under binocular conditions. Minor degrees of monocular distortion can produce major alterations in binocular spatial perception. Consider, for example, a patient with symmetrical oblique astigmatism wearing a +1.00 diopter cylinder, axis 135° before the right eye and a +1.00 diopter cylinder, axis 45° before the left eye. If the patient looks at a vertical rod 3 meters away, the retinal images of the rod will be tilted toward each other at the top (declination error) approx-

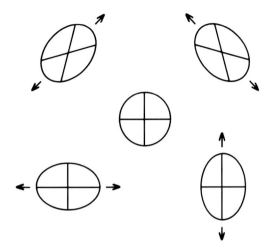

Figure A-1 Monocular distortion caused by meridional magnification. If the retinal image is magnified more in one direction than the other (as indicated by the arrows), vertical lines may become slanted, horizontal lines may become tilted, and objects may appear taller or shorter.

imately 0.4° each, a barely perceptible amount under monocular conditions. But under binocular conditions, the vertical rod will theoretically appear tilted toward the patient (inclination) approximately 35°! Such large errors in stereoscopic spatial localization are clearly intolerable, seemingly out of proportion to the amount of monocular distortion that produces them. Oblique distortion in one or both eyes causes more distressing binocular symptoms than vertical or horizontal distortion, and movement accentuates the symptoms.

Fortunately, errors in stereoscopic spatial localization are usually compensated for in most patients by experiential factors: perspective clues, the known size and shape of familiar objects, the knowledge of what is level and what is perpendicular, etc. The possibility of permanent adaptation to binocular distortion will be discussed later, but the fact remains that some patients cannot or will not tolerate binocular spatial distortion, and herein lies our problem.

We have no effective means of treating binocular spatial distortion except by altering or eliminating the monocular distortion that produces it. Complete understanding of the causes and management of monocular distortion is difficult, involving several areas of physiological optics that the average practitioner would prefer to avoid: blur theory, spectacle lens design, obliquely crossed cylinders, and theory of the Jackson cross cylinder. However, with a few key facts from each of these areas, we can suddenly gain a working understanding of astigmatic spectacle corrections.

Sources of Monocular Distortion

As illustrated in Figure A-1, monocular distortion is caused by meridional magnification. We can identify two basic sources of meridional magnification, one involving the design of the spectacle lens, and the other involving the location of the spectacle lens with respect to the entrance pupil of the eye.

"Shape Factor" of the Spectacle Lens

All spectacle lenses having curved front surfaces produce a magnification inherent to the lens itself. The more convex the front surface and the thicker the lens, the greater will be this "shape factor" magnification. If the front surface of the lens is spherical, the shape factor magnification will be the same in all meridians, producing only an overall size change in the retinal image. On the other hand, if the front surface of the lens is cylindrical or toric, the shape factor magnification will vary from one meridian to another, producing distortion of the retinal image. Again, this only occurs with lenses having the cylinder ground on the front surface of the lens, the so-called *plus cylinder form* or anterior toric spectacle lens. Lenses having the cylinder ground on the back surface (minus cylinder lenses, posterior toric lenses, "iseikonoid" lenses) do not produce differential meridional magnification due to the shape factor, because the front surface power is the same in all meridians. The lens clock may be used to check the front and back curves.

Meridional magnification arising from the shape factor of plus cylinder spectacle lenses is rarely more than 1% to 2%. Many patients can perceive this difference, however, and for this reason and others, since the mid-1960s, minus cylinder spectacle lenses have become the preferred form for routine dispensing.

Distance of the Spectacle Lens From the Entrance Pupil

More important than the shape factor of the spectacle lens in producing distortion is the location of the spectacle lens relative to the entrance pupil of the eye. We shall consider both the conventional method and the general method of analyzing the magnification produced.

The Conventional Analysis: A Special Case

The conventional method of calculating the total magnification produced by a spectacle lens is to multiply the shape factor magnification times the "power factor" magnification. The power factor magnification is a function of the dioptric power of the correcting lens and the distance of the correcting lens from the "seat of ametropia." For example, consider a +4.00 D cylindrical lens placed at a vertex distance of 12 mm from an eye with simple hyperopic astigmatism. Assume that the eye's astigmatism arises in the cornea and that the +4.00 D cylindrical lens fully corrects the astigmatic error. This lens will produce a power factor magnification of 0% in the axis meridian and 5% in the meridian perpendicular to the axis meridian, for a differential meridional magnification of 5%. Figure A-2 shows the (differential) meridional magnification to be expected for this lens as a function of vertex distance. The shorter the vertex distance, the less will be the meridional magnification, an important point to remember when trying to minimize distortion.

The conventional analysis is only valid, though, when the spectacle lens actually *corrects* the corneal astigmatism. What sort of meridional magnification and resulting distortion can we expect with *uncorrected* astigmatism, or with astigmatism that is only partially, or inappropriately, corrected?

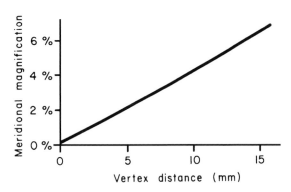

Figure A-2 Meridional magnification as a function of vertex distance for a +4.00 diopter cylindrical spectacle lens.

The General Case: Blurred Retinal Images

To investigate the general nature of meridional magnification, we must consider what happens in the case of blurred retinal images. The size of a blurred retinal image is defined as the distance between the centers of those blur circles which represent the extremities of the object.[1] Each blur circle is formed by a bundle of rays limited by the entrance pupil of the eye with the chief ray of the bundle passing toward the center of the entrance pupil and forming the center of the blur circle on the retina. Therefore, the chief rays from the extremities of the object determine the size of the retinal image, and because the chief rays pass toward the center of the entrance pupil, the angle subtended by the object *at the entrance pupil* is proportional to the size of the retinal image.[2]

We need not be concerned here with *computing* meridional magnification of blurred retinal images; we simply need to examine the relationship of the entrance pupil to meridional magnification in a qualitative sense. The entrance pupil of the eye (Fig A-3) is the pupil we see when we look at a patient's eye. It is actually the image formed by the cornea of the real pupil and is located about 0.5 mm in front of, and is about 14% larger than, the real pupil.

Figure A-3 The entrance pupil of the eye. Note the approximate location of the entrance pupil with respect to the cornea, to the crystalline lens, and to the corrective spectacle lens.

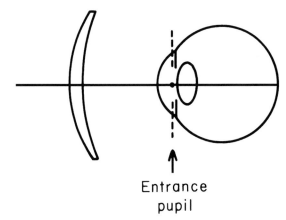

Entrance
pupil

Illustrating the Location Effect of Cylindrical Lenses

Figure A-4 illustrates the general case of distortion of the retinal image produced by a cylindrical lens placed before a nonastigmatic eye. In Figure A-4, rays *ef* and *gh* represent the chief rays from the vertical extremities of the object. These chief rays cross at the center of the entrance pupil and continue on to form the vertical extremities of the retinal image.[3] No distortion of the retinal image is present in Figure A-4a.

In Figure A-4b, a cylindrical lens is placed before the eye in the usual spectacle plane with its axis *xy* oriented in the 45° meridian. Chief rays *ijk* and *lmn* pass through the cylindrical lens at points away from the axis *xy* and are therefore bent by the lens. Chief ray *ijk* undergoes a small prismatic deviation down and to the patient's left, while chief ray *lmn* undergoes a small prismatic deviation up and to the patient's right. The chief rays continue on through the center of the entrance pupil to the retina, but the ray segments *jk* and *mn* lie in a tilted plane because of the prismatic deviations that occurred in opposite horizontal directions at the cylindrical lens. (Note that ray segments *i* and *I* do not lie in the same common plane as the segments *jk* and *mn,* and neither do they follow the same paths as ray segments *e* and *g* in Figure A-4a.) Because ray segments *jk* and *mn* lie in a tilted plane, the vertical arrow in the retinal image of Figure A-4b is tilted. In fact, the entire retinal image in Figure A-4b is distorted. In the case of this retinal image as a whole, we may speak of the distortion as arising from meridional magnification caused by the cylindrical lens—a meridional magnification in the direction of the double arrows, perpendicular to axis *xy* of the cylindrical lens.

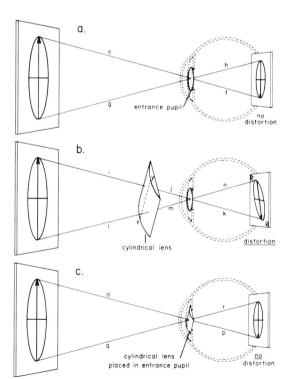

Figure A-4 The relationship between the position of a cylindrical lens relative to the entrance pupil of a nonastigmatic eye and the distortion of the retinal image produced. *a,* No distortion in the absence of the cylindrical lens. *b,* Distortion produced by the cylindrical lens located in the usual spectacle plane. *c,* No distortion when the cylindrical lens is placed hypothetically in the entrance pupil of the eye.

In Figure A-4c the cylindrical lens has been moved toward the eye until it is located hypothetically within the entrance pupil. Chief rays *op* and *qr* pass to the center of the entrance pupil where they now pass *undeviated* through the cylindrical lens because they strike the lens along its axis. Chief rays *op* and *qr* continue on to the retina and may be seen to be identical with rays *ef* and *gh* of Figure A-4a, causing no distortion of the retinal image.

Summary of the General Case

To summarize the lesson of Figure A-4, astigmatic refracting surfaces located away from the entrance pupil of the eye cause meridional magnification and distortion of the retinal image. The direction of meridional magnification is determined by the axis orientation of the astigmatic refracting surface, and the amount of meridional magnification increases not only with the power of the astigmatic refracting surface but also with increased distance of the astigmatic refracting surface from the entrance pupil of the eye.[4]

Distortion With Uncorrected and Inappropriately Corrected Astigmatism

We can now predict what sort of meridional magnification and resultant distortion to expect in the case of uncorrected astigmatism or inappropriately corrected astigmatism. In uncorrected astigmatism the astigmatic refracting surfaces are those of the cornea or lens. Because these surfaces are located near the entrance pupil (see Fig A-3), meridional magnification and distortion will be minimal. The meridional magnification produced by uncorrected corneal astigmatism is approximately 0.3% per diopter of astigmatism, which is a rather small amount.

The situation with inappropriately corrected astigmatism is much the same as the situation with properly corrected astigmatism. Whenever an astigmatic spectacle lens is placed before an eye, whether it is the correct lens or not, significant meridional magnification is likely to occur because of the relatively remote location of the spectacle lens from the entrance pupil (see Fig A-3). Even though the eye may be astigmatic, the effect of astigmatic surfaces located near the entrance pupil is so small that the direction and amount of meridional magnification are primarily determined not by the astigmatism of the eye itself, but by the axis and power of the astigmatic spectacle lens—whatever the axis and power may be, correct or not.

Common Misconceptions

It is time to correct some common misconceptions in clinical teaching. It is almost universally taught in clinical ophthalmology, with a rare exception, that retinal images slant in uncorrected oblique astigmatism and are straightened by the proper astigmatic spectacle correction. The opposite, of course, is closer to the truth. Undoubtedly, this misconception has arisen from the simple experiment of holding a cylindrical lens before one's emmetropic eye to "simulate" astigmatism, and noting the distortion produced. The fallacy, of course, is that the trial lens simulates the effect of a *spectacle* lens and not the effect of an astigmatic cornea. It is easily confirmed that as the trial lens is brought closer and closer to the entrance pupil of the eye, the observed distortion progressively decreases.

A second misconception in clinical teaching, again with only a rare exception, deals with the effect of residual astigmatism on distortion. When an axis error is made in correcting an astigmatic eye with a spectacle lens, the general rules for combination of cylinders having obliquely crossed axes may be used to calculate the axis and power of the residual astigmatism. It is taught that the axis and power of this residual astigmatism determine the direction and amount of distortion that will be present. From the preceding discussion it should be evident that the axis and power of the residual astigmatism are only coincidental and that the primary determinants of distortion are simply the axis and power of the spectacle lens itself. For example, if a correcting cylindrical lens is rotated to produce an axis error, the amount of distortion will remain substantially the same, but the direction of distortion will rotate an amount corresponding to the rotation of the cylindrical lens.

Relative Contributions From Sources of Distortion

The various sources of meridional magnification do not make equal contributions to the amount of magnification produced. The relative contributions may be appreciated more easily from the graphs in Figure A-5. These graphs show the meridional magnification to be expected with various degrees of astigmatism, both in the uncorrected state and in the corrected state, using for correction a common form of astigmatic spectacle lens. Note that with uncorrected astigmatism, the meridional magnification that occurs is much less than, and in the opposite direction to, the meridional magnification produced by the correcting spectacle lens. Also note that the shape factor of the spectacle lens, if a plus cylinder lens is used, increases the meridional magnification only about 2%.

Photographic Simulation of Distortion

Figure A-6 illustrates by exaggerated photographs the monocular distortion that is produced by spectacle correction of oblique astigmatism. Note that despite the presence of

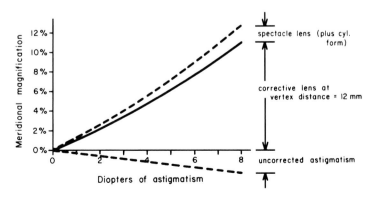

Figure A-5 Contributing factors to meridional magnification in uncorrected and corrected astigmatism. Calculations are for a positive cylindrical spectacle lens having no spherical power, with base curve of 6 D, thickness of 3 mm, and vertex distance of 12 mm.

Figure A-6 Photographic simulation of distortion with oblique astigmatism. *Left,* no astigmatism. *Center,* uncorrected oblique astigmatism with the circle of least confusion on the retina. No significant distortion is present. *Right,* spectacle-corrected oblique astigmatism producing significant distortion.

blur in the uncorrected state, no significant distortion is present. With spectacle correction of the astigmatism, the distortion becomes painfully apparent.

Minimizing Monocular Distortion

Having discussed the sources of monocular distortion, we can now explore various ways to minimize meridional magnification and, with it, monocular distortion. This will be necessary in patients who cannot tolerate their present spectacles or in those whose new refractions demand a change in prescription such that we might anticipate problems with distortion. How can we minimize meridional magnification? We can specify minus cylinder spectacle lenses, minimize vertex distance, and sometimes alter the astigmatic correction by rotating the axis or reducing the power of the correcting cylinder.

Specifying Minus Cylinder (Posterior Toric) Spectacle Lenses

The small amount of meridional magnification caused by plus cylinder (anterior toric) spectacle lenses is avoided simply by specifying minus cylinder lenses in the prescriptions. In practice, this distinction is rarely necessary, for minus cylinder lenses have become the preferred form for routine dispensing. Most dispensers will choose the minus cylinder form automatically and reserve the plus cylinder form only for duplication of an old pair of plus cylinder lenses.

Minimizing Vertex Distance

As previously discussed, meridional magnification decreases as the correcting spectacle lens is placed closer and closer to the eye (see Fig A-2). There is often little room for manipulation of vertex distance with common styles of frames, but when distortion is anticipated, we can at least avoid the so-called fashionable glasses that sit at the end of the patient's nose.

With contact lenses, the vertex distance is reduced to zero and distortion is practically eliminated. Contact lenses should always be considered as an alternative to spectacle correction if the patient remains unsatisfied with other attempts to reduce distortion. In fact, contact lenses may be the only means available (other than iseikonic corrections) to reduce distortion while maintaining clear imagery, for further attempts to reduce distortion by manipulating the spectacle lens correction, as we shall see in the next section, involve a certain sacrifice in the sharpness of the retinal image.

Altering the Astigmatic Correction

Rotating the cylinder axis

Clinical experience suggests that new astigmatic spectacle corrections in adults are better tolerated if the axis of the cylinder is at 90° or 180° rather than in an oblique meridian. In fact, it has long been taught that oblique axes should be rotated toward 90° or 180°, if visual acuity does not suffer too much, to avoid problems from oblique distortion. This makes sense, for the *direction* of meridional magnification is determined principally by the axis orientation of the correcting cylinder, whether or not the axis is correct, and vertical or horizontal aniseikonia is known to be more tolerable than oblique aniseikonia.

There have been recurrent arguments in the literature regarding why cylinder axes should not be rotated away from the correct position, but these arguments are primarily based on the misconception stated earlier that the axis and power of the *residual* astigmatism determine the direction and amount of distortion. As we have seen, it is the axis and power of the spectacle lens itself, correct or not, that principally determine the direction and amount of distortion. With this concept understood, and on the basis of clinical experience, we may thus state that the *direction* of distortion may be made more tolerable, if necessary, by rotating the cylinder axis toward 90° or 180°.

There is another situation in which the cylinder axis should sometimes be rotated away from the correct position. An older patient may have *adapted* to an incorrect axis position in his or her previous spectacles, and may not tolerate the change in direction of distortion produced by rotating the cylinder axis to the correct position. The nature of such adaptation will be discussed later, but there is no question that it occurs and can cause problems. In this case, the cylinder axis should be rotated toward the position of the *old* cylinder axis, even if the old cylinder axis is oblique. This maneuver does not *reduce* distortion but does change the *direction* of distortion back toward the position of adaptation.

Reducing the cylinder power

The other method that is commonly used to lessen distortion is reduction of the power of the correcting cylinder. This makes sense, for we have seen that the *amount* of meridional magnification is largely determined by the power of the correcting cylinder—the less the cylinder power, the less the meridional magnification.

Photographic simulation

Figure A-7 illustrates by exaggerated photographs the reduction of distortion by altering the astigmatic correction. In each case when the cylinder power is altered, the spherical correction is changed the appropriate amount to keep the circle of least confusion on the retina, as will be discussed later. Note that distortion may be decreased by reducing the cylinder power or changed in direction by rotating the cylinder axis, but either of these manipulations causes blurring of the image. We have decreased distortion, but at the expense of visual acuity. What produces the blur? Residual astigmatism.

Figure A-7 Photographic simulation of altering the astigmatic correction to reduce distortion. *Left,* distorted image resulting from full spectacle correction of oblique astigmatism. *Center,* decreased amount of distortion obtained by reducing the cylinder power. *Right,* improved direction of distortion (vertical) as well as decreased amount of distortion obtained by rotating the plus cylinder axis to 180° and reducing the cylinder power.

Residual astigmatism

Whenever the cylinder power is reduced from its correct value, or the cylinder axis is rotated away from its correct position, residual astigmatism appears. The residual astigmatism does not produce distortion, but it does produce blur of the retinal image, limiting the amount that the cylinder power may be reduced or the amount that the cylinder axis may be rotated away from its correct position. If we must minimize distortion, we must be careful at the same time not to create excessive blur from residual astigmatism.

It is the *amount* of residual astigmatism that produces the blur, not the axis[5] of the residual astigmatism. It is easy to judge the amount of residual astigmatism when reducing the cylinder power of a spectacle correction, for the residual astigmatism is simply equal to the amount the cylinder power is reduced. It is more difficult, however, to judge the amount of residual astigmatism induced by rotating the cylinder axis away from the correct position. The resulting residual astigmatism may always be calculated using the rules for combination of obliquely crossed cylinders, but this calculation requires considerable mental gymnastics. A simple graph may be easier to remember. Figure A-8 should provide a working knowledge of the amount of residual astigmatism induced by rotating the cylinder axis.

As indicated by the graphs in Figure A-8, when we rotate the cylinder axis away from its correct position and keep the cylinder at its full value, we rapidly introduce residual astigmatism.[6] If the cylinder axis is rotated 30° from its correct position, the residual astigmatism becomes equal to the original uncorrected astigmatism. If the cylinder axis is rotated 90° from its correct position, the residual astigmatism becomes *twice* the value of the original uncorrected astigmatism!

From the mathematics of obliquely crossed cylinders, it may be shown[7] that as the cylinder axis is rotated away from its correct position, the power of the cylinder should be reduced in order to minimize residual astigmatism. For each position of the cylinder axis, there exists an optimal value for the cylinder power that minimizes residual astigmatism as indicated by the graphs in Figure A-8.

Figure A-8 Residual astigmatism produced when a cylinder axis is shifted away from its correct position. Graphs illustrate how reducing the cylinder power to an optimal value can minimize residual astigmatism.

Optimal value for cylinder power

Thus, if we choose to shift the cylinder axis to make the direction of meridional magnification more tolerable, we should also reduce the cylinder power slightly to minimize residual astigmatism. But how can we know the optimal value for cylinder power without performing complicated trigonometric calculations? Here we are lucky, for we may simply use the Jackson cross cylinder test for cylinder power. It may be shown from cross cylinder theory that for *any* setting, this test automatically gives us the optimal cylinder power to result in minimum residual astigmatism. The axes of the cross cylinder are simply aligned with the principal meridians of the correcting lens, and the patient is asked, "Which is better, one or two?" as the cross cylinder is flipped. From the patient's responses, the refractionist adjusts the cylinder power until both flipped positions of the cross cylinder appear equally clear.

It is generally known that the cylinder axis should be refined first with cross cylinder testing, for the correct axis will be found even if the cylinder power is incorrect. The cylinder power is generally refined *after* the axis is refined, for the correct cylinder cannot be found if an axis error is present. It has never been pointed out, however, that the cylinder power which *is* found in the presence of an axis error is truly the optimal cylinder power for that axis error, resulting in the least residual astigmatism possible for that axis error.[8]

This is a profound coincidence—a coincidence which, as previously explained, greatly simplifies our task of reducing distortion while maintaining acceptable visual acuity.

Optimal value for sphere power

When reducing the cylinder power by *any* method, we must take care to maintain the proper spherical correction for best visual acuity. The usual teaching is that the spherical equivalent of the refractive correction must be kept constant when reducing the cylinder power, a concept based on the conoid of Sturm and the supposition that visual acuity is best when the circle of least confusion falls on the retina. Although this is probably true in many cases, it is certainly not true in every case. For example, a patient with residual astigmatism with the rule may obtain best visual acuity with the vertical focal line of the conoid of Sturm falling on the retina—simply because more of our customary test letters are recognizable when the vertical strokes are clear. Thus, the spherical equivalent concept is not always strictly applicable when reducing the power of the cylinder.

When refining the cylinder power by cross cylinder testing, the sphere should be adjusted for best visual acuity during the refinement and also as the final step. When *empirically* reducing the cylinder power, the spherical equivalent concept provides a useful estimate for adjusting the sphere, but it should not be relied upon without a final subjective check.

Adaptation to Distortion

It is a common clinical observation that children adapt readily to induced distortion from astigmatic spectacle corrections. Adults adapt less readily. Little is known of the actual mechanism of adaptation. Experiments in adults with induced aniseikonia for periods of up to two weeks have suggested that adaptation to spatial distortion is primarily an interpretive process rather than a physiological process. In these adult subjects, the sense of distortion usually disappeared completely in several days, but in unfamiliar surroundings, where there were few monocular perspective cues, the spatial disturbance returned. In these experiments, however, there appeared to be some physiological adaptation to distortion. A physiological component was measured as being responsible for 20%–60% of the total adaptation, and there was an aftereffect of aniseikonia in the opposite direction when the distorting lenses were discontinued.

There is evidence that physiological adaptation to distortion is age-dependent. In a large study at the Dartmouth Eye Institute in 1945, adults with astigmatism at oblique axes tended to show a larger physiological component of adaptation to distortion if their astigmatism had been corrected at an early age.

Physiological adaptation to distortion appears to involve a reordering of the retinal meridians and may therefore be thought of as a form of rotational anomalous retinal correspondence. Indeed, the ability to physiologically adapt to distortion appears to parallel in patient age the ability to develop conventional anomalous retinal correspondence. The ability is well developed in children and decreases rapidly with advancing age.

The ability to reorder the retinal meridians on a permanent basis is further evidenced by patients having oblique extraocular muscle dysfunction with large anatomical cyclodeviations (5°–15°) of the eyes. Patients having these cyclodeviations since birth or since early childhood experience no spatial distortion and have no measurable cyclophoria. Acute cyclodeviations in older patients (for example, after bilateral oblique muscle surgery) produce both measurable cyclophorias and spatial distortion. This spatial distortion disappears in a few days, but the measurable cyclophoria remains much longer—months to possibly years—indicating the poor ability of the older patient to develop a rotational type of anomalous retinal correspondence. Physiological adaptation to cyclodeviations requires a pure rotational reordering of the retinal meridians, while adaptation to astigmatic distortion requires a scissors-type of reordering of the retinal meridians, but the neurological mechanisms are probably quite similar.

Regardless of the mechanism and extent of physiological adaptation to distortion, the greater portion of adaptation to astigmatic distortion appears to be the interpretive type of adaptation. Monocular perspective cues, if they are abundant enough, prevail over the altered binocular stereoscopic cues. Usually in a few days the distorted spatial frame of reference comes to be interpreted in view of the known monocular cues, and the sense of spatial distortion disappears—to reappear only if the monocular cues are removed.

Occasional older patients cannot even adapt to distortion by the interpretive mechanism, and it is for these patients that we must be able to reduce or minimize distortion by manipulating the astigmatic spectacle correction.

Revised Guidelines for Prescribing Cylinders

We can now formulate a revised set of guidelines for prescribing cylinders.

1. In *children,* give the full astigmatic correction.
2. In *adults,* try the full astigmatic correction first. Give warning and encouragement. If problems are anticipated, try a walking-around trial with trial frames before prescribing.
3. To minimize distortion, use minus cylinder lenses and minimize vertex distances.
4. Spatial distortion from astigmatic spectacle corrections is a *binocular* phenomenon. Occlude one eye to verify that this is indeed the cause of the patient's complaints.
5. If necessary, reduce distortion still further by rotating the cylinder axis toward 180° or 90° (or toward the *old* axis) and/or by reducing the cylinder power. Balance the resulting blur with the remaining distortion, using careful adjustment of cylinder power and sphere. Residual astigmatism at *any* position of the cylinder axis may be minimized with the Jackson cross cylinder test for cylinder power. Adjust the sphere using the spherical equivalent concept as a guide, but rely on a final subjective check to obtain best visual acuity.
6. If distortion cannot be reduced sufficiently by altering the astigmatic spectacle correction, consider contact lenses (which cause no appreciable distortion) or iseikonic corrections.

Special cases occasionally arise. If a patient's sense of spatial distortion seems out of proportion to his astigmatic correction, consider the possibility of spherical aniseikonia as the cause of his symptoms, and prescribe accordingly.

If the patient with moderate to high astigmatism has no complaints about distance spectacle correction but has difficulty reading at near, remember that changes in the astigmatic axes of the eyes (from cyclorotations) and changes in the effectivity of astigmatic corrections may cause problems at near. Such patients may require separate reading glasses.

Finally, patients who desire spectacles only for part-time wear may not be able to adapt to distortion during short periods of wear. In such cases, the astigmatic correction should be altered to reduce distortion according to the principles outlined above.

The revised set of guidelines for prescribing cylinders is now complete. With a rational basis for these guidelines, we should be able to place our confidence in them and prescribe cylinders more from knowledge and less from empirical rumors.

For a complete list of references see the original article: Guyton DL. Prescribing cylinders: The problem of distortion. *Surv Ophthalmol.* 1977;22:177–188.

NOTES

1. In the case of astigmatism, the blur patches on the retina may be ellipses or lines instead of blur circles, and the size of the blurred retinal image may appear somewhat altered by the effect of the *shape* of the blur patches on the outline of the image. This effect, however, only affects the *outline* of the retinal image and does not cause the type of monocular distortion (tilting of lines, etc) which concerns us here.

2. The size of the retinal image is usually computed as being proportional to the angle subtended by the object at the first nodal point of the eye (which is approximately 4 mm posterior to the center of the entrance pupil), but this is true only for sharp retinal images. The nodal point cannot be used to compute the size of blurred retinal images.

3. Chief rays such as those in Figure A-4, although they initially pass *toward* the center of the entrance pupil, are actually refracted by the cornea, pass through the center of the *real* pupil, and are further refracted by the crystalline lens before continuing on to the retina. However, each pair of chief rays such as *ef* and *gh*, or *jk* and *mn*, because of the axial symmetry of the ocular media, remain *in the same plane* with each other as they pass through the eye's optics. Therefore, while the retinal images in Figure A-4 are not exactly the proper size because of the simplified representation of the chief rays, the presence or absence of distortion is accurately represented.

4. An alternate way to analyze the effect of a cylindrical lens is to consider the lens as an integral part of the eye's optical system and calculate the position of the entrance pupil for the system as a whole in each principal meridian. The pairs of chief rays in the two principal meridians would then cross the optical axis at different points, producing the same differential meridional magnification as obtained with the present analysis.

5. The axis of residual astigmatism is of no consequence in the consideration of blur except perhaps as it may affect the reading of letters that have predominantly vertical strokes. If the axis of the residual astigmatism is vertical or horizontal, and if the patient is able to clear the vertical strokes of the letters by accommodating, his reading ability may be somewhat better than would otherwise be predicted.

6. The residual astigmatism in this case is approximately equal to $2C \sin \theta$, where C is the dioptric value of the cylinder and θ is the angle that the cylinder axis has been rotated away from its correct position.

7. By differentiating the trigonometric expression for residual astigmatism with respect to the correcting cylinder power and setting the expression equal to zero, the optimal cylinder power for minimal residual astigmatism may be shown to be equal to $C \cos 2\theta$, where C is the original full dioptric power of the correcting cylinder and θ is the angle the cylinder axis has been rotated away from its correct position. With this "optimal value" for the cylinder power, the residual astigmatism is equal to $C \sin 2\theta$.

8. Other methods of determining cylinder power may also be used for determining the optimal cylinder power for a given axis error. For example, the rotating types of astigmatic dials, if aligned with the correcting cylinder at *any* axis setting, will measure the "optimal" power at that axis setting.

Basic Texts

Clinical Optics

Campbell CJ. *Physiological Optics.* Hagerstown, MD: Harper & Row; 1974.

Corboy JM. *The Retinoscopy Book: An Introductory Manual for Eye Care Professionals.* 4th ed. Thorofare, NJ: Slack; 1996.

Duke-Elder S, Abrams D. *System of Ophthalmology.* Volume V, *Ophthalmic Optics and Refraction.* St Louis: Mosby; 1970.

Michaels DD. *Visual Optics and Refraction: A Clinical Approach.* 3rd ed. St Louis: Mosby; 1985.

Milder B, Rubin ML. *The Fine Art of Prescribing Glasses Without Making a Spectacle of Yourself.* 3rd ed. Gainesville, FL: Triad; 2004.

Rubin ML. *Optics for Clinicians.* Gainesville, FL: Triad; 1993.

Stein HA, Slatt BJ, Stein RM. *Fitting Guide for Rigid and Soft Contact Lenses: A Practical Approach.* 3rd ed. St Louis: Mosby; 1990.

Steinert RF, Puliafito CA. *The Nd:YAG Laser in Ophthalmology: Principles and Clinical Applications of Photodisruption.* Philadelphia: Saunders; 1985.

Tasman W, Jaeger EA, eds. *Duane's Clinical Ophthalmology.* Philadelphia: Lippincott-Raven; 1995.

Related Academy Materials

Focal Points: Clinical Modules for Ophthalmologists

Hiatt RL. Diagnostic and therapeutic applications of prisms. Module 5, 1986.

Hill WE, Byrne SF. Complex axial length measurements and unusual IOL power calculations. Module 9, 2004.

Kastl PR. Contact lens fitting for irregular astigmatism. Module 11, 1997.

Liegner JT. Rehabilitation of the low vision patient. Module 5, 2002.

Nichamin LD. IOL update: new materials, designs, selection criteria, and insertional techniques. Module 11, 1999.

Spencer JB. A practical approach to refraction in children. Module 4, 1993.

Strauss L. Spectacle lens materials, coatings, tints, and designs. Module 11, 2005.

Wisnicki HJ. Bifocals, trifocals, and progressive-addition lenses. Module 6, 1999.

Publications

Fletcher DC, ed. *Low Vision Rehabilitation: Caring for the Whole Person.* Ophthalmology Monograph 12, 1999.

Lane SS, Skuta GS, eds. *ProVision: Preferred Responses in Ophthalmology,* Series 3. Self-Assessment Program, 1999.

Skuta GL, ed. *ProVision: Preferred Responses in Ophthalmology,* Series 2. Self-Assessment Program, 1996.

Wilson FM II, ed. *Practical Ophthalmology: A Manual for Beginning Residents,* 5th ed. 2005.

Continuing Ophthalmic Video Education

Farrell TA, Alward WLM, Verdick RE. *Fundamentals of Slit-Lamp Biomicroscopy,* 1993.

Freeman MI, Rakow PL, Campbell RC. *Basic Principles of Contact Lens Fitting,* 1993.

Guyton DL. *Retinoscopy: Minus Cylinder Technique,* 1986.

Guyton DL. *Retinoscopy: Plus Cylinder Technique,* 1986.

Guyton DL. *Subjective Refraction: Cross-Cylinder Technique,* 1987.

Preferred Practice Patterns

Preferred Practice Patterns Committee, Refractive Errors Panel. *Refractive Errors,* 2002.

Preferred Practice Patterns Committee, Refractive Errors Panel. *Visual Rehabilitation for Adults,* 2001.

Ophthalmic Technology Assessments

Ophthalmic Technology Assessment Committee, Refractive Surgery Panel. *Excimer Laser Photorefractive Keratectomy (PRK) for Myopia and Astigmatism,* 1999.

Ophthalmic Technology Assessment Committee, Refractive Surgery Panel. *Intrastromal Corneal Ring Segments for Low Myopia,* 2001.

Complementary Therapy Assessments

Task Force on Complementary Therapy. *Visual Training for Refractive Errors,* 2004.

To order any of these materials, please call the Academy's Customer Service number at (415) 561–8540, or order online at www.aao.org.

Credit Reporting Form

Basic and Clinical Science Course, 2007–2008
Section 3

The American Academy of Ophthalmology is accredited by the Accreditation Council for Continuing Medical Education to provide continuing medical education for physicians.

The American Academy of Ophthalmology designates this educational activity for a maximum of 40 *AMA PRA Category 1 Credits™*. Physicians should only claim credit commensurate with the extent of their participation in the activity.

If you wish to claim continuing medical education credit for your study of this Section, you may claim your credit online or fill in the required forms and mail or fax them to the Academy.

To use the forms:

1. Complete the Study Questions and mark your answers on the Section Completion Form.
2. Complete the Section Evaluation.
3. Fill in and sign the statement below.
4. Return this page and the required forms by mail or fax to the CME Registrar (see below).

To claim credit online:

1. Log on to the Academy website (www.aao.org/cme).
2. Select Review/Claim CME.
3. Follow the instructions.

Important: These completed forms or the online claim must be received at the Academy within 3 years of purchase.

I hereby certify that I have spent _____ (up to 40) hours of study on the curriculum of this Section and that I have completed the Study Questions.

Signature: _____
_____ Date

Name: _____

Address: _____

City and State: _____ Zip: _____

Telephone: (_____) _____ Academy Member ID# _____
        area code

Please return completed forms to: **Or you may fax them to:** 415-561-8575
American Academy of Ophthalmology
P.O. Box 7424
San Francisco, CA 94120-7424
Attn: CME Registrar, Customer Service

2007–2008
Section Completion Form

Basic and Clinical Science Course

Answer Sheet for Section 3

Question	Answer	Question	Answer
1	a b c d e	26	a b c d e
2	a b c d e	27	a b c d
3	a b c d e	28	a b c d e
4	a b c d e	29	a b c d e
5	a b c d e	30	a b c d
6	a b c d e	31	a b c d e
7	a b c d e	32	a b c d
8	a b c d e	33	a b c d
9	a b c d e	34	a b c d
10	a b c d	35	a b c d
11	a b c d e	36	a b c d
12	a b c d	37	a b c d
13	a b c d	38	a b c d
14	a b c d e	39	a b c d
15	a b c d e	40	a b c d
16	a b c d	41	a b c d e
17	a b c d e	42	a b c d e
18	a b c d	43	a b c d
19	a b c d e	44	a b c d e
20	a b c d	45	a b c d e
21	a b c d	46	a b c d e
22	a b c d	47	a b c d e
23	a b c d e	48	a b c d
24	a b c d e	49	a b c d
25	a b c d	50	a b c d

Section Evaluation

Please complete this CME questionnaire.

1. To what degree will you use knowledge from BCSC Section 3 in your practice?

   ☐ Regularly

   ☐ Sometimes

   ☐ Rarely

2. Please review the stated objectives for BCSC Section 3. How effective was the material at meeting those objectives?

   ☐ All objectives were met.

   ☐ Most objectives were met.

   ☐ Some objectives were met.

   ☐ Few or no objectives were met.

3. To what degree is BCSC Section 3 likely to have a positive impact on health outcomes of your patients?

   ☐ Extremely likely

   ☐ Highly likely

   ☐ Somewhat likely

   ☐ Not at all likely

4. After you review the stated objectives for BCSC Section 3, please let us know of any additional knowledge, skills, or information useful to your practice that were acquired but were not included in the objectives. [Optional]

5. Was BCSC Section 3 free of commercial bias?

   ☐ Yes

   ☐ No

6. If you selected "No" in the previous question, please comment. [Optional]

7. Please tell us what might improve the applicability of BCSC to your practice. [Optional]

Study Questions

Although a concerted effort has been made to avoid ambiguity and redundancy in these questions, the authors recognize that differences of opinion may occur regarding the "best" answer. The discussions are provided to demonstrate the rationale used to derive the answer. They may also be helpful in confirming that your approach to the problem was correct or, if necessary, in fixing the principle in your memory. Where relevant, additional textbook and journal references are given.

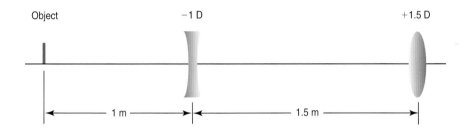

Questions 1–6 concern the figure above. An object is placed 1 m in front of a −1 D spherical lens. The −1 D lens, in turn, is positioned 1.5 m in front of a +1.5 D spherical lens.

1. Where does the −1 D lens form an intermediate image?
   a. at optical infinity
   b. 2 m in front of the lens
   c. 1 m in front of the lens
   d. 0.5 m in front of the lens
   e. 2 m behind the lens

2. Describe the intermediate image.
   a. upright, real, magnified
   b. upright, real, minified
   c. upright, virtual, magnified
   d. upright, virtual, minified
   e. inverted, virtual, minified

3. What is the size of the intermediate image as compared to the object?
   a. indeterminate
   b. one fourth the size
   c. half the size
   d. same size
   e. twice the size

4. What is the location of the final image?

    a. 1 m in front of the second lens

    b. 1 m behind the second lens

    c. 4 m behind the second lens

    d. 10 m behind the second lens

    e. at optical infinity

5. Describe the final image.

    a. upright, real, magnified

    b. upright, real, minified

    c. inverted, real, magnified

    d. inverted, real, minified

    e. inverted, virtual, minified

6. What is the size of the final image as compared to the object?

    a. indeterminate

    b. one fourth the size

    c. half the size

    d. same size

    e. twice the size

7. The ability of a light wave from a laser to form interference fringes with another wave from the same beam, separated in time, is a measure of its

    a. temporal coherence

    b. spatial coherence

    c. polarization

    d. directionality

    e. intensity

8. How much does a 15Δ prism bend light, in degrees?

    a. 7.51°

    b. 8.53°

    c. 12.40°

    d. 15.00°

    e. 86.20°

9. The anterior and posterior focal points of a thin lens are located at different distances from the lens. In addition, the nodal point of the lens does not correspond with the anatomic center of the lens. Which of the following is *true*?

    a. This is not possible.

    b. The lens is a spherocylinder.

    c. The optical characteristics described are seen only in thick lens or multielement lens systems.

    d. Media of different refractive indices bound the lens.

    e. Two separated principal planes must be used to define the lens mathematically.

10. The far point of the nonaccommodated myopic eye
    a. and the fovea are corresponding points
    b. is posterior to the eye, optically speaking
    c. is nearer to the eye than the point of focus of the fully accommodated eye
    d. cannot be moved by placing a lens in front of the eye

11. The near point of the fully accommodated hyperopic eye
    a. is beyond infinity, optically speaking
    b. is between infinity and the cornea
    c. is behind the eye
    d. is beyond minus infinity, optically speaking
    e. cannot be determined without additional information

12. You are about to write the postoperative spectacle prescription for a cataract surgery patient with macular degeneration. The best choice for a reading add for the patient with 20/70 best-corrected vision is
    a. +3.00 D
    b. +3.50 D
    c. +7.00 D
    d. a 3.5× magnifier

13. Proper distance visual acuity testing for a low vision patient includes all *except*
    a. a testing chart with symbols arranged in rows of decreasing size that are equally legible
    b. nonstandardized room illumination
    c. a Snellen visual acuity chart
    d. a +1.00 D lens placed over the patient's distance refraction

14. A patient with moderately low vision (20/160 in each eye) wishes a prescription to be able to read; the best choice would be a(n)
    a. +8.00 D single-vision reading spectacle
    b. +4.00 D half-glass reader with a total of 6Δ BI prism
    c. +8.00 D half-glass reader with a total of 10Δ BI prism
    d. +8.00 D half-glass reader with 10Δ BI prism per lens
    e. 8.0× magnifier

15. A patient with congenital nystagmus has a null point measured to be 10° to the left of fixation. The appropriate prism prescription to rectify the induced head turn is
    a. 10Δ BI OS, 10Δ BO OD
    b. 10Δ BI OD, 10Δ BO OS
    c. 20Δ BI OS, 20Δ BI OD
    d. 20Δ BI OD, 20Δ BO OS
    e. 20Δ BI OS, 20Δ BO OD

16. What is the retinal magnification of an eye with a refractive error of $+5$ D when viewed with a direct ophthalmoscope?

    a. 13.75×

    b. 15.00×

    c. 10.75×

    d. 5.00×

17. If a cornea has an anterior radius of curvature of 7.7 mm, a posterior radius of curvature of 6.8 mm and a center thickness of 0.5 mm, what will its dioptric power be if it is submerged in water?

    a. 0 D

    b. −0.29 D

    c. +2.47 D

    d. +14.30 D

    e. +37.60 D

18. The power of an intraocular lens should be increased

    a. as the power of the cornea increases and the axial length increases

    b. as the power of the cornea decreases and the axial length increases

    c. as the power of the cornea increases and the axial length decreases

    d. as the power of the cornea decreases and the axial length decreases

19. Which of the following laser properties is not clinically important in ophthalmic applications?

    a. energy level

    b. power level

    c. pulse duration

    d. polarity

    e. focal spot size

20. Multifocal IOLs

    a. offer increased image clarity and contrast for both near and far viewing

    b. are independent of pupil size if they are well centered

    c. offer a trade-off between decreased image quality and increased depth of focus

    d. are indicated for patients who do not wish to minimize the use of spectacles

21. Considered as a whole, the focal planes of a Keplerian telescope are located

    a. at the objective lens

    b. at the ocular lens (eyepiece)

    c. between the ocular and the objective

    d. nowhere; the planes do not exist

22. The SRK formula does not specifically require a measurement of anterior chamber depth because

    a. the formula was specifically designed to eliminate the need for this measurement

    b. regression analysis did not show increased accuracy when anterior chamber depth was included in the IOL formula

    c. modern IOLs are all at about the same anterior chamber depth

    d. the postoperative anterior chamber depth is not necessarily the same as the measured preoperative anterior chamber depth

23. The glasses of a patient with myopia are prescribed incorrectly and he is overminused by 1 D. When he wears them, his near point of accommodation is 20 cm. What is his refractive error and amplitude of accommodation?

    a. There is not enough information to solve this problem.

    b. −1 D, 6 D

    c. −5 D, 6 D

    d. −6 D, 6 D

    e. −6 D, 5 D

24. In bifocal design, image jump may be minimized by

    a. placing the optical center of the segment as close as possible to the top of the segment

    b. placing the top of the segment as close as possible to the distance optical center

    c. using a smaller bifocal segment

    d. using a blended bifocal segment having no visible line of separation

    e. lowering the bifocal segments by 3 mm

25. An angle of $45°$ corresponds to how many prism diopters?

    a. 45

    b. 22.5

    c. 90

    d. 100

26. A patient with a comitant 3Δ right hyperphoria wears the following spectacle correction:

    OD +3.00 +1.00 × 180°
    OS −1.00 +0.50 × 090°

    What is the vertical imbalance in the reading position, 8 mm below the optical centers of the lenses?

    a. 1Δ right hyperphoria

    b. 1Δ left hyperphoria

    c. 4Δ right hyperdeviation

    d. 5Δ right hyperdeviation

    e. 7Δ right hyperdeviation

27. In the derivation of the IOL formula using geometrical optics

    a. the index of refraction of the IOL is ignored because it does not differ significantly from that of the aqueous and vitreous

    b. the refractive contribution of the cornea may be neglected because the light reaches the IOL plane after it has already passed through the corneal surface

    c. the formula for change of vergence with change in location must be modified because of the index of refraction of the aqueous

    d. the anterior chamber depth may be neglected, as studies have shown a negligible increase in accuracy if it is included in power calculations

28. All the following pairs are matched correctly *except*

    a. diopter—reciprocal meter

    b. prism diopter—centimeters per meter

    c. refractive index—dimensionless

    d. wavelength—nanometers

    e. frequency—cycles per degree

29. When prescribing bifocal lenses for a patient with myopia,

    a. the practitioner should leave the choice of the segment type to the optician

    b. a round-top segment is preferred because of its thin upper edge, which causes less prismatic effect

    c. a flat-top segment is preferred because it lessens image jump

    d. the one-piece shape is indicated for adds greater than $+2.00$ D

    e. a split bifocal should be used because patients with myopia do not accept bifocals easily

30. If K measurements are 7.90 (horizontal)/7.70 (vertical), the refractive error is $-3.25 + 0.50$ axis 90°, and the base curve of the RGP contact lens is chosen to be 7.80 mm, what is the anticipated (1) power needed by the contact lens and (2) amount of the residual astigmatism?

    a. (1) -3.25 sphere and (2) -0.50 axis 90°

    b. (1) -3.75 sphere and (2) -0.50 axis 90°

    c. (1) -3.25 sphere and (2) -0.50 axis 180°

    d. (1) -3.75 sphere and (2) -0.50 axis 180°

31. Which of the following statements regarding dispersion and chromatic aberration is *false*?

    a. Inside of the eyes, blue rays focus in front of red rays.

    b. Blue print appears nearer than red print when both are displayed against a black background.

    c. Image sharpness is reduced by chromatic aberration in the eyes of patients with achromatopsia.

    d. Retinal image quality is limited by chromatic aberration and diffraction even if all monochromatic refractive errors are eliminated by wavefront-guided LASIK.

    e. Blue-blocking and red-blocking sunglasses improve image sharpness by eliminating part of the chromatic interval, thereby reducing chromatic aberration.

32. An object is placed 25 cm in front of a concave spherical mirror with a radius of curvature of 1 m (see the following figure). The image is

   a. virtual with a transverse magnification of 1.77

   b. virtual with a transverse magnification of −0.56

   c. real with a transverse magnification of −1.77

   d. real with a transverse magnification of 0.56

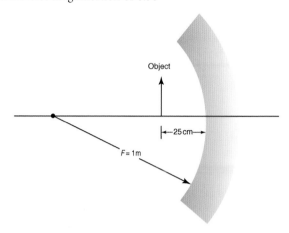

33. Following are the results of a streak retinoscopy performed at a testing distance of 0.67 m on a 5-year-old with an accommodative esotropia. In the right eye, a +5 D sphere neutralizes the 180° meridian and a +3.5 D sphere neutralizes the 90° meridian. In the left eye, a +7 D sphere neutralizes the 180° meridian and a +6 D sphere neutralizes the 90° meridian. Which of the following statements is *false*?

   a. The spherocylindrical notation for the full hyperopic correction can be expressed as

      RE: +3.5 −1.5 × 180
      LE: +5.5 −1.0 × 180

   b. The child will have an induced 0.5Δ left hyperphoria looking 1 cm below the centers of spectacle lenses containing the full hyperopic correction.

   c. The child will have an induced 2Δ exophoria looking 1 cm to the right of the centers of spectacle lenses containing the full hyperopic correction.

   d. If the examiner decreases the working distance to 0.5 m after neutralizing the retinoscopic reflex, "with" motion will be seen in all meridians.

34. A 92-year-old patient with dry AMD complains of deteriorating vision in 1 eye. Best-corrected visual acuity 12 months earlier was 20/30. With the same spectacle correction, it is now 20/100. Attempted refinement of the manifest refraction using ±0.25 D and ±0.50 D spherical lenses and a ±0.50 D Jackson cross cylinder elicits no change in the refraction. What is the next step?

   a. Perform a darkroom pinhole test.

   b. Repeat the manifest refraction using a ±0.75 D or ±1.00 D change in sphere and a ±0.75 D or ±1.00 D Jackson cross cylinder.

   c. Perform a slit-lamp examination for cataract or other media opacity.

   d. Dilate the pupil and examine for a choroidal neovascular membrane.

35. You fit a patient who has -3.50 D of myopia with an RGP contact lens that is flatter than K. If the patient's average K reading is 7.80 mm and you fit a lens with a base curve of 8.00 mm, what is the shape of the tear lens?

    a. plano

    b. tear drop

    c. concave

    d. convex

36. For the patient in Question 35, what power RGP lens should you order?

    a. -3.50 D

    b. -4.00 D

    c. -2.00 D

    d. -2.50 D

37. You fit a toric soft contact lens on a patient with a refractive error of -2.50 D -1.50×175. The trial lens centers well, but the lens mark at the 6 o'clock position appears to rest at the 4 o'clock position when placed on the patient's eye. What power contact lens should you order?

    a. -2.50 D -1.50×175

    b. -2.50 D -1.50×115

    c. -2.50 D -1.50×55

    d. -2.50 D -1.00×175

38. Which of the following statements about piggyback IOLs is *true*?

    a. Piggyback IOLs modify the vergence of light entering the eye after it leaves the incorrectly powered primary IOL.

    b. Piggyback IOLs can be used in a second operation only if the original IOL power was too low and additional dioptric strength is indicated.

    c. A piggyback IOL may be useful after removal of an incorrectly powered IOL.

    d. Piggyback IOLs may be less necessary as standard IOL power ranges increase.

39. Aiming for a slight residual myopia in IOL power selection may be desirable because

    a. weaker lenses are thinner and are less likely to cause surgical or postoperative complications due to size, disruption of tissues, inflammation, and so on

    b. the A constant is calculated for a slight degree of residual myopia

    c. residual myopia is closer to emmetropia than residual hyperopia

    d. an error in power calculation is less likely to produce a resultant hyperopia, in which the patient is in focus for no real distance

40. The advantage of the A constant, as used in the SRK formulas, is that

    a. it eliminates the need for anterior chamber depth measurement for all formulas

    b. the A constant is universal for all eyes and need not be measured for each patient preoperatively

    c. the A constant in effect includes the anterior chamber depth measurement

    d. it eliminates the need to consider near vision requirements

41. Which of the following statements regarding a patient with a central scotoma is *false*?

    a. Most patients will fixate using an eccentric retinal location called the *preferred retinal locus (PRL)*.

    b. The location, shape, and number of scotomata variably affect visual function.

    c. Eccentric fixation and PRL training can sometimes help patients improve coordination, tracking, and scanning and thereby facilitate function.

    d. Reading is usually not possible because central macular function is required to read.

    e. The best device for mapping a central scotoma is a scanning laser ophthalmoscope (SLO).

42. Which of the following statements regarding the prescription of visual aids is *false*?

    a. Kestenbaum's rule provides a starting point to determine the appropriate addition required to read 1-M size print.

    b. Base-in prisms increase effective magnification for binocular patients using reading spectacles.

    c. Illuminated stand-magnifiers help overcome stability and lighting problems associated with higher-power magnification.

    d. Optical magnification without contrast enhancement may be insufficient for patients with severely reduced contrast sensitivity function.

    e. In some states it is legal to drive with bioptic telescopes even when visual acuity falls below the normally accepted cutoff limit.

43. The principle of the astronomical telescope is used for magnification in which of the following ophthalmic instruments?

    a. indirect ophthalmoscope

    b. direct ophthalmoscope

    c. retinal fundus camera

    d. a and c

44. When using a binocular indirect ophthalmoscope on a patient with small pupils, binocular visualization can be improved by

    a. moving the ophthalmoscope's mirror closer to the observer

    b. narrowing the observer's effective interpupillary distance

    c. moving the ophthalmoscope's eyepieces farther apart

    d. increasing the distance between the observer's head and the patient

    e. all of the above

45. Which of the following is a recognized notation of visual acuity?

    a. Snellen fraction

    b. minimum angle of resolution

    c. logMAR

    d. 4-m standard fraction

    e. all of the above

46. In which type of astigmatism do the focal lines straddle the retina?

    a. mixed astigmatism

    b. compound myopic astigmatism

    c. compound hyperopic astigmatism

    d. simple myopic astigmatism

    e. simple hyperopic astigmatism

47. The nodal point of the reduced schematic eye

    a. represents a point through which light rays enter or leave the eye undeviated

    b. is equivalent to the posterior focal point of the cornea

    c. allows the size of a retinal image to be calculated if the size and distance of the object are known

    d. a and c

    e. all of the above

48. The Brewster angle is defined as the angle

    a. of incidence at which only 1 polarization of light is reflected for a given interface

    b. at which nystagmus is most reduced

    c. at which the greatest amount of specular reflection occurs for a given interface

    d. at which prism effectivity doubles

49. All of the following statements regarding irregular astigmatism are true *except*

    a. Manifest refraction and automated refraction may be dissimilar if there is significant irregular astigmatism.

    b. Irregular astigmatism may cause a poor endpoint in clinical refraction.

    c. Irregular astigmatism may be induced by a decentered refractive surgical procedure, pellucid marginal degeneration, and keratoconus.

    d. Best-corrected visual acuity is usually better with spectacles than with rigid contact lenses in the setting of significant irregular astigmatism.

50. A patient comes for refractive surgery with keratometry readings of 43.0 D/42.0 D and a manifest refraction of −9.5 D. If LASIK were performed, you would expect the postoperative average keratometry reading to be

    a. 36.8 D

    b. 36.3 D

    c. 37.3 D

    d. 34.0 D

Answers

1. **d.** Light from the object, which is 1 m in front of the first lens, has a vergence of −1 D as it enters the lens (see the following figure). Vergence (diopters) = n/distance (meters) = −1/1 = −1 D. The lens adds an additional −1 D of vergence. Light leaving the lens, therefore, has a vergence of −2 D. Light rays with a vergence of −2 D appear to be coming from a point 0.5 m in front of the lens.

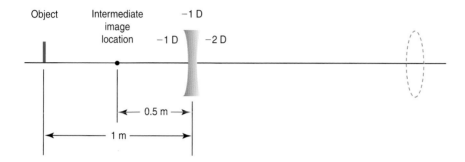

2. **d.** A −1 D lens has an anterior focal point, F_a, 1 m behind the lens and a posterior focal point, F_p, 1 m in front of the lens (see the following figure). A light ray from the tip of the object that enters the lens heading toward F_a will exit the lens parallel to the optical axis. A light ray that enters the lens parallel to the optical axis will exit the lens divergent, as if it had come from F_p. A ray traversing the nodal point of the lens, which corresponds to the optical center of the lens, will exit the lens undeviated. Back tracing the 3 rays as they leave the lens produces an upright virtual image at the location determined previously. The image is virtual because it is on the same side of the lens as the object. If a screen were placed at this location, no image would form. The raytracing diagram shows that the image is minified.

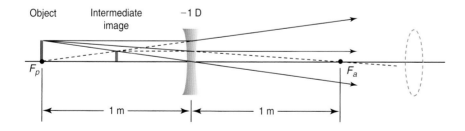

3. **c.** By similar triangles, the height of the intermediate image is one half the height of the object (see the following figure). The transverse magnification is 0.5.

4. **b.** To answer questions 4–6, one makes the intermediate image the new object and forgets the first lens (see the following figure). The intermediate image is 2 m in front of the second lens. The vergence of light entering the second lens is, therefore, −0.5 D. The lens adds +1.5 D of vergence. The light exiting the lens, therefore, has a vergence of +1 D. Light rays with a vergence of +1 D come to a focus 1 m behind the second lens.

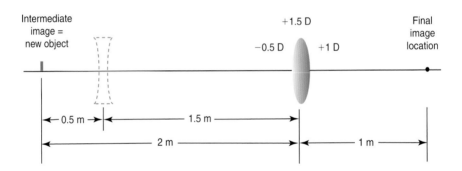

5. **d.** The $+1.5$ D spherical lens has an anterior focal point, F_a, 67 cm (2/3 m) in front of the lens and a posterior focal point, F_p, 67 cm behind the lens (see the following figure). A light ray from the tip of the object that enters the lens after going through F_a will exit the lens parallel to the optical axis. A light ray that enters the lens parallel to the optical axis will exit the lens and travel through F_p. A ray traversing the nodal point of the lens, which corresponds to the optical center of the lens, will exit the lens undeviated. All 3 rays intersect at the final image location determined previously. The image is real because it is on the opposite side of the lens as the object. A screen placed at this location would form a real image. The raytracing diagram shows that the image is inverted and minified.

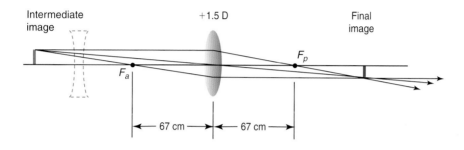

6. **b.** By similar triangles, the height of the final image is one half the height of the intermediate image (see the following figure). Because the intermediate image is one half the height of the object, the final image is one fourth the height of the object. The transverse magnification is -0.25.

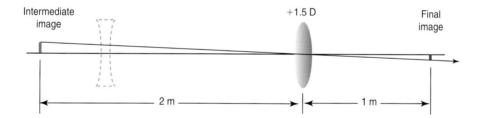

7. **a.** *Temporal coherence* is the principle by which the Michelson interferometer works. Spatial coherence, on the other hand, is a measure of the ability of 2 separated portions of the same wave to interfere. It is the principle by which wavefront splitting interferometers work. Polarization, directionality, and intensity refer to other important properties of laser light.

8. **b.** A 15Δ prism deflects light 15 cm at a distance of 100 cm. The tangent of the angle of the deflection is 15/100. The angle, therefore, is arctan $(0.15) = 8.53°$.

9. **d.** A spherocylinder has 2 sets of focal lines equidistant from the lens on either side of the lens. Although a thick lens or multielement lens system could have these features, the lens in the example is described as thin. By definition, a single principal plane can represent it. When media with different refractive indices bound a thin lens, the anterior and posterior focal lengths are different. The nodal point is "pulled" in the direction of the medium with the higher refractive index.

10. **a.** The far point of the eye and the fovea are always corresponding points when accommodation is relaxed. All the other statements are false.

11. **e.** The nonaccommodated hyperopic eye has a far point behind the eye. A virtual image of the retina forms at this location. As the eye begins to accommodate, the point of focus recedes to minus infinity. Minus infinity and plus infinity are essentially the same optically. As the eye continues to accommodate through optical infinity, the point of focus moves in front of the eye to a point between plus infinity and the cornea. The near point of the eye, in diopters, is equal to the far point location, in diopters, plus the amplitude of accommodation. Because we are told neither the amount of hyperopia nor the amplitude of accommodation, we cannot determine the location of the near point.

12. **b.** The best reading add for a low vision patient can easily be obtained from the visual acuity by using Kestenbaum's rule. The VA is expressed as a fraction 1/x. The *dioptric* power of the add is simply x. In this example, x is determined to be 3.50. Note that a 3.5× magnifier is equivalent to a + 14.0 D lens.

13. **c.** Distance visual acuity testing for a low vision patient is best done at 1 m (hence, an extra + 1.00 D of power is needed). The chart, such as the ETDRS or Colenbrander chart, should show a proportional decrease in the size of the letters from line to line. A Snellen chart has only 1 or 2 letters in the lines at the top of the chart and is not useful. Room or chart illumination does not need to be standardized and should be optimized for each patient.

14. **d.** A patient with 20/160 vision should still be able to maintain binocularity with reading despite requiring a reading add of + 8.00 D (see Kestenbaum's rule). This will require adding to each lens a base-in prism that is 2.0Δ more than the dioptric strength of the lens. A half-glass reader is the most convenient spectacle form for this type of lens because the lens bulk and weight are minimized.

15. **e.** Parallel prisms can be used to help reduce a head turn induced by nystagmus. This patient has a 10° head turn to the right to compensate for the null point position. This requires a 20Δ prism over each eye (each 1° is roughly equal to 2Δ). Placing the prisms with their bases to the right (BI over OS and BO over OD) allows the patient to directly face the object of regard. The virtual image of the object is displaced 10° to the left, enabling the patient to view it with eyes deviated 10° to the left (to the null point).

16. **a.** When viewed with a direct ophthalmoscope, the patient's eye acts like a simple magnifier, with a magnification equal to power divided by 4. An emmetropic schematic eye has a refractive power of 60 D, so an eye that is + 5 D hyperopic would have a refractive power of 55 D. Therefore, the magnification is 55/4, or 13.75×.

17. **b.** The refracting power of a spherical surface in the paraxial region is given by the equation

$$p = \frac{n_2 - n_1}{r}$$

For the anterior surface, n_2 is 1.376 (cornea) and n_1 is 1.333 (water). P_1, the power of the anterior surface under water, is

$$P_1 = \frac{1.376 - 1.333}{0.0077} = +5.58 \text{ D}$$

For the posterior surface, n_2 is 1.336 (aqueous humor) and n_1 is 1.376 (cornea). P_2, the power of the posterior surface, is

$$P_2 = \frac{1.336 - 1.376}{0.0068} = -5.89 \text{ D}$$

The total power of a cornea submerged in water is calculated using the equation

$$P = P_1 + P_2 - \frac{tP_1P_2}{n}$$

$$= +5.58 + (-5.89) - \frac{(0.0005)(+5.58)(-5.89)}{1.376} = -0.29 \text{ D}$$

It is apparent from this calculation that the cornea has little refracting power underwater. In this environment, the lens has more power than the cornea in the average eye. This explains why things are blurry when you open your eyes underwater if you are not wearing goggles.

18. **d.** A certain vergence of light is necessary to focus incoming light on the retina. As the power of the cornea decreases, a corresponding amount of vergence power (corrected for the different location of the refractive element) must be added. Similarly, as the eye becomes shorter, more vergence power is needed to bring the light into focus on the now-less-distant retina.

19. **d.** Many lasers emit a polarized beam. However, medical applications do not currently use this specific laser property.

20. **c.** Multifocal IOLs present both near and distant foci to the retina at the same time. This leads to an unavoidable decrease in image quality and contrast sensitivity, particularly at low levels of illumination. Pupil size may be a factor, particularly with certain types of multifocal IOLs. (Smaller pupil size results in increased depth of focus regardless!)

21. **d.** A Keplerian telescope is an afocal optical system: it does not have focal planes, principal planes, or nodal points.

22. **b.** Formula accuracy did not differ significantly whether anterior chamber depth was included or not. The formula was not specifically designed to do anything; rather, it was derived from the regression analysis of large numbers of cases. All IOLs are not at the same anterior chamber depth—the SRK formula works for anterior chamber lenses, too. Although the postoperative anterior chamber depth may not be exactly what the measured preoperative depth was, there is a correlation: an eye with a relatively shallow anterior chamber depth preoperatively is likely to have a relatively shallow depth postoperatively as well. In the SRK formula, the A constant, which is different for different lens types, probably accounts for the average postoperative anterior chamber depth for a particular IOL.

23. **a.** There is insufficient information to solve this problem. We know the patient's amplitude of accommodation is 6 D because it takes 1 D of accommodation to focus to infinity and an additional 5 D of accommodation to focus to the false near point at 20 cm. However, we are given no information by which to calculate the patient's refractive error.

24. **a.** As the direction of gaze travels downward from the distance optical center into the bifocal segment, there will be an abrupt upward image jump at the top edge of the segment. This jump is due to the prismatic effect of the plus lens (segment). Based on Prentice's rule, the amount of jump will depend on the power of the segment and on the distance from the top of the segment to the optical center of the segment.

25. **d.** As a rule of thumb, the number of prism diopters is approximately twice the angle in degrees. However, this works only for small angles ($<20°$). An angle of $45°$ means that at 1 m, a beam is deviated by 1 m (100 cm). Thus, $45°$ corresponds to 100Δ. An angle of $90°$ is infinity in prism diopters.

26. **e.** To solve this problem, you will find it helpful to convert the spectacle prescription to power cross notation, as shown here.

There is $+4$ D acting in the vertical meridian of the right eye and -1 D acting in the vertical meridian of the left eye. In the reading position, 8 mm below the optical centers of the lenses, the plus sphere produces base-up prism effect and the minus sphere produces base-down prism effect. By Prentice's rule, the net prismatic effect of the spectacles is

OD	$4 \times 0.8 = 3.2\Delta$ BU
OS	$1 \times 0.8 = 0.8\Delta$ BD
Net difference	4.0Δ BU OD

The spectacles cause an additional 4Δ right hyperdeviation in the reading position. Added to the comitant 3Δ hyperphoria already present, the resultant right hyperdeviation measures 7Δ in the reading position. This amount of vertical imbalance almost always produces a heterotropia, or manifest misalignment of the eyes.

27. **c.** The IOL must, of course, have an index of refraction different from that of the aqueous/vitreous for it to have any significant refractive effect at all. The refractive contribution of the cornea must not be neglected; in fact, it must be specifically considered. The IOL must provide only the vergence that is still required at the IOL plane, which is the total vergence required minus that already provided (at the IOL plane) by the cornea. Although the anterior chamber depth appears to have little importance in regression-derived formulas, it is essential in ones based on geometrical optics. The formula for the change in vergence with change in location is the familiar $P/(1 - Pd)$, where a vergence of power P is moved a distance d. If the refractive index n of the material is not 1, a "reduced distance" of d/n must be substituted.

28. **e.** A diopter is the reciprocal of distance in meters. A prism diopter measures the deviation in centimeters at 1 m, or centimeters per meter. Refractive index is the ratio of speeds and, therefore, has no dimensions. Wavelength can be measured in any unit of length. For optical wavelengths, the nanometer is convenient. Frequency is measured in cycles per second or hertz (Hz). Spatial frequency is measured in cycles per degree.

29. **c.** In general, patients perceive image jump as more of a problem than image displacement. Flat-top segments minimize image jump because the optical center is near the top. In patients with myopia, flat tops also reduce prism displacement because the base-down effect of the distance portion is reduced by the base-up effect of the segment.

30. **a.** The first step is to convert the plus cylinder refractive error to the minus cylinder format: −2.75 −0.50 axis 180°. In calculating the power needed by the contact lens, consider only the spherical component of the refraction (−2.75) and the flattest corneal meridian (7.90). The chosen base curve of 7.80 mm is 0.10 mm steeper than flat K, which is equivalent to 0.50 D (0.25 D for each 0.05 mm difference in radius of curvature). This should be added to the spherical component of the refraction ("steeper add minus"). The corneal astigmatism is 1.00 D with-the-rule, whereas the refractive astigmatism is only 0.50 D. This means that 0.50 D of with-the-rule astigmatism must have been neutralized by 0.50 D of against-the-rule lenticular astigmatism, which remains uncorrected when the corneal astigmatism is neutralized by the tear lens created by the contact lens.

31. **b.** Because red rays focus behind blue rays, the eye must make an accommodative effort to focus on red print after looking at blue print. It must relax accommodation to focus on blue print after looking at red print. The brain therefore perceives that the red print is in front of the blue print when both are displayed against the same background.

32. **a.** Light from the object has a vergence of −4 D when it strikes the mirror. The mirror adds +1 D, so light exiting the mirror has a vergence of −3 D. Because the mirror reverses image space, the image appears 0.33 m to the right of the mirror. The image can be drawn by tracing rays, as shown in part A of the figure. The image is upright. Image height can be determined by similar triangles, as shown in part B. The transverse magnification is 1.33/0.75 = 1.77. A negative transverse magnification would indicate an inverted image.

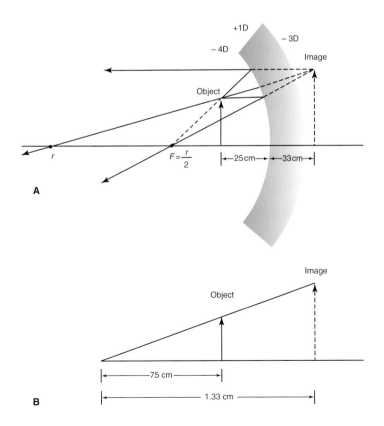

33. **b.** The power cross for this retinoscopy, before subtracting the effect of the working distance, is shown in the figure. In plus cylinder terms, the corresponding spherocylinder refraction is

RE: +3.50+1.50×090
LE: +6.00+1.00×090

Subtracting 1.50 D to compensate for the effect of the working distance produces a spherocylinder refraction of

RE: +2.00+1.50×090
LE: +4.50+1.00×090

This result can be expressed in minus cylinder terms. Referring again to the power cross, note the 2.5 D difference between the eyes acting in the vertical meridian. This anisometropia produces a net 2.5Δ base-up prism effect in front of the left eye, creating a 2.5Δ left hyperphoria. There is a 2 D difference between the eyes in the horizontal meridian. This meridional anisometropia produces a net 2Δ base-in prism effect before the left eye, resulting in a 2Δ exophoria. Once a retinoscopic reflex has been neutralized at the peephole of a retinoscope, the far point of the eye is at 0.67 m. Moving closer produces "with" motion, and moving away produces "against" motion.

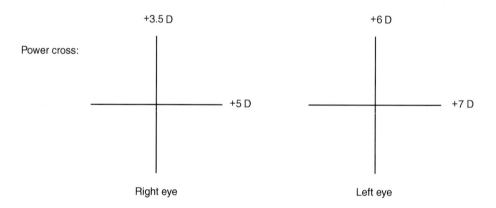

34. **b.** Changes of ±0.25 D and ±0.50 D in sphere and cylinder are likely to be below the "just noticeable" threshold for a patient with 20/100 visual acuity. Because the first thing to rule out when vision changes is a change in refraction, an additional attempt should be made to refine the refraction using larger-step changes in sphere and cylinder. The darkroom pinhole test is a test of potential vision. It should be performed after the refraction has been maximized.

35. **c.** The tear lens is formed by the posterior surface of the contact lens and the anterior surface of the cornea. If these 2 curvatures are the same, as with a soft contact lens, the tear lens is plano. If they are different (as is typical of RGP contact lenses), a + or − tear lens will be formed. In this case, the contact lens is flatter than K, so the tear lens is negative, or concave, in shape.

36. **d.** Use the rule of thumb that for every 0.05-mm radius of curvature difference between the base curve and K, the induced power of the tear film is 0.25 D. The power of the concave tear lens in this case is −1.00 D. The power of the RGP contact lens you should order is −3.50 D − (−1.00 D) = −2.50 D. An easy way to remember this is to use the following rule: *SAM* = *steep add minus* and *FAP* = *flat add plus.*

37. **b.** The amount and direction of rotation should be noted. In this case, they are, respectively, 2 clock-hours and rotation to the right. Each clock-hour represents 30° (360°/12 = 30°), so the adjustment needs to be 60°. Because the rotation is to the right, you should order a contact lens with axis 115 instead of 175—that is, −2.50 D −1.50×115. An easy rule to remember is *LARS* = *left add, right subtract.*

38. **d.** Piggyback IOLs have been used to reach a total dioptric power that was unavailable in a single lens. As IOLs are becoming available in a wider range of powers, it is less likely that a piggyback IOL will be needed to reach an unusually high or low power. Piggyback IOLs are placed anterior to the primary lens and thus modify the light vergence *before* it reaches the primary IOL, not after. These IOLs may be used to correct inaccurate primary IOLs in a second operation if the original IOL power was too low *or* too high. Piggyback IOLs are not used after removal of an incorrectly powered IOL—"piggyback" implies that a second IOL is in the eye.

39. **d.** No IOL power formula is 100% accurate. Aiming for a small degree of myopia increases the chances that the patient will have good uncorrected vision at some useful distance. There is no significant increase in surgical risks or complications related to different lens thicknesses due to different dioptric powers for a given IOL model. The *A* constant of the SRK formulas is related to the IOL type and is unaffected by the choice of refractive endpoint.

40. **c.** The *A* constant, empirically derived, seems to include the anterior chamber depth measurement. In the derivation of the SRK formula, no additional accuracy was obtained by including the specific anterior chamber depth measurement. The *A* constant, of course, is not used in all formulas—only SRK formulas. The *A* constant is not universal for all eyes; it differs for each model IOL and is a property of the IOL and not of the eye in which the IOL is to be implanted. The *A* constant has nothing to do with near versus distance vision requirements.

41. **d.** Patients with central scotomata can still read by using eccentric fixation, along with appropriate magnification and enhanced contrast, if necessary. Reading speed is usually decreased, but reading ability can often be improved with training and practice.

42. **b.** Base-in prisms should be incorporated into high-power reading spectacles to assist accommodative convergence in patients who have similar visual function binocularly. They do not affect magnification.

43. **d.** Both the indirect ophthalmoscope and the retinal fundus camera use the principle of the astronomical telescope, thereby producing magnified, real, and inverted images of the retina. The direct ophthalmoscope, however, applies the principle of a simple magnifier, using the refractive power of the patient's eye to produce magnified, virtual, upright images of the retina.

44. **e.** When looking through a small pupil, the observer can improve visualization by narrowing his or her effective interpupillary distance. This can be accomplished by several means. Moving the ophthalmoscope's mirror closer to the observer (the "small-pupil feature" available on some ophthalmoscopes) decreases the distance between the light paths to the observer's left and right eyes, effectively narrowing the observer's interpupillary distance. Moving the ophthalmoscope's eyepieces farther apart also decreases the distance between the light paths to the observer's eyes, similarly narrowing the observer's effective interpupillary distance. Increasing the distance between the observer and the patient decreases the angle formed by the observer's 2 eyes and the patient's eye, thereby allowing the light paths from the observer's eyes to "squeeze through" a smaller pupil.

45. **e.** The Snellen fraction (eg, 20/20), the minimum angle of resolution (eg, 1.0), logMAR (eg, 0.0), and the 4-m standard (eg, 4/4) are all measures of visual acuity.

46. **a.** In mixed astigmatism, 1 focal line forms in front of the retina and the other line forms behind the retina. In compound myopic astigmatism, both focal lines fall in front of the retina. In compound hyperopic astigmatism, both focal lines fall behind the retina. In simple myopic astigmatism, 1 line forms on the retina and the other falls in front of it. In simple hyperopic astigmatism, 1 line forms on the retina and the other falls behind it.

47. **d.** The nodal point of an optical system is the point through which light rays entering or leaving the system are undeviated. In the reduced schematic eye, the nodal point is located 5.6 mm posterior to the corneal surface. Because all light rays passing through this point are undeviated, a ray of light that leaves the tip of an object will pass through the nodal point and strike the retina undeviated. Retinal image size can be calculated by similar triangles.

48. **a.** The Brewster angle is the angle of incidence of light (defined with respect to the normal) at an optical interface, such that the reflected light beam contains only 1 polarization. Gas lasers often take advantage of the Brewster angle to produce linearly polarized light from reflections off the mirrored surfaces positioned near the ends of the laser cavity.

49. **d.** *Irregular astigmatism* is a catchall phrase for higher-order monochromatic aberrations. Most irregular astigmatism arises at the anterior surface of the cornea. RGP contact lenses create a smooth air–lens interface when they sit on the surface of an irregular cornea. Soft contact lenses cannot do this; rather, they mold to the surface of the cornea. If glasses could be manufactured to compensate for higher-order aberrations, they would work in 1 gaze direction only. For this reason, RGP contact lenses provide the best acuity for patients with irregular corneas and irregular astigmatism.

50. **a.** The formula is keratometry change = 0.6 × refractive change. Here, the keratometry change = 0.6 × 9.5 D = 5.7 D, so the calculated final postoperative average is K = (43.0 D + 42.0 D)/2 − 5.7 D = 36.8 D.

Index

(i = image; t = table)